www.wadsworth.com

Antisocial Behavior in School: Evidence-Based Practices

SECOND EDITION

HILL M. WALKER
University of Oregon

ELIZABETH RAMSEY
Peninsula School District, Gig Harbor, Washington

FRANK M. GRESHAM
University of California, Riverside

THOMSON

WADSWORTH

Australia • Canada • Mexico • Singapore • Spain • United Kingdom • United States

THOMSON

WADSWORTH

Publisher: Vicki Knight
Education Editor: Dan Alpert
Development Editor: Tangelique Williams
Editorial Assistant: Heather Kazakoff
Technology Project Manager: Barry Connolly
Marketing Manager: Dory Schaeffer
Advertising Project Manager: Shemika Britt
Project Manager, Editorial Production: Trudy Brown
Print/Media Buyer: Karen Hunt

Permissions Editor: Joohee Lee
Production Service: Strawberry Field Publishing
Text Designer: Adriane Bosworth
Photo Researcher: Terri Wright
Copy Editor: Tom Briggs
Cover Designer: Bill Stanton
Cover Image: Eric O'Connell/Getty Images
Compositor: Pre-Press Co., Inc.
Text and Cover Printer: Transcontinental Printing/Louiseville

Printed in Canada
1 2 3 4 5 6 7 07 06 05 04 03

For more information about our products, contact us
at:
Thomson Learning Academic Resource Center
1-800-423-0563

For permission to use material from this text, contact
us by:
Phone: 1-800-730-2214
Fax: 1-800-730-2215
Web: http://www.thomsonrights.com

Library of Congress Control Number: 2003108595

ISBN 0-534-25884-0

Wadsworth/Thomson Learning
10 Davis Drive
Belmont, CA 94002-3098
USA

Asia
Thomson Learning
5 Shenton Way #01-01
UIC Building
Singapore 068808

Australia/New Zealand
Thomson Learning
102 Dodds Street
Southbank, Victoria 3006
Australia

Canada
Nelson
1120 Birchmount Road
Toronto, Ontario M1K 5G4
Canada

Europe/Middle East/Africa
Thomson Learning
High Holborn House
50/51 Bedford Row
London WC1R 4LR
United Kingdom

Latin America
Thomson Learning
Seneca, 53
Colonia Polanco
11560 Mexico D.F.
Mexico

Spain/Portugal
Paraninfo
Calle/Magallanes, 25
28015 Madrid, Spain

This book is dedicated to the Oregon Social Learning Center and its research scientists whose work and tireless efforts have contributed so much to our understanding of the developmental pathways and effective treatments for antisocial youth and their families.

About the Authors

Hill M. Walker, Ph.D. is the founder and co-director of the Institute on Violence and Destructive Behavior at the University of Oregon. He has been a professor in the University of Oregon College of Education since 1967 and has focused his research career on youths having school-related behavior disorders including antisocial behavior, disruption, aggression, and internalizing problems. He and his colleagues have a long record of contributions in the areas of early screening and intervention for behaviorally at risk children and have developed the *Early Screening Project,* the *Systematic Screening for Behavior Disorders Procedure,* and the *First Step to Success* program. Dr. Walker received the Outstanding Research Award from the Council for Exceptional Children in 1993. His name was included in a list of the 54 most influential persons in the history of Special Education—a list that includes Helen Keller, John Kennedy, and Maria Montessori compiled and published by the journal, *Remedial and Special Education.* In June 2000 he was awarded the University of Oregon's highest honor, the Presidential Medal, in recognition of his contributions to the university and is the only faculty member to have received this award in its history.

Elizabeth Ramsey, Ph.D. is a middle school counselor at Kopachuck Middle School in Gig Harbor, Washington. She served as a post-doctoral research scientist at the Oregon Social Learning Center for two years following her graduate work. Dr. Ramsey is a coauthor of the Seattle-based Committee for Children's violence prevention program entitled *Second Step.* This program has been rated as the most effective school safety intervention available by a panel of experts assembled by the U.S. Office of Education. It is currently used in over 15,000 U.S. schools and a number of foreign countries. Currently, Dr. Ramsey consults daily with students, parents, and teachers in guiding preteen and teenage youths in their struggle for success. She enjoys putting into actual practice the ideas, concepts, and suggestions found within this book.

Frank M. Gresham, Ph.D. is Distinguished Professor and Director of the School Psychology Program at the University of California–Riverside. He has conducted extensive research in the area of social skills assessment and training, interventions with children and youth with emotional and behavioral disorders, and issues in ensuring high quality, evidence-based interventions in classrooms. He was given the Senior Scientist Award from the American Psychological Association's Division of School Psychology and he is a Fellow of two divisions within that organization. Dr. Gresham is a frequent presenter to school districts and professional organizations in the United States and Canada. He is coauthor of the *Social Skills Rating System* and is Co-Principal Investigator for Project REACH, a national center funded by the Office of Special Education Programs for developing and implementing interventions for children and youth with severely challenging emotional, social, and behavioral difficulties.

Brief Contents

Contents

4   Preventing Antisocial Behavior by Addressing Risk Factors Within Family, School, and Community Contexts   117

5   Proven Principles and Practices for Managing Antisocial Behavior   147

6   Assessment and Classification of Social Competence Deficits Among Antisocial Youths   177

7   Principles and Procedures of Social Skills Instruction and Generalization Programming for Antisocial Children and Youths   205

8 Bullying, Harassment, Peer-Related Aggression, and Mean-Spirited Teasing in School   236

9 Parent Involvement in the Schooling of Antisocial Students: Critical Issues and Best Practices   279

10 Case Study Applications of Best Practices with Antisocial Students   317

11 Youth Violence, Gangs, and School Safety: Reducing Risks and Enhancing Protections   350

Foreword

Teachers of difficult students—just about all teachers—need all the help they can get. They need practical suggestions grounded in reliable research, and not merely anecdotal reports or philosophical speculation. This book provides invaluable practical help to teachers or anyone else working with antisocial children and youths. I used the first edition as a text in my course in behavior management from the year of its publication (1995). My students and I loved it. I strongly endorse this second edition. It is the kind of book that will help teachers *identify* antisocial behavior, *understand why* students exhibit such behavior, and—more importantly—*know what to do about it when they see it.* This book should be read by everyone who cares about children's socialization.

Walker, Ramsey, and Gresham offer a realistic appraisal of the difficulty of reversing antisocial behavior once it is firmly established in a child's repertoire. They highlight the importance of early intervention, but they don't dismiss any youngster as hopeless. Even though kids may present tough problems and need continuing support, they maintain, teachers should not give up. It is an extraordinarily realistic yet hopeful book.

The authors' analysis of the need for early intervention goes beyond the usual plea for working with children when they are young. These experts help teachers understand how problems look when they are just starting and why it is important to intervene early in an episode or incident, and not merely early in a child's life. Not only do they help teachers identify the earliest signs of problems, but they also give teachers research-tested ideas for how to keep misbehavior from evolving into bigger problems or reaching a peak or blow-up stage. I have seen first-hand the benefits of the kind of sensitivity and action they recommend (Kauffman, Bantz, & McCullough, 2002). But their tactics do not depend on such observation, for their suggestions are backed up by decades of careful research about what works and what does not. If teachers consistently implemented the ideas the authors present in this book, the education of our children would be much enhanced. We would see more prosocial and less antisocial behavior in schools, and the school climate would improve. Students would learn more, and schools would be kinder places for both students and teachers.

Unfortunately, the forces arrayed against early identification of problems and early intervention to resolve these problems are many and strong (Kauffman, 1999, 2003, 2004). Nearly a half century ago, Bower (1960) noted the ambivalence people feel toward early identification and asked who would "bell the cat"—that is, risk his or her professional life for the good of the community. Ironically, some of the people who suggest the importance of early intervention still become very angry with anyone who goes on to suggest what is required for early intervention, such as providing scientific evidence, labeling problems, providing funding, identifying more students, identifying the behavior that should trigger intervention regardless of the child's personal identity, and risking false identification more often. If anything, in the past half century, our society has become more tolerant of social deviance, less willing to intervene early, and less willing to label deviance as such (see Hendershott, 2002; Kauffman, 2003; Ravitch, 2003). To use Bower's metaphor, the "cat" of antiprevention pressure has grown bigger and stronger (it's more like a tiger nowadays), and no one has been able to put a bell on it that will keep it from "killing prevention."

The authors and others who show the way toward early intervention face tremendous odds. But the overwhelming odds against early intervention must not deter us from the task. In accepting a significant award for leadership in special education for students with emotional and behavioral disorders, Walker (2003) commented:

> Our society is now reaping a bitter harvest of our own making of damaged children and youth that is sown with the seeds of domestic violence, neglect and abuse and made much worse by the toxic conditions of our society. Collectively, we seem to have a greatly reduced capacity to safely raise and socialize our children.
>
> I believe our field stands as a lighthouse beacon of hope, caring and unconditional support for these at-risk children and youth to whom life has dealt such a cruel hand. I have been a researcher in the area of school-related behavior disorders for over three decades. During that time, I have been proud to call myself a member of the field [of behavioral disorders] which brings together dedicated professionals from diverse backgrounds who work together so well on behalf of at-risk children. Our field models and demonstrates positive values and best practices that can make a real difference in the lives of children and youth with emotional and behavioral disorders and those of their families.

Such sentiments keep many of us going. But sentiment alone is not sufficient—we must have tools for doing our work. Walker, Ramsey, and Gresham give us those tools. They explain how to recognize the signs that a child's behavior is going "off track," how to know when the child's behavior (including what the child says) is leading somewhere we don't want to go, and how to turn the child toward more productive interaction. They help teachers see recurrent patterns in behavior and make predictions about what is likely to happen next.

Seeing recurrent patterns and making predictions are the stuff of the arts and of math and science and of communication. We call this anticipation. In fact, being able to discern patterns—anticipating notes and chords, shapes and colors, and words, sequences, and relationships—is fundamental to all creativity. Unfortunately, some educators deny that behavior patterns are recurrent and that behavior is predictable; in doing so, they deny that education is art *or* science. Of course, no prediction is perfect, and the unanticipated or "surprise" element keeps art and communication fresh and drives science to find out new things.

However, if no pattern can be discerned, then both science and art are impossible because there is no background against which to see or hear anything meaningful. Another way of putting this is to say that when *everything* is a surprise, the world (including communication, art, and science) is simply uninterpretable. Teaching involves both art and science, and the teacher who cannot discern a pattern—who cannot make predictions of what is likely to come next—is not going to be successful. We cannot prevent what we cannot or will not anticipate (Kauffman, 2003).

Good sentiments *and* good science are a combination necessary to help children and their teachers and parents. I am thankful to Hill Walker, Elizabeth Ramsey, and Frank Gresham for giving us both.

James M. Kauffman
Professor Emeritus
University of Virginia
Charlottesville, VA

References

Bower, E. M. (1960). *Early identification of emotionally handicapped children in school.* Springfield, IL: Thomas.

Hendershott, A. B. (2002). *The politics of deviance.* San Francisco: Encounter Books.

Kauffman, J. M. (1999). How we prevent the prevention of emotional and behavioral disorders. *Exceptional Children, 65,* 448–468.

Kauffman, J. M. (2003). Appearances, stigma, and prevention. *Remedial and Special Education, 24,* 195–198.

Kauffman, J. M. (2004). How we prevent the prevention of emotional and behavioral difficulties in education. In P. Garner, F. Yuen, P. Clough, & T. Pardeck (Eds.), *Handbook of emotional and behavioral difficulties in education.* London: Sage.

Kauffman, J. M., Bantz, J., & McCullough, J. (2002). Separate and better: A special public school class for students with emotional and behavioral disorders. *Exceptionality, 10,* 149–170.

Ravitch, D. (2003). *The language police: How pressure groups restrict what students learn.* New York: Knopf.

Walker, H. M. (2003, February 20). *Comments on accepting the Outstanding Leadership Award from the Midwest Symposium for Leadership in Behavior Disorders.* Kansas City, KS: Author.

Preface

Our society experienced a tidal wave of youth violence in the 1980s and early 1990s, driven primarily by the crack cocaine epidemic and the increase in the number of youths carrying weapons—especially handguns (Satcher, 2001). In the mid-to-late 1990s, this wave of violence threatened to overwhelm our schools as reflected in the number and magnitude of school shootings. These tragic events exemplified a trend in which the number of victims per school shooting increased substantially and culminated in the Littleton, Colorado, and Springfield, Oregon, attacks. Parents, school officials, and society in general were in a state of shock over these terrible events. These developments resulted in a vigorous and broad-based response by the federal government, state and federal agencies, and school districts to address a problem that threatens the very foundations of our society. The *Surgeon General's Report on Youth Violence* analyzed the risk factors and societal conditions associated with youth violence and provided a valuable roadmap for addressing it through policy- and empirically based interventions that meet the highest standards of treatment effectiveness and integrity (see Satcher, 2001).

Some of the initial responses were reactionary and quite disappointing in their promotion of simplistic solutions to a very complex problem. These included permanently excluding from the schooling process students who are accused of violent acts and profiling students to identify those who are likely to commit future violent acts. Although these ineffective and potentially destructive approaches still retain their advocates, they have been largely discounted by proponents of more rational and conservative solutions. These approaches include (1) addressing systematically the risk and protective factors operating in the lives of potentially at-risk youths; (2) creating secure and confidential hot lines in school settings that allow students to report concerns about the intentions or actions of other students who may be planning violent acts; (3) doing something about the rampant mean-spirited teasing, harassment, and bullying in many of our schools that demean and humiliate students to the point at which they seek revenge; (4) creating student-friendly mental health services in school and nonschool settings where students can access supports and services for their problems; (5) investing in evidence-based practices that address prevention goals at the primary, secondary, and tertiary levels; and (6) establishing schoolwide systems that simultaneously enhance school safety and security and create school climates that are respectful of all persons who participate in the school culture. Although there is still much to be learned and to do in this regard, considerable progress has been made in recent decades in understanding the causal factors and influences that account for antisocial, destructive, and violent behavior. In addition, we are now in a position to implement approaches and practices that will address many of the risk factors associated with these outcomes within collaborative partnerships involving parents, schools, and community agencies.

This book focuses on the role that schools can play in contributing to solutions that will ultimately make our society safer and produce citizens who lead productive lives and experience a high quality of life. Schools provide an important setting for accessing those students who are behaviorally at risk and who bring attitudes, beliefs, and behavioral histories with them that legitimize violence and aggression as viable means for achieving social goals. Due to the diminished capacity of many families to effectively raise and socialize their children, schools are now called upon to socialize many students to standards of behavior that are civil and acceptable. This is not a role that school systems should have to or necessarily want to assume, but it is a fact of life as we enter the 21st century in America.

The specific content of this book comprehensively addresses the challenges that schools face in the mass processing of all students—particularly antisocial and behaviorally at-risk students. It details promising intervention approaches, practices, and procedures in educating and managing antisocial students in school, home, and community contexts. The classroom teacher in today's school environment has one of the most challenging and important assignments in our society. The teacher's role is particularly critical in the preschool and early years of students' schooling. The kind of start that children experience in school and the quality of the classroom settings to which they are first exposed have everything to do with their subsequent school adjustment and success. Students who succeed in school are much more likely to succeed in life. It is incumbent upon all who are concerned with the schooling process to assist students in engaging, bonding with, and fully participating in school. This is very important not only in facilitating school success but also in protecting students from a host of adolescent health-risk behaviors including delinquency, heavy drinking, and teenage sex and pregnancy (see Hawkins, Catalano, Kosterman, Abbott, & Hill, 1999).

Schools have enormous potential to achieve these important societal goals, but they have been largely unsupported for doing so. However, the violence of the past two decades has changed the landscape regarding prevention, and there are palpable differences in the way that school administrators now listen and react to this message. It has resulted in a greater willingness to embrace programs and approaches that can positively change the school's culture, atmosphere, and operations. We are strong believers in early identification and screening and in early intervention approaches that enable true prevention and that catch problems early on in their development in the lives of children and youths. Achieving these outcomes will yield value-added, positive benefits for everyone, but they require that the bureaucratic and philosophical objections to addressing problems early on be addressed systematically and that the resistance that so often emerges around this issue abates. These are political problems that our society must solve. We have the means to address effectively the needs of our most vulnerable children and youths in the context of schooling. The purpose of this book is to make that information available to a wide range of individuals and systems (teachers, related-services personnel, family members, social service workers, courts, legislatures, and mental heath professionals) that influence whether best practices are actually applied to the problems of today's students.

Acknowledgments

The authors wish to acknowledge their collective indebtedness to the influence of the Oregon Social Learning Center in furthering their understanding of antisocial behavior patterns as they are expressed in family, school, and community contexts. OSLC scientists have generously shared their knowledge and findings in a myriad of ways over the years that have proved invaluable in our own work and particularly within the development of this book's content. The work of Del Elliott, Ph.D., of the Center for the Study and Prevention of Violence at the University of Colorado, has also been an invaluable resource in this regard. Finally, our respective colleagues, with whom we collaborate, have been an important shaping influence in our work and ideas about how things work.

We wish to acknowledge the role that Ann Thurber played in attending to the many details that go into producing a volume of this type. Her skills and attention to these details made all the difference in the quality and accuracy of the final product. Bonnie McClure also provided very able assistance at key points in the manuscript's development and her efforts are sincerely appreciated.

We are also indebted to and most appreciative of the roles played by the Wadsworth editorial and production staff (Dan Alpert, Heather Kazakoff, Melanie Field, Tom Briggs) in bringing this project to fruition. Their expertise and prompt responses made many of the onerous tasks of book writing much more palatable.

Finally, we wish to thank the reviewers of this edition: Rhonda W. Buford, Clemson University; Deborah G. Hammond, Arizona State University; Kelly A. Heckaman, Northwestern State University of Louisiana; James Jacobs, Indiana State University; James M. Kauffman, University of Virginia; Jennifer J. Olson, University of Idaho; and Daryl J. Wilcox, Wayne State College.

References

Hawkins, D., Catalano, R., Kosterman, R., Abbott, R., & Hill, K. (1999). Preventing adolescent health-risk behaviors by strengthening protection during childhood. *Archives of Pediatrics & Adolescent Medicine, 153*, 226–234.

Satcher, D. (2001). *Youth violence: A report of the surgeon general.* Washington, DC: Author. Available on the internet at: www.surgeongeneral.gov/cmh.childreport.htm

Antisocial Behavior, Conduct Disorder, Delinquency, and Violence Among At-Risk Children and Youth: Characteristics, Causes, and Outcomes

Introduction

This book examines antisocial behavior in all its destructive manifestations and adverse social outcomes. Specifically, we describe the negative impact of anti-social behavior patterns on those children and youths who display them (victimizers of others); on their targets (victims), many of whom are peers and classmates, as well as family members; and on the schools that must deal with them—often unsuccessfully. Child aggression, antisocial behavior, delinquency, and sometimes violence are strongly connected links in a developmental chain of behavior that U.S. children and youths are adopting in large numbers. These unfortunate developments are due primarily to social and economic changes that occurred in our society during the second half of the 20th century (e.g., poverty, family disfunction, drug use, and social fragmentation) (see American Psychological Association, 1993; Loeber & Farrington, 1998; 2001; Reid, Patterson, & Snyder, 2002). As a result, increasing numbers of children from at-risk backgrounds are bringing well-developed patterns of antisocial behavior to the schooling process, and many of them also have extreme deficits in their school readiness skills.

Increasingly, society looks to the schools to solve youth problems that are largely not of their making (e.g., school dropout, aggression, bullying, depression, and harassment). Rather, these problems are, to a substantial degree, a result of our society's diminishing capacity to effectively rear its children and to socialize them to acceptable standards of responsibility, conscientiousness, achievement, self-regulation, caring, and empathy.

Schools are now charged with the mass processing of an increasingly diverse student population in terms of prevailing attitudes and beliefs, behavior styles, racial-ethnic and language backgrounds, socioeconomic levels, and risk status. In addition, pressures for higher academic standards and outcomes for *all* students currently approach excruciating levels. Those students who bring challenging, antisocial behavior patterns to this pressurized school context can wreak considerable havoc, forcing extraordinary school accommodations and disrupting the learning and achievement of other students. Too often, these students are extremely difficult to teach and manage effectively, and they sometimes overwhelm teachers and classrooms. As a rule, educators are not well trained to deal with moderate-to-severe levels of antisocial behavior. And the farther along the educational track these students progress, the more serious their problems become, and the more difficult they are to manage. To make matters worse, school personnel generally do not have a thorough understanding of the origins and developmental course of such behavior, which further complicates their reactions to it.

However, there is reason for optimism given the progress that has been made in understanding and developing solutions for antisocial behavior and similar patterns of challenging behavior (e.g., attention deficit/hyperactive disorder and oppositional-defiant disorder) (see Burns, 2002; Burns & Hoagwood, 2002; Jensen & Cooper, 2002). In recent decades, enormous strides have been made in treating antisocial behavior, particularly early on in its developmental course. Through longitudinal and retrospective studies conducted in the United States,

© Bonnie Kamin/PhotoEdit

Aggression, fighting, and bullying are externalizing types of antisocial behavior. Students who are depressed, avoid peer contact, and have low self-esteem display internalized behaviors that are not hostile or disruptive.

Australia, New Zealand, Canada, and various western European countries, a great deal of knowledge has been acquired and replicated regarding the long-term outcomes that result from the early adoption of this behavior pattern by behaviorally at-risk youths, especially those who bring it to school with them or manifest it as they begin their school careers (see Kazdin, 1987, 1993; Patterson, Reid, & Dishion, 1992; Reid et al., 2002). Of equal importance, a strong knowledge base has been assembled on evidence-based interventions to prevent this serious disorder (Greenberg, Domitrovich, & Bumbarger, 2001; Loeber & Farrington, 1998, 2001; Reid et al., 2002).

Antisocial behavior patterns have been the subject of intense study by researchers in various disciplines and fields including biology, sociology, psychiatry, corrections, education, and psychology. The field of psychology, in particular, has developed a powerful empirical literature around antisocial behavior that can assist school personnel in coping with this most problematic of behavior disorders. To date, however, this invaluable knowledge base has been infused into educational practices and decision-making processes concerning at-risk students in only a limited fashion. A major goal of this book is to communicate and adapt this knowledge base for effective use by educators who must cope with the rising tide of antisocial students populating today's schools.

Antisocial Behavior Defined

Early on within the developing professional interest, antisocial behavior was defined by Simcha-Fagan, Langner, Gersten, and Eisenberg (1975) as involving the repeated violation of social norms across a range of contexts (e.g., home, school, and community). In this sense, an antisocial behavior pattern is characterized as traitlike in nature. That is, traits such as conscientiousness and responsibility are assumed to operate in a constant or predictable fashion across multiple environmental contexts and are considered to be largely unaffected by the social contingencies operating within these specific settings (Mischel, 1969; Weiner, 2003). Antisocial is the polar opposite of prosocial, which refers to cooperative, positive, and mutually reciprocal forms of social behavior. Antisocial behavior might entail hostility and aggression toward others, willingness to commit rule infractions, defiance of adult authority, and violation of social norms and mores. Indeed, the dictionary definition of *antisocial* is "hostile to the well-being of society and aversive to others."

This behavior pattern thus involves deviations from accepted rules and expected standards governing appropriate behavior across a range of settings. In fact, antisocial behavior is one of the most common forms of psychopathology among children and youths. It ranks as *the* most frequently cited reason for referral of young people to mental health services, accounting for nearly one-half of all such referrals (see Achenbach, 1985; Miller, Brehm, & Whitehouse, 1998; Quay, 1986; Reid et al., 2002). An antisocial behavior pattern, as reflected in school-based referrals, typically involves acts of defiance, noncompliance, aggression, bullying, stealing, and truancy.

Many researchers and professionals working in the area of corrections and delinquency prevention refer to antisocial behavior as involving actual illegal acts. In contrast, Loeber and Farrington (2001) view antisocial behavior patterns as *precursors* to subsequent delinquent and criminal acts. Specifically, they cast antisocial behavior as the first stage of a three-stage progression from disruptive behavior, to child delinquency, and finally to serious and/or violent juvenile offending. Other researchers conceptualize the school- and non-school-based mental health problems of children and youths as either externalizing or internalizing in nature, with antisocial behavior patterns a subclass of externalizing problems (see Achenbach, 1985; Greenberg et al., 2001; Ross, 1980). Externalizing behavior problems are directed outward, toward the external social environment (e.g., aggression, disruption), whereas internalizing problems are directed inward, and away from the external social environment (e.g., depression, social avoidance, phobias).

There is considerable implied agreement as to the meaning of antisocial behavior across diverse professional and lay constituencies. The term tends to elicit impressions of behavior that is not only destructive but intractable, aversive, and difficult to tolerate. The accuracy of this characterization is perhaps best reflected in research findings showing that antisocial behavior tends to be highly persistent over time and frequently leads, by the middle school years, to social rejection by teachers, peers, and caregivers (Eddy, Reid, & Curry, 2002; Loeber & Farrington, 2001). In sum, antisocial behavior is perhaps *the* most destructive behavior pattern that children and youths can adopt, one that sets them up for a lifetime of sadness, disappointment, and failure.

The Prevalence of Antisocial Behavior and Conduct Disorder

To a large extent, antisocial acts provide the behavioral content and clinical foundation for conduct disorder (CD), which is a psychiatric diagnosis used to describe a condition involving aggression, property destruction, and deceitful behavior that persists over time (usually one-plus years). Forms of antisocial behavior that lead to a diagnosis of conduct disorder include truancy, fighting, cruelty to others, cheating, and destruction of others' property and possessions. Formal surveys generally indicate that between 2% and 6% of the general population of U.S. children and youths manifest some form of conduct disorder (Institute of Medicine, 1989; Kazdin, 1993). Half of these youths will maintain the disorder into adulthood, and the other half will experience significant adjustment problems during their adult lives (Kazdin, 1993; Robins, 1978).

Eddy, Reid, and Curry (2002) argue that conduct disorder, when combined with oppositional-defiant disorder (which often precedes and co-occurs with conduct disorder), characterizes between 2% and 16% of the U.S. youth population. Hoagwood and Erwin (1997) estimate that the pool of youths with serious conduct disorders, and related conditions, who are in need of comprehensive mental health services comprises slightly more than 20% of the school-age population. Although school-age students can and do access mental health services, both within and outside the school setting, school systems typically refer and ultimately serve slightly less than 1% of the public school population with emotional and behavioral problems (e.g., via the federal entitlement authorizing special education services delivered via the Individuals with Disabilities Education Act [IDEA]).

Antisocial students are no doubt included in this 1% figure at some level, because they tend to represent high-end, intensive cases that force school accommodations. However, schools are also well known for denying students who are considered "maladjusted" access to special education services, because these students typically are regarded as not having a "legitimate" disability. But problematic behavior patterns appear to be increasing dramatically, which severely constrains the ability of school systems to educate all students effectively (Burns & Hoagwood, 2002; Horne & Sayger, 1990; Kauffman, 1989; Reid, 1990). In addition, changing societal conditions are producing a much larger class of children and youths who are designated as "at-risk" or as "special needs" populations. Many of these individuals will ultimately develop severe conduct disorders and antisocial behavior patterns leading to such negative outcomes as delinquency, school dropout, vocational adjustment problems, adult criminality, interpersonal adjustment problems, and appearance on community psychiatric registers in adulthood (Eddy et al., 2002; Loeber & Farrington, 2001; Parker & Asher, 1987).

Antisocial Behavior: Emotional Disturbance or Behavioral Disorder?

Expert opinion and substantial empirical evidence indicate that school systems vastly underserve the school-age population having serious emotional and behavioral problems (Walker, Nishioka, Zeller, Severson, & Feil, 2000). As noted previously, the proportion of the school population falling in this category can range upwards of 20% (Hoagwood & Erwin, 1997). Angold (2000) argues that, according to criteria specified by the American Psychiatric Association, this same proportion of school-age students could qualify for psychiatric services or counseling. Given the huge disparity that exists between the percentage of school-age students who need mental health services (20+%) and the proportion

Socially maladjusted students benefit from proven intervention programs. However, these students are often under-served by schools.

actually served through special education (1%), it is highly unlikely that the needs of most antisocial students are addressed by school systems.

The reasons underlying this marked pattern of underservice appear to be primarily philosophical and fiscal in nature. In philosophical terms, schools have long believed that they should not be held responsible or accountable for the mental health needs of students. Further, for many years, the definition of emotional disturbance incorporated into federal legislation authorizing special education services specifically excluded students whose behavior patterns could be characterized as "socially maladjusted." These students were not perceived as having a *legitimate* disabling condition and were blamed for the problems they caused in school, on the assumption that they had a choice about displaying such aversive and destructive forms of behavior. Today, antisocial students are widely perceived to fit this profile of the maladjusted student. In contrast, students with internalizing-type problems (e.g., depression, low self-esteem, anxiety, affective disorders, fears, and social avoidance) were considered to be emotionally disturbed—victims of circumstances beyond their control that did result in a legitimate disability.

The fiscal issues raised by students with emotional and behavioral problems are regarded as very serious by school district officials. If a student is certified as emotionally disturbed and then qualifies for special education services, the school and district are obligated to provide an appropriate education program for him or her. Failing that, parents and advocates have the right to sue the school district to absorb the costs of an out-of-district placement, which can cost up to $200,000 annually. This possibility creates a powerful incentive for school districts to deny students access to special education programs and services that could be instrumental in addressing their needs. Further, the legal protections attendant upon special education certification mean that special care must be taken in sanctioning students' behavioral transgressions. Because antisocial youths are likely targets for school-based punishments, this policy requirement provides an added incentive for denying them special education certification.

Traditionally authorizing legislation and policy governing delivery of special education services have selectively ruled out students who are considered aggressive, maladaptive, and/or antisocial. However, in spite of these efforts, there continues to be substantial overlap in the behavioral characteristics of students with emotional and behavioral problems who are certified for special education compared with those who either are not referred for evaluation or are referred, evaluated, and then denied such certification.

Walker and his colleagues (2000) examined this issue in a study involving three groups of middle school boys—emotionally disturbed (ED), learning disabled (LD), and socially maladjusted (SM)—who were compared on a range of social and behavioral measures. Boys in the ED and LD groups had been previously referred, evaluated, and certified to receive special education services by school district child study teams. Boys in the SM group had been placed on a wait-list for placement in an alternative school program for students with severe behavior problems (e.g., antisocial or destructive). Fourteen of the 15 SM boys had been previously evaluated for but denied IDEA eligibility as emotionally disturbed. Study measures included school records, parent interviews, and parent and teacher ratings of the boys' behavior at school and home.

Although results indicated that the LD boys differed significantly from those in the ED and SM groups on some of the study measures, there were no statistically significant differences between the ED and the SM boys. On one of the measures, a social skills teacher rating scale (the School Social Behavior Scale), which contained an antisocial behavior subscale (see Merrell, 1993), there were also no differences between the ED and the SM boys. This study showed an absence of detectable differences on measures and domains in which ED and SM boys would be expected to differ. If these results can be replicated with larger samples, they will call into question the validity of the judgments that school personnel have traditionally been asked to make regarding so-called emotionally disturbed and socially maladjusted (read "antisocial") children and youths. They may also reflect a pervasive school practice of using special education to serve the most difficult, acting-out students regardless of their emotional problems.

We have long believed that forcing related services personnel and special educators to distinguish between emotional problems and maladaptive behavior (aggression, oppositional defiance, disruption) is an unfortunate practice that does not serve the interests of children, youth, and their families—or educators for that matter. Its principal outcome is to deny needed services and supports to all but a tiny sliver of the school-age student population who are behaviorally at risk due to the family, community, school, and societal risks to which they have been and are exposed. The comorbidity of emotional and behavioral disorders of functioning is now an established fact and is something that is commonly encountered in children's mental health (Lane, Gresham, MacMillan, & Bocian,

2001). We need authorizing legislation that recognizes this fact, and policies and practices that accommodate it. In our view, we would be far better off in ordering at-risk children and youth along a pattern of severity or intensity of problems than continuing to engage the task of determining whether a referred student is or is not emotionally or behaviorally disordered.

Antisocial Behavior Patterns and Comorbidity

Comorbidity refers to the fact that individuals with a single disorder may be at elevated risk for a second or multiple disorders, which may, in turn, negatively affect their developmental course (Seeley, Rhode, Lewinsohn, & Clarke, 2002). Comorbidity represents perhaps the highest risk status for destructive outcomes, as the existence of multiple disorders (e.g., hyperactivity and conduct disorder or antisocial behavior combined with a learning disability) can produce a negative "multiplier effect."

Comorbidity was first introduced into the medical literature in 1970 (Seeley et al., 2002). Although actual comorbid disorders have likely been around for some time, the concept of comorbidity in the psychological literature on antisocial behavior has been highlighted and illustrated only recently by Lynam (1996), who developed a theoretical formulation of the future chronic offender. He framed his formulation around this question: "Who is the fledgling psychopath?" In attempting to answer this provocative question, Lynam reviewed and synthesized empirical evidence that points to at-risk youths who fit the profile of conduct disorder (CD) mixed with hyperactivity-impulsivity-attention (HIA) problems. He argues that the presence of HIA increases risk for destructive outcomes (e.g., school failure and social behavior problems) and that HIA also leads to CD. Lynam suggests that the mixture of HIA and CD produces a virulent strain of CD, best described as "fledgling psychopathy," that is associated with future chronic offending.

Gresham and his associates (Gresham et al., 2001; Gresham, Lane, & Lambros, 2000; Gresham, MacMillan, Bocian, Ward, & Forness, 1998) have replicated Lynam's findings on comorbidity with a longitudinal, at-risk sample of elementary-aged students. These investigators found that those students who were comorbid for HIA and CD were also at elevated risk on a host of social-behavioral measures as compared with samples of students who manifested only one disorder or problem.

Antisocial youths are most likely to be comorbid for three common disorders given their backgrounds and the environmental influences to which they are exposed from an early age. These disorders are hyperactivity, depression, and learning disabilities. The destructive effects of conduct problems mixed with hyperactivity, impulsivity, and attention problems have been increasingly well documented (Jensen & Cooper, 2002). Seeley and his colleagues (2002) have researched the comorbidity of adolescent depression with a range of psychiatric disorders including CD. Like other researchers on this topic, they report that depressed youths with comorbidity for other disorders are at much higher risk for destructive outcomes (e.g., suicide). Antisocial youths are commonly found to have learning disabilities and lower academic achievement (Walker, Block-Pedego, Todis, & Severson, 1991). Walker, Colvin, & Ramsey (1995) report that,

TABLE 1.1 ◆

Students in Grades 7–12 Reporting One or More Health-Risk Behaviors.

Behavior	Percent Reporting the Behavior	Percent Reporting at Least One Other Problem Behavior
Regular tobacco use	11	85
Regular alcohol use	11	92
Regular binge drinking	7	97
Marijuana use	14	88
Other illicit drugs	5	95
Fighting	33	56
Weapon carrying	6	89
Suicide attempt	13	100
Unprotected sex	12	76

Source: Lindberg, Boggess, and Williams (1999).

within a sample of 206 boys who had previously been selected for participation in a longitudinal study of antisocial behavior, antisocial ninth-graders who were receiving special education services and had been arrested one or more times were at the highest levels of risk.

With extremely at-risk populations, vulnerability for multiple-risk conditions and associated disorders is probably the norm rather than the exception (Biglan, 2001). Screening and assessment procedures applied to antisocial students should focus on the identification of multiple problems, disorders, and conditions as outlined by Lane and her colleagues (2001). The co-occurrence of multiple conditions of risk has been documented by Biglan (2001). Table 1.1 shows the conditional probabilities of problem behaviors for a national sample of adolescents. The data indicate a strong pattern of comorbidity for the problems listed.

The design of interventions for comorbid antisocial youths should be ecological and comprehensive in nature, should span multiple settings (home and school), and should involve multiple social agents (parents, teachers, and peers). The responsiveness of antisocial youths to typical interventions depends on several factors as described in the next section.

The Responsiveness of Conduct Disorder and Antisocial Behavior Patterns to Intervention

Conduct disorder is regarded by most experts as a chronic, lifelong condition that is highly resistant to intervention and tends to be unresponsive to adult-controlled tactics of social influence (Coie & Jacobs, 1993; Kazdin, 1985; Patterson et al.,

1992). Although there are numerous promising interventions for CD currently available, very few have *permanently* altered this condition (Greenberg et al., 2001). However, a number of effective early interventions have emerged that have the potential to divert at-risk children and youths from a trajectory leading to a host of long-term, negative developmental outcomes (see Burns & Hoagwood, 2002; Eddy et al., 2002; Greenberg et al., 2001).

The earlier such intervention occurs in the child's life and in the trajectory of the antisocial pattern of development, the greater will be the return on the investment in the intervention. In fact, Kazdin (1987) has argued that, after about age 8, antisocial behavior and conduct disorder should be viewed as a chronic disorder (like diabetes) that has no cure but that can be controlled and managed with a sensible regimen of supports and appropriate interventions. Having said this, it is important to note that it is *never* too late to intervene with behaviorally at-risk children and youths, no matter how remote the possibility of a "cure." We must never give up on at-risk students simply because they seem unlikely to benefit sufficiently from a proposed intervention.

The Stability of Antisocial Behavior

If a pattern of antisocial behavior persists into adulthood (i.e., to age 18 and beyond), it is referred to as antisocial personality disorder, as opposed to conduct disorder. If an at-risk child brings a well-developed antisocial behavior pattern to school, and if this pattern ultimately leads to a diagnosis of conduct disorder, it will likely persist into adulthood (assuming that it becomes elaborated during the elementary and middle school years). Often, this behavior disorder is exacerbated severely by adoption of a delinquent lifestyle in adolescence and comorbidity for other disorders, particularly depression (Seeley et al., 2002).

As previously noted, a tremendous amount has been learned about conduct disorder and its expression through antisocial behavior patterns among at-risk children and youths (see Cicchetti & Nurcombe, 1993; Patterson et al., 1992; Reid et al., 2002). We have considerable information about the causal factors that contribute to the development and expression of antisocial behavior among at-risk children and youths. This knowledge (1) helps us to understand and predict the path and likely outcomes of antisocial behavior, (2) allows us to recognize and identify its early behavioral signs, and (3) provides a road map of sorts for the development of strategies for its treatment and prevention. Box 1.1 summarizes some of the most important findings to date on antisocial behavior patterns.

These findings indicate that antisocial behavior is a very destructive and difficult-to-manage disorder. Given its relative stability and its strong association with delinquency in adolescence, most experts agree that antisocial behavior requires the earliest possible intervention that targets three primary settings and the key social agents within them: (1) the home and parents, (2) the classroom and teachers, and (3) the playground and peers (see Dodge, 1993; Reid, 1993).

Box 1.1　　Facts on Antisocial Behavior

◆ The vast majority of antisocial children are boys; antisocial behavior in girls is less evident and expressed differently than in boys. For example, antisocial behavior among girls is more often self-directed than outer-directed.

◆ There are two types of antisocial behavior: overt and covert. Overt involves acts against people; covert involves acts against property and/or self-abuse. By adolescence, many at-risk children display both forms, which escalates their risk status substantially.

◆ Antisocial behavior early in a child's school career is the single best predictor of delinquency in adolescence.

◆ Three years after leaving school, 70% of antisocial youths have been arrested at least once.

◆ The stability of aggressive behavior over a decade is approximately equal to that for intelligence. The correlation for IQ over ten years is .70; for aggressive behavior, it approximates .80.

◆ Antisocial children can be identified very accurately at age 3 or 4.

◆ The more severe the antisocial behavior pattern, the more stable it is over the long term and across settings (e.g., home to school); severity is also associated with higher risk for negative developmental outcomes and for police contacts/arrest.

◆ If an antisocial behavior pattern is not changed by the end of grade 3, it should be treated as a chronic condition, much like diabetes. That is, it cannot be cured but can be managed with appropriate supports and continuing interventions.

◆ Early intervention in the home, school, and community is the single best way of diverting children from the path of antisocial behavior.

◆ Children who grow up antisocial are at severe risk for a host of long-term, negative developmental outcomes, including school dropout, vocational adjustment problems, drug and alcohol abuse, relationship problems, and higher hospitalization and mortality rates.

◆ Using three measures of school-related adjustment in grade 5, the arrest status of a high-risk sample can be correctly predicted in 80% of cases five years later. These measures are (1) a 5-minute teacher rating of social skills, (2) two 20-minute observations of negative-aggressive behavior on the playground involving peers, and (3) the number of discipline contacts with the principal's office that are written up and placed in the child's permanent school record.

School Adjustment and Antisocial Behavior

When children enter school, they have to negotiate two important social-behavioral adjustments: teacher-related and peer-related (see Walker, McConnell, & Clarke, 1985). *Teacher-related* adjustment refers to the process of students meeting the minimal behavioral demands and expectations that the majority of teachers require in order to manage instructional environments (Hersh & Walker, 1983; Walker, 1986). *Peer-related* adjustment refers to the ability to forge satisfactory relationships with peers, to develop friendships, and to establish and maintain social support networks (Dodge, 1993; Hollinger, 1987; Patterson et al., 1992). Satisfactory adjustment in these two domains is essential to gaining teacher and peer acceptance. During the middle school years, a third form of adjustment, self-related, comes into play as well. *Self-related* adjustment involves managing one's emotions, being organized, regulating one's behavior, asserting oneself, coping successfully with relational aggression, and protecting one's reputation. This form of adjustment is most relevant to adolescent development (Williams, Walker, Holmes, Todis, & Fabre, 1989).

If children and youths fail to satisfactorily negotiate either teacher-related or peer-related adjustment relatively early in their school careers, they are at increased risk for later school failure. And if they fail in *both* adjustment areas, they are at risk for an array of negative, long-term developmental outcomes (Strain, Guralnick, & Walker, 1986). Figure 1.1 presents a conceptual model of teacher- and peer-related adjustment with associated long-term outcomes. Enhancers (student adaptive behaviors) and impairers (student maladaptive behaviors) of each form of adjustment are also listed. According to Gresham and colleagues (Gresham, Lane, MacMillan, & Bocian, 1999; Lane et al., 2001), the behavioral correlates associated with these teacher- and peer-related adjustments are model behavioral profiles that are strongly preferred by teachers and peers, respectively. In fact, researchers have clearly documented associations between the success or failure of teacher- and peer-related adjustments and the enhancers and impairers listed in Figure 1.1 (Parker & Asher, 1987; Robins, 1978).

Students with conduct disorder and antisocial behavior patterns are at risk for failure in both of these adjustment areas. Due to their coercive behavior, antisocial students are especially vulnerable to social rejection by their nonantisocial peers. If they are also noncompliant with teacher directives or engage in oppositional-defiant behavior, then rejection by teachers is also a real possibility. In such cases, failure in both teacher- and peer-related adjustment areas is virtually assured, with all of the associated negative outcomes.

Long-Term Outcomes for Antisocial and At-Risk Boys

The senior author and his colleagues conducted an eight-year follow-up study of their ongoing longitudinal sample of antisocial ($N = 39$) and at-risk ($N = 41$) boys. These boys were identified in the fourth grade using parent and teacher ratings on the Aggression Subscale of the Achenbach Child Behavior Checklist (Achenbach, 1991) and an antisocial risk index developed by Patterson and his associates (see

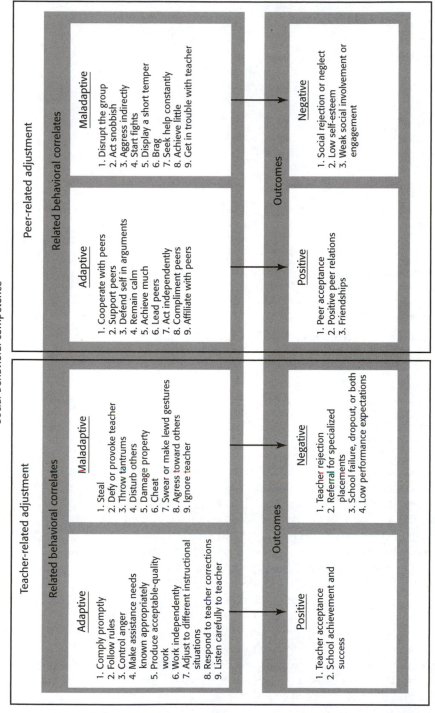

Social-behavioral competence

Teacher-related adjustment

Related behavioral correlates

Adaptive

1. Comply promptly
2. Follow rules
3. Control anger
4. Make assistance needs known appropriately
5. Produce acceptable-quality work
6. Work independently
7. Adjust to different instructional situations
8. Respond to teacher corrections
9. Listen carefully to teacher

Maladaptive

1. Steal
2. Defy or provoke teacher
3. Throw tantrums
4. Disturb others
5. Damage property
6. Cheat
7. Swear or make lewd gestures
8. Agress toward others
9. Ignore teacher

Outcomes

Positive

1. Teacher acceptance
2. School achievement and success

Negative

1. Teacher rejection
2. Referral for specialized placements
3. School failure, dropout, or both
4. Low performance expectations

Peer-related adjustment

Related behavioral correlates

Adaptive

1. Cooperate with peers
2. Support peers
3. Defend self in arguments
4. Remain calm
5. Achieve much
6. Lead peers
7. Act independently
8. Compliment peers
9. Affiliate with peers

Maladaptive

1. Disrupt the group
2. Act snobbish
3. Aggress indirectly
4. Start fights
5. Display a short temper
6. Brag
7. Seek help constantly
8. Achieve little
9. Get in trouble with teacher

Outcomes

Positive

1. Peer acceptance
2. Positive peer relations
3. Friendships

Negative

1. Social rejection or neglect
2. Low self-esteem
3. Weak social involvement or engagement

FIGURE 1.1

Model of Interpersonal Social-Behavioral Competence Within School Settings.

Source: From "A Construct Score Approach to the Assessment of Social Competence: Rationale, Technological Considerations, and Anticipated Outcomes," by H. M. Walker, L. K. Irvin, J. Noell, and G. H. S. Singer, in *Behavior Modification, 16* (1992), 448–474. Reprinted by permission.

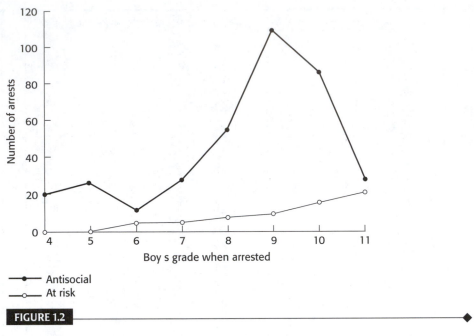

FIGURE 1.2

Frequency of Arrests for Antisocial and At-Risk Boys.
Source: Patterson et al. (1992).

Capaldi & Patterson, 1989). The relative risk status of the two participant groups was considered extreme for the antisocial boys and mild for the at-risk boys.

During their high school years, the dropout rate was 62% for the antisocial group and 12% for the at-risk group. The antisocial boys had a far higher rate of alcohol, tobacco, and drug use than the at-risk boys. Approximately half the antisocial boys reported using drugs, and 80% of those who did said they came to school stoned. Between grades 4 and 12, the at-risk boys had a total of 45 arrests; the antisocial boys had 350 arrests over this same time span.

Figure 1.2 plots the yearly frequency of the arrests for the two groups. The transition from middle school to high school was associated with a dramatic increase in arrest rate for the antisocial boys, perhaps partly due to their association with deviant peers (Patterson et al., 1992; Reid et al., 2002). In contrast, the boys in the at-risk group showed only a gradual increase over the high school years. However, by the end of grade 11, the arrest rates for the two groups were nearly equivalent. Approximately half of all antisocial children go on to become adolescent delinquent offenders, and one-half to three-quarters of adolescent offenders become adult criminals. Patterson, Capaldi, and Bank (1990) note that, at some point in late adolescence, the incidence of delinquent acts as a function of age begins to decline, and this trend continues into men's late 20s. The data in Figure 1.2 show a clear drop-off effect for the sample of antisocial boys. The reasons underlying this phenomenon are not well understood at present. Burnout, among other factors, has been suggested as partially accounting for this effect. In any case, it is likely that those offenders who continue their criminal activity do so at a very high rate.

Behavioral Characteristics and Correlates of Antisocial Behavior

Few individuals go through their lives without engaging in some form or type of antisocial behavior on occasion (Bullis & Walker, 1995; Reid et al., 2002). This is particularly true of young children who, through the socialization efforts of parents and guardians, gradually reduce their levels of antisocial behavior as they approach school age. However, those children who develop conduct disorder, while following a similar trend, often maintain much higher-than-normal levels of antisocial behavior (Patterson, DeBaryshe, & Ramsey, 1989; Reid, 1993).

The Problem of Aggression

In a very real sense, antisocial behavior is about aggression—physical, gestural, and verbal. The aggression that is characteristic of antisocial children and youths is directed at multiple targets, including social agents (peers, siblings, parents, teachers, other adults), property (vandalism, theft, arson), and self (drug and alcohol abuse, impulsive, high-risk behavior). Hunt (1993) identified and described five neurobiological patterns of aggression; these patterns and their behavioral manifestations are summarized in Box 1.2. There is some degree of overlap among the types of aggression Hunt described. Further, an aggressive individual rarely manifests the characteristics of only a single pattern of aggression. Still, these distinctions are a useful way to characterize the types of aggressive behavior that are seen increasingly in school and community settings. Although the strategies and practices described in this book have implications for all five patterns of aggression, they are most closely geared to the affective and instrumental types of aggression. This is because antisocial behavior patterns typically involve a strong investment by at-risk youths in the use of instrumental aggression.

Aggressive behavior is highly aversive to others and often leads to rejection and social avoidance from peers. Aggression also produces powerful short-term rewards, including getting one's way, achieving social control over situations, and dominating and humiliating others. Aggressive children and youths have a strong impact on peer groups. However, children who adopt aggression as a characteristic behavior pattern are likely to win battles but to lose the larger war. That is, they may be able to control and dominate specific social situations in the short run, but over the long term, they are likely to suffer social avoidance and rejection by peers (Patterson et al., 1992).

Coie and Kupersmidt (1983) conducted an intriguing study in which they demonstrated just how quickly antisocial, aggressive youths, in effect, *train* their peer groups to socially reject them. The researchers identified a group of boys who were highly aggressive and who were also socially rejected by their peer groups. They formed play groups of same-age children, all of whom were unfamiliar with each other, and placed one of these boys in each group. Within a matter of minutes, each of the play groups showed clear signs of rejecting the aggressive boy assigned to them! Reid (1993) argues convincingly that many of

Box 1.2	Patterns of Neurobiological Aggression

- **Overaroused aggression.** This form of aggressive behavior is due primarily to a state of overarousal, such as that seen in children and youths with attention deficit/hyperactive disorder. Aggressive behavior of this type is largely a side effect of heightened arousal and activity levels and is not characterized by intent to inflict pain or by attempts to use aggression for instrumental purposes. Victims or targets of these aggressive acts are generally randomly involved in the aggressive episode.

- **Impulsive aggression.** Aggression of this type occurs in a sudden burst, without any identifiable precursors or signs that it is coming. It is thought to be neurologically based and is often associated with irritability or long periods of passivity. Aggressive episodes are very brief in duration and subside as quickly as they emerge. Children and youths displaying this pattern of aggression are subject to frequent and intense mood swings.

- **Affective aggression.** Aggression arising out of states of intense anger and rage, such as that seen among abused children, is characteristic of this pattern. It is emotionally charged and includes a range of affective states involving intense passion; it is sometimes motivated by vindictiveness or self-protectiveness. Violent episodes are typical of this pattern of aggression. It is highly destructive to both the perpetrators and the victims of the aggression. It may be dangerous to be closely associated with such children and youths.

- **Predatory aggression.** This form of aggression is most prevalent among those at adolescent and adult levels of development. It is often associated with a thought disorder involving paranoia. Such youths have a conspiratorial view of social relations and tend to misinterpret neutral social behavior directed toward them as intentionally harmful. Much of their aggressive behavior is revenge-based and thoughtfully planned. Often it is designed to "settle scores," real or imagined, and contains elements of the predator–prey relationship.

- **Instrumental aggression.** This very common form of aggression is adopted by many children and youths as a standard way of operating on the social environment (i.e., a modus operandi) and involves using aggressive tactics to maximize their advantage and to get their way. Instrumental aggression is used to intimidate, humiliate, and coerce others. There is a strong drive to achieve dominance and social control underlying this aggressive pattern. Instrumental aggression is associated with sociopathic tendencies and is commonly viewed as representing a character disorder. Such children and youths often come from unstable, chaotic family environments.

Source: Hunt (1993).

Box 1.3   The Case of Ritchie

The senior author first encountered Ritchie in the process of developing the RECESS program for aggressive children in the K–3 grade range (Walker et al., 1993). Ritchie was in the second grade and was referred for involvement in the program by his school counselor and regular homeroom teacher. Teacher ratings of his classroom and general social behavior were quite negative and were well below normative standards. Direct observations of Ritchie's playground behavior on three separate occasions showed a frequent pattern of coercing peers, dominating playground activities, making up his own rules for games, breaking playground rules, verbally abusing and ridiculing others, and physically provoking smaller and less powerful children.

During one of these observation sessions on the playground, Ritchie began choking a smaller boy (a kindergartner) for no apparent reason. He appeared to have a clear goal of hurting the younger child. The recess supervisor broke up the encounter and called the principal and counselor to deal with the situation. As this entourage was escorting Ritchie into the principal's office to call his parents, I asked him why he was choking the other boy like that. He looked at me in amazement and said, "Well, it was recess!"

these aggressive boys are probably unaware that their own behavior is responsible for such rejection.

Dodge and his colleagues have conducted some seminal research on how aggressive, rejected children process social information, interpret interpersonal cues, and make decisions based on this information (Dodge, 1985; Dodge, Pettit, McClaskey, & Brown, 1986). Dodge and Crick (1990) have illustrated how this information-processing model applies to aggression. The model consists of a series of steps dealing with the encoding and interpretation of information within social contexts wherein aggression is one behavioral option. Studies have shown that antisocial, aggressive children and youths tend to be deficient in each of the steps within this model (Crick, Grotpeter, & Bigbee, 2002). For example, they frequently make errors in evaluating the motives and intent underlying the social behavior directed toward them by peers and adults. They often misinterpret important social cues that guide appropriate responses in everyday situations with peers. They are likely to attribute hostile intentions to accidental or ambiguous behavior from others and to respond quite inappropriately as a result. Further, they are often frequent teasers of others but respond negatively to similar provocations from others. Finally, they appear to have quite abnormal standards and expectations regarding their own behavior. These beliefs may, in turn, legitimize much of their deviant, aversive behavior and may also insulate them from accurately decoding negative and disapproving feedback about their behavior.

The case of Ritchie, touched on in Box 1.3, illustrates this point. By second grade, Ritchie showed all the signs of being well along the path to antisocial behavior. Students like Ritchie who persist in this behavior pattern into the intermediate grades and who affiliate with deviant peer groups have a severely elevated risk of delinquency (Patterson et al., 1992). We find in our research that we can correctly identify predelinquent children, like Ritchie, in the fifth grade using three easy-to-record measures: (1) a 5-minute rating of classroom-related social skills, (2) the number of discipline contacts in the student's school records, and (3) the total amount of negative social behavior occurring between the student and peers at recess recorded during two 20-minute observation sessions. The arrest status of antisocial and at-risk students ($N = 80$) who met cutoff points on these three measures could be accurately predicted in 80% of cases five years later when they were in the tenth grade (Walker & McConnell, 1995). It is no exaggeration to say that the path to prison begins very early in a child's school career, usually in the elementary grades, and that schools often serve merely as a way station along this well-traveled road (Walker & Sylwester, 1991).

This is powerful testimony to the stability of antisocial behavior patterns, and it supports the opinion of many experts that young bullies often get worse, rather than better, as they progress through school. For example, about 50% of children up to age 10 who get into trouble in school because of their aggressive behavior continue to have serious behavior problems in adolescence (Kutner, 1993). And, noted previously, the stability of well-developed antisocial behavior over a 10-year period rivals that of measured IQ over the same time span.

Most children and youths who are antisocial have skilled repertoires of bullying others. As a result of court decisions and parental pressures, schools are becoming increasingly concerned with the effects of bullying behavior on both its victims and the perpetrators. They are investing in social skills training programs to teach methods for reducing such aggression and strategies for coping with it (Colvin, Tobin, Beard, Hagan, & Sprague, 1998; Epstein, Plog, & Porter, 2001; Hoover & Juul, 1993; Snell, MacKenzie, & Frey, 2002).

Antisocial children and youths often have moderate-to-severe academic skill deficits, which are reflected in below-average achievement (see Coie & Jacobs, 1993; Hinshaw, 1992; Offord, Boyle, & Racine, 1991; Reid, 1993). It is not clear whether these academic problems are primarily the causes or consequences of antisocial behavior; however, there is little doubt that they greatly exacerbate it. Table 1.2 lists academic achievement scores in reading, math, and total achievement for a longitudinal sample of 39 antisocial boys and 41 at-risk boys that the senior author and his colleagues have been following since 1984. Scores are reported for these two groups when they were in grades 5, 6, and 7. In each year and on each achievement test, the at-risk students were above the 50th percentile. In contrast, the antisocial boys had average scores that fell well below the 50th percentile, ranging from a low of 23.80 in math during grade 7 to a high of 43.36 in reading during grade 6. In sum, the antisocial boys had serious academic underachievement problems. Further, as these boys progressed through their school careers, their academic deficits and achievement problems became even more severe.

Classroom Behavior

As a rule, antisocial students make relatively poor adjustments to the demands of schooling and to instructional environments controlled by teachers. They often put extreme pressures on the management and instructional skills of class-

TABLE 1.2

Standardized Achievement Test Percentile Scores for Antisocial and At-Risk Students Across Grades 5, 6, and 7.

	Grade 5		Grade 6		Grade 7	
	Antisocial	At Risk	Antisocial	At Risk	Antisocial	At Risk
Reading	42.38	56.63	43.36	56.62	37.00	56.46
Math	32.00	58.68	38.36	55.74	23.80	52.18
Total	35.75	58.88	41.59	53.51	28.29	54.15

Source: Walker et al. (1987).

room teachers and disrupt the instructional process for other students. Antisocial students are increasingly being placed outside the regular classroom—in self-contained classes, day-treatment centers, and residential settings. About two-thirds of the students assigned to self-contained classrooms for severely emotionally disturbed children and youths have acting-out behavior patterns (Wagner, 1989). This is a potentially serious problem, given that research reported by Dishion and Andrews (1995), and replicated by other investigators, suggests that students with challenging behavior patterns who are placed in socially restrictive settings tend to socialize each other to higher levels of deviance than would otherwise be the case. This is especially true if the intervention is weak and the alternative program is relatively unstructured. These findings have been strongly embraced by the community of psychological researchers on antisocial behavior and children's mental health (Burns & Hoagwood, 2002), and have begun to inform policies and practices in treating the emotional and behavioral problems of behaviorally at-risk children and youths (see Burns & Hoagwood, 2002).

Teacher ratings of antisocial students' social skills tend, not surprisingly, to be low and are predictive of future adjustment problems (Patterson et al., 1992; Reid et al., 2002; Walker & McConnell, 1995). We find in our own longitudinal research that regular teachers annually rate our antisocial students as highly deficient in their social skills, particularly those skills that support a successful classroom adjustment (e.g., cooperates with others, is personally organized, and listens carefully to instructions).

The amount of time students spend academically engaged in the classroom is an important skill that is a correlate of academic achievement as measured by standardized tests (Rosenshine, 1979). Academic engagement (academic learning time) means that the student is working on assigned tasks, attending to and involved with the assignment, and making appropriate motor responses (e.g., writing or computing) (see Brophy & Evertson, 1981; Brophy & Good, 1986). Studies indicate that, on average, academic engagement levels in the elementary grades vary between about 70% and 90% of allocated instructional time. In an observational study of 230 elementary school students with disabilities, Rich and Ross (1989) assessed the amount of academically engaged time (AET) displayed

TABLE 1.3

Profiles of the Classroom Behavior of Antisocial and At-Risk Students, Grade 5.

Code Category	Antisocial (%)	At Risk (%)	Difference (%)	p
Attending	76.30	86.00	9.70	.0001
Positive initiation to teacher	1.32	0.74	0.58	.0108
Group compliance	1.25	1.90	0.65	.0531
Negative initiation to teacher	0.34	0.05	0.29	.0105
Physical aggression	0.21	0.07	0.14	.0162
Noise	2.80	0.46	2.34	.0005
Out of seat	3.40	1.03	2.37	.0005

Source: Walker et al. (1987).

by their sample as follows: regular classrooms ($N = 39$), resource rooms ($N = 55$), special classrooms ($N = 84$), and special schools ($N = 52$). The academic engagement levels for students in the resource room were highest (93%), followed by the regular classroom (81%). These two placements had higher levels of both allocated and actual engaged time than the other two placements in the study; in contrast, the special class placement group had the lowest levels on these measures. It should be noted, however, that the students with milder disabling conditions were assigned to resource rooms and regular classrooms, whereas the students with more severe disabilities were in the special class and special school placements.

The academic engagement levels of the antisocial youths studied by Walker, Shinn, O'Neill, and Ramsey (1987) were consistently below regular classroom, normative standards for AET, averaging between 60% and 70% of observed time in regular classroom settings. Table 1.3 contains profiles of the behavior of the antisocial and at-risk students in our ongoing longitudinal study (Walker et al., 1987). These profiles are based on a series of direct observations recorded by professionally trained observers when the target students were in the fifth grade. The observation sessions were conducted during structured academic periods in regular classrooms. The table lists the average amount of time spent in three categories of appropriate behavior and four categories of inappropriate behavior. The antisocial students had significantly less favorable profiles than the at-risk students on each of the appropriate categories except for positive initiation to the teacher. As expected, the antisocial students had substantially less favorable profiles on all of the inappropriate categories.

Interestingly, the antisocial students had higher rates of positive *and* negative initiations to the teacher. This may be a consequence of their having relatively low levels of engagement with academic tasks, poor attending rates, and weak academic skills. These attributes would cause them to be substantially more dependent on the teacher's assistance in order to perform academically.

This profile shows a very poor classroom adjustment for the antisocial students and a surprisingly good one for the at-risk students.

Playground Behavior

Antisocial students have equally serious adjustment problems with peers on the playground as they do with teachers in the classroom. In fact, the aggressive tendencies of antisocial students are more easily expressed in the less structured setting of the playground. Also, the ratio of adults to students on the playground is much less favorable than in the classroom. Studies by the senior author and his colleagues indicate that antisocial children produce anywhere from two to nine times more negative-aggressive behavior than their nonantisocial peers in free-play settings (Walker, Hops, & Greenwood, 1993). Table 1.4 contains a profile of the playground social behavior of the antisocial and at-risk students in this ongoing longitudinal study. Specifically, the table shows the average proportion of time spent in seven observation code categories (five negative, one positive, and one structured) for the antisocial and at-risk students during a series of behavioral observations recorded on the playground. As in the classroom, the antisocial students had significantly less favorable profiles on each of these categories than

---

TABLE 1.4

Profiles of the Playground Social Behavior of Antisocial and At-Risk Students.

Code Category*	Antisocial (%)	At Risk (%)	Difference (%)	p
Negative target verbal	6.20	2.40	3.80	.0407
Negative target physical	0.85	0.45	0.40	.0011
Negative peer verbal	5.50	2.57	2.93	.0041
Negative peer physical	3.90	1.50	2.40	.0007
Ignore	0.82	0.43	0.39	.0252
Positive target verbal	5.60	6.90	1.30	.0124
Structured activity	38.80	50.20	11.40	.0407

*Code categories are defined as follows:
Negative target verbal: Hostile, verbally aggressive language by the target student.
Negative target physical: Hostile behavior involving physical contact by the target student (for example, hitting).
Negative peer verbal: Hostile, verbally aggressive language by a peer of the target student directed toward the target student.
Negative peer physical: Hostile behavior involving physical contact by a peer of the target student directed toward the target student (for example, hitting).
Ignore: A student does not respond to the social initiation of a peer.
Positive target verbal: Positive comments (such as compliments or praise) by the target student directed toward a peer.
Structured activity: An organized game or activity with an identifiable set of rules.
Source: Walker et al. (1993).

the at-risk students. The two groups were much more nearly equivalent in their positive social behavior than in their negative behavior. In addition, the antisocial students had substantially more negative social behavior directed toward them than did the at-risk students. Finally, the antisocial students spent much less time in structured activities at recess than did the at-risk students.

Overall, these studies of the playground social behavior of antisocial students indicate that their positive social behavior nearly matched the levels of their normal peers. However, their frequency of negative social behavior was much higher than is normal for the playground. For their part, peers tended to reciprocate these students' negative-aggressive behavior at nearly identical levels (Walker et al., 1987). They were biased against antisocial children due to their history of aversive, negative interactions with them. Peers tended to attribute malevolent intentions to even the neutral social behavior of antisocial children (Hollinger, 1987).

Gender, Conduct Disorder, and Antisocial Behavior

Conduct disorder and antisocial behavior have been studied much more extensively among boys than girls. Perhaps this is because of the frequency with which boys engage in these forms of behavior and so come into contact more often with police and the juvenile justice system (Chamberlain & Reid, 1994; Zoccolillo, 1993). In spite of the fact that girls are a far less serious threat to the public safety than boys, adolescent girls now make up the fastest-growing segment of the juvenile justice system (Acoca, 1998). Boys are much more likely to express their antisocial behavior in confrontational, externalizing (outer-directed) forms whereas girls are more covert and internalizing (inner-directed).

In a major review of gender and conduct disorder, Zoccolillo (1993) reported overwhelming evidence of a greater prevalence of antisocial behavior patterns among preadolescent boys than girls. Other studies, however, offer a more balanced interpretation of the available research, noting that approximately 60% of youths from the general population, both boys and girls, report participating in a broad array of delinquent acts (Loeber & Hay, 1994; Talbott & Thiede, 1999). The research on antisocial behavior, conduct disorder, and delinquency in boys and girls seems to support the following conclusions:

◆ The first step along girls' pathway into the juvenile justice system typically involves victimization as opposed to arrest (Acoca, 1998).

◆ The antisocial and delinquent behavior of girls is much more likely to emerge during adolescence than earlier, as is so often the case with boys (Chesney-Lind & Sheldon, 1998; Talbott & Thiede, 1999).

◆ Delinquent girls self-report more psychological symptoms and tend to have higher rates of *DSM-IV* mental disorders than delinquent boys. They also tend to have higher rates of physical, emotional, and sexual abuse and of neglect, as well as increased incidence of family histories of mental illness (see McCabe et al., 2002).

◆ When adolescent girls are identified as having conduct problems, they are more than twice as likely to be diagnosed as having comorbid emotional disorders and are substantially less likely to receive services for their problems (Chamberlain & Reid, 1994; Offord, Boyle, & Racine, 1991).

◆ Girls with conduct disorder are at least equal to if not at greater risk for serious long-term disorders than are males with CD. Further, girls appear to be far less well served than boys by the courts and social service agencies for their problems, and at-risk girls are more likely to be assigned to out-of-home placements than are boys (Chamberlain & Reid, 1994).

◆ Boys are more invested in physical forms of overt aggression whereas girls are primarily invested in relational aggression in which nonphysical but destructive forms of covert aggression are practiced (e.g., the trashing of others' reputations, social exclusion from all-girl groups, and delivery of verbal punishment) (see Crick, 1995; Crick et al., 2002; Tomada & Schneider, 1997).

These research findings indicate that, although there is some degree of overlap in the antisocial and delinquent behavior of girls and boys (Talbott & Thiede, 1999), it would be a huge mistake to assume that the same detection procedures and intervention approaches are appropriate for each gender. Indeed, quite the opposite is the case. Girls have different risk profiles than do boys and appear to be in much greater need of treatment for psychological problems resulting from abuse and victimization when they enter the juvenile justice system. Further, in their judgments, disposition of cases, and general actions, the courts and social service agencies frequently seem to exhibit systemic biases that favor boys over girls.

A focus on feminine values, the development of social support networks, and the forging of good social relationships are of paramount importance in treatment programs for girls. Gender-specific programming guidelines are now beginning to emerge that will prove useful in designing and implementing interventions for girls who have CD and who are at risk of adopting a delinquent lifestyle (see *Oregon's Guidelines for Effective, Gender-Specific Programming for Girls* [Patton & Morgan, 2000] and also *Investing in Girls: A 21st Century Strategy* [Acoca, 1999], available from the U.S. Office of Juvenile Justice and Delinquency Prevention). These documents are highly recommended for professionals who work with female delinquents and girls exhibiting antisocial behavior. They also contain curricular resources and materials for use by online practitioners in programming effectively for at-risk and non-at-risk girls.

The Causes and Origins of Antisocial Behavior

Conduct disorder and antisocial behavior are considered to be multiply determined; that is, a host of constitutional (genetic, neurobiological) and environmental (family, community) factors may influence the development of these behavior patterns (Kazdin, 1985; Loeber & Farrington, 1998, 2001; Patterson et al., 1992; Reid et al., 2002). In terms of causal factors, the family situation(s) in which at-risk children are embedded should be considered within a community context. As a rule, the child with CD is exposed to high levels of risk in both the family and community settings, and the development of antisocial behavior patterns is often the unfortunate result of such exposure within these two contexts.

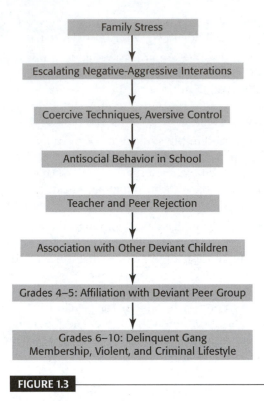

FIGURE 1.3 ◆

Causal Events for Antisocial Behavior.

Patterson and his colleagues (Patterson et al., 1992; Reid et al., 2002) offer a detailed explanation of the causal events and processes in the development of antisocial behavior patterns among at-risk children and youths. They present a causal model in which a host of family stressors (e.g., poverty, divorce, drug and alcohol problems, and abuse) play a role. Under the influence of these stressors, normal parenting practices are disrupted, and family routines become chaotic, unpredictable, and ruled by coercion processes (e.g., escalating in order to force the submission of other family members, to get one's way, and to escape from unpleasant circumstances and tasks). Disrupted parenting practices, in turn, lead to negative-aggressive interactions among family members and attempts to control each others' behavior through aversive means. Family pathology can become extremely destructive under these conditions, providing a fertile breeding ground for the development of antisocial behavior patterns. Children from such homes come to school with negative attitudes about schooling, a limited repertoire of cooperative behavior skills, a predilection to use coercive tactics to control and manipulate others, and a well-developed capacity for emotional outbursts and confrontation.

Figure 1.3 illustrates the developmental phases of this causal process and the way it plays out over time. Children from this kind of family context are socialized to antisocial behavior very efficiently. Unfortunately, these shaping forces and their negative effects tend to flow across generations, much like inherited traits (Patterson et al., 1992).

If a young child brings a pattern of antisocial behavior to school that is characterized by (1) a high frequency of occurrence, (2) occurrence across multiple settings and contexts, and (3) expression in multiple forms, he or she will be at serious risk for both peer and teacher rejection. This rejection, in turn, is associated with academic failure and further isolation. Because of this rejection and resulting social isolation, the antisocial child seeks out as peer affiliates those who share the same status, attitudes, and behavioral characteristics. Sociometric studies consistently indicate that antisocial students' best friends tend to be the other antisocial students in their school (Patterson et al., 1992). Around grade 4 or 5, these antisocial children become eligible for, and are recruited into, deviant peer groups comprised of other children like themselves. Due to social rejection by normal peers, other at-risk, antisocial children are often the only friendship options available to them. Of these children, 70% have their first felony arrest within two years of becoming a fully enfranchised member of this deviant peer group. (And note that approximately 1 arrest occurs for every 10 to 11 arrestable offenses committed.) If this pattern of delinquency continues, it becomes an excellent predictor of adult criminality.

In sum, the path to delinquency, criminality, and, ultimately, prison begins for many individuals very early in their lives. It usually starts with the early acquisition of an antisocial behavior pattern within the home and family that is often well developed prior to entering school. And if this behavior pattern becomes elaborated during the primary grades, it usually leads to social rejection, acceptance by a deviant peer group, and, frequently, to criminal behavior. This is a highly predictable path, and one that, sadly, is being trod by many thousands of young people as conditions have deteriorated socially, economically, and culturally.

Pathways to Antisocial Behavior and Conduct Disorder

As noted previously, longitudinal and descriptive studies in the United States and other countries have contributed enormously to our knowledge of the developmental course of conduct disorder and antisocial behavior among at-risk children and youths (see Cicchetti & Nurcombe, 1993; Eddy et al., 2002; Loeber & Farrington, 1998, 2001; Reid et al., 2002). Research reported by these investigators over the past two decades provides support for two observations:

- ◆ Many at-risk children demonstrate a progression in their antisocial behavior from trivial to severe antisocial acts.
- ◆ Antisocial children and youths tend to follow one or more of the following paths to conduct disorder: covert, overt, and/or disobedience or conflict with authority.

Patterson and his associates have studied the ecology and dynamics of family interactions of antisocial children and youths more thoroughly than perhaps any group to date. They were the first to document that many antisocial

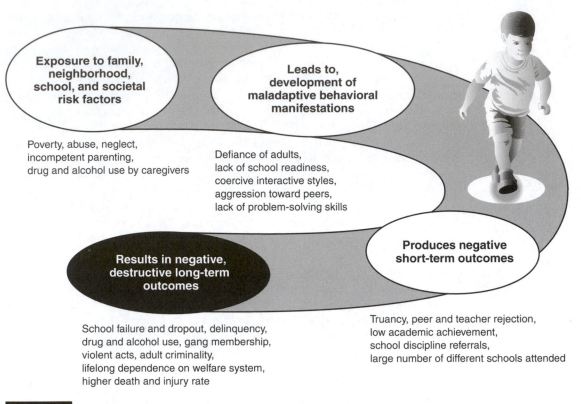

Exposure to family, neighborhood, school, and societal risk factors

Poverty, abuse, neglect, incompetent parenting, drug and alcohol use by caregivers

Leads to, development of maladaptive behavioral manifestations

Defiance of adults, lack of school readiness, coercive interactive styles, aggression toward peers, lack of problem-solving skills

Produces negative short-term outcomes

Truancy, peer and teacher rejection, low academic achievement, school discipline referrals, large number of different schools attended

Results in negative, destructive long-term outcomes

School failure and dropout, delinquency, drug and alcohol use, gang membership, violent acts, adult criminality, lifelong dependence on welfare system, higher death and injury rate

FIGURE 1.4 ◆

The Path to Long-Term Negative Outcomes for At-Risk Children and Youths.

children progress from trivial to severe antisocial acts over time. Often, this process involves an unskilled parent caring for an infant with a difficult temperament. Tense infant–caregiver interactions and relationships emerge, affected by the parent's limited ability to influence the child. This may lead to the child not complying with parental requests, commands, and even demands. Noncompliance eventually evolves into oppositional-defiant behavior, which can include tantrums. The parent may weakly monitor and supervise the child's activities, whereabouts, schedule, and affiliations. This, in turn, can lead to maladaptive child behavior involving acts such as stealing, lying, and cheating, as well as affiliation with deviant peers. These forms of antisocial behavior are often precursors to delinquent acts, especially if they are accompanied by membership in a deviant peer group (Loeber & Farrington, 1998, 2001; Patterson et al., 1992).

Figure 1.4 shows the connections that exist between risks, their behavioral effects, and the short- and long-term outcomes that result from them. Longitudinal evidence suggests that thousands of behaviorally at-risk children are on this path, which is fueled by ongoing risk exposure in family, neighborhood, school, and societal contexts. Our goal should be to keep vulnerable children off this path and to divert, as soon as possible, those who are already on it. Early intervention is the best option available for doing so.

Loeber and his colleagues (Loeber, Wei, Stouthamer-Loeber, Huizina, & Thornberry, 1999) have identified three different pathways to the development of antisocial behavior, conduct disorder, and delinquency; these pathways are summarized in Table 1.5. Individuals on a *covert* path are characterized by stealth and concealment, and they direct their attention toward property (vandalism, theft, arson), toward themselves (substance abuse), or both. The dishonesty involved in a covert path (lying, cheating, stealing) is strongly objectionable to teachers and other school personnel. In contrast, individuals on an *overt* path directed their attention toward other persons; they confront and victimize others, act aggressively, and use coercive tactics to obtain their way or to force the submission of others. Cruelty, bullying, and fighting are commonly associated with this path. The *defiance-disobedience* path involves opposition to adult-imposed rules and behavioral expectations.

Considerable research has been done the past two decades regarding the age of onset of delinquent acts. Juvenile delinquents can be divided into early versus later starters based on the age at which they first begin committing delinquent

---

TABLE 1.5

Developmental Pathways to Antisocial Behavior, Conduct Disorder, and Delinquency.

Covert Behavior
Stealing
Lying
Burglary
Drug and Alcohol involvement

Overt Behavior
Aggression
Coercion
Bullying
Manipulation of others
Escalated interactions with teachers, parents, and peers

Disobedience
Noncompliance
Oppositional-defiant behavior
Resistance to adult influence

Source: Loeber et al. (1993).

acts. *Early* starters are socialized to antisocial behavior from infancy by the family environment and family stressors that disrupt parenting practices. In contrast, *later* starters are thought to be socialized to delinquency by peer group influences and not by pathological family conditions. According to Moffitt (1993), early starters have life course antisocial behavior, and later starters have adolescent-limited antisocial behavior.

Patterson and his colleagues (Patterson et al., 1990) analyzed a longitudinal sample of 206 boys and their families according to those who had committed one or more delinquent acts. They found that early starters were substantially more at risk for a host of adjustment problems than were later starters. These authors hypothesize that later starters have not been exposed to negative family conditions and disrupted parenting practices in the same way that early starters have; they also have not experienced the same degrees of academic failure and peer rejection. Thus, their risk profiles tend to be quite different from those of early starters (i.e., much less serious), with a better long-term prognosis.

The distinction between early and later starters enables us to assess the risk status of antisocial delinquents in a more precise manner. It also has clear implications for intervention. It is especially important to closely monitor later starters, who typically begin their antisocial acts in the intermediate grades, and to implement interventions (e.g., mentoring programs) to "pull them back." Also, at-risk girls typically do not begin engaging in antisocial acts until early adolescence and are often denied access to intervention supports and services when they do.

Antisocial Behavior and Youth Violence

Our society is concerned, quite justifiably, with the escalating patterns of violence that have emerged in recent decades. The U.S. Office of Juvenile Justice and Delinquency Prevention (OJJDP), for example, reports that between 1985 and 1994 there was a 40% increase in murders, rapes, robberies, and assaults reported to law enforcement agencies nationally. Despite their comparatively low numbers within the general population, youths accounted for 26% of this increase in violence. And during this same period, there was a 249% increase in gun-related murders committed by juveniles.

The National Center for Juvenile Justice estimates that the number of youths age 10–17 arrested annually for violent crime could double by the year 2010. If offense and arrest rates remain at current levels, the following increases in violent crimes are projected to occur by 2010: murder, 142%; rape, 66%; robbery, 58%; and assault, 129% (APA Online, 2002). In our view, these grim prospects call for a national action plan, heavily weighted toward prevention, in order to reduce the potential social, human, and economic costs.

The majority of criminal acts are committed by approximately 6–8% of the population. As Lipsey and Derzon (1998) note, identifying who these individuals are and intervening very early with them, as well as their families, would be a highly cost-effective strategy. In fact, the OJJDP has proposed an 8% solution that would focus intensively on just this portion of the youth population. However, this strategy, like prevention approaches in general, is highly dependent on the ability to identify likely correlates of future violence and to detect populations who share these attributes.

Violence predictors have been investigated across four broad constructs or dimensions: (1) categories of antisocial behavior, (2) personal characteristics, (3) family characteristics, and (4) social factors. Youth violence predictors have been identified by Lipsey and Derzon (1998) for 6- to 11-year-olds and for 12- to 14-year-olds. The strongest predictors for these two groups are a pattern of general offending and substance abuse. Other predictors include involvement with antisocial peers, antisocial parents, low socioeconomic status, aggression, and weak school performance. The good news is that most of these predictors are amenable to change through appropriate intervention. For example, having friends who behave in a conventional manner is an important protective factor in buffering and offsetting the risk of violent and delinquent behavior (Satcher, 2001). Thus, teaching at-risk youths to seek friendships among groups of normative peers is an important prevention strategy.

Patterson and his colleagues (Patterson et al., 1991, 1992; Reid et al., 2002) have shown that youths who are chronic offenders (i.e., having three or more arrests by age 12) are much more likely to be early starters in their pattern of antisocial behavior. They found that 100% of boys arrested before age 10 had at least three arrests before reaching age 17. They also identified 17 boys in their longitudinal sample who had committed violent acts; each of these 17 boys was found to be a chronic offender. Thus, a severe pattern of antisocial behavior that is clearly in evidence early in the schooling process, coupled with an early start in committing delinquent acts, may identify the future chronic offender. A significant proportion of violent acts are committed by chronic offenders—many of whom fit the profile of the fledgling psychopath as described by Lynam (1996).

Violent behavior remains one of the most difficult problems with which society must cope. In spite of our increasing knowledge of the conditions from which it springs, we are still relatively limited in our ability to predict and prevent its occurrence (Satcher, 2001). We can identify groups of at-risk youths who share certain characteristics including antisocial behavior and who as a group will have higher-than-normal rates of violence over time. However, when it comes to predicting which of these individuals will commit such violent acts in the future, our prediction models tend to fare poorly. Still, our current knowledge does enable the early detection and treatment of groups of at-risk individuals.

The recently released Surgeon General's Report on Youth Violence (Satcher, 2001) provides the most complete synthesis to date on the causes and correlates of youth violence. As the report makes clear, U.S. society suffered an epidemic of violence between the early 1980s and mid-1990s, fueled primarily by the surge in the crack cocaine trade and a huge increase in the number of weapons-carrying youths. However, over the past decade, the rates of youth violence have, for the most part, reverted to their pre-1980 levels. Figure 1.5 depicts the rates, over a 20-year period, of the four crimes that form the FBI's violent crime index. All of these crime rates have returned to their approximate early-1980s levels with the exception of aggravated assault, which remains well above its level prior to the surge in youth violence. Policymakers are concerned that, should youths resume carrying weapons on a broad scale, the possibility exists for another surge in the rate of violent acts (Satcher, 2001).

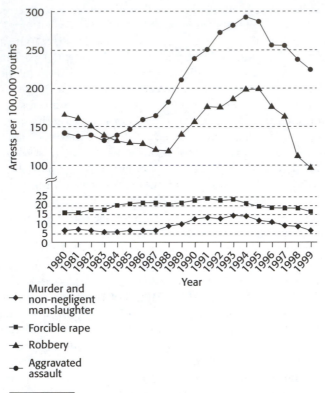

Arrest Rates of Youths Age 10–17 for Serious Violent Crime, by Type of Crime, 1980–99.
Source: Satcher (2001).

Youth violence spilled over into the school setting in a tragic manner in the second half of the 1990s. School shootings with multiple victims—in Arkansas and Oregon and Colorado—traumatized society by the sheer numbers killed and wounded, by the conspiratorial aura of the attacks, and by the apparent randomness with which victims were selected. The student shooters had been teased and bullied by peers, tended to be consumed with rage, were bent on seeking redress for their grievances through violent means, and in some cases had mental health problems.

The mass murders resulted in a huge federal investment in school safety and security measures for school systems. Indeed, ensuring the safety of schools has emerged as a high national priority in the past decade (Green, 1999). An early study by the National School Boards Association (1993), along with the shock associated with the school shootings, proved to be influential in galvanizing the government to address the problem of violence in schools. The study involved more than 700 school districts nationwide and concluded that such violence results primarily from the breakdown of the family and the portrayal of violent acts in the media. Other major causes of violence cited in the survey included alcohol and drug abuse, easy access to guns, and poverty. We would add mean-spirited teasing, harassment, and bullying to this list of causal factors.

According to the study, 39% of responding urban districts reported a shooting or knife attack in school during the previous year, and 23% reported a drive-by shooting. Suburban and rural school districts also reported an increase in the number and seriousness of violent incidents, including rapes and shootings. Further, more than 80% of the 700 participating districts reported increases in school violence, with 35% noting that the increase was substantial. Seventy-seven percent of the districts cited changing family situations as being primarily responsible for this increase, and 60% cited the media.

The report noted that common methods schools have traditionally used to address violence include suspending offenders, increasing the police presence on campus, teaching students alternative ways of handling conflict, and setting up separate schools for disruptive students. Thirty-nine percent of urban schools reported using metal detectors, and 11% had installed closed circuit television systems. And these numbers are far higher today than they were when this study was conducted (see Green, 1999).

During the past decade, the landscape of school violence has changed, and we now have a much deeper knowledge of the causal factors associated with it and strategies for reducing its likelihood. This general landscape and accompanying knowledge base, as it relates to school security and safety, are dealt with in detail later in this book.

A Perspective on Violence

Violent acts committed within the family, school, and community threaten the very fabric of our society. Like tornadoes and earthquakes, violent acts usually occur without warning, do incredible damage, and require long periods for recovery. Just as we know that tornadoes, for example, arise out of volatile thermo-convectional conditions, we understand something of the conditions associated with violent acts: (1) family stressors such as poverty, alcohol, and drug abuse; (2) a history of physical, sexual, and/or psychological abuse and neglect; (3) depression, frustration, and a sense of hopelessness; and (4) exposure to the modeling or display of violence. As with tornadoes, we can sometimes identify the mix of volatile conditions and triggering events that make violent acts more likely to occur. However, once triggered and unleashed, they must run their course, often leaving a wake of destruction in their path.

Because violent acts are so difficult to predict and nearly impossible to control once they occur, far greater efforts must be made to prevent or ameliorate the conditions out of which they arise (Satcher, 2001; Schorr, 1988). We have the scientific knowledge and overall capability to address this social problem in a more effective manner than we currently do. Further, violence is a *societal* problem that we must solve collectively. Schools have an important role to play in this regard, particularly in relation to preventing school violence. Ultimately, however, reducing violence in society will require working partnerships between families, schools, social service agencies, legislators, policymakers, churches, public safety officials, corrections departments, and advocacy organizations, which collectively must forge a new set of normative standards and values in which violence is eschewed as a means of solving problems. A blueprint and action plan for doing so will probably have to begin with and be coordinated by our national political leadership.

Making Schools More Supportive for At-Risk Students

Our society's social and economic problems are spilling over into schools in an unfortunate, but not unexpected, manner. They are greatly complicating the basic task of educating our students safely and effectively. The school's primary role is to facilitate the academic achievement and social development of all students. Students who bring maladaptive behavior patterns to school or who are prone to violence must be *directly taught* a replacement adaptive behavior pattern that will enhance their chances of (1) staying in school for as long as possible (80% of all crimes are committed by high school dropouts), (2) achieving school success, (3) gaining acceptance from teachers and peers, and (4) going on to lead productive lives.

Even though today many children and youths come from and return to chaotic home environments, they can still succeed in school if given the proper supports and access to good instruction. Keeping our young people engaged in school and helping them to be successful therein are two of the very best things that can be done for them—and for ourselves—in terms of potential long-term benefits. There is no better investment our society can make in its own future than this one.

We have substantial knowledge about how to divert at-risk children, youths, and families from destructive outcomes, and successful model programs have been reviewed and described extensively by Catalano, Loeber, and McKinney (1999), by Loeber and Farrington (1998, 2001), and by Reid and his colleagues (2002). Schools, we believe, are willing participants in developing comprehensive solutions to the complex problems of children and youths that threaten our overall quality of life. But they need our society's investments in time, money, support, and expertise as never before.

In the mass processing of individuals by schools, educators are faced with ever-increasing numbers of children who are severely disadvantaged in their ability to meet the normal demands of schooling. Many antisocial children do not have the school readiness skills and preschool experiences necessary for getting off to a solid start in school, which is so important for school success. The long-term prospects for many of these children are truly dismal.

Miller and his colleagues (1998) have observed that successful school-based efforts to prevent these outcomes require a sustained commitment to schoolwide reform, and not simply application of time-limited programs. They argue that prevention requires a major institutional commitment to empower staff, students, and parents to participate in the design and implementation of changes that will positively affect their lives. Schools can make important contributions to reducing dropout rates and increasing graduation rates among marginalized student populations, enhancing attachment to schooling, and facilitating school connectedness (see Baker et al., 2001; McNeely, Nonnemaker, & Blum, 2002).

Gary and Denise Gottfredson and their associates have conducted the most thorough national investigation on what schools actually do, and should do, in addressing problem behavior, delinquency, and violence in the context of schooling (Gottfredson & Gottfredson, 2001; Gottfredson et al., 2000). Schools that successfully prevent these problems and outcomes tend to do the following: (1) ensure the principal's support, (2) provide high-quality staff training, (3) supervise prevention activities, (4) use structured materials and programs when possible, (5) integrate programs into normal school operations, (6) embed programs in a school planning activity, and (7) create structures and systems to promote the use of best practices and to implement them with high degrees of fidelity. We believe the problem is not one of not knowing what to do, but rather one of forging a marriage between research-based intervention programs and practices that are known to work, and also reforming school structures and systems in ways that support their effective use and sustainability over the long term. The role of the schools in addressing antisocial behavior patterns is discussed more fully in the next chapter.

Conclusion

The remainder of this book is devoted to providing guidelines and strategies for use by school personnel in working with antisocial students. There are no magic bullets in the material presented herein. Dealing with the antisocial student population in today's pressurized school environment is difficult and frustrating, and often there is no identifiable reward. However, of all those who suffer from conditions and disorders that impair school performance, these students are among the most capable, with the greatest capacity for change. We believe that antisocial students deserve access to the best practices and model programs—ones that have proved to be effective in prior research. Our basic purpose herein is to describe and illustrate these practices and programs.

InfoTrac College Edition Research Terms

Antisocial behavior
Oppositional defiant disorder
Behaviorally at-risk
School Social Behavior Scale

References

Achenbach, T. (1985). *Assessment and taxonomy of child and adolescent psychopathology*. Beverly Hills, CA: Sage.

Achenbach, T. (1991). *The child behavior checklist: Manual for the teacher's report form.* Burlington: University of Vermont, Department of Psychiatry.

Acoca, L. (1998). Outside/inside: The violation of American girls at home, on the streets, and in the juvenile justice system. *Crime & Delinquency, 44,* 561–589.

Acoca, L. (1999). Investing in girls: A 21st century strategy. *Journal of the Office of Juvenile Justice and Delinquency Prevention, 6*(1)*, 3–13.

American Psychological Association. (1993). *Violence and youth: Psychology's response. Volume I: Summary report of the American Psychological Association Commission on Violence and Youth.* Washington, DC: American Psychological Association.

Angold, A. (2000). *Preadolescent screening and data analysis.* Paper presented to the 2nd Annual Expert Panel Meeting on Preadolescent Screening Procedures. Sponsored by the Substance Abuse and Mental Health Services Administration, National Institutes of Health, Washington, DC.

APA Online. (2002). *Is youth violence just another fact of life?* American Psychological Association, Public Interest Directorate, 750 First Street NE, Washington, DC 20002.

Baker, J., Derrer, R., Davis, S., Dinklage-Travis, H., Linder, D., & Nicholson, M. (2001). The flip side of the coin: Understanding the school's contribution to dropout and completion. *School Psychology Quarterly, 16*(4), 406–426.

Biglan, T. (2001). *The Palo Alto Project.* Unpublished document. Eugene: Oregon Research Institute.

Brophy, J., & Evertson, C. (1981). *Student characteristics and teaching.* New York: Longman.

Brophy, J., & Good, T. (1986). Teacher behavior and student achievement. In M. Wittrock (Ed.), *Handbook of research on teaching* (3rd ed., pp. 328–375). New York: Macmillan.

Bullis, M., & Walker, H. M. (1995). Characteristics and causal factors of troubled youth. In C. M. Nelson, B. I. Wolford, & R. B. Rutherford, Jr. (Eds.), *Comprehensive and collaborative systems that work for troubled youth: A national agenda* (pp. 15–28). Richmond: Eastern Kentucky University, National Coalition for Juvenile Justice Services, Training Resource Center.

Burns, B. (2002). Reasons for hope for children and families: A perspective and overview. In B. Burns & K. K. Hoagwood (Eds.), *Community treatment for youth: Evidence-based interventions for severe emotional and behavioral disorders* (pp. 1–15). New York: Oxford University Press.

Burns, B., & Hoagwood, K. (2002). *Community treatment for youth: Evidence-based interventions for severe emotional and behavioral disorders.* New York: Oxford University Press.

Capaldi, D. M., & Patterson, G. R. (1989). *Psychometric properties of fourteen latent constructs from the Oregon Youth Study.* New York: Springer-Verlag.

Catalano, R., Loeber, R., & McKinney, K. (1999). School and community interventions to prevent serious and violent offending. *Juvenile Justice Bulletin,* U.S. Department of Justice, Office of Juvenile Justice and Delinquency Prevention, Washington, D.C.

Chamberlain, P., & Reid, J. (1994). Differences in risk factors and adjustment for male and female delinquents in Treatment Foster Care. *Journal of Child and Family Studies, 3*(1), 23–39.

Chesney-Lind, M., & Sheldon, R. (1998). *Girls, delinquency, and juvenile justice.* Belmont, CA: Wadsworth.

Cicchetti, D., & Nurcombe, B. (Eds.). (1993). *Toward a developmental perspective on conduct disorder,* [Special issue], *Development and Psychopathology, 5*(1/2), 1–344. London: Cambridge University Press.

Coie, J., & Kupersmidt, J. (1983). A behavioral analysis of emerging social status in boys' groups. *Child Development, 54,* 1400–1416.

Coie, J., & Jacobs, M. (1993). The role of social context in the prevention of conduct disorder. *Development and Psychopathology, 5*(1/2), 263–276.

Colvin, G., Tobin, T., Beard, K., Hagan, S., & Sprague, J. (1998). The school bully: Assessing the problem, developing interventions, and future research directions. *Journal of Behavioral Education, 8*(3), 293–319.

Crick, N. (1995). Relational aggression: The role of intent attributions, feelings of distress, and provocation type. *Development and psychopathology, 7,* 313–322.

Crick, N., Casas, J., & Mosher, M. (1997). Relational and overt aggression in preschool. *Developmental Psychology, 33*(4), 579–588.

Crick, N., Grotpeter, J., & Bigbee, M. (2002). Relationally and physically aggressive children's intent attributions and feelings of distress for relational and instrumental peer provocations. *Child Development, 73*(4), 1134–1142.

Dishion, T., & Andrews, D. (1995). Preventing escalation in problem behaviors with high-risk, young adolescents: Immediate and one-year outcomes. *Journal of Consulting and Clinical Psychology, 63*(4), 1–11.

Dodge, K. (1985). A social information processing model of social competence in children. In M. Perlmutter (Ed.), *Minnesota symposium in child psychology.* Hillsdale, NJ: Erlbaum.

Dodge, K. (1993). The future of research on conduct disorder. *Development and Psychopathology, 5*(1/2), 311–320.

Dodge, K., & Crick, N. (1990) Social information-processing bases of aggressive behavior in children. *Personality and Social Psychology Bulletin, 53,* 1146–1158.

Dodge, K., Pettit, G., McClaskey, C., & Brown, M. (1986). Social competence in children. *Monographs of the Society for Research in Child Development* [Serial No. 213], *51*(2), 1–84.

Eddy, J. M., Reid, J. B., & Curry, V. (2002). The etiology of youth antisocial behavior, delinquency and violence and a public health approach to prevention. In M. R. Shinn, H. M. Walker, & G. Stoner (Eds.), *Interventions for academic and behavior problems II: Preventive and remedial approaches* (pp. 27–51). Bethesda, MD: National Association for School Psychologists.

Epstein, L., Plog, A., & Porter, W. (2002). Bullying-proofing your school: Results of a four-year intervention. *Emotional and Behavioral Disorders in Youth, 2*(3), 55–56, 73–78.

Gottfredson, G., & Gottfredson, D. (2001). What schools do to prevent problem behavior and promote safe environments. *Journal of Educational and Psychological Consultation, 12*(4), 313–344.

Gottfredson, G., Gottfredson, D., Czeh, E., Cantor, D., Crosse, S., & Hantman, I. (2000). *National study of delinquency prevention in schools.* Available from Gottfredson Associates, Inc., 3239 B Corporate Court, Ellicott City, MD 21042.

Green, M. (1999). *The appropriate and effective use of security technology in U.S. schools.* U.S. Department of Justice, Office of Juvenile Justice Programs, 810 Seventh Street NW, Washington, DC 20531.

Greenberg, M. T., Domitrovich, C., & Bumbarger, B. (2001). *Preventing mental disorders in school-age children: A review of the effectiveness of prevention programs.* Available from the Prevention Research Center for the Promotion of Human Development, College of Health and Human Development, Pennsylvania State University, State College, PA.

Gresham, F. M., Lane, K. L., & Lambros, K. M. (2000). Comorbidity of conduct problems and ADHD: Identification of "fledging psychopaths." *Journal of Emotional and Behavioral Disorders, 8*(2), 83–93.

Gresham, F. M., Lane, K. L., MacMillan, D. L., & Bocian, K. M. (1999). Social and academic profiles of externalizing and internalizing groups: Risk factors for emotional and behavioral disorders. *Behavioral Disorders, 24*(3), 231–245.

Gresham, F., Lane, K., McIntyre, L.,Olson-Tinker, H., Dolstra, L., MacMillan, D., Lambros, K., & Bocian, K. (2001). Risk factors associated with the co-occurrence of hyperactivity-impulsivity-inattention and conduct problems. *Behavioral Disorders, 26*(3), 189–199.

Gresham, F., MacMillan, D., Bocian, C., Ward, S., & Forness, S. (1998). Comorbidity of hyperactivity-impulsivity-inattention + conduct problems: Risk factors in social, affective, and academic domains. *Journal of Abnormal Child Psychology, 26,* 393–406.

Hersh, R. H., & Walker, H. M. (1983). Great expectations: Making schools effective for all students. *Policy Studies Review, 2*(Special No. 1), 147–188.

Hinshaw, S. (1992). Externalizing behavior problems and academic underachievement in childhood and adolescence: Causal relationships and underlying mechanisms. *Psychological Bulletin, 111,* 127–155.

Hoagwood, K., & Erwin, H. (1997). Effectiveness of school-based mental health services for children: A 10-year research review. *Journal of Child and Family Studies, 6*(4), 435–451.

Hollinger, J. (1987). Social skills for behaviorally disordered children as preparation for mainstreaming: Theory, practice and new directions. *Remedial and Special Education, 8*(4), 17–27.

Hoover, J., & Juul, K. (1993). Bullying in Europe and the U.S. *The Journal of Emotional and Behavioral Problems, 2*(1), 25–29.

Horne, A., & Sayger, T. (1990). *Treating conduct and oppositional disorders in children.* Elmsford, NY: Pergamon Press.

Hunt, R. (1993). Neurobiological patterns of aggression. *The Journal of Emotional and Behavioral Problems, 2*(1), 14–20.

Institute of Medicine, (1989). *Research on children and adolescents with mental, behavioral, and developmental disorders.* Washington, DC: National Academy Press.

Jensen, P., & Cooper, J. (2002). *Attention deficit hyeractive disorder: State of the science: Best practices.* New York: Civic Research Institute.

Kauffman, J. (1989). The regular education initiative as Reagan-Bush Education Policy: A trickle-down theory of education of the hard-to-teach. *Journal of Special Education, 23,* 256–278.

Kazdin, A. E. (Ed.). (1985). *Treatment of antisocial behavior in children and adolescents.* Homewood, IL: Dorsey Press.

Kazdin, A. (1987). Treatment of antisocial behavior in children: Current status and future directions. *Psychological Bulletin, 102,* 187–203.

Kazdin, A. (1993). Adolescent mental health: Prevention and treatment programs. *American Psychologist, 48,* 127–141.

Kutner, L. (1993, January). Young bullies often get worse. *Eugene Register Guard.*

Lane, K., Gresham, F., MacMillan, D., & Bocian, K. (2001). Early detection of students with antisocial behavior and hyperactivity problems. *Education and Treatment of Children, 24*(3), 294–308.

Lindberg, L. D., Boggess, S. & Williams, S. (1999). Multiple threats: The co-occurrence of teen health risk behaviors. In *Trends in the well-being of America's children and youth* (HHS-100-95-0021). Washington, DC: Office of the Assistant Secretary for Planning and Evaluation, USDHHS.

Lipsey, M., & Derzon, J. (1998). Predictors of violence or serious delinquency in adolescence and early adulthood: A synthesis of longitudinal research. In R. Loeber & D. Farrington (Eds.), *Serious and violent juvenile offenders: Risk factors and successful intervntions.* Thousand Oaks, CA: Sage.

Loeber, R., & Farrington, D. P. (Eds.). (1998). *Serious and violent juvenile offenders: Risk factors and successful interventions.* Thousand Oaks, CA: Sage.

Loeber, R., & Farrington, D. P. (2001). *Serious and violent juvenile offenders: Risk factors and successful interventions.* Thousand Oaks, CA: Sage.

Loeber, R., & Hay, D. (1994). Developmental approaches to aggression and conduct probems. In M. Rutter & D. Hay (Eds.), *Development through life: A handbook for clinicians* (pp. 488–516). Oxford: Blackwell Scientific.

Loeber, R., Wei, E., Stouthamer-Loeber, M., Huizina, D., & Thornberry, T. (1999). Behavioral antecedents to serious and violent juvenile offending: Joint analyses from the Denver Youth Survey, the Pittsburg Youth Study, and the Rochester Development Study. *Studies in Crime and Crime Prevention, 8,* 245–263.

Lynam, D. (1996). Early identification of chronic offenders: Who is the fledgling psychopath? *Psychological Bulletin, 120,* 209–234.

McCabe, K., Lansing, A., Garland, A., & Hough, R. (2002). Gender differences in psychopathology, functional impairment, and familial risk factors among adjudicated delinquents. *Journal of the American Academy of Child and Adolescent Psychiatry, 41*(7), 860–867.

McNeely, C., Nonnemaker, J., & Blum, R. (2002). Promoting school connectedness: Evidence from the national longitudinal study of adolescent health. *Journal of School Health, 72*(4), 138–146.

Merrell, K. W. (1993). *The school social behavior scales (SSBS).* Brandon, VT: Clinical Psychology Publishing, Inc.

Miller, G., Brehm, K., & Whitehouse, S. (1998). Reconceptualizing school-based prevention for antisocial behavior within a resiliency framework. *School Psychology Review, 27*(3), 364–379.

Mischel, W. (1969). Continuity and change in personality. *American Psychologist, 24*(11), 1012–1018.

Moffitt, T. (1993). Adolescence-limited and life-course-persistent antisocial behavior: A developmental taxonomy. *Psychological Review, 100*(4), 674–701.

National School Boards Association. (1993, January). Report of the National School Boards Association on violence in schools. *The Los Angeles Times.*

Offord, D., Boyle, M., & Racine, Y. (1991). The epidemiology of antisocial behavior in childhood and adolescence. In D. J. Pepler & K. H. Rubin (Eds.), *The development and treatment of childhood aggression* (pp. 31–54). Hillsdale, NJ: Erlbaum.

Parker, J. G., & Asher, S. R. (1987). Peer relations and later personal adjustment: Are low-accepted children at risk? *Psychological Bulletin, 102*(3), 357–389.

Patterson, G. R., Capaldi, D., & Bank, L. (1990). An early starter model for predicting delinquency. In D. Pepler & K. H. Rubin (Eds.), *The development and treatment of childhood aggression* (pp. 139–168). Hillsdale, NJ: Lawrence Erlbaum.

Patterson, G. R., DeBaryshe, B. D., & Ramsey, E. (1989). A developmental perspective on antisocial behavior. *American Psychologist, 44,* 329–335.

Patterson, G. R., Reid, J. B., & Dishion, T. J. (1992). *Antisocial boys.* Eugene, OR: Castalia.

Patton, P., & Morgan, M. (2000). *Oregon's Guidelines for Effective Gender-Specific Programming for Girls.* Available from Gender-Specific Consultants, Inc., 830 NE Holladay, Suite 125, Portland, OR 97232.

Quay, H. (1986). Conduct disorders. In H. Quay & J. Werry (Eds.), *Psychopathological disorders of childhood.* New York: Wiley.

Reid, J. (1990). *Prevention research in conduct disorders.* NIMH prevention center proposal, available from Oregon Social Learning Center, 207 E. 5th Avenue, Suite 202, Eugene, OR 97401.

Reid, J. B. (1993). Prevention of conduct disorder before and after school entry: Relating interventions to developmental findings. *Development & Psychopathology, 5,* 311–319.

Reid, J. B., Patterson, G. R., & Snyder, J. J. (Eds.). (2002). *Antisocial behavior in children and adolescents: A developmental analysis and the Oregon Model for Intervention.* Washington, DC: American Psychological Association.

Rich, H., & Ross, S. (1989). Students' time on learning tasks in special education. *Exceptional Children, 55*(6), 508–515.

Robins, L. N. (1978). Sturdy childhood predictors of adult antisocial behavior: Replications from longitudinal studies. *Psychological Medicine, 8,* 611–622.

Rosenshine, B. (1979). Content, time, and direct instruction. In P. Peterson & H. Wahlberg (Eds.), *Research on teaching: Concepts, findings and implications.* Berkeley, CA: McCutcheon.

Ross, A. (1980). *Psychological disorders of children: A behavioral approach to theory, research and therapy* (2nd ed.). New York: McGraw-Hill.

Satcher, D. (2001). *Youth violence: A report of the Surgeon General.* Washington, DC: U.S. Public Health Service, U.S. Department of Health and Human Services.

Schorr, L. (1988). *Within our reach: Breaking the cycle of disadvantage.* New York: Doubleday.

Seeley, J. R., Rohde, P., Lewinsohn, P. M., & Clarke, G. N. (2002). Depression in youth: Epidemiology, identification, and intervention. In M. R. Shinn, H. M. Walker, & G. Stoner (Eds.), *Interventions for academic and behavior problems II: Preventive and remedial approaches* (pp. 885–911). Bethesda, MD: National Association of School Psychologists.

Simcha-Fagan, O., Langner, T., Gersten, J., & Eisenberg, J. (1975). *Violent and antisocial behavior: A longitudinal study of violent youth.* (OCD-CB-480). Unpublished report of the Office of Child Development.

Snell, J. L., MacKenzie, E. P., & Frey, K. S. (2002). Bullying prevention in elementary schools: The importance of adult leadership, peer group support, and student social-emotional skills. In M. R. Shinn, H. M. Walker, & G. Stoner (Eds.), *Interventions for academic and behavior problems II: Preventive and remedial approaches* (pp. 351–372). Bethesda, MD: National Association of School Psychologists.

Strain, P., Guralnick, M., & Walker, H. M. (Eds.). (1986). *Children's social behavior: Development, assessment, and modification.* New York: Academic Press.

Talbott, E., & Thiede, K. (1999). Pathways to antisocial behavior among adolescent girls. *Journal of emotional and behavioral disorders, 7*(1), 31–39.

Tomada, G., & Schneider, B. (1997). Relational aggression, gender, and peer acceptance: Invariance across culture, stability over time, and concordance among informants. *Developmental Psychology, 33*(4), 601–609.

Wagner, M. (1989, April). *The national transition study: Results of a national, longitudinal study of transition from school to work for students with disabilities.* Paper presented at the Council for Exceptional Children's Annual Convention, San Francisco.

Walker, H. M. (1986). The Assessments for Integration into Mainstream Settings (AIMS) assessment system: Rationale, instruments, procedures, and outcomes. *Journal of Clinical Child Psychology, 15*(1), 55–63.

Walker, H. M., Block-Pedego, A., Todis, B., & Severson, H. (1991). *School archival records search (SARS): User's guide and technical manual.* Longmont, CO: Sopris West.

Walker, H. M., Colvin, G., & Ramsey, E. (1995). *Antisocial behavior in schools: Strategies and best practices.* Pacific Grove, CA: Brooks/Cole.

Walker, H. M., Hops, H., & Greenwood, C. R. (1993). RECESS: Research and development of a behavior management package for remediating social aggression in the school setting. In P. Strain (Ed.), *The utilization of classroom peers as behavior change agents* (pp. 261–303). New York: Plenum.

Walker, H. M., & McConnell, S. R. (1995). *The Walker-McConnell scale of social competence and school adjustment (SSCSA)*. Florence, KY: Thomson Learning.

Walker, H. M., McConnell, S. R., & Clarke, J. Y. (1985). Social skills training in school settings: A model for the social integration of handicapped children into less restrictive settings. In R. McMahon & R. D. Peters (Eds.), *Childhood disorders: Behavioral-developmental approaches* (pp. 140–168). New York: Brunner/Mazel.

Walker, H. M., Nishioka, V., Zeller, R., Severson, H., & Feil, E. (2000). Causal factors and potential solutions for the persistent under-identification of students having emotional or behavioral disorders in the context of schooling. *Assessment for Effective Intervention, 26*(1), 29–40.

Walker, H. M., Shinn, M., O'Neill, R., & Ramsey, E. (1987). A longitudinal assessment of the development of antisocial behavior in boys: Rationale, methodology and first year results. *Remedial and Special Education, 8*(4), 7–16, 27.

Walker, H. M., & Sylwester, R. (1991). Where is school along the path to prison? *Educational Leadership, 49*(1), 14–16.

Williams, S. L., Walker, H. M., Holmes, D., Todis, B., & Fabre, T. R. (1989). Social validation of adolescent social skills by teachers and students. *Remedial and Special Education, 10*(4), 18–27, 37.

Weiner, I. (2003). *The Handbook of Psychology*. New York: Wiley.

Zoccolillo, M. (1993). Gender and the development of conduct disorder. *Development and Psychopathology, 5*(1/2), 65–78.

Issues, Guidelines, and Resources for Use in Implementing School-Based Interventions for Antisocial Behavior and Violence

Introduction

This chapter sets the stage for understanding and applying the material presented in the rest of this book. The chapter focuses on the culture and social ecology of schools as they relate to interventions for antisocial students. It also offers procedural guidelines and recommendations for implementing intervention programs that are evidence-based and either proven or promising in their efficacy.

With this information, we believe it is more likely that best-practice interventions for behaviorally at-risk children and youths can be delivered that will actually have a chance of positively impacting their myriad adjustment problems. The term *school-based interventions* refers to behavior change procedures that either originate in the school and are extended to other settings or are restricted to the school setting. Often, antisocial students require interventions that address issues and needs extending beyond school boundaries.

Schools provide an important setting and a powerful context for intervening with antisocial students. However, schools are, at once, complex and fragile organizations, and infusing effective interventions for antisocial behavior into a school's ongoing operations requires sensitivity, tact, and careful attention to details. The overall goals of this chapter are twofold: (1) to document the external factors that impact antisocial behavior patterns and also constrain the school's ability to address them effectively, and (2) to describe specific techniques to facilitate the identification and implementation of best-practice interventions for reducing and replacing antisocial behavior patterns. Some of the information presented is empirically derived and has stood the tests of replication and time. Other information is experiential in nature and less formal; it reflects the authors' collective experiences, as well as those of other professionals with expertise in school-based interventions. We believe that both types of information are valuable, containing useful wisdom for those who venture bravely into classroom, playground, and other settings intent on improving the adjustment of antisocial students.

The School's Role in Addressing Antisocial Behavior

Policymakers and legislators view schools as the ultimate vehicle for accessing children who need services, supports, and interventions that can impact their physical and mental health (e.g., medical and sensory screenings, vaccinations, and treatments of various kinds). Schools are also important settings for identifying children who suffer from various forms of neglect and abuse at home. As families continue to abandon their parenting responsibilities on a broad scale, schools increasingly must assume the role of protector, socializing agent, and caregiver. Instruction in sex education, drug awareness, wellness and health promotion, and rudimentary parenting skills are part of the curricula of many public schools. Further, schools are now expected to instruct children and youths in how to protect themselves from violence. In the past, the school was one of the only safe havens available for at-risk children and youths; now, even that safety has been seriously eroded in many urban, suburban, and even rural areas of our country.

Schools have few answers for dealing with young people who are hungry, who are unable to sleep well at night because of myriad anxieties about their personal safety, and who must suffer the indignities of sexual, physical, and psychological abuse on a daily basis. If present trends continue, we will have produced generations of children and youths who will be in long-term states of rage and anger at the treatment they have received at the hands of family members, acquaintances, and the larger society. Complex obstacles stand between such children and youths and their achievement of desirable life outcomes.

To make matters even worse, in the face of all these unfortunate developments, we are (1) reducing our investment in public schools, (2) asking schools to restructure and reform themselves to achieve higher academic standards, and (3) becoming more and more critical of school systems for their failure to compensate for our failures as a society. Survey after survey shows that we invest far less in our educational system and infrastructure than do other modern, industrialized nations. We also lead the world in the rate of incarcerating our citizens—particularly our youths. In a speech in the early 1900s, Mark Twain offered an anecdote that has compelling relevance for us in the 21st century. He told the story of a farmer in Missouri who had heard that a local township wanted to close some of its schools because they were too expensive. After listening to the debate on this issue at a town meeting, the farmer said, "Well, I don't see how we are going to save any money. For every school we close, we'll just have to build a new jail." At this moment, we are disinvesting in schools and building new jails and prisons at a rate perhaps unparalleled in our history!

Differences among first-grade children in beginning reading literacy provide a good example of how many antisocial children from impoverished backgrounds are severely disadvantaged as they begin their school careers. Juel (1988) investigated this problem extensively and concluded that, if a child is a good reader in grade 1, the probability of staying a good reader in grade 4 is .87; however, if the child is a poor reader in grade 1, the probability of remaining a poor reader in grade 4 is equally likely at .88. In other words, the good news is that, if you start school ready to learn and are a good reader, you will remain so; the bad news is that, if you start school not ready to learn and you are a poor reader, you will also remain so. These findings speak to the critical importance of school readiness skills and the early development of literacy for all children. There is also an interesting parallel between reading success or failure in grade 1 and emerging antisocial behavior patterns. If challenging forms of behavior are not addressed effectively at the point of school entry, the behavior likely will increase in severity as these students move through their school careers.

An estimated 20–40% of the school-age population is at risk of school failure and dropout because of long-term exposure to societal conditions of risk (Lyon, 2002). A significant number of these same children will also follow a trajectory leading to antisocial behavior and, ultimately, conduct disorder, delinquency, and adult criminality. We believe that the federal government must galvanize and focus public attention on the true dimensions of the problems and develop a national action plan to address them. These problems are so massive that they will likely require a coordinated national effort, involving a broad range of stakeholders and implemented across a number of years, in order to be successful. The Individuals with Disabilities Education Act of 1997 mandates early screening, intervention services, and supports for children and families who suffer from recognized disabilities and handicapping conditions. We need a parallel law that addresses the needs of young children who are at risk for developing antisocial behavior patterns, school failure, violent behavior, and delinquency. Our current legal mandates for providing essential services are not adequate for coping with the increasing levels of antisocial behavior that we are seeing in our schools and in society.

Equally important, schools must be broadly supported and encouraged to engage in partnership arrangements with families and social service agencies that have the capacity to address those critical, unmet needs of children that affect their education and quality of life. School districts, private foundations, and consortia of social service agencies across the country are beginning to develop school-linked models of services and supports targeted to families and their children who are at risk. The New Beginnings program of the San Diego, California, school district is an outstanding example. The Robert Wood Johnson Foundation has been a strong supporter of such models in a number of states including Kentucky and California. And the Center for the Future of Children, supported by the David and Lucile Packard Foundation, has produced a major study of school-linked models for at-risk students in which critical issues such as funding, coordination and integration of services, infrastructure, and evaluation procedures are examined and reviewed. (For more information, contact the David and Lucile Packard Foundation, 300 Second Street, Suite 102, Los Altos, CA 94022.) Private foundations, school districts, and social service agencies are to be commended for their efforts in this important domain. However, it is essential that federal, state, and local governments invest aggressively in a school-linked services approach if we are to have any chance of dealing effectively with the problems confronting us. Schools can play a critical role in this process if they are allowed to do so and are supported in the process.

Factors Affecting the Development of Antisocial Behavior

Numerous conditions can influence the development of antisocial behavior among today's at-risk children and youths. However, debates in professional and lay public forums have tended to focus on a cluster of key factors, including media violence, nature versus nurture, and family, community, and societal conditions. Each of these influences is briefly discussed. In addition, we touch on our society's relentless promotion of pharmacological remedies for solving its problems and the increasing incivility we see in our social relations with one another.

Media Violence

Informed laypersons tend to believe that media violence has played some role in the youth violence of recent decades. Televised violence, and its relationship to societal violence, has been the subject of intense debate since the early days of television. Portrayals of violence in the media and acts of violence that occur in real life *are* connected to each other, but not in any simple or direct way (Murray, 1997). Societal violence is nearly always multiply determined, and media violence is only one potential cause (Satcher, 2001). Major national studies of media violence include (1) the U.S. Surgeon General's Commission Report (1972), (2) the National Institute of Mental Health's Ten-Year Followup (1982), and (3) the report of the American Psychological Association's Task Force on Television in Society (1992). After reviewing hundreds of individual studies of media violence (descriptive, correlational, and experimental), the three groups agreed that *heavy* exposure to televised violence has at least a correlational relation to societal violence (see APA Online, 2002).

A more recent review of the scientific evidence by Murray (1997) cites empirical evidence of a documentable relationship between exposure to media violence and the violent attitudes, values, and behavior of children and youths. Murray identified two studies that are particularly relevant for behaviorally at-risk youths—one by Gadow and Sprafkin (1993) and one by Grimes, Cathers, and Vernberg (1996). These studies demonstrated that children with emotional disorders are particularly vulnerable to televised violence. For example, according to Grimes and his colleagues (1996), 8- to 12-year-olds with either attention deficit/hyperactivity disorder (ADHD), oppositional-defiant disorder (ODD), or conduct disorder (CD) showed less emotional concern for victims and were more willing to accept violence as justified than a matched group of children who did not have these disorders. Thus, heavy exposure to media violence may actually accelerate the aggressive and violent tendencies of antisocial children and youths.

Dr. Carole Lieberman, a psychiatrist and noted expert on violence in the media, states that the media have played a key role in desensitizing our society to violence in such a way that it is now considered by many to be endemic and culturally normative (Lieberman, 1994). However, media industry leaders continue to deny the possibility that such exposure increases violent, aggressive tendencies among children and youths, in much the same way that the tobacco industry has denied the health risks of tobacco use. Box 2.1 presents some of Lieberman's conclusions.

Lieberman is chair of the National Coalition on Television Violence (NCTV), which is dedicated to deglamorizing violence in the media. In 1992, on behalf of the NCTV, Lieberman presented a ten-point plan to the House Judiciary's Subcommittee on Crime and Criminal Justice designed to sweep violence off television. Box 2.2 contains a copy of this plan, which offers numerous suggestions for change but does not recommend censorship.

What can schools do about this issue? Their most valuable contribution might be teaching students about the risks of consistent exposure to media violence and informing them of its subtle, psychological effects. Students, and their parents or caregivers, could also be taught how to become more selective in their viewing habits and how to interpret violent events to which they are exposed in the media. Curricula and instructional models are available that are designed to achieve these goals vis-à-vis media violence.

Nature Versus Nurture

The nature–nurture controversy is never more evident than in the debate over the true roots of antisocial behavior and violence. It is difficult to identify and clearly separate the roles of inherited versus social-environmental factors in the development of antisocial behavior patterns; it is even more difficult to reliably isolate an early predilection toward committing violent acts. However, it is possible that such attributes as activity levels, hormone levels, temperament, and impulsivity are at least partially inherited and could thus serve as precursors (i.e., predisposing factors) for the development of antisocial behavior.

On the nurture side of the issue, considerable evidence suggests that the family context and parenting practices play strong, contributing roles in the development of antisocial behavior patterns (see Kazdin, 1987; Patterson, 1982; Patterson, Reid, & Dishion, 1992). The specific parenting practices and family stressors that account for this outcome are reviewed in a later chapter. It is also possible that traumatic head injury and the resulting neurological damage may be a contributing factor in the development of aggression and could, in some instances, trigger violent episodes. Drug-affected babies who are exposed prenatally are often born with high activity levels, which predispose them toward a number of disorders including CD, ADHD, and antisocial behavior.

Schools have to function in the contexts of neighborhoods, communities, and the larger society, and they must educate and manage students who are

Box 2.2   **The NCTV Ten-Point Plan to Sweep Violence off TV and Off Our Streets**

1. *No censorship.* There should be no government censorship of the media. It must be recognized that upholding the separation of government and media (as well as religion and media) is even more vital to the citizens of the United States than curbing violence.

2. *Ratings system for violence.* A ratings system which describes the violent content of TV shows should be agreed upon by the networks and cable channels. Ratings would delineate the quantity of violence (in terms of violent acts per show) and the quality of violence (in terms of how graphic and lethal the violence is, whether the overall message is pro- or anti-violence, and how gratuitous the violence is). Ratings would be determined by an independent review board comprised of experts in the field of media violence.

3. *Ingredient labels.* Using the precedent of requiring labels on food products which detail the ingredients contained inside, TV shows should be required to broadcast ingredient labels and use them in TV publicity/listings. Such labels would reflect the results of the ratings system: the quantity and quality of the violence contained in the show.

4. *Warning labels on TV shows.* Using the precedent established for products such as cigarettes, TV shows should be required to flash a warning label before those shows rated high in violence. The warning label should read: "The TV show you are about to watch may be hazardous to your psychological and/or physical health due to its highly violent content."

5. *Warning labels on TV ads.* Commercials for war toys (including, but not limited to, action figures, video games, guns, and other weapons) and other violent-themed products would need to carry appropriate warning labels. These would read: "The toy you have just seen advertised may be hazardous to the psychological and/or physical health of a child due to its theme which inspires violent play."

6. *Violence advisors on staff.* At least one psychiatrist and/or researcher on TV violence should be on staff at each network and cable channel to review its shows and determine the psychological impact of any violence portrayed. This person would then advise the producers and TV executives of the findings and make recommendations as to how the violence can be toned down without compromising artistic integrity.

7. *Public service announcements.* Networks and cable channels should be strongly advised to carry PSAs [public service announcements] which educate viewers about the harmful effects of media violence. Each channel would be advised to carry a number of PSAs per day which would be in proportion to how much violent programming it broadcasts.

Box 2.2   *(Continued)*

8. *"Just say no" in government institutions.* No violent TV programming should be offered to residents of government institutions, such as jails and psychiatric hospitals. These residents are often exposed to countless hours of TV viewing, while in a condition which they are particularly vulnerable to its effect, instead of receiving more appropriate psychotherapy and rehabilitation. No children residing in government institutions should be exposed to TV violence.

9. *Tax breaks.* Tax breaks should be given to networks and cable channels, production companies, foundations, private donors, etc. who provide money to support research and education on the effects of TV violence [and] development of nonviolent TV programming for children.

10. *Media literacy public health campaign.* A public health campaign should be launched, in the same spirit as campaigns against drunk driving and against the consumption of alcohol by pregnant women, to promote awareness of the effects of media violence. Schools and TV itself would participate in this campaign to create better-educated media consumers. Obviously, safeguards must be built in to disallow government and media resources from promoting self-serving agendas.

◆

often products of negative family conditions and parenting practices. All of these contexts can influence the development of antisocial behavior patterns. Figure 2.1 provides an overview of the factors, within and across such contexts, related to the development of antisocial behavior patterns among children and youths. As the figure shows, social-environmental factors operate at four levels: family, school and neighborhood, community, and society. The family has the most direct influence and is most proximal to the child development process. Societal factors operate at the most distal (i.e., removed) level and exert the least direct influence on the development of antisocial behavior. Within each level, we identify important variables from the literature that seem to suggest an influencing role of some type.

Schools can do relatively little on their own to attenuate the effects of social-environmental factors operating at a societal, community, or neighborhood level. However, with the cooperation and active support of social service agencies, churches, neighborhood associations, volunteer community groups, and families, they can do a great deal. To prevent and remediate antisocial behavior patterns, schools need to (1) start as early as possible in students' lives, (2) work with families to develop their parenting skills and build strong school–home communication bonds that foster cooperation, mutual respect, and positive regard, (3) serve as a site for the delivery and integration of interagency services and resources, and (4) work collaboratively with other agencies to provide distressed families with the support, technical assistance, and training they need to

Level One: Family Factors

    1. Disrupted and unskilled parenting practices
    2. Family stressors: poverty, alcohol and drug abuse, parent criminality, single caregiver, and so on

Level Two: School and Neighborhood Factors

    1. Early labeling of antisocial student as deviant
    2. Rejection by teachers and peers
    3. Social disorganization of neighborhood and loss of ability to monitor, supervise, and control youths

Level Three: Community Factors

    1. Crime rate
    2. Socioecomic level
    3. Availability of recreation and leisure activities for children and youth
    4. Gang activity

Level Four: Societal Factors

    1. Problems with job and career path availability
    2. Depictions of violent acts in the media (film, TV programs, and news)
    3. Social discrimination and ethnic conflict
    4. Lack of cultural cohesion and social harmony

Left axis: Proximal ... Distal. Right axis: Direct ... Indirect.

FIGURE 2.1

Social-Environmental Influence Factors in the Development of Antisocial Behavior Among Children and Youths.

cope with the stressors and problems that spill over into their children's lives and negatively affect their school performance. School-based interventions are now available that provide for the meaningful involvement of parents and caregivers in the intervention process. Examples of these programs include (1) Multisystemic Therapy, (2) Linking the Interests of Families and Teachers, and (3) the Second Step Violence Prevention Program. These interventions will be profiled in a later chapter.

In certain situations, schools may be able to enhance the cohesiveness and social ecology of the neighborhoods they serve by playing a leadership role in (1) developing a sense of community, (2) connecting families and neighborhood members to each other, and (3) making the school a center for neighborhood and community activities. Sociological research indicates that a community or neighborhood's level of social disorganization is a predictor of gang activity, delinquency, and crime victimization (Sampson, 1992). Social disorganization refers to the absence of a sense of neighborhood cohesion, a lack of neighborhood support networks, conflicting values, and social isolation. This disorganization is directly related to a neighborhood's ability to control delinquent activities.

Sampson and Groves (1989) identified three dimensions of social disorganization that are relevant to delinquency. The first is the ability of a community or neighborhood to supervise and control teenage peer groups. Where low levels of cohesion and high levels of social disorganization exist, gangs often develop from spontaneous play groups. The second dimension consists of local friendship and acquaintance networks that empower neighborhood members to recognize strangers and to engage in guardianship behavior that protects against victimization. The third dimension relates to participation in formal and voluntary organizations, which allows a neighborhood to advocate and defend its local interests. A weak base in this area impairs the neighborhood's ability to exercise effective social control.

The full integration of schools into neighborhood and community life can do much to rebuild the social infrastructure that has been so devastated by the societal problems of the past quarter century. Community psychology, which is focused on the study of groups within natural contexts, has been used to influence communities to adopt more effective parenting and schooling practices (see Biglan, 1992, 1993; Biglan, Lewin, & Hops, 1990). The tools of community psychology should be an integral part of any larger attempts to address problems in this area.

Pharmacological Overreliance

Our society has been described as drug obsessed and is constantly pummeled with advertising campaigns by drug manufacturers that promote prescription and nonprescription pharmacological solutions to huge numbers of ailments. It seems, in some instances, that drugs are developed first and that ailments or disease conditions are then either identified or created to match the alleged benefits of the drug being promoted. For example, the condition of "social anxiety" comes to mind as one for which a drug solution has been heavily promoted. One can argue that acceptance of a drug-based solution for a condition such as social anxiety is not a good idea and may actually keep consumers of such drugs from realistically evaluating and solving whatever problems are contributing to their social anxiety. In this sense, such drugs can absolve individuals of the responsibility of working through their problems. And the heavy promotion of such anxiety-relieving and behavioral coping drugs is sending patients to their doctors in droves. Medical professionals are under heavy pressure to prescribe these drugs even though their appropriateness is dubious in many instances.

The use of psychotropic medications for ADHD and other, related conditions of childhood and youth has surged in the last 20 years. There is an ongoing, rather vitriolic public debate about the benefits versus drawbacks of such medications (Jensen & Cooper, 2002), and opposition to their widespread use has substantial support among some professional and consumer groups. Many of these drugs are even used with preschool children in attempts to control their behavior. Just recently, approval was granted by the federal Food and Drug Administration for the use of Prozac with children, which ranks as a most controversial decision. Some have argued that the continuing widespread use of these drugs is poisoning our children. Good parenting and socialization practices and the use of proven methods of behavior management in home and school settings would go a long way toward eliminating the need for such powerful drugs.

What does this have to do with antisocial behavior among children and youths? Increasing numbers of antisocial and conduct-disordered students are labeled as having ADHD as a means of legitimately controlling their behavior through a prescribed drug regimen. Because an ADHD diagnosis can be ambiguous, and given the condition's overlap with antisocial behavior and CD, this practice is not often questioned. More ominously, our "drug culture" of heavy consumption of legitimate drugs by adults, along with relentless promotion by drug companies, may set the stage for early drug experimentation (tobacco, alcohol, illegal substances) by vulnerable youths who otherwise may not be drawn to it. Early substance abuse remains one of the most potent risk factors for antisocial behavior and serious, violent offending (Lipsey & Derzon, 1998; Satcher, 2001). Aside from educating our children about the negative effects and dangers of substance use of all types, we need to provide better adult models for our children of the *appropriate* consumption of both prescription and nonprescription drugs.

The Growing Incivility of Society

In recent decades, there has been a shift in the degree of civility that we show each other in our daily interactions. We used to respect adults and institutional authority in ways that have not been in evidence since the late 1960s.

Now it appears almost normative for individuals to express palpable levels of anger in their daily interactions with others. The overarching term commonly used to describe this phenomenon is *incivility*. It can be observed in the way customers react to service personnel, in the manners (or lack thereof) that motorists display in traffic situations, and in the behavior of politicians as expressed through extreme forms of partisanship and in attributions of the self-interested and malevolent motives of their colleagues.

Our society needs a large dose of civility and common good manners. We have experienced a huge paradigm shift in the opposite direction, which has proved damaging to society and has significantly lowered our collective quality of life. Now we need a shift back, such that consideration, empathy, kindness, and belief in the best rather than the worst about others, are highly valued (and actually practiced) emotions and acts in our social relations with others. The bumper sticker that says "Practice random acts of kindness" has it right.

Unfortunately, adults in our society have provided very poor models for our children in how to relate to the world around them. Media portrayals of human interactions are saturated with displays of incivility and overt disrespect of fellow human beings. This incivility can be observed in the ordinary interactions of many individuals on a daily basis. We need to carefully address how we model and teach acceptable attitudes and forms of behavior regarding the treatment of others, especially family members. Schools should also be a participant in this effort. It is in their best interest to do so, as incivility toward and lack of respect for teachers is a huge complicating factor in the education of children and youths.

The problem of incivility is macro in nature and certainly not amenable to short-term improvement, and positive change is likely to be glacial in nature. Nevertheless, given the powerful albeit distal influences on the adoption of antisocial behavior patterns by our children and youths, it is worthy of policy considerations and corrective legislation where appropriate.

Factors Affecting the Magnitude of Outcomes of School-Based Interventions

The efficacy of school-based interventions for antisocial behavior is a source of continuing discourse among professionals and laypersons. Such interventions have been described as reflecting a search for a "magic bullet" that works every time, lasts indefinitely, and is easy to implement. Unfortunately, such an intervention is not on the horizon for antisocial students who, as a rule, require powerful, multicomponent interventions applied across settings and school years.

Too often, we are not bound by empirical outcomes in adopting school-based interventions for problem behavior (Gottfredson & Gottfredson, 2001). The most effective, proven interventions are typically not those applied most frequently. Instead, intervention approaches are selected that allow the implementer to address the problem (by doing something about it) and that appeal, for whatever reason(s), to him or her. When dealing with antisocial behavior patterns, however, we do not have the luxury of selecting interventions on this basis. Although no current intervention approach can claim to have effected a "cure" for antisocial behavior, some practices clearly are more effective than others (Greenberg, Domitrovich, & Bumbarger, 2001; Loeber & Farrington, 1998, 2001; Reid, Patterson, & Snyder, 2002).

Approaches to teaching beginning reading provide a good example. It would seem practicable to select the teaching method that produces the lowest rate of reading failure among students in general, which happens to involve phonics. In spite of the accumulated empirical evidence on this issue, schools continue to invest in a variety of less effective approaches to teach children beginning reading. The social and human costs of this failure are reflected in the 4 out of 10 beginning readers who need structured assistance and teaching to master the complexities of reading (Lyon, 2002). This is analogous to a surgeon choosing to perform a procedure that has a 19% mortality rate over one that has a 10% rate because (1) it is easier to do, (2) the surgeon is trained in it, and (3) the surgeon simply likes it better. Given the stakes involved, it is not possible for medical personnel to operate in this manner, yet such a practice continues in many of our schools today. It is likely that this practice is driven by such factors as educators not being trained in more effective intervention or instructional methods or being invested in philosophical approaches that are counter to more effective approaches and that account for their rejection.

Currently, there is a national push to teach all children to learn to read as well as possible by the end of the primary grades, as expressed in the federal "No Child Left Behind" legislation. Under the auspices of this act, states are required to demonstrate that they are using effective research-based methods of teaching reading in order to qualify for federal assistance. Federal leadership of this type is long overdue.

Given the socioeconomic costs of antisocial behavior, we cannot afford to invest in any but the best intervention practices currently available. Figure 2.2 shows four variables that play key roles in determining the magnitude of intervention outcomes. They are particularly salient in relation to students who are

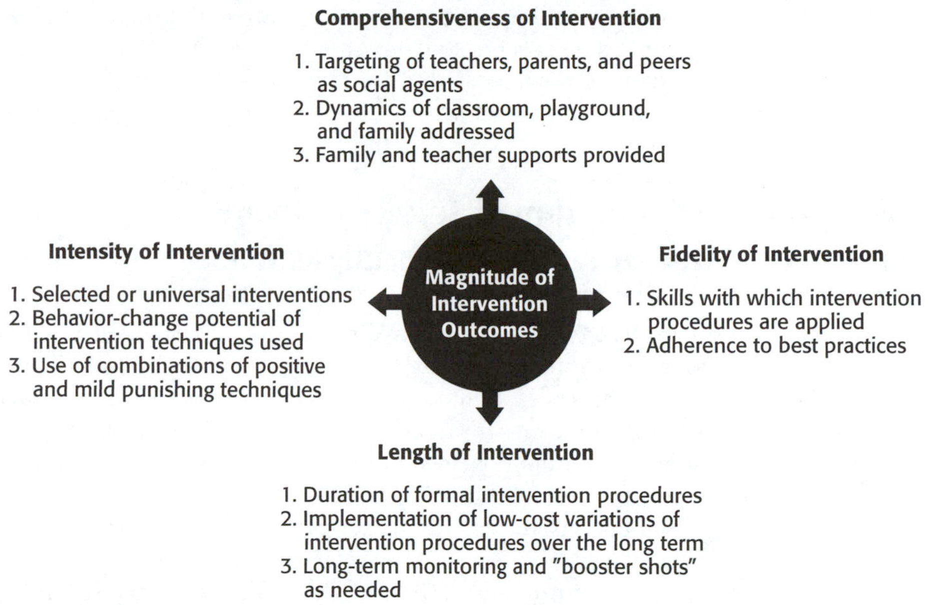

Comprehensiveness of Intervention

1. Targeting of teachers, parents, and peers as social agents
2. Dynamics of classroom, playground, and family addressed
3. Family and teacher supports provided

Intensity of Intervention

1. Selected or universal interventions
2. Behavior-change potential of intervention techniques used
3. Use of combinations of positive and mild punishing techniques

Magnitude of Intervention Outcomes

Fidelity of Intervention

1. Skills with which intervention procedures are applied
2. Adherence to best practices

Length of Intervention

1. Duration of formal intervention procedures
2. Implementation of low-cost variations of intervention procedures over the long term
3. Long-term monitoring and "booster shots" as needed

FIGURE 2.2

Factors Affecting the Magnitude of Intervention Outcomes.

invested in antisocial behavior patterns. Differentially weighting the importance of these four factors in determining intervention outcomes is difficult. The empirical literature and experiential knowledge have established each of them as important; that is, these factors are applicable to all school-based interventions, regardless of their philosophical underpinnings or characteristics. However, careful attention to them is of crucial importance in implementing interventions for antisocial students. Specifically, such interventions must be comprehensive, be applied according to best-practice standards and guidelines, and be of maximal power and of sufficient duration to produce enduring effects.

Fidelity of intervention is critical in maximizing outcomes for antisocial students. This dimension involves a careful adherence to best practices and key guidelines in the delivery of interventions designed to change the behavior of antisocial students (Greenberg et al., 2001). Throughout the remainder of this book, we present guidelines and recommendations that will assist educators in achieving this goal.

The entries under each of the four dimensions in Figure 2.2 are guidelines for maximizing the influence or power of that factor. If closely followed during the implementation process, they will produce better and more powerful effects across intervention applications. And when combined with each other, they will produce the best possible outcomes for a particular intervention or approach. When working with antisocial students, it is particularly important to carefully assess their responses to the intervention and to monitor, track, and support their changed behavior over the long term. This means implementing low-cost variations of the intervention or ongoing maintenance procedures for antisocial students across school years. One-shot interventions, implemented only within the span of a single school year, will not be sufficient to adequately impact antisocial behavior patterns in the vast majority of cases (Greenberg et al., 2001).

Developmental Continuum of Service Delivery and Expected Outcomes for Antisocial Behavior

Bullis and Walker (1994) have noted the importance of establishing benchmarks governing intervention expectations for antisocial behavior patterns and deciding how to invest limited resources in their prevention, remediation, continuing management, or simple accommodation. They propose a four-stage developmental continuum of prevention, remediation, amelioration, and accommodation goals; this continuum is illustrated in Figure 2.3. This figure contains four developmental phases relating to services and interventions for antisocial behavior patterns.

If a comprehensive intervention is applied consistently from preschool to grade 3 with high levels of treatment fidelity, it may be possible to divert the at-risk child from the pathway leading to antisocial behavior and conduct disorder (Reid et al., 2002). Bullis and Walker (1994) recommend an approach involving active remediation of antisocial behavior in the early middle school years. Although anything resembling a cure for antisocial behavior is highly unlikely at this developmental level, a considerable impact can be achieved on the deficits associated with this disorder (e.g., remediating social skills deficits, teaching self-control, improving study and academic skills, and enhancing peer relations).

By grades 7 and 8, goals and expectations should shift from prevention or remediation to attenuation of the negative effects of the behavior pattern on the antisocial student, peers, family members, and society at large. This developmental phase, referred to as amelioration, focuses on buffering the damaging effects of the behavior through teaching coping and survival skills that provide some protection against its ravages. Strategies for anger management and control are particularly important in this context.

Finally, in the developmental period spanning grades 9–12, the focus shifts from amelioration to simple accommodation. Bullis and Walker (1994) argue that antisocial students at this stage have a high risk of remaining invested in an antisocial behavior pattern well into adulthood. Realistically, there is little that either schools or social agencies can do at this point to affect the antisocial behavior pattern. Accommodation carries the assumption that this disorder will likely not change for the better. Efforts should be made to keep these students in school as long as possible and to prepare them, to the maximum extent possible, for the transition from the school to the work world and adult life.

This continuum suggests that far more resources should be invested in the early developmental stages of antisocial behavior patterns than in attempts to manage or control their destructive manifestations later on. Making this transi-

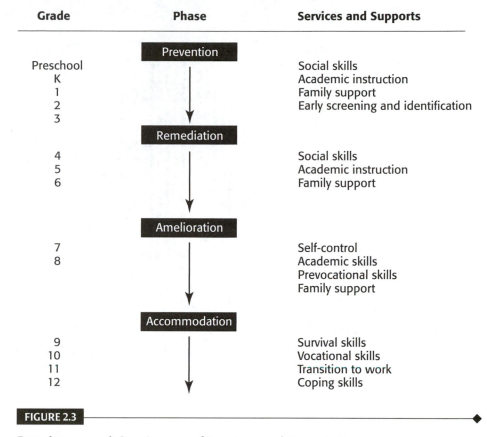

Grade	Phase	Services and Supports
Preschool K 1 2 3	**Prevention**	Social skills Academic instruction Family support Early screening and identification
4 5 6	**Remediation**	Social skills Academic instruction Family support
7 8	**Amelioration**	Self-control Academic skills Prevocational skills Family support
9 10 11 12	**Accommodation**	Survival skills Vocational skills Transition to work Coping skills

FIGURE 2.3

Developmental Continuum of Services and Expectations for Antisocial Behavior.

Source: Bullis and Walker (1994).

tion will not be easy, however, given (1) the numbers of children and youths who currently manifest antisocial behavior patterns, (2) the intensity and aversiveness of their behavioral acts, (3) the increasingly limited resources available, and (4) society's seeming reluctance to "catch problems early."

Authorizing legislation and statutes actually prohibit certain federal agencies from engaging in prevention efforts. This is a particularly unfortunate constraint in addressing antisocial behavior patterns early in their developmental trajectory. Small children often exhibit the "soft" signs of antisocial behavior that are relatively trivial (e.g., noncompliance, arguing, lying) and gradually progress to much more severe "hard" signs (e.g., cruelty, aggression, bullying, harassment, violence, theft, arson) as they mature (Patterson, 1982; Patterson et al., 1992; Reid et al., 2002). Thus, it is important to address these early signs and less serious acts while we still have a chance to affect them. Far too often, we wait until it's too late to turn around vulnerable children before we define their problem behavior as in need of intervention.

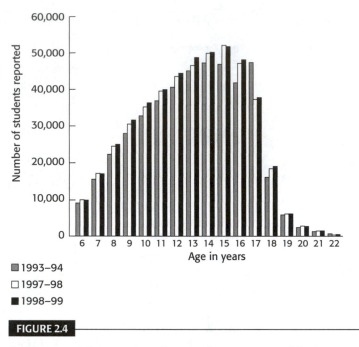

1993–94
□ **1997–98**
■ **1998–99**

FIGURE 2.4 ◆

Students with Emotional Disturbance Served by Age, Selected School Years.

Figure 2.4 provides a stark example of this practice, which is more typical than not in today's public school systems. Walker, Nikiosha, Zeller, Severson, and Feil (2000) examined students in the K–12 grade range who were certified as eligible for special education supports and services under authority of the Individuals with Disabilities Education Act (IDEA) for the 1998–99 school year. The data in the figure represent all the states reporting and were compiled by the U.S. Office of Special Education Programs for its annual report to Congress on progress in implementing the IDEA. As the figure shows, the number of students certified as emotionally disturbed reaches its peak around age 15 (approximately 50,000 cases during the 1998–99 school year); the lowest number reported was at age 6 (grade 1) during this same year. These results suggest that a large number of students, who were no doubt in need of ED (emotionally disturbed) supports and services in their elementary and middle school years, were not referred, evaluated, or served under special education. Only when their behavior problems become so intractable and difficult to accommodate in adolescence are many of these students finally defined as being in need, referred, certified and, ultimately, served. This practice is the polar opposite of a proactive, preventive approach and confirms the findings of Hoagwood and Erwin (1997) that the mental health needs of the vast majority of today's students are not being served.

Design and Application of Comprehensive, Coordinated Interventions Early in School Careers

In an influential and comprehensive review of empirical evidence on the prevention of delinquency, Zigler, Taussig, and Black (1992) noted that intervention and accommodation programs developed specifically for delinquency prevention have produced consistently disappointing outcomes. After evaluating the outcomes associated with juvenile foster homes, diversion programs, and retribution-restitution programs, they concluded that *none* have worked. However, interventions aimed at reducing or preventing the precursors of delinquency (i.e., antisocial, aggressive, acting-out forms of behavior) have shown some promising results (see Michelson, Kazdin, & Marchione, 1986; Patterson, Chamberlain, & Reid, 1982). Ironically, the most powerful evidence in support of the prevention of delinquency comes from long-term, follow-up studies of childhood programs targeting at-risk children very early in their school careers. These intervention programs were designed not to prevent delinquency, but rather to prevent the school failure of at-risk populations. Some of the most effective early-intervention programs were multidimensional and included noneducational supports related to health care, parental involvement, and needed services to families.

Zigler and his colleagues (1992) highlighted the features of three such programs that have proved effective in preventing the adoption of a delinquent lifestyle: the Perry Preschool Project, the Syracuse University Family Development Research Project, and the Yale Child Welfare Research Program. These findings provide clear evidence about the importance of prevention efforts based on well-designed and well-implemented early intervention programs.

Early Screening and Identification of Antisocial Behavior

To achieve early intervention for preventive purposes, it is necessary to systematically screen and identify at-risk children early—some of whom will show only the soft, beginning signs of antisocial behavior. Preschool children, particularly boys, often engage in oppositional, overly active, and pestering behavior that may not seem serious at this developmental level. However, the manifestations of this behavior pattern in adolescence are very different and can be quite destructive.

Phillip Strain, a distinguished early-childhood educator and researcher, is a strong advocate of the earliest possible identification of at-risk children. He has developed a videotape to illustrate its importance for use in in-service training sessions for preschool staff. The videotape opens by showing some small boys who are shoving each other and being unresponsive to a teacher's attempts to correct their behavior. The next scene shows a female teacher approaching a surly, sulking adolescent. When she attempts to engage him in conversation, he assaults her and breaks her jaw. Strain's key point is that these two acts are of the same general type or response class, only separated by about 10 years of physical development and elaboration!

© Richard Hutchings/PhotoEdit/PictureQuest

Unchecked, this type of behavior can prove highly destructive.

It is important to note that preschoolers who show signs of emerging antisocial behavior do not necessarily outgrow them—particularly if the antisocial behavior is well developed prior to the point of school entry and the children are continually exposed to risk factors for antisocial behavior outside school. Rather, as they move through their school careers, these young people grow into these unfortunate behavior patterns, with often disastrous results for themselves and others (see Loeber & Farrington, 2001; Reid et al., 2002). The myth that preschoolers will outgrow their antisocial behavior is pervasive among many teachers and early educators. Unfortunately, this belief leads many professionals to do nothing early on, when the problem can often be addressed successfully.

The social behavior of preschool children is sufficiently well differentiated that antisocial behavior patterns are identifiable at this developmental stage (Loeber & Farrington, 2001). Once they enter elementary school, it is even easier to identify such students because of the more intense performance demands and greater structure operating at this level (Hersh & Walker, 1983). Box 2.3 presents some guidelines for the early screening and identification of children and youths who are at risk for developing antisocial behavior patterns.

Studies of the referral process in public schools show that (1) regular (general education) teachers are involved in the vast majority of referrals, (2) the referral frequency peaks around grade 2 or 3, and (3) students are far more likely to be referred for academic than social-behavioral problems. In an important study, Lloyd, Kauffman, Landrum, and Roe (1991) systematically analyzed school records to determine how and why a sample of regular teachers referred students in their classes for special education. Their findings indicated that 69% of referrals were for boys, and 67% of all referrals occurred in grades K–3; in addition, the problems most likely to prompt teacher referrals were academic difficulties (35%), reading problems (31%), and attention problems (23%).

By rank ordering the frequency of each referral reason, these researchers found that the seven most frequent reasons involved academic problems; aggressive, disruptive, and delinquent behavior was only the 10th-most-frequent reason given for referral. Thus, it does not seem likely that teachers, on their own, are inclined to refer children, early in their school careers, who may be at risk for developing antisocial behavior patterns. In fact, teacher referrals for problem behavior tend to peak in grades 9 or 10. Yet teachers, more than anyone, have

---

Box 2.3   **Guidelines for Screening and Identifying Antisocial Behavior Patterns**

1. Use *proactive* rather than a *reactive* process to screen and identify students at risk for antisocial behavior.

2. Whenever possible, use a multi-agent (teacher, parent, observer) and multi-setting (classroom, playground, home setting) screening-identification approach in order to gain the broadest possible perspective on the dimensions of target students' at-risk status.

3. Screen and identify at-risk students as early as possible in their school careers—ideally at the preschool and kindergarten levels.

4. Use teacher nominations and rankings or ratings in the early stages of screening, and supplement them later in the process, if possible, by direct observations, school records, peer or parent ratings, and other sources as appropriate.

---

an important reservoir of information concerning the behavioral characteristics of such children. They have the advantage of being able to make literally thousands of normative comparisons among students as they teach and manage the classroom. This information is essential in making sensitive judgments about the at-risk status of individual students.

Left on their own, regular teachers are more likely to reactively refer students than to proactively screen them on a regular basis and then refer suspected at-risk students for further evaluation and/or treatment (Gerber & Semmel, 1984). It is essential that proactive, universal screening procedures be implemented at least twice annually (preferably in October and February) in order to (1) provide all students with an equal chance to be identified for their problem behavior; (2) provide access to mental health services for antisocial students, for students who may be comorbid for several conditions (e.g., antisocial behavior plus ADHD, or CD plus depression), and for students with nondisruptive, but potentially serious, behavior problems that are not typically the focus of teacher concern (e.g., fears, anxiety, social avoidance, depression, peer neglect, and rejection); and (3) take advantage of the store of knowledge about student characteristics that teachers develop over time.

Issues and procedures for accomplishing the proactive, early screening of behaviorally at-risk students are dealt with in considerable detail in a later chapter. This chapter illustrates a variety of screening and assessment approaches covering identification processes and the design of interventions.

Key Target Areas of School-Based Interventions for Antisocial Behavior

Greenberg and his colleagues (2001) and Reid and his colleagues (2002) argue that a single intervention program rarely, if ever, is sufficient to deal with the complex and multidimensional nature of antisocial behavior. Children and youths who are at risk for antisocial behavior are also at risk for a host of other negative conditions including (1) academic failure, (2) child abuse and neglect, (3) drug and alcohol involvement, (4) sexually transmitted diseases, (5) accidents, (6) tobacco use, (7) gang membership, and (8) delinquency (Biglan, 2001). Schools alone obviously cannot address all these risk factors, but in working partnerships with families, social service agencies, and community groups, they can be effective contributors to comprehensive interventions.

The first responsibility of schools in this regard should be to teach alternative, replacement behavior that is adaptive and functional. This is a complex process that involves not only direct teaching but also the use of systematic behavior management methods, the provision of both positive consequences and negative sanctions, and access to support systems. Schools should assume a leadership role in developing intervention strategies for the following intervention target areas in order to help reduce or eliminate associated risk factors:

◆ Study skills to improve academic performance and competence (see Archer & Gleason [2002], *Skills for School Success,* Curriculum Associates, 5 Esquire Road, North Billerica, MA 01862-2589; 508-667-8000)

◆ Social skills training to improve teacher-, peer- and self-related forms of adjustment (see Alberg, Petry, & Eller [1994], A *Resource Guide for Social Skills Instruction,* Sopris West, Inc., 1140 Boston Avenue, Longmont, CO 80501; 303-651-2829)

◆ Health awareness to identify the consequences of a high-risk lifestyle (see Severson & James [2002], "Prevention and Early Interventions for Addictive Behaviors: Health Promotion in the Schools," in M. Shinn, H. Walker, & G. Stoner [Eds.], *Interventions for Academic and Behavior Problems II: Preventive and Remedial Approaches,* National Association of School Psychologists, 4340 East West Highway, Suite 402, Bethesda, MD 20814)

These three areas represent risks that affect nearly all antisocial children and youths and have everything to do with the quality of life they will likely experience. Whenever possible, social service agencies that can provide support, technical assistance, training, and relief to distressed families should be marshaled and coordinated through a school-linked services approach (see Behrmann, 1992). Schorr (1988) makes the case that flexible, individually tailored services, applied from outside the family, can help reduce family stressors and their negative effects. The seminal work of Patterson and his associates has certainly validated this assumption (Patterson et al., 1992; Reid et al., 2002). School-linked services of this type are likely to be one of the only effective approaches available in comprehensively addressing the complex problems of antisocial children, youths, and their families.

It is also essential to focus on the dimension of resiliency when dealing with antisocial children and youths. There has been a surge of research interest in the concept of social resilience since the ground-breaking work of Garmezy, Rutter, and Werner was reported in the 1980s (see Katz, 1997; Miller, Brehm, & Whitehouse, 1998; Werner & Smith, 1988). As defined by Garmezy (1985), *resiliency* has to do with the interaction or relationship between risk and protective factors. A relatively small percentage of children who have many of the risk factors for developing antisocial behavior patterns and are on a path to destructive outcomes actually end up prevailing over the adverse situations into which they are born. In fact, children and youths who are considered resilient often turn out to have productive lives.

Garmezy (1985) identified three broad categories of nonintellectual, protective factors that contribute to resiliency: (1) personality dispositions of the child, (2) a supportive family milieu, and (3) an external support system that encourages and reinforces a child's coping efforts. In addition, Rutter (1979) identified positive temperament as an important correlate of resiliency. Rutter and his colleagues also found that a family support system characterized by warmth and support operates as a protective factor.

Miller and his colleagues (1998) present a persuasive case for reconceptualizing the school-based prevention of antisocial behavior in terms of resilience rather than risk. They point out that (1) epidemiological studies have demonstrated that a significant number of children exposed early on to adverse conditions actually experience prosocial outcomes; (2) some youths who have CD and/or well-developed antisocial behavior patterns avoid the outcomes (delinquency, school failure, violence) normally expected of them; and (3) an array of individual and contextual resources predictive of social competence and/or adaptive coping under conditions of adversity have been identified. Given this body of empirical evidence, it does indeed make sense to consider reframing antisocial behavior in terms of social resilience.

Miller and her colleagues (1998) describe three broad categories of resources of social resilience: (1) individual characteristics including intellectual ability, self-regulation, and positive temperament; (2) parenting characteristics and skills including family cohesion and parent–child attachment; and (3) contextual factors that promote prosocial values and support for displays of prosocial behavior. These resources buffer and offset the damaging effects of risk exposure and make it possible for social competence repertoires to emerge. Social competence, in turn, is predictive of successful outcomes in a number of domains (e.g., employment, social relations, and education) (Catalano & Hawkins, 1996; Mastern & Coatsworth, 1998; Reid et al., 2002; Strain, Guralnick, & Walker, 1986).

The identification and development of social resilience among at-risk youths is critical to the prevention of antisocial behavior, especially among younger children. Miller and colleagues (1998) have developed a road map, of sorts, as to how this might be partially accomplished within the context of schooling and have reviewed a series of intervention programs that could be used for this purpose.

The emergence of strengths-based assessment over the past decade is a reflection of an increasing emphasis upon social resilience (see Epstein & Sharma, 1998). Comprehensive assessment approaches often include tools to measure social skills, individual assets, and strengths in a number of areas (e.g., self-control and intrapersonal and interpersonal domains).

Social skills training procedures have been in place for at-risk and non-at-risk students in school settings for nearly two decades, albeit with mixed results (see Elksnin & Elksnin, 2001). (See the chapters herein on the assessment and training of social skills.) More recently, social skills curricula and instruction have been incorporated into classroom sequences via universal intervention approaches (see

Bullis, Walker, & Sprague, 2001; Committee for Children, 1992). Other programs extend social skills values and practices throughout the entire school setting (Embry & Flannery, 1999).

In terms of the role of schools in developing resiliency, it is important that antisocial students (1) be able to recruit and maintain a positive support network of nonantisocial peers and (2) be mentored and socially valued by adults and older peers in the school. Assisting antisocial students to become involved in school activities is another method of broadening their social engagement within the school culture. Any investment of effort to increase students' capacity for resiliency will be time well spent and should be a high-priority strategy for use with antisocial students. Also, many social skills curricula have parenting components built into them for teaching and strengthening social skills at home. Alberg, Petry, and Eller (1994) have developed an excellent resource guide for selecting and implementing social skills curricula and have conducted evaluative reviews of scores of such curricula regarding their construction, instructional integrity, ease of teaching, and user friendliness.

Prevention as an Outcome of Intervention

The issue of prevention versus intervention has been a polarizing one in policy debates among professionals and laypersons alike. The argument over whether and how to invest public dollars in prevention nearly always raises the specter of diverting scarce resources from intervention, sanctions, and incarceration. Indeed, there are large and vocal constituencies arrayed against the use of intervention resources in this way. Clearly, however, we need to address the complex problems of our young people as early as possible in their developmental trajectories. In this regard, prevention is best viewed as an *outcome* rather than as a means to an end or an approach, as is commonly the case (Walker & Sprague, 2002).

The U.S. Public Health Service has developed a valuable schema for classifying different types of prevention outcomes. Instead of viewing prevention as a means to an end, this classification conceptualizes intervention as a tool or instrument for achieving prevention outcomes. Figure 2.5 illustrates three types of prevention and the approximate proportions of the school-age population that would be appropriate targets for each of these prevention outcomes. Primary prevention refers to intervention efforts designed to keep problems from emerging—that is, to *prevent* harm. Secondary prevention refers to interventions whose purpose is to *reverse* harm to children and youths who already exhibit the behavioral signs of prior risk exposure. Finally, tertiary prevention refers to the use of interventions implemented for the most severely involved, at-risk children and youths (e.g., those who suffer from abuse, neglect, or family dysfunction). The goal of tertiary prevention is to *reduce* harm.

The lead author and his colleagues adapted this model of prevention for addressing antisocial behavior and other forms of challenging behavior within the school setting (Walker et al., 1996). We demonstrated how this classification schema can be used to integrate and coordinate different intervention types

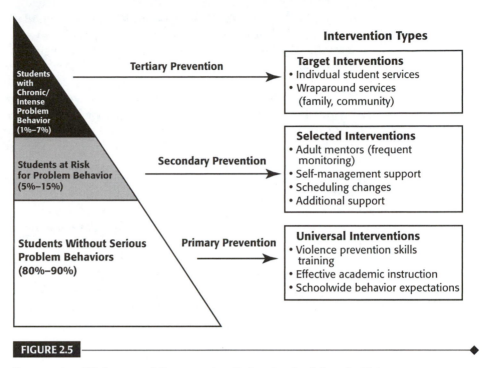

Intervention Types

Tertiary Prevention

Target Interventions
- Indivdual student services
- Wraparound services (family, community)

Secondary Prevention

Selected Interventions
- Adult mentors (frequent monitoring)
- Self-management support
- Scheduling changes
- Additional support

Primary Prevention

Universal Interventions
- Violence prevention skills training
- Effective academic instruction
- Schoolwide behavior expectations

Students with Chronic/ Intense Problem Behavior (1%–7%)

Students at Risk for Problem Behavior (5%–15%)

Students Without Serious Problem Behaviors (80%–90%)

FIGURE 2.5

Preventing Violent and Destructive Behavior in Schools: Primary, Secondary, and Tertiary Systems of Intervention.

(e.g., universal, small group, individual) to achieve prevention outcomes for at-risk students within the context of schooling. We also described its potential application for producing better, more cost-effective outcomes. This adaptation has proved to be very popular among educational researchers and has been broadly adopted by practitioners in the selection and delivery of model interventions for school-based problem behavior. It is sometimes referred to in professional educational forums as the "Oregon model." However, this model or approach to prevention is clearly a matter of public domain and is not "owned" by anyone. The types of interventions that are appropriate for achieving differing types of prevention outcomes are described in the next section.

Universal and Selected Interventions for Addressing Antisocial Behavior in School

Universal interventions are those designed to impact all students in the same manner under the same conditions. Each student receives the intervention at the identical dosage level; it is delivered in a common format and generally repeated on a daily or weekly basis. These interventions are ideally suited for classwide and schoolwide applications. Examples of universal interventions include school vaccinations, social skills training of all students in a regular classroom, school-wide discipline plans or instruction in violence prevention social skills (e.g., anger management, conflict resolution, impulse control, or empathy), and the development, posting, and monitoring of rules governing classroom behavior and performance. In contrast, *selected* interventions are those designed for an identified (or selected) target student or small group of at-risk students. These procedures are individually tailored and fine-tuned to fit the specific needs of the target student and/or the characteristics of the small group. Examples of selected interventions include individual counseling, individualized programs to remediate antisocial students' aggressive behavior with peers, and establishment of a small group of at-risk students, for instructional purposes, who share common social skills deficits.

Students for whom the universal intervention is ineffective select themselves out from the pool of regular students as needing more intensive intervention supports and services. Selected interventions are commonly used as backups for universal interventions. It is extremely rare that a universal intervention will be effective for all students within a classroom or school. As a general rule, universal interventions are effective for only about 85% of the students in a school and are insufficient for the remaining 15%.

During the Civil War, both Union and Confederate generals planned defensive battle tactics in a manner analogous to the notion of a universal–selected dichotomy. That is, based on the assumption that a certain number of attacking soldiers would break through the first and second lines of defense, the defending army was deployed so that there was a third line of defense as well. In the same sense, antisocial students are very likely to "break through" most universal interventions; these strategies will be insufficiently powerful to control or to adequately change the aversive, destructive features of their behavior. A later chapter presents a series of case studies that illustrate the application of both universal and selected interventions for antisocial behavior patterns.

Universal interventions are commonly used to achieve primary prevention outcomes in the context of schooling. They create an important foundation and context for the application of more intensive and costly selected interventions. Selected interventions are generally of two types. In type-1 interventions, individual and small groups of moderately at-risk students are identified who become candidates for exposure to intensive interventions that address secondary prevention goals (i.e., to reverse harm that has been previously inflicted). Type-2 selected interventions are reserved for the most problematic students and generally involve case management and the participation of social service agencies and families. The Multisystemic Therapy (MST) program for seriously delinquent-violent adolescents (Schoenwald, Brown, & Henggeler, 2000) is an example of a type-2 tertiary intervention. Interventions such as MST are geared toward reducing harm, not reversing or preventing it, due to the severity of tertiary-level students' problems.

The coordination of differing interventions to achieve the three types of prevention outcomes makes it possible to address the needs of all students in a school in a cost-effective fashion. With careful planning and integration, intervention resources can be allocated well using this model at the level of the school. There are a number of ongoing research investigations into this integrated approach to prevention within school systems, and results should be available in several years. In the meantime, in our view, this approach represents a major conceptual advance in the coordinated delivery of school interventions for serving the needs of *all* students.

Because universal interventions are generally less demanding to implement and because all students are exposed to them in the same manner, they are more likely to be acceptable to teachers. They do not compromise fairness and equity issues in the management of individual students, which is important to most teachers. Selected interventions have the disadvantage of appearing to treat individual students in a special manner, different from that accorded other students. Although a selected intervention can be highly effective and is recommended for use with antisocial behavior patterns, it can stigmatize and label the students who are exposed to it.

Universal interventions have their greatest impact among students who "are on the margins"—for example, those students who are mildly at risk or who are just beginning to invest in an antisocial behavior pattern. Sometimes, systematic exposure to an intervention of this type will be sufficient to tip them in the right direction and divert them from a negative path. However, if they bring well-developed antisocial behavior patterns to their early school careers, this outcome is highly unlikely.

The most appropriate way to judge the effectiveness of a universal intervention is to assess the extent to which it reduces the expected base rate of disorders or problems among groups of students, over the long term, within classroom, school, home, and neighborhood contexts (see Eddy, Reid, & Curry, 2002). Selected interventions, in contrast, are appropriately evaluated in terms of how effective they are in changing the behavior of an individual student or the members of a small group of at-risk students. Thus, judgments about the efficacy of selected interventions are usually, though not always, made on a case-by-case basis.

Universal interventions have an important role to play in achieving the two main goals of schooling: academic and social development. These twin goals can be achieved by (1) implementing, according to best-practice standards, strategies and tactics of instruction that have been derived through studies of effective schooling and (2) teaching positive mental health principles and interpersonal skills as instructional content and using peer tutoring strategies to assist in this process.

Algozzine and Ysseldyke (1992) have developed a teaching manual for use in implementing effective instructional practices called *Strategies and Tactics for Effective Instruction* (available from Sopris West, Inc., 4093 Specialty Place, Longmont, CO 80504). They provide strategies, tactics, and activities to support the application of the following ten principles governing effective instruction and classroom management:

1. Goals and expectations for performance and success are stated clearly and understood by the student.

2. Classroom management is effective and efficient.

3. There is a sense of positiveness in the school environment.

4. There is an appropriate match between student skills and the demands of classroom tasks.

5. Lessons are presented clearly and follow specific instructional procedures.

6. Instructional support is provided for the individual student.

7. Sufficient time is allocated to academics, and instructional time is used efficiently.

8. Student opportunity to respond is high.

9. The teacher actively monitors student progress and understanding.

10. Student performance is evaluated appropriately and frequently.

Adherence to these critical features of effective instruction will benefit all students, especially those at risk for antisocial behavior patterns. All other things being equal, doing so will also produce superior academic outcomes for all students. Their systematic use is highly recommended.

The second broad goal of schooling is to facilitate students' mental health and development of a repertoire of interpersonal and interactional skills. Two of the chapters in this book are devoted to the topic of social skills and social competence; they describe critical conceptual and procedural issues involved in improving the social competence and resilience of at-risk students.

Strayhorn, Strain, and Walker (1993) have advocated for the use of peer tutoring strategies in teaching social interaction skills in order to facilitate positive mental health and social competence outcomes among general student populations. The model they propose is based on the following assumptions:

◆ Positive, friendly, kind, and cooperative interactions are highly relevant to the prevention of psychiatric disorders and antisocial behavior.

◆ Academic competence (e.g., in reading, mathematics, and writing) is also an important psychological health skill for children.

◆ Prevention attempts encounter a major obstacle when they depend on programs into which only a fraction of the target population will ever enter.

◆ One of the most promising ways of overcoming these obstacles is a transformation and restructuring of schools so that the nurturance and academic training of younger students by older students is part of the daily experience of each student and a training ground in which important psychological skills can be modeled, instructed, practiced, monitored, and reinforced.

These authors also proposed a school reorganization plan, based on principles of effective peer tutoring, that would allow this universal intervention to be implemented in a cost-effective manner without unduly burdening teachers and other school personnel. As more and more children enter school with deficits in their basic socialization training, it is essential that schools invest themselves in directly teaching and supporting this type of content.

Intervention Techniques, Programs, and Resources for Antisocial Behavior and Violence in School Settings

Literally hundreds of intervention techniques have been reported in the professional literature in the last three decades. In this section, we focus on a small subset of these techniques that we have found to be highly effective in producing rapid, economical changes in the behavior of antisocial students. Online Appendix A on your companion Web site provides information on the specific details of how these techniques are implemented and the effects they produce among aggressive, antisocial children and youths.

When dealing with well-established antisocial behavior patterns, our experience has been that a combination of (1) systematic social skills training, (2) behavior-specific praise, (3) positive reinforcement contingencies (individual and group), (4) time-out, and (5) response costs or cost contingencies is usually necessary to produce socially valid outcomes (Kazdin, 1977; Wolf, 1978). By "socially valid," we mean intervention outcomes or results that (1) justify the time and effort invested by the implementers, (2) move the antisocial student into the normative range on the target behaviors to which the intervention is applied, and (3) are acceptable to and valued by consumers of them (Walker et al., 1998).

These procedures can be classified as positive, accelerative techniques to encourage desirable behavior and as reductive techniques that rely on negative sanctions to discourage undesirable behavior. Unfortunately, the behavior patterns of antisocial children and youths can be so resistant to tactics of social influence that they often require the application of both types of procedures. We do not wish to be perceived as advocates of negative sanctions—indeed, we are not. (See Repp and Singh [1990] for a seminal treatment of this issue involving vulnerable, at-risk populations.) Nevertheless, ample evidence suggests that the combined application of limits setting, negative sanctions, careful monitoring, and reinforcement contingencies is necessary to substantively impact the overall behavior of antisocial students (see Greenberg et al., 2001; Kazdin, 1985, 1987; Loeber & Farrington, 2001; Reid et al., 2002; Patterson, 1983; Patterson et al., 1992; Shinn, Walker, & Stoner, 2002).

Just as no single intervention is sufficient to solve all the adjustment problems of antisocial individuals, no single technique (positive or negative) is sufficient to change their behavior to within normal limits. If the goal is to

© Jeff Greenberg/PhotoEdit

Time-out is one of many positive intervention techniques teachers and parents can implement for antisocial behavior patterns. Combining timeouts with other types of methods often increases the likelihood of improved behaviors.

simply change how antisocial children and youths *perceive* and *talk about* their behavior, then counseling and psychotherapy will be adequate. But if the goal is to produce changes in how they *act* and *behave,* then the application of scientifically derived behavior change procedures is necessary.

In addition to the intervention procedures and implementation guidelines contained in subsequent chapters of this book, some excellent resources have become available in the past decade that provide the "nuts and bolts" of the behavior management mechanics necessary to achieve socially valid outcomes for antisocial students and those with challenging behavior patterns. In addition, these valuable resources treat the issues of violence and criminal behavior in school and nonschool contexts in great depth. The reader is referred to the following highly recommended sources:

- Burns, B., & Hoagwood, K. (2002). *Community treatment for youth: Evidence-based interventions for severe emotional and behavioral disorders.* New York: Oxford University Press.

- Elias, M., Zins, J., Weissenberg, R., Frey, K., Greenberg, M., Hayes, N., Kessler, R., Schwab-Stone, M., & Shriver, T. (1997). *Promoting social and emotional learning: Guidelines for educators.* Alexandria, VA: Association for Supervision and Curriculum Development.

- Elliott, D., Hamburg, B., & Williams, K. (1998), *Violence in American Schools.* Cambridge: Cambridge University Press.

- Gottfredson, G., Gottfredson, D., & Czeh, E. (2000), *National Study of Delinquency Prevention in Schools.* Elliott City, MD: Gottfredson Associates.

- Greenberg, M., Domitrovich, C., & Bumbarger, B. (2001). The prevention of mental disorders in school-aged children: Current state of the field. *Prevention and Treatment, 4,* 1–61.

- Jensen, P. & Cooper, J. (2002). *Attention deficit hyperactivity disorder: State of the science-best practices.* New York: Civic Research Institute.

- Loeber, R., & Farrington, D. (2001). *Child delinquents: Development, intervention and service needs.* Thousand Oaks, CA: Sage.

- Osofsky, J. (1997). *Children in a violent society.* New York: Guilford Press.

- Reid, J., Patterson, G., & Snyder, J. (2002). *Antisocial behavior in children and adolescents: A developmental analysis and model for intervention.* Washington, DC: American Psychological Association.

- Satcher, D. (2001). *Youth violence: A report of the surgeon general.* Washington, DC: U.S. Public Health Service, U.S. Department of Health and Human Services.

- Shinn, M., Walker, H., & Stoner, G. (2002). *Interventions for academic and behavior problems II: Prevention and remedial approaches.* Bethesda, MD: National Association of School Psychologists.

- Thornton, T., Craft, C., Dahlberg, L., Lynch, B., & Baer, K. (2000). *Best practices of youth violence prevention: A sourcebook for community action.* Atlanta: Centers for Disease Control and Prevention.

Guidelines for Implementing Best-Practice Interventions

The following guidelines are derived from our collective experiences and are presented for the reader's consideration in designing and implementing interventions for antisocial students in school. They are divided into two major types: generic strategies and implementation recommendations. Generic strategies have to do with the appropriate approach to this population and the kinds of decisions made within this context. Implementation recommendations are suggestions for maximizing the cost-effective application of specific intervention techniques and applying them according to best-practice standards.

Generic Strategies

It's important to conduct a functional behavioral assessment and analysis of the target student's behavior to determine the specific purposes or goals that the behavior in question may serve (e.g., to avoid a task, to escape from a situation, to establish control or dominance over others, or to seek a positive outcome that is valued). (See the chapter on assessing antisocial behavior for an overview of this procedure.) Before designing an intervention to change specific forms of behavior, it is essential to know, or at least have some idea about, the purpose(s) the problematic behavior serves. Problematic behavior that is aversive to others is nevertheless maintained because it serves the antisocial student's own behavioral goals. As a rule, training is required in order to conduct a functional analysis in a valid manner. (See O'Neill, Horner, Albin, Storey, & Sprague [1997] for a comprehensive treatment of the issues and procedures involved in conducting a functional analysis of problem behavior.)

Armed with this knowledge, you can do the following:

1. Attempt to build a positive, trusting relationship with the antisocial student as a first step in positively influencing her or his behavior and development. Young (1993) calls this an essential step in "setting the stage" for intervening with students in school. Because antisocial students come from such chaotic and unpredictable environments, they need exposure to caring adults who value them and who establish school settings that are consistent, predictable, and supportive (see Young, 1993). This strategy should be implemented as a precursor to full intervention. It will not only help to establish a bond, and perhaps friendship, with the student but also create the possibility of actually influencing the student's behavior in more positive directions.

2. Establish the best universal intervention procedures you can for improving academic performance and social adjustment before resorting to selected interventions. Although there is a high probability that antisocial students will spend some part of their school day and even school career in a more restrictive setting, they should have as much exposure as possible to normal peers and general education settings.

3. Be sensitive to the behavioral efficiency of the responses you are trying to reduce and replace in comparison with those you are replacing them

with. Often, maladaptive forms of behavior are much more efficient at producing reinforcement from the social environment than are appropriate forms. When this occurs, it makes the behavior change process very difficult because the adaptive strategies you are teaching compete poorly with the antisocial behavior you are seeking to eliminate. As a rule, newly taught forms of behavior extinguish unless they are strongly supported by the social environment. This situation calls for careful selection of the target responses, monitoring of their usage, and provision of long-term support to ensure their integration into students' ongoing behavioral repertoires.

4. Begin your intervention approach or strategy with positive procedures only (e.g., social skills training, limits setting, statement of rules, daily debriefings about difficult situations and the ways in which they were handled, and school- or home-based incentive systems). Add time-out, brief suspension, or cost contingency procedures only if the antisocial student's behavior remains unaffected or is only marginally so. In most cases, you will have to resort to this far more powerful strategy in which adaptive, appropriate behavior is reinforced and supported while maladaptive, inappropriate behavior is *simultaneously* mildly punished and reduced or eliminated. (See online Appendix A on the companion Web site for details of these procedures and their effects.)

5. Do all that you can to involve the antisocial student's primary caregivers in the intervention process while recognizing that, in some cases, you will receive little cooperation or interest from them in this regard. (The chapter on parenting strategies contains suggestions and procedures for approaching this task with parents.)

6. Systematically screen and begin intervening as early as possible in the school careers of any student at risk for antisocial behavior patterns. Preschool and kindergarten are good times to begin. Plan on monitoring, tracking, and reintervening with "booster shots" during subsequent school years, as necessary, after the end of your initial intervention. Effecting positive behavior change is a two-stage process. Stage 1 involves implementing procedures to produce reliable and socially valid changes in the target student's behavior; stage 2 involves monitoring, tracking, and supporting the student's changed behavior over the long term to ensure that it is sustained (Walker, 1995). Booster shots are one effective method of achieving this goal.

7. Be sure to teach empathy and socially responsible decision making as part of your intervention. As noted previously, antisocial students tend to have weak social skills repertoires and tend to be especially vulnerable in these two skill areas.

8. Be aware that the academic demands and ordinary classroom management procedures that most teachers and students take for granted, as a normal part of schooling, may be highly aversive events for the antisocial student (see Gunter, Denny, Jack, Shores, & Nelson, 1993; Shores, Gunter, & Jack, 1993). Often, antisocial students display highly agitated forms of behavior that can quickly spin out of control due to frustration with their inability to

meet minimal academic demands or to accept the constraining effects of classroom rules. The natural response of most antisocial students to such frustration is either to withdraw from the situation or to initiate an escalating confrontation with the teacher. Either one is a destructive outcome for the student and/or the student–teacher relationship.

It is important to remember that considerable overlap exists between antisocial, aggressive behavior patterns and ADHD. Estimates vary, but experts generally agree that there is a 50–60% degree of overlap between these two commonly occurring disorders (see Barkley, 1990; DuPaul & Stoner, 2002; Jensen & Cooper, 2002; McKinney, Montague, & Hocutt, 1993). Thus, students who are routinely screened or referred for antisocial behavior should also be assessed for ADHD, and vice versa. Barkley, DuPaul, and McKinney, and their respective associates (as previously cited) provide excellent resource materials and tools for accomplishing this task, as do Jensen and Cooper (2002). In addition, Pfiffner and her colleagues (Pfiffner & Barkley, 1990) offer some useful recommendations for teachers in managing the behavior of ADHD students within classrooms. The *CH.A.D.D. Educator's Manual,* produced by the national organization Children and Adults with Attention Deficit Disorders (CH.A.D.D.), is essential reading for teachers and other school personnel who are concerned with the problem of ADHD in school and its overlap with antisocial behavior patterns. It contains a superb compilation of research-based, proven strategies for intervening with these students. The manual is available from CASET Associates, Ltd. (10201 Lee Highway, #180, Fairfax, VI 22030). The U.S. Department of Education, Office of Special Education Programs, has sponsored a number of forums, research studies, and materials development projects for addressing ADHD in school. The Chesapeake Institute (2030 M Street NW, Suite 810, Washington, DC 20036) distributes these materials for the cost of publication and mailing. They are designed for use in educational settings and are both practical and easy to use.

There is a strong connection between antisocial behavior patterns, conduct disorder, and depression (see Seeley, Rohde, Lewinsohn, & Clarke, 2002). Many antisocial children and youths are at elevated risk for adolescent depression; the mixture of depression and CD places antisocial children and youths at elevated risk for many destructive outcomes. The material in this book does not address the problem of depression; however, it is very important for teachers, counselors, and school psychologists to be on the alert for this disorder among antisocial students and to refer those who are suspected of having it for appropriate evaluation and treatment.

Antisocial students also have an elevated risk of school failure and dropout. They have behavioral characteristics that are highly aversive to others and that directly conflict with teacher expectations associated with the management of the classroom environment (see Hersh & Walker, 1983; Walker, 1986). It is strongly recommended that attempts be made to teach antisocial students to understand, accept, and adhere to established classroom rules and teacher expectations. Although this is no easy task, it is an important one that could directly influence the school careers of antisocial students. Learning to accept and abide by the structures of rule-governed systems such as schools and classrooms is a significant life skill. In this context, we recommend giving careful attention to the issue of antisocial students responding to teacher requests and commands. This is one of the most important skills antisocial students can learn, and one in which they are very often deficient (see Walker & Walker, 1991). (This topic will be discussed in detail in the chapter on managing the social interactions of antisocial students.)

Implementation Recommendations

The following recommendations for implementing a series of intervention techniques are ones that we and others have found to be effective in addressing the behavior problems of antisocial students in grades K through 5 or 6. In the online Appendix A on your companion Web site, we illustrate these techniques and present results to demonstrate their efficacy. It is unrealistic to expect that a single technique (e.g., adult praise or time-out), applied in isolation, will have an enduring impact on the behavioral adjustment and teacher or peer acceptance of antisocial students. Rather, it is almost always necessary to implement multiple techniques within a larger intervention program when dealing with this student population.

Adult Praise. Adult praise (from teachers, parents, or others) is a form of focused attention that communicates approval and positive regard. It is an abundantly available, natural resource that is greatly underutilized. This is unfortunate because praise that is behavior specific and delivered in a positive and genuine fashion is one of our most effective tools for motivating students and teaching them important skills. A technical manual on praising, which was developed for Utah's BEST Project, provides detailed guidelines on how to use this technique effectively. These authors note that praise should be immediate, frequent, enthusiastic, descriptive, and varied, and should involve eye contact. We would also suggest that the ratio of praises to criticisms and reprimands be at least 4:1—and higher if possible. Finally, it is important to recognize that antisocial students may not be initially responsive to adult praise incorporated into a school intervention because of their long history of negative interactions with the adults in their lives. However, through pairing with other incentives (e.g., points exchangeable for privileges at school or home), the positive consequences of praise will eventually increase.

Individual and Group Reinforcement Contingencies. A contingency refers to and defines the relationship between a positive consequence and the target behavior of an individual or a group of individuals. It has to do with the arrangement of details between earnable consequences and the performance criteria that must be met to access them. Contingencies can be individual or group oriented. Individual contingencies are a private, one-to-one arrangement between a teacher or parent and a student in which certain consequences (e.g., privileges) are made available dependent upon the student's performance. Earning a minute of free time for every ten or fifteen math problems correctly solved, or attempted, is an example of an individual contingency. Group contingencies are arrangements in which an entire group of individuals (e.g., a class) is treated as a single unit and the group's performance, as a whole, is evaluated to determine whether a positive consequence is earned. For example, if the level of academic engagement for the entire class meets or exceeds 70% for a 30-minute instructional period, then the class earns 5 minutes of extra recess. A combined individual–group contingency arrangement is also possible in which the target student, through acceptable performance, earns a group activity reward or consequence that is shared equally with the entire class. Applications of these three types of contingency arrangements are illustrated in (1) online Appendix A, (2) *Utah's Best Practices: Behavioral and Educational Strategies for Teachers* (Reavis et al., 1996), and (3) *The Acting Out Child* (see Walker, 1995).

Social Skills Training.   The social skills training chapter provides extensive coverage of this topic and presents detailed guidelines for conducting effective training. Recommended curricular resources are also provided.

Time-Out.   Time-out is sometimes a necessary tool for use with disruptive, aggressive students particularly when they are younger. Time-out is commonly used by parents but much less often by school personnel. Time-out refers to removal of students for a brief time (usually 5–15 minutes) from situations in which (1) they have problems controlling their behavior and/or (2) the attention of peers is drawn to their inappropriate behavior. Time-out is a controversial technique that *must* be used according to prescribed guidelines in order to meet essential ethical standards governing its application, to control potential undesirable side effects, and to achieve the desired outcomes (i.e., reduction or elimination of undesirable, destructive, or maladaptive forms of behavior). *Utah's BEST Project Technical Manual* and *The Acting Out Child* provide guidelines for using time-out effectively. We recommend that procedures be set up to provide for both in-classroom time-out for minor infractions and out-of-classroom time-out (the principal's office) for more serious infractions. Further, students should be given the option of volunteering for brief periods of time-out when they temporarily cannot control their own behavior. Finally, teachers should *never* physically engage with students in order to forcibly put them in time-out. We recommend as well that time-out be used sparingly, as a last resort, and that its use be avoided with older students.

Response Cost (RC) or Cost Contingency.   Unlike time-out, *cost contingency* (or *response cost*) removes a privilege or earned points for a behavioral infraction of some sort. Instead of removing the student from the situation, it removes a point or privilege from the student; thus, it is much easier to manage than time-out. Cost contingency is the basis for fines, traffic tickets, penalties in football, foul shots in basketball, and other sanctions in public life that are applied for the purpose of controlling illegal or maladaptive forms of behavior (e.g., speeding, running red lights, or committing tax fraud). In combination with praise, a carefully implemented point system, and time-out as a backup procedure, cost contingency can be quite effective in reducing maladaptive behavior. The technique is versatile and can be used with equal effectiveness in classroom and playground settings.

Online Appendix A contains a number of studies illustrating the effective use of this technique in the classroom and on the playground. We suggest that the following general guidelines be strictly followed in using cost contingency:

1. Carefully explain the RC system before applying it.
2. Always tie RC to a reinforcement system, preferably involving points.
3. Develop an appropriate delivery system.
4. Implement RC immediately after the target behavior or response occurs.
5. Apply RC each time an instance of a target behavior occurs.
6. Never allow students to accumulate negative points (i.e., to go in the hole with point totals).
7. Control the ratio of points earned to those lost.
8. Never be intimidated from using RC by the target student.
9. Never let the subtraction of points be punitive or personalized.
10. Praise positive, appropriate behavior as frequently as opportunities permit.

(See Walker [1995] for a detailed treatment of RC's use with disruptive, aggressive students within classroom and playground settings.)

Program–Environment Fit or Match Considerations

A central principle of social ecology is person–environment fit or match (Romer & Heller, 1983). This principle concerns the degree to which an individual's characteristics (i.e., attitudes, skills, and performance) fit or match up with the demands and expectations of the environment (e.g., the classroom or playground). As a rule, the better the fit or match, the more likely it is that a satisfactory adjustment will be achieved.

Horner, Sugai, and Todd (1994) have extended this concept to intervention programs that match up or fit with the contexts in which they are implemented. Program–environment fit is an extremely important dimension that is often ignored in the delivery of school interventions. We argue that (1) there is a growing need for the provision of behavioral supports within school settings and (2) too often, interventions are designed and delivered in a manner that is technically sound but contextually inappropriate.

Unless an intervention is a good contextual fit—in the sense of being acceptable to teachers and students, being consistent with their values and beliefs, not requiring too much effort, being relatively unobtrusive, and holding the promise of effectiveness—it is likely to fail no matter how well designed it is. Knowledge of schools and their operations is essential if maximally effective interventions are to be designed and implemented for students, and especially for antisocial students.

School interventions must be designed and implemented so as to be sensitive to and systematically take into account the cultural backgrounds of an increasingly diverse student body. Punishing students for culturally normative behavior, beliefs, or attitudes is fraught with unfortunate consequences and is something that is to be avoided. Hernandez and Isaacs (1998) provide an excellent resource on promoting cultural competence in children's mental health services. They address special issues in serving culturally diverse populations in a sensitive and comprehensive manner.

We recommend careful attention to the literature on the acceptability of interventions in schools. Witt and his colleagues have conducted the seminal work in this area (see Elliott, Witt, Kratochwill, & Stoiber, 2002; Witt & Martens, 1983; Witt, Noell, LaFleur, & Morrison, 1997; Witt & Robbins, 1985). This literature indicates that teachers are concerned about the following factors in relation to school-based interventions: (1) risk to the target child, (2) amount of teacher time required, (3) effects of the intervention on other children, and (4) amount of teacher skill required. With regard to reductive intervention techniques, teachers universally find corporal forms of punishment to be unacceptable and differential reinforcement of alternative forms of appropriate behavior to be highly acceptable. Teachers have reported varying degrees of acceptability for such techniques as reprimands, staying after school, and time-out. As a general rule, teachers prefer positive, accelerative intervention approaches to negative, reductive ones.

A careful analysis of the influence of the setting on an intervention's potential effectiveness is highly recommended in the design of any intervention. It is essential that this dimension be attended to carefully in working with antisocial students. There is increasing evidence that a carefully implemented universal intervention provides a solid foundation for the application of more intensive, individualized interventions. Selected interventions are much more likely to be effective if they are implemented within the context of a universal intervention (Burns & Hoagwood, 2002; Eddy et al., 2002; Sugai et al., 2002). Interventions delivered within school settings must be integrated and carefully coordinated with each other in order to maximize their cost effectiveness.

Conclusion

This chapter presented information designed to empower the reader to understand the complexity of antisocial behavior patterns and the role of schooling as a powerful context for intervening with them. We still have much to learn, but we have discovered a great deal that is not being applied consistently or effectively in this regard. If we make a good-faith effort to implement well that which we currently know regarding antisocial children and youths, we can collectively make a huge difference in their lives. The material in the remainder of this book attempts to make that information accessible to educators and other professionals.

InfoTrac College Edition Research Terms

Second Steps Violence Prevention Program

Social skills training

Teacher praise

Youth violence intervention

References

Alberg, J., Petry, C., & Eller, S. (1994). *A social skills planning guide*. Longmont, CO: Sopris West.

Algozzine, R., & Ysseldyke, J. (1992). *Strategies and tactics for effective instruction*. Longmont, CO: Sopris West.

APA Online. (2002). *Is youth violence just another fact of life?* American Psychological Association, Public Interest Directorate, 750 First Street NE, Washington, DC 20002.

Barkley, R. (1990). *Attention-deficit hyperactive disorder: A manual for diagnosis and treatment*. New York: Guilford.

Behrman, R. (1992). *The future of children: School-linked services*. Los Altos, CA: Center for the Future of Children, the David and Lucile Packard Foundation.

Biglan, T. (1992). Family practices and the larger social concept. *New Zealand Journal of Psychology, 21*(1), 37–43.

Biglan, T. (1993). A functional contextualist framework for community interventions. In S. C. Hayes, L. J. Hayes, H. Reese, & T. Sarbin (Eds.), *Varieties of scientific contextualism* (pp. 251–276). Reno, NV: Context Press.

Biglan, T. (2001). *The Palo Alto Project*. Unpublished document. Eugene: Oregon Research Institute.

Biglan, T., Lewin, L., & Hops, H. (1990). A contextual approach to the problem of aversive practices in families. In G. Patterson (Ed.), *Depression and aggression: Two facets of family interactions* (pp. 103–129). Hillsdale, NJ: Erlbaum.

Bullis, M., & Walker, H. M. (1994). *Comprehensive school-based systems for troubled youth*. Eugene: University of Oregon, Institute on Violence and Destructive Behavior.

Bullis, M., Walker, H. M., & Sprague, J. R. (2001). A promise unfulfilled: Social skills training with at-risk children and youth. *Exceptionality, 9*(1/2), 67–90.

Burns, B., & Hoagwood, K. (2002). *Community treatment for youth: Evidence-based interventions for severe emotional and behavioral disorders*. New York: Oxford University Press.

Catalano, R., & Hawkins, J. (1996). The social development model: A theory of antisocial behavior. In J. D. Hawkins (Ed.), *Delinquency and crime: Current theories* (pp. 149–197). New York: Cambridge University Press.

Committee for Children. (1992). *Second Step: A violence prevention curriculum*. Seattle: Author.

DuPaul, G. J., & Stoner, G. (2002). Interventions for attention problems. In M. Shinn, H. Walker, & G. Stoner (Eds.), *Interventions for academic and behavior problems, II: Preventive and remedial approaches* (pp. 913–938), Bethesda, MD: National Association of School Psychologists.

Eddy, J. M., Reid, J. B., & Curry, V. (2002). The etiology of youth antisocial behavior, delinquency and violence and a public health approach to prevention. In M. R. Shinn, H. M. Walker, & G. Stoner (Eds.), *Interventions for academic and behavior problems II: Preventive and remedial approaches* (pp. 27–51), Bethesda, MD: National Association of School Psychologists.

Elksnin, L., & Elksnin, N. (Eds.). (2001). *Exceptionality, 9*(1/2).

Elliott, S., Witt, J., Kratochwill, T., & Stoiber, K. (2002). Selecting and evaluating classroom interventions. In M. Shinn, H. Walker, & G. Stoner (Eds.), *Interventions for academic and behavior problems, II: Preventive and remedial approaches* (pp. 243–294), Bethesda, MD: National Association of School Psychologists.

Embry, D. E., & Flannery, D. (1996). Two sides of the coin: Multilevel prevention and intervention to reduce youth violent behavior. In D. Flannery & R. Huff (Eds.), *Youth violence: prevention, intervention, and social policy* (pp. 47–72), Washington, D.C.: American Psychiatric Press.

Epstein, M. H., & Sharma, J. M. (1998). *Behavioral and emotional rating scale: A strength-based approach to assessment—Examiner's manual.* Austin, TX: Pro-Ed.

Gadow, K. D., & Spraftkin, J. (1993). Television violence and children with emotional and behavorial disorders. *Journal of Emotional and Behavorial Disorders, 1*(1), 54–63.

Garmezy, N. (1985). Stress-resistant children: The search for protective factors. In J. E. Stevenson (Ed.), *Recent research in developmental psychopathology* (pp. 213–233). New York: Pergamon Press.

Gerber, M. M., & Semmel, M. I. (1984). Teacher as imperfect test: Reconceptualizing the referral process. *Educational Psychologist, 19*(3), 137–148.

Gottfredson, G., & Gottfredson, D. (2001). What schools do to prevent problem behavior and promote safe environments. *Journal of Educational and Psychological Consultation, 12*(4), 313–344.

Greenberg, M., Domitrovich, C., & Bumbarger, B. (2001). *Preventing mental disorders in school-age children: A review of the effectiveness of prevention programs.* Available from the Prevention Center for the Promotion of Human Development, College of Health and Human Development, Pennsylvania State University, State College, PA.

Grimes, T., Cathers, T., and Vernberg, E. (1996). *Emotionally disturbed children's reaction to violent media segments.* Unpublished manuscript, School of Journalism and Mass Communication, Kansas State University.

Gunter, P., Denny, K., Jack, S., Shores, R, & Nelson, M. (1993). Aversive stimuli in academic interactions between students with serious emotional disturbance and their teachers. *Behavioral Disorders, 18*(4), 265–274.

Hernandez, M., & Isaacs, M. (1998). *Promoting cultural competence in children's mental health services.* Baltimore: Paul Brookes.

Hersh, R. H., & Walker, H. M. (1983). Great expectations: Making schools effective for all students. *Policy Studies Review, 2*(Special No. 1), 147–188.

Hoagwood, K., & Erwin, H. (1997). Effectiveness of school-based mental health services for children: A 10-year research review. *Journal of Child and Family Studies, 6*(4), 435–451.

Horner, R., Sugai, G., & Todd, A. (1994). *Effective behavioral support in schools.* Field-initiated research proposal submitted to the U.S. Department of Education. Available from Educational and Community Supports, University of Oregon, Eugene, OR 97403.

Jensen, P., & Cooper, J. (2002). *Attention deficit hyperactivity disorder: State of the science: Best practices.* New York: Civic Research Institute.

Juel, C. (1988). *Learning to read and write: A longitudinal study of 54 children from first through fourth grade.* Paper presented at the Annual

Conference of the American Educational Research Association, New Orleans.

Kazdin, A. (1977). Assessing the clinical or applied importance of behavior change through social validation. *Behavior Modification, 5,* 427–452.

Kazdin, A. E. (Ed.). (1985). *Treatment of antisocial behavior in children and adolescents.* Homewood, IL: Dorsey Press.

Kazdin, A. (1987). *Conduct disorders in childhood and adolescence.* London: Sage.

Katz, M. (1997). *On playing a poor hand well.* New York: Norton.

Lieberman, C. (1994, May). *Television and violence.* Paper presented at the Council of State Governments Conference on School Violence, Westlake Village, CA.

Lipsey, M., & Derzon, J. (1998). Predictors of violent or serious delinquency in adolescence and early adulthood: A synthesis of longitudinal research. In R. Loeber & D. Farrington (Eds.), *Serious and violent juvenile offenders: Risk factors and successful interventions.* Thousand Oaks, CA: Sage.

Lloyd, J. W., Kauffman, J. M., Landrum, T. M., & Roe, D. L. (1991). Why do teachers refer pupils for special education? An analysis of referral records, *Exceptionality, 2*(3), 115–126.

Loeber, R., & Farrington, D. P. (Eds.). (1998). *Serious and violent juvenile offenders: Risk factors and successful interventions.* Thousand Oaks, CA: Sage.

Loeber, R., & Farrington, D. (2001). *Child delinquents: Development, intervention, and service needs.* Thousand Oaks, CA: Sage.

Lyon, R. (2002, November). The current status and impact of U.S. reading research. Keynote address to the National Association of University Centers for Excellence in Developmental Disabilities, Bethesda, MD.

Mastern, A. & Coatsworth, J. (1998). Development of competence in favorable and unfavorable environments: Lessons from research on successful children. *American Psychologist, 53,* 205–220.

McKinney, J., Montague, M., & Hocutt, A. (1993). *A synthesis of the research literature on the assessment and identification of attention deficit disorder.* Coral Gables, FL: University of Miami.

Michelson, L., Kazdin, A., & Marchione, K. (1986). *Prevention of antisocial behavior in children.* Pittsburgh: University of Pittsburgh School of Medicine, Western Psychiatric Institute and Clinic.

Miller, G., Brehm, K., & Whitehouse, S. (1998). Reconceptualizing school-based prevention for antisocial behavior within a resiliency framework. *School Psychology Review, 27*(3), 364–379.

Murray, J. (1997). Median violence and youth. In J. Osofsky (Ed.), *Children in a violent society* (pp. 72–96). New York: Guilford Press.

O'Neill, R. E., Horner, R. H., Albin, R. W., Storey, K., & Newton, S. (1997). *Functional analysis of problem behavior: A practical assessment guide.* Pacific Grove, CA: Brooks/Cole.

Patterson, G. R. (1982). *Coercive family process (Vol. 3): A social learning approach.* Eugene: Castalia.

Patterson, G. R. (1983). *Longitudinal investigation of antisocial boys and their families* Research grant from the National Institute of Mental Health. Eugene: Oregon Social Learning Center.

Patterson, G. R., Reid, J. B., & Dishion, T. J. (1992). *Antisocial boys.* Eugene: Castalia.

Patterson, G., Chamberlain, P., & Reid, J. (1982). A comparative evaluation of parent training procedures. *Behavior Therapy, 13,* 638–650.

Pfiffner, L., & Barkley, R. (1990). Educational placement and classroom management. In R. Barkley (Ed.), *Attention-deficit hyperactivity disorder: A handbook for diagnosis and treatment.* New York: Guilford Press.

Reavis, H. K., Taylor, M., Jenson, W., Morgan, D., Andrews, D., & Fister, S. (1996). *Best practices: Behavioral and educational strategies for teachers.* Longmont, CO: Sopris West.

Reid, J. B., Patterson, G. R., & Snyder, J. J. (Eds.). (2002). *Antisocial behavior in children and adolescents: A developmental analysis and the Oregon Model for Intervention.* Washington, DC: American Psychological Association.

Repp, A., & Singh, N. (1990). Perspectives on the use of nonaversive interventions for persons with developmental disabilities. Sycamore: IL: Sycamore.

Romer, D., & Heller, T. (1983). Social adaptation of mentally retarded adults in community settings: A social-ecological approach. *Applied Research in Mental Retardation, 4,* 303–314.

Rutter, M. (1979). Protective factors in children's responses to stress and disadvantage. In M. Kent & J. Rolf (Eds.), *Primary prevention of psychopathology, Volume III: Social competence in children* (pp. 49–74). Hanover, NH: University Press of New England.

Sampson, R. (1992). Family management and child development: Insights from social disorganization theory. In J. McCord (Ed.), *Facts, frameworks, and forecasts: Advances in criminological theory* (Vol. 3, pp. 63–93). New Brunswick, NJ: Transaction Books.

Sampson, R., & Groves, W. (1989). Community structure and crime: Testing social disorganization theory. *American Journal of Sociology, 94,* 774–802.

Satcher, D. (2001). *Youth violence: A report of the Surgeon General.* Washington, DC: U.S. Public Health Service, U.S. Department of Health and Human Services.

Schoenwald, S., Brown, T., & Henggeler, S. W. (2000). Inside Multisystemic Therapy: Therapist, supervisory, and program practices. *Journal of Emotional and Behavioral Disorders, 8*(2), 113–127.

Schorr, L. (1988). *Within our reach: Breaking the cycle of disadvantage.* New York: Doubleday.

Seeley, J. R., Rohde, P., Lewinsohn, P. M., & Clarke, G. N. (2002). Depression in youth: Epidemiology, identification, and intervention. In M. R. Shinn, H. M. Walker, & G. Stoner (Eds.), *Interventions for academic and behavior problems II: Preventive and remedial approaches* (pp. 885–911). Bethesda, MD: National Association of School Psychologists.

Shinn, M. R., Walker, H. M., & Stoner, G. (Eds.). (2002). *Interventions for academic and behavior problems II: Preventive and remedial approaches.* Bethesda, MD: National Association of School Psychologists.

Shores, R., Gunter, P., & Jack, S. (1993). Classroom management strategies: Are they setting events for coercion? *Behavioral Disorders, 18*(2), 92–102.

Strain, P., Guralnick, M., & Walker, H. M. (eds.). (1986). *Children's social behavior: Development, assessment, and modification.* New York: Academic Press.

Strayhorn, J., Strain, P. S., & Walker, H. M. (1993). The case for interaction skills training in the context of tutoring as a preventative mental health intervention in the schools. *Behavioral Disorders, 19*(1), 11–26.

Sugai, G., Horner, R., & Gresham, F. (2002). Behaviorally effective school environments. In M. Shinn, H. Walker, & G. Stoner (Eds.), *Interventions for academic and behavior problems II: Preventive and remedial approaches* (pp. 315–350), Bethesda, MD: National Association of School Psychologists.

Walker, H. M. (1986). The Assessments for Integration into Mainstream Settings (AIMS) assessment system: Rationale, instruments, procedures, and outcomes. *Journal of Clinical Child Psychology, 15*(1), 55–63.

Walker, H. M. (1995). *The acting-out child: Coping with classroom disruption* (2nd ed.). Longmont, CO: Sopris West.

Walker, H. M., Forness, S. R., Kauffman, J. M., Epstein, M. H., Gresham, F. M., Nelson, C. M., & Strain, P. S. (1998). Macro-social validation: Referencing outcomes in behavioral disorders to societal issues and problems. *Behavioral Disorders, 24*(1), 7–18.

Walker, H. M., Horner, R. H., Sugai, G., Bullis, M., Sprague, J. R., Bricker, D., & Kaufman, M. J. (1996). Integrated approaches to preventing antisocial behavior patterns among school-age children and youth. *Journal of Emotional and Behavioral Disorders, 4,* 193–256.

Walker, H. M., Nishioka, V., Zeller, R., Severson, H., & Feil, E. (2000). Causal factors and potential solutions for the persistent under-identification of students having emotional or behavioral disorders in the context of schooling. *Assessment for Effective Intervention, 26*(1), 29–40.

Walker, H. M., & Sprague, J. R. (2002). Intervention strategies for diverting at-risk children and youth from destructive outcomes. *Report on Emotional and Behavioral Disorders in Youth, 1*(1), 5–8, 18–19.

Walker, H. M., & Walker, J. E. (1991). *Coping with noncompliance in the classroom: A positive approach for teachers.* Austin, TX: Pro-Ed.

Werner, E., & Smith, R. (1988). *Vulnerable but invincible: A longitudinal study of resilient children and youth.* New York: McGraw-Hill.

Witt, J., Noell, G., LaFleur, L., & Mortenson, B. (1997). Increasing teacher usage of interventions in general education settings. *Journal of Applied Behavior Analysis, 30,* 693–696.;

Witt, J., & Robbins, J. (1985). Acceptability of reductive interventions for the control of inappropriate child behavior. *Journal of Abnormal Child Psychology, 11,* 59–67.

Witt, J., & Marsten, D. (1983). Assessing the acceptability of behavioral interventions. *Psychology in the Schools, 20,* 510–517.

Wolf, M. M. (1978). Social validity: The case for subjective measurement, or how applied behavior analysis is finding its heart. *Journal of Applied Behavior Analysis, 11,* 203–214.

Young, K. (1993). The role of social skills training in the prevention and treatment of behavioral disorders. In B. Smith (ed.), *Focus '93—Teaching students with learning and behavior problems* (pp. 341–367). Victoria, British Columbia: Smith.

Zigler, E., Taussig, C., & Black, K. (1992). Early childhood intervention: A promising preventative for juvenile delinquency. *American Psychologist, 47,* 997–1006.

Best Practices in Assessment of Antisocial Behavior

Introduction

This chapter describes the types of assessment that are important for understanding and dealing effectively with school-based antisocial behavior. Reliable, valid, and accurate assessment of antisocial behavior is an indispensable first step in intervening effectively with this behavior pattern. The main purpose of any assessment process is to collect information that will lead to correct decisions about the individuals involved (Witt, Elliott, Daly, Gresham, & Kramer, 1998). This fact is no less important for antisocial students than for students in general. At least five types of decisions can be made in the assessment process: (1) screening, (2) classification and placement, (3) monitoring of student progress, (4) intervention and instruction, and (5) documentation of program effectiveness (Salvia & Ysseldyke, 1991). Different consumers of assessment information use and differentially value this information; Table 3.1 lists the purposes of assessment from the perspectives of various consumers of this information.

Decision Making in Assessment

Screening decisions are based on the evaluation of an entire population of individuals to determine if they require more specialized, comprehensive assessment procedures. For example, hearing screenings are routinely conducted in schools to determine whether certain students should be referred for more comprehensive and expensive audiological examinations. Screening tools are advantageous because they are brief, easy to administer, and generally effective in identifying students who are at risk for certain kinds of problems (Witt et al., 1998). Early screening and identification of children at risk for antisocial behavior is essential for effective prevention efforts. The longer these children go without effective interventions, the more intense and resistant their problem behavior will be later in their school careers (Kazdin, 1987a, b; Severson & Walker, 2002).

Note that we are willing to tolerate more false positives in making screening decisions than we would be in making classification, placement, or program evaluation decisions. A false positive is the inaccurate identification of individuals as having a problem when, in fact, they do not. For example, all commercially developed home pregnancy test kits have established acceptable levels of false positive identification. The primary risk in the false positive identification of antisocial behavior patterns may be exposing individuals to potentially costly early interventions that they do not need.

A false negative identification creates much more serious risks. A false negative refers to *not* identifying a student as having a problem when, in fact, she or he does. In oncology, for example, the failure to identify patients in the early stages of cancer can result in much higher mortality rates. False negative identifications are problematic because they deny early intervention services for students who need them and could benefit most from them. With respect to antisocial behavior patterns, the failure to identify and intervene with at-risk children by 8 years of age most often results in a lifelong pattern of antisocial behavior that is

TABLE 3.1 ◆

Purposes of Assessment for Different Consumer Groups.

Consumer Group	Purposes
Policymakers	Set standards
	Select goals
	Monitor quality of interventions
	Encourage best practices
	Formulate policies
	Distribute resources (personnel and money)
Administrators	Monitor program effectiveness
	Identify program strengths and weaknesses
	Designate program priorities
	Compare alternative strategies
	Plan and improve programs
Teachers and other personnel	Make classification decisions
	Make placement decisions
	Monitor student progress
	Plan instruction
	Design interventions
Parents and students	Gauge student progress
	Assess student behavioral excesses and deficits
	Assess student academic strengths and weaknesses
	Evaluate school accountability

highly resistant to intervention efforts (Kazdin, 1987b; Lipsey & Derzon, 1998; Walker, Severson, & Feil, 1995).

Classification and placement decisions are based on more comprehensive and expensive assessments than screening decisions. Information used in making classification decisions might include norm-referenced tests of ability and academic achievement, behavior rating scales completed by teachers and parents, direct observations of students' behavior, school records, and interviews with significant others in students' lives. Classification decisions are based on performances of students that differ substantially from their "normal" peers and that also correspond to the characteristics that define a particular condition or disorder (e.g., depression, anxiety, or attention deficit/hyperactivity disorder [ADHD]). For example, the recent literature on antisocial behavior shows that it is desirable to identify and classify students who demonstrate characteristics of *both* ADHD and conduct disorder (CD) as early as possible (Lynam, 1996; Waschbush, 2002).

Placement decisions, as distinct from classification decisions, are based on what a team of individuals considers to be the most appropriate setting for a student with a particular classification status. For example, many students classified as emotionally disturbed in schools might be placed in a self-contained special education class or an alternative program in order to remediate their social-emotional and behavioral difficulties. Other students might be placed in a residential treatment program for 24 hours a day, seven days a week, depending on the severity and intensity of their problem behaviors. Still other students who are chronic law violators might be placed in juvenile justice lockdown facilities for several years based on their repeated offenses against property and/or persons.

Progress monitoring of student performance in school settings is highly valued by teachers, parents, and administrators. One cannot determine whether a given intervention is effective or ineffective without some form of objective progress monitoring. Examples of progress monitoring include curriculum-based measurements of academic performance, systematic observations of students' social behavior in classroom and playground settings, and work samples of academic performance. Progress monitoring uses individuals' baseline levels of performance as the criterion against which the effects of interventions are compared or evaluated later on (Gresham & Lambros, 1998).

Intervention decisions are based on assessment information that relates directly to choices of particular curricula or behavioral programs. The most important concept in making intervention decisions is treatment validity, which refers to the degree to which assessment information contributes to beneficial treatment outcomes (Hayes, Nelson, & Jarrett, 1987). The key in establishing treatment validity is to show a clear relationship between the assessment information collected and the treatment planning process. Specifically, for any assessment procedure to have treatment validity, it must lead to identification of target behaviors, result in more effective treatments, and be useful in evaluating treatment outcomes (Gresham & Lambros, 1998). The practice of functional behavioral assessment (described later in this chapter) is based on a treatment validity notion. In functional behavioral assessment, interventions are selected and implemented based on a systematic assessment of the function or specific purpose that a particular behavior serves for an individual (Gresham, Watson, & Skinner, 2001).

Program effectiveness decisions are often of greatest interest to administrators who are responsible for various educational and other treatment programs in schools. Data concerning program effectiveness are important in making decisions about continuing, modifying, or discontinuing specific intervention programs in schools. Program evaluation data can also be used to conduct cost-benefit analyses to support continued or increased funding for specific programs.

Assumptions in Assessment

Central to the assessment process are the assumptions that underlie the use of assessment procedures to make decisions about individuals. The rules by which we judge whether assessment procedures are reliable, accurate, and valid are well established. A particularly valuable heuristic to guide assessment practices was presented by Messick (1995), who argues that the validity of any assessment process must be based on (1) whether it attains some clearly specified purpose and (2) whether the consequences of using it are beneficial for the individuals involved. Consistent with our earlier definition, valid assessment leads to correct decisions about individuals. In turn, these decisions should lead to beneficial outcomes for individuals.

It is important to understand the assumptions upon which assessment practices are based. The following assumptions are from the assessment model developed by Witt and his colleagues (Witt, Elliot, Daly, Gresham, & Kramer, 1998), which we strongly support:

- Assumption 1: Individual differences among students are relative rather than absolute.

- Assumption 2: Assessments are samples of behavior.

- Assumption 3: The primary reason for assessment is to improve intervention.

- Assumption 4: All forms of assessment contain error.

- Assumption 5: Good assessment involves gathering information about the environment.

With regard to assumption 1, students often differ from peers on at least one dimension. The key question is whether we should be concerned about such differences. Making this determination often depends on a student's situation and acculturation and on the expectations placed on the student in a particular situation. Specific forms of behavior might be considered normal in one setting or situation and deviant in another, depending on the context. For example, a boy who is reading at the 25th percentile might not be considered to have a reading problem if he attends a school in which average reading achievement is at the 10th percentile. However, if that same boy were to move to a school in which average reading achievement is at the 80th percentile, he most likely would be considered to have a reading problem and might be referred for special education services.

According to assumption 2 (assessments are samples of behavior), any given assessment procedure should not be used to make decisions. Rather, people should make decisions about students based on a full consideration and analysis of all issues. For example, basing a decision about a student's antisocial behavior on a 10-minute playground observation would not be considered a best practice because it would be based on an inadequate sample of behavior. Similarly, basing a decision about a student's behavior solely on the results of a brief, Likert rating scale completed by a teacher would be inappropriate. The collection of samples of behavior from multiple sources can go a long way to ensure that decisions are based on an adequate knowledge base. Whenever possible, the collection of assessment information about antisocial behavior patterns should be multimethod, multi-agent, and multisetting in nature.

With regard to assumption 3 (the primary reason for assessment is to improve intervention), assessment can have many goals ranging from determining

Direct observation helps identify at-risk and antisocial students. Direct observation is also an essential part of student classification, placement, and programming for special services.

the causes of students' problem behavior to determining the most appropriate placement. However, the ultimate goal of assessment should be to guide the selection, implementation, and evaluation of intervention efforts. As previously discussed, this requires that the assessment procedures have adequate treatment validity, reliability, and sensitivity.

A study by Broussard and Northrup (1995) illustrates this point well. These authors found that students who exhibited high rates of off-task behavior responded differentially to teacher attention, peer attention, and classroom demands. In some cases, they engaged in off-task behavior in order to engage either teacher or peer attention; in other cases, they used off-task behavior as an instrument to get out of assigned work (i.e., escape from task demands). Following this assessment process, these authors designed effective interventions to increase students' on-task behavior based on information as to why the students were off-task. In short, the assessment was essential to designing the most appropriate intervention.

According to assumption 4, error is present in any assessment activity, test, or evaluation procedure. For example, lie detector tests (polygraphs) are inadmissible in courts of law because they contain 10–25% error (Bersoff, 1983). Many tests used in schools by educators and psychologists contain even greater amounts of error; however, we frequently use these tests anyway to make important, long-term educational decisions about students.

Measurement error is a direct reflection of the unreliability of test scores. Unreliability in test scores comes from a variety of sources. First, the items on a test may not correlate highly with each other, thereby creating inconsistency in the measurement of a particular trait. Second, test scores may fluctuate over time, thus creating instability in the measurement process. Finally, observers who code behavior may disagree among themselves regarding the quality, frequency, or duration of observed behavior, thereby introducing error into the assessment process.

Accepting the fact that error is always present in all forms of assessment influences practice in two ways. First, it dictates that we be aware of and try to minimize factors that contribute to such errors of measurement. Second, knowing that error is present makes it essential that we use and interpret assessment data in a cautious and professional manner.

Finally, according to assumption 5 (good assessment involves gathering information about the environment), the kinds of assessment information that are gathered can directly influence the kinds of inferences we make about students' behavior. If we collect information only about the student in question, then we will likely view the situation as a *within-student* problem. For example, if we collect information using only a norm-referenced teacher rating scale, then we will base our conclusion(s) primarily on how the student compares with other students.

An alternative assessment practice would be to collect not only teacher rating scale information on the student but also data on specific environmental factors that may contribute to the student's behavioral excesses. For instance, we might find that problem behaviors are much more common in unstructured settings and activities (e.g., on the playground or in the hallway) than in structured ones (e.g., during classroom instruction). We might also discover that problem behaviors are less likely to occur with preferred peers and more likely to do so with nonpreferred peers on the playground. Finally, we might learn that these problem behaviors result in peer social attention, which reinforces their continued occurrence. Clearly, by not collecting this type of information, we risk making some faulty assumptions about the causes of the behavior problems.

Assessment Within a Problem-Solving Model

Good assessment practice takes place within a problem-solving model focused on making screening, classification, placement, progress monitoring, and program effectiveness decisions (Witt et al., 1998). Problem solving can be defined as the process by which it is determined that (1) a significant discrepancy exists between an individual's current level of performance and a desired level of performance and (2) strategies are investigated to reduce or eliminate this discrepancy (Gresham, 1991, 2002).

In this model, "problem" is a relative concept because a discrepancy may vary according to the perceptions of different social agents in the student's environment. For instance, parents may not report a discrepancy between how the child is behaving and how they want their child to behave. In contrast, the child's teacher and principal may see a huge discrepancy between current and desired levels of performance in academic, social, personal, and behavioral domains.

Once current and desired levels of performance are defined in operational terms, this discrepancy becomes the focus of the problem-solving assessment process. Defining problems in this manner is based on the belief that problems are a result of unsuccessful or discrepant interactions between persons (e.g., child and peers, child and teacher, child and parent, or parent and teacher). As such, the person identified as having a problem, as well as his or her interactions with the environment, must be examined in order to understand and change the problem behavior (Witt et al., 1998). Many children with antisocial behavior patterns come to the school setting with a long list of nonschool-related risk factors operating in their lives and a learning history that has shaped many of their problems. However, the focus of a problem-solving model is to identify and intervene on those variables over which educators and other professionals have some control.

In this model, problem solving takes place in a four-step process, with specific objectives for each step (Kratochwill & Bergan, 1990). The four steps or phases are (1) problem identification, (2) problem analysis, (3) plan implementation, and (4) problem evaluation. The first step in this process is to obtain a clear, objective definition of the problem behavior(s). As we shall see later in this chapter, the screening process uses objective operational definitions of externalizing and internalizing behavior patterns for this purpose (Walker & Severson, 1990). Once the problem behavior is clearly defined, the next step is to analyze factors that may be contributing to the acquisition and maintenance of the behavior. After defining behavior problems and analyzing factors contributing to their occurrence, the next step is to implement an intervention to change the target behaviors. The final step in this problem-solving process is to evaluate the degree to which the implemented intervention was effective in reducing or eliminating the problem behaviors.

Assessment information in each of these four steps is gathered from a variety of sources. Some information is obtained from archival records, school cumulative folders, and other available records. Other information is gathered by interviewing teachers, parents, and students themselves. Still other information is obtained by direct observation of students in classroom or playground settings. The overarching goal in this problem-solving, assessment process is to integrate information from multiple sources and informants. Table 3.2 shows the objectives for each of the four steps or stages in the problem-solving process.

The following sections describe specific problem-solving assessment strategies for making decisions about children and youths at risk for or displaying antisocial behavior patterns. We begin with a discussion of risk and protective factors that either contribute to or buffer students from the destructive effects of serious antisocial behavior. The ensuing sections illustrate procedures for making decisions regarding early screening, identification, and intervention approaches based on functional behavioral assessments that can also be used in progress monitoring and program evaluation.

TABLE 3.2 ◆

Objectives of Each Stage of Problem-Solving Assessment.

Stage	Objectives
1. Problem identification	Define behaviors in operational, measurable terms
	Prioritize behavioral concerns
	Describe planned methods of assessment
	Describe events preceding target behavior
	Describe events following behavior
	Describe discrepancy between observed and expected performance
	Set goals for intervention outcomes
2. Problem analysis	Formulate reasonable hypotheses about factors affecting the problem
	Focus on factors over which we have control
	Generate solution based on presumed function of target behaviors
3. Plan implementation	Define responsibilities of all parties involved
	Determine need for training intervention implementers
	Conduct skills training as necessary
	Assess and monitor treatment integrity
4. Problem evaluation	Evaluate degree to which intervention was implemented
	Evaluate effectiveness of intervention
	Evaluate social validity from perspectives of different consumers

Identification of Risk and Protective Factors

A useful way of understanding the social, emotional, and behavioral challenges experienced by children and youths is known as the risk factor model (Hawkins, VonCleve, & Catalano, 1991; Patterson, Reid, & Dishion, 1992). This model identifies macro, molar variables (i.e., those that are broad in scope) that influence behavior across multiple settings and over a relatively long time. Research suggests that systematic exposure to risk factors (e.g., dysfunctional families, caregiver substance abuse, child neglect or abuse, poverty, and unemployment) predicts the development of maladaptive behavior patterns (Elliott, 2001; Walker & Sprague, 1999). These maladaptive behavior patterns include defiance, noncompliance, aggression, impulsivity, and negative school attitudes. Short-term outcomes of these maladaptive behavior patterns include low academic achievement, truancy, school discipline referrals, and teacher and peer rejection (Gresham, Lane, MacMillan, & Bocian, 1999; Walker, Irvin, Noell, & Singer, 1992). In turn, these short-term outcomes are associated with more serious long-term outcomes such as gang membership, arrests, school dropout, and substance abuse (Cicchetti & Nurcombe, 1993; Patterson, 2002; Walker & Severson, 2002).

Walker and Sprague (1999) suggest that, if we want to understand variables that are associated with students' problem behaviors in a general sense and to predict future behavior, then a risk factor assessment model is required. Walker and Severson (2002) divided risk factors into four categories: (1) child factors (e.g., prematurity, poor social skills, impulsivity), (2) family factors (e.g., teenage motherhood, single parenthood, poor parenting practices), (3) school context (e.g., deviant peer group, poor school attachment, peer rejection), and (4) community/cultural factors (e.g., socioeconomic disadvantage, lack of support services, social or cultural discrimination).

It is also important to understand which factors operate in each of these categories to moderate or buffer the pernicious effects of risk factors. Adequate social skills, problem-solving strategies, stable family relationships, peer acceptance, and access to support services operate as protective factors. An understanding of these risk and protective factors assists greatly in designing and implementing interventions for students with antisocial behavior. Table 3.3 lists a number of risk and protective factors associated with antisocial and criminal behavior. (Loeber and Farrington [2001] offer recommended measurement tools for assessing risk and protective factors.)

Serious antisocial behavior patterns are known to be highly stable over time (Eddy, Reid, & Curry, 2002; Olweus, 1979). Approximately 50% of elementary-age children who demonstrate antisocial behavior patterns will continue this behavior pattern into adolescence, and 40–75% of adolescents who demonstrate this behavior pattern will continue it into early adulthood (Eddy, 2001). It is important to keep in mind that the presence of a single risk factor does not necessarily mean that an individual will develop antisocial behavior in the future. A meta-analysis by Lipsey and Derzon (1998) showed that the single strongest risk factor for future antisocial behavior is past antisocial behavior, followed by gender (being male), socioeconomic status, antisocial parents, ethnicity (being a minority), and a mental health condition. These risk factors do not operate in isolation, but rather interact jointly to accurately predict future antisocial behavior patterns (Eddy et al., 2002).

Lipsey and Derzon (1998) estimate that the base rate for juveniles identified as violent or seriously delinquent is approximately 8% of the population. Using the risk factors just discussed, we can predict that 47–84% of at-risk individuals will develop antisocial behavior between age 15–25 (depending on the weighting of the risk factor). The majority of children classified as not at risk will have a low probability of becoming antisocial; however, 20–23% of those who do not become antisocial will show up as false positives (i.e., inaccurately predicted to be antisocial when they are not) (Lipsey & Derzon, 1998). (The reader is referred to Loeber and Farrington [2001] for resource information on assessment instruments and procedures for the appropriate assessment of risk and protective factors.)

TABLE 3.3 ◆

Risk and Protective Factors Associated with Antisocial Behavior.

	Risk Factors		
Child Factors	Family Factors	School Context	Community and Cultural Factors
Prematurity	*Parental characteristics:*	School failure	Socioeconomic disadvantage
Low birth weight	Teenage mothers	Normative beliefs about aggression	Population density and housing conditions
Disability	Single parents	Deviant peer group	Urban area
Prenatal brain damage	Psychiatric disorder, especially depression	Bullying	Neighborhood violence and crime
Birth injury	Substance abuse	Peer rejection	
Low intelligence	Criminality	Poor attachment to school	Cultural norms concerning violence as acceptable response to frustration
Difficult temperament	Antisocial models	Inadequate behavior management	
Chronic illness	*Family Environment:*		Media portrayal of violence
Insecure attachment	Family violence and disharmony		Lack of support services
Poor problem solving	Marital discord		Social or cultural discrimination
Beliefs about aggression	Disorganization		
Attributions	Negative interaction/ social isolation		
Poor social skills	Large family size		
Low self-esteem	Father absence		
Lack of empathy	Long-term parental unemployment		
Alienation	*Parenting Style:*		
Hyperactivity/disruptive behavior	Poor supervision and monitoring of child		
Impulsivity	Harsh or inconsistent discipline style		
	Rejection of child		
	Abuse		
	Lack of warmth and affection		
	Low involvement in child's activities		
	Neglect		

(continued)

TABLE 3.3 ◆

(Continued)

Protective Factors

Child Factors	Family Factors	School Context	Community and Cultural Factors
Social competence	Supportive, caring parents	Positive school climate	Access to support services
Social skills		Prosocial peer group	Community networking
Above-average intelligence	Family harmony	Responsibility and required helpfulness	Attachment to community
Attachment to family	More than two years between siblings	Sense of belonging/bonding	Participation in church or other community group
Empathy	Responsibility for chores or required helpfulness	Opportunities for success at school and recognition of achievement	Community/cultural norms against violence
Problem-solving ability	Secure and stable family		Strong cultural identity and ethnic pride
Optimism	Supportive relationship with other adult	School norms against violence	
School achievement	Small family size		
Easy temperament	Strong family norms and morality		
Internal locus of control			
Moral beliefs			
Values			
Self-related cognitions			
Good coping style			

Early Identification and Screening for Antisocial Behavior

Many fields have well-established practices of early identification of problems that lead to more effective treatments. For instance, in medicine, routine screening procedures such as prostate-specific antigen (PSA) tests to detect prostate cancer, mammograms to detect breast cancer, and Papanicolaou (Pap) tests to identify early stages of cervical cancer have been routine for years. Unfortunately, similar proactive early-identification approaches are not universal practices for identifying children with or at risk for antisocial behavior. As discussed in the previous section, we know a great deal about the risk factors that predict quite accurately those children who will develop social and emotional behavioral problems later in life. The technology for making these predictions is gradually becoming more accurate for children at younger ages, yet the practice of early identification remains relatively static (Severson & Walker, 2002).

Bullis and Walker (1994) have discussed the irony of teachers' consistently ranking children with severe behavior disorders as one of their highest service priorities, even though prevalence studies indicate that this school population continues to be seriously underidentified (Walker, Nishioka, Zeller, Severson, &

Feil, 2000). In fact, Kauffman (1999) suggests that the field of education actually "prevents prevention" of behavior disorders of at-risk children through well-meaning efforts to "protect" them from such factors as labeling and stigmatization associated with the screening–identification process.

We know that children who have not learned to achieve their social goals other than through coercive behavioral strategies by around 8 years of age (end of third grade) will likely continue displaying some degree of antisocial behavior throughout their lives (Bullis & Walker, 1994; Kazdin, 1987b; Loeber & Farrington, 1998). We also know that the longer such children go without access to effective intervention services, the more resistant their behavior problems will be to later intervention efforts (Gresham, 1991). In the absence of early intervention, these problem behaviors will escalate and morph into more serious and violent behavior patterns.

Technical Considerations in Early Identification and Screening

Screening instruments and approaches must have established levels of technical adequacy before they can be used to identify accurately children who are at risk for antisocial behavior. Technical adequacy subsumes the concepts of reliability and validity. Reliability refers to the consistency with which individuals are identified as being either at risk or not at risk over time. The key question in assessing the reliability of screening approaches is this: Does the individual obtain the same relative risk status at two points in time? For example, does a child who is identified as having an antisocial behavior pattern in grade 1 show this same behavior pattern in grade 6?

The validity of screening approaches is reflected in their accuracy in the identification or detection of at-risk status. In other words, is the level of predictive accuracy sufficiently high to justify use of the screening procedure (Severson & Walker, 2002)? Table 3.4 shows the dimensions that are germane to assessing predictive accuracy. Sensitivity reflects the proportion of persons with a given outcome (e.g., antisocial behavior pattern) who have a particular risk indicator (e.g., poor social skills). Specificity is the proportion of persons without the outcome who do not have the risk indicator present. Positive predictive power (PPP) is the proportion of individuals classified as high risk who develop the outcome. Negative predictive power (NPP) is the proportion of persons classified as low risk who do not develop the outcome. The base rate of the outcome is the prior probability or prevalence of the outcome in a given population. The overall accuracy of a risk assessment method is the proportion of individuals correctly classified by the screening method.

Two types of errors in predictive accuracy are inherent in the use of behavioral screening measures. As noted previously, false positive errors involve the identification of individuals as having a problem when they do not. Thus, a person with a risk indicator present (e.g., poor social skills) would be inaccurately predicted to have the outcome when, in fact, she or he did not (e.g., antisocial behavior). False positive errors are shown in cell B of Table 3.4. False negative errors, in contrast, result from a failure to predict that individuals will have a given outcome when, in fact, they do. In this case, the risk factor is absent (poor

TABLE 3.4 ◆

Dimensions of Predictive Accuracy.

Risk Indicator	Present	Absent
Present	*Sensitivity* (proportion of children with the outcome who have the indicator present: % of children who are antisocial who are aggressive)	*False Positive* (proportion of children with the indicator who do not develop the outcome: % of children who are aggressive who are not antisocial)
Absent	*False Negative* (proportion of children without the indicator who develop the outcome: % of children who are not aggressive who are antisocial)	*Specificity* (proportion of children without the outcome who do not have the indicator: % of children who are not antisocial who are not aggressive)

Positive predictive power: Proportion of children with the indicator who develop the outcome (Sensitivity/ Sensitivity + False Positive)

Negative predictive power: Proportion of children without the indicator who do not develop the outcome (Specificity/Specificity + False Negative)

Prevalence: Prior probability of the outcome being predicted (Sensitivity + False Negative/Sensitivity + False Positive + False Negative + Specificity)

Accuracy: Proportion of children correctly classified (Sensitivity + Specificity/Sensitivity + False Positive + False Negative + Specificity)

social skills), but the outcome is present (antisocial behavior). False negative errors are shown in cell C.

Screening: Multiple Gating Procedures

A particularly valuable approach to screening that is more valid than approaches using single risk indicators is known as multiple gating. Multiple gating procedures have been shown to be accurate in the identification of children at risk for subsequent serious behavior disorders and delinquency (Loeber, Dishion, & Patterson, 1984). Loeber and colleagues used a three-gate system whereby they predicted the presence of delinquency risk by using teacher and parent reports of externalizing behavior. Multiple gating is a process in which a series of progressively more expensive and precise assessments (i.e., gates) are used to identify children at risk for antisocial behavior. Several of these multiple gating procedures are described here.

Systematic Screening for Behavior Disorders.   The Systematic Screening for Behavior Disorders (SSBD) procedure (Walker & Severson, 1990) is a multiple gating screening device for the identification of children having behavior disorders in grades 1–6. It provides for the cost-effective, mass screening of all students in regular education classrooms on both externalizing and internalizing behavioral dimensions. The SSBD is a multiple gating device because it contains a series of linked, sequential assessments known as "gates." The SSBD utilizes a combination of teacher nominations (Gate 1), teacher rating scales (Gate

2), and direct observations of classroom and playground behavior (Gate 3) to accomplish the early identification of children who are at risk for serious behavior disorders.

The SSBD contains three interrelated stages for screening that are graphically shown in Figure 3.1. The first gate of the SSBD uses teacher nominations in which teachers are asked to identify three students in their classes who match each of two profiles or types of behavior patterns. The first behavior pattern is known as externalizing, which refers to behavior problems that are directed outward by the child toward the external environment. Externalizing behavior problems (sometimes called "undercontrolled" behavior patterns) are viewed as behavioral excesses because they occur too often. Examples include defying teachers, aggressing toward others, failing to comply with teacher directions, and arguing (Walker & Severson, 1990). The second pattern, known as internalizing (sometimes called "overcontrolled" behavior patterns), refers to behavior problems that are directed inward and that represent problems with the self. Internalizing behavior problems are known as "behavioral deficits" and include depression, anxiety, and social withdrawal.

The second gate of the SSBD involves the use of teacher ratings of externalizing and internalizing behavior patterns. Teachers are asked to rate the three children ranked highest on the externalizing dimension and the three children ranked highest on the internalizing dimension from Gate 1 (for a total of six students) on two brief rating scales that measure, respectively, the frequency of adaptive and of maladaptive forms of behavior. Teachers also rate these children on a Critical Events Index (CEI) or checklist that assesses whether a student has exhibited any of 33 externalizing and/or internalizing behavior problems within the past six months. Those students exceeding normative cutoff points in the second gate of the SSBD are then independently assessed in Gate 3 via classroom and playground observations by professionally trained observers.

In Gate 3, a school professional (e.g., school psychologist, guidance counselor, or social worker) assesses students on two measures of school adjustment using direct observation procedures. Both measures utilize duration recording procedures, which estimate the amount of time a target behavior occurs during a specified observation session. The first measure, known as academic engaged time (AET), is recorded during independent seatwork periods. The second measure, the peer social behavior observation code, measures the quality, distribution, and level of students' social behavior during recess periods on the playground. Students who exceed normative criteria on these two measures are then considered to "pass" Gate 3 and are referred for more comprehensive assessments of their behavior.

The SSBD was nationally standardized on 4,500 cases for the Gate 2 measures and approximately 1,300 cases for the Gate 3 measures. These cases were collected from 18 school districts in eight states: Oregon, Washington, Utah, Illinois, Wisconsin, Rhode Island, Kentucky, and Florida. The SSBD has extensive empirical evidence in support of its reliability and validity, which is reported in the SSBD technical manual and in other sources (Severson & Walker, 2002; Walker et al., 1990, 1994).

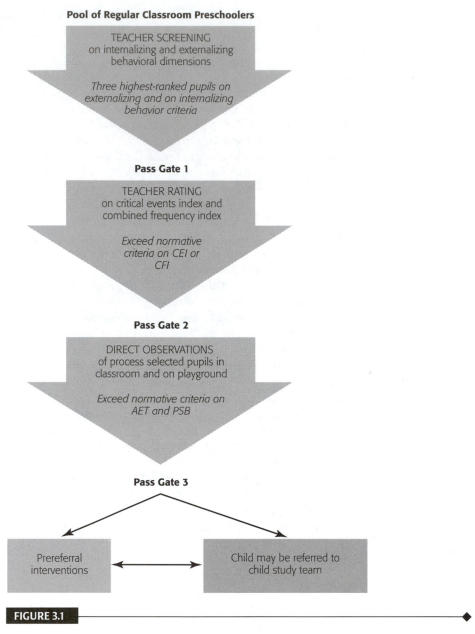

Pool of Regular Classroom Preschoolers

TEACHER SCREENING
on internalizing and externalizing
behavioral dimensions

*Three highest-ranked pupils on
externalizing and on internalizing
behavior criteria*

Pass Gate 1

TEACHER RATING
on critical events index and
combined frequency index

*Exceed normative
criteria on CEI or
CFI*

Pass Gate 2

DIRECT OBSERVATIONS
of process selected pupils in
classroom and on playground

*Exceed normative criteria on
AET and PSB*

Pass Gate 3

Prereferral
interventions ⟷ Child may be referred to
child study team

FIGURE 3.1

Systematic Screening for Behavior Disorders (SSBD).

The SSBD represents a significant advance in the systematic and comprehensive screening for behavior problems of general education students (Forness, Kavale, MacMillan, Asarnow, & Duncan, 1996; Gresham, Lane, & Lambros, 2000, 2002; Kauffman, 1999). The major advantage of the SSBD is its provision of behaviorally referenced criteria and a common set of standards for teachers to use in evaluating students' behavioral risk status. It identifies both students who are "acting out" (externalizers) and those who are "acting in" (internalizers), and it removes most of the idiosyncratic subjectivity endemic to the current referral process (Severson & Walker, 2002). Proactive universal approaches to early identification such as the SSBD provide opportunities for early-intervention efforts that can prevent the escalation of problem behavior into more virulent and resistant strains.

Early Screening Project. The Early Screening Project (ESP) is a downward extension of the SSBD developed for use in preschool and day-care settings for children age 3–5 (Walker, Severson, & Feil, 1995). Like the SSBD, the ESP assesses young children who are at risk for developing externalizing and internalizing behavior problems. The ESP was normed on 2,853 children in eight states. The process used by the ESP is the same as in the SSBD except that it incorporates parent ratings of problem behavior at Gate 3 of the screening process. There is strong empirical support for the ESP in terms of its reliability and validity, as reported in the technical manual for the instrument, and it is a user-friendly and highly useful instrument. The ESP has been shown to be an important component of early-intervention programs in which systematic screening occurs on a regular basis (Walker, Severson, & Feil, 1998). Use of the ESP in Head Start programs has been particularly beneficial in the early-identification process (Del'Homme, Sinclair, & Kasari, 1994; Sinclair, 1993; Sinclair, Del'Homme, & Gonzalez, 1993). The ESP is versatile in that it can be used for making screening, classification, placement, and intervention planning decisions, and for monitoring progress in evaluating outcomes of interventions (Severson & Walker, 2002).

Student Risk Screening Scale. The Student Risk Screening Scale (SRSS) (Drummond, 1993) has identified a number of behavioral indicators that are predictive of the development of conduct disorders and later adoption of a delinquent lifestyle (Loeber, 1991; Loeber & LeBlanc, 1990). Adults (parents and teachers) are able to accurately rate these behavioral indicators very early in the child's life (i.e., preschool). Drummond (1993) has ingeniously adapted these indicators into a universal, mass screening procedure for use by elementary school teachers in identifying at-risk students. He has extensively developed and researched a seven-item scale (SRSS), using these five criteria to guide its development:

◆ *Brief:* A screening instrument of this type should have no more than 10 items.

◆ *Research based:* The items should be those that most powerfully discriminate and predict antisocial behavior patterns.

◆ *Easily understood:* The format, scoring, and administration instructions should be as clear and self-explanatory as possible.

◆ *Valid:* The instrument should be accurate and valid for the screening and identification of at-risk students.

◆ *Powerful:* The instrument should be efficient in identifying those students who are truly at risk and who could benefit from early intervention programs.

TABLE 3.5 ◆

Student Risk-Screening Scale (SRSS) Screening for a Classroom.

Name	Steal	Lie, Cheat, Sneak	Behavior Problem	Peer Rejection	Low Academic Achievement	Negative Attitude	Aggressive Behavior	Totals
Jamie	1	3	3	2	2	0	1	12
Susan	0	0	0	3	3	2	3	11
Fred	1	1	3	3	2	3	3	16

These criteria are carefully reflected in the final form of the SRSS. This instrument has proved to be easy to use, highly effective, and technically sound. It has excellent validity and reliability and powerfully distinguishes non-at-risk students from those who show early signs of antisocial behavior (i.e., it has excellent positive predictive power).

The seven items of the SRSS are:

1. Stealing
2. Lying, cheating, sneaking
3. Behavior problems
4. Peer rejection
5. Low academic achievement
6. Negative attitude
7. Aggressive behavior

Students are rated on each of the seven items on a 0-to-3 scale: 0 = never, 1 = occasionally, 2 = sometimes, and 3 = frequently. Total scores on the SRSS can therefore range from 0 to 21. Based on his use of the SRSS, Drummond has established the following risk-score range categories for determining at-risk status: high risk = 9–21, moderate risk = 4–8, and low risk = 0–3. Thus, a student who receives a score of between 9 and 21 should be evaluated carefully for possible early school or family intervention to address the indicated problems.

Table 3.5 shows how the SRSS can be used to assess an entire classroom. The actual SRSS screening form can accommodate up to 30 students. Student names are listed down the left side of the form, and the seven SRSS items are listed across the top of the form. The teacher then simply evaluates each student on the individual items across the rows and enters a rating (0–3) that characterizes the student's behavior for each item.

As the profiles in Table 3.5 show, three students have an elevated (i.e., high) risk for antisocial behavior as indicated by their total scores on the SRSS (12, 11, and 16, respectively). Jamie seems to have more of the indicators of a covert pattern of antisocial behavior while Fred's profile suggests investment in an overt pattern. Susan seems to have problems that fall between these two poles; her problems may be more in the realm of disobedience and low academic achievement.

Table 3.6 illustrates behavioral and academic profiles for three groups of students identified by the SRSS. As these profiles show, the SRSS has great sensitivity

TABLE 3.6 ◆

Profiles of Risk Groups Using the Student Risk-Screening Scale (SRSS).

Variable	Low Risk	Moderate Risk	High Risk
Number of students	117	40	27
Grade point average	3.10	2.43	2.24
Number of classes failed	0.52	1.42	1.88
Metropolitan Achievement Test (<15th percentile)	9%	27%	45%
Academic remediation	19%	35%	52%
Minor discipline infractions per student	0.76	1.90	2.37
Major discipline infractions per student	0.09	0.30	0.89
Serious academic problems	22%	48%	67%
Serious discipline problems	3%	18%	33%
Academic and discipline problems	0%	10%	30%

in identifying students whose risk status is confirmed by existing school records. The SRSS is a highly cost-effective screening instrument that allows teachers to identify at-risk students very early in their school careers so appropriate interventions and support services can be provided for them. Its use is highly recommended as a cost-effective, best practice.

Classification Decisions: Comorbid Conduct and Attention Problems

The two most common classes of behavior problems bringing children to the attention of mental health professionals are (1) hyperactivity-impulsivity-inattention (HIA) and (2) antisocial behavior (Hinshaw, 1987). Based on a review of 60 studies, Hinshaw determined that the correlation between antisocial behavior and HIA based on teacher and parent ratings is .56 and that 30–90% of children in one of these categories could be correctly classified in the other. Thus, it appears that antisocial behavior and HIA are correlated, and not completely independent behavior problems.

Throughout this book, we emphasize that antisocial behavior represents persistent violations of socially acceptable behavior patterns and includes verbal and physical hostility toward others, defiance toward authority figures, and aggressive, coercive acts. In a recent meta-analysis based on over 24,000 participants age 4–20 years, the prevalence rate for antisocial behavior (conduct problems) was 3.92%. And the prevalence rate for boys is over six times higher than that for girls (6.16% versus 0.95%) (Waschbush, 2002).

Prevalence Rates. Recently, the research community has identified a group of children who are at high risk for developing lasting, insidious patterns of antisocial and delinquent behavior. These children are characterized as having characteristics of *both* HIA problems and conduct problems (CP). In his meta-analysis,

Teacher observations of student behavior are an invaluable part of classification and placement decisions, as well as progress monitoring.

Waschbush (2002) found that the prevalence rate for HIA-only was 3.50%, for CP-only was 3.92%, and for HIA+CP was 2.98%. The prevalence rate data suggest that HIA and CP co-occur more highly than would be expected by chance and therefore are not an artifact of sampling biases. In fact, the expected prevalence rate of HIA+CP in the population is only 0.45%, but the actual, observed prevalence rate is almost 3% (Waschbush, 2002).

Characteristics.   Lynam (1996) has referred to children showing characteristics of HIA+CP as "fledgling psychopaths" because his review suggested that these children are more likely to maintain this behavior pattern into adulthood. So-called psychopathic individuals may be described as self-centered, manipulative, lacking in empathy, and coercive or forceful (Hare, 1981).

A pervasive but inaccurate assumption is that these individuals suffer from a low self-concept, which leads them to develop violent and aggressive behavior patterns. However, an important review by Baumeister, Smart, and Boden (1996) suggests that the major cause of aggressive and violent behavior is an *unrealistically high* level of self-esteem that is challenged by external evaluations which contradict or question these perceptions of high self-regard. In other words, when individuals' self-evaluations are more positive than their objective characteristics would indicate are warranted, they may react unfavorably, and sometimes aggressively or violently, to disconfirming feedback regarding these characteristics (Baumeister et al., 1996). These authors referred to this phenomenon as "threatened egotism."

In their review of serious and violent juvenile offending and problem behaviors, Huizinga and Jakob-Chien (1998) found no differences in self-esteem between children with different levels of offenses (serious violent, serious nonviolent, and nondelinquent [control] youths). Similar findings have been reported by other researchers (see Gresham et al., 1999; Gresham, Lane, MacMillan, Bocian, & Ward, 2000; Gresham, MacMillan, Bocian, Ward, & Forness, 1998; Hughes, Cavell, & Grossman, 1997; Schneider & Leitenberg, 1989). Given this body of research, it would seem that interventions for this subpopulation should focus more on developing accurate self-appraisals than on enhancing artificially inflated and inaccurate self-perceptions (i.e., "humility training").

Clearly, children with HIA+CP tend to be characterized by the worst features of both attention deficits and conduct problems. Compared with children with CP-only or HIA-only children, those with HIA+CP have (1) much higher levels of aggression and delinquency based on parent and teacher reports, (2) higher levels of HIA, (3) lower verbal IQ scores, (4) more difficulties in peer relationships, (5) earlier age of onset, and (6) more conduct and attention problems in early adulthood (20 years of age). These data indicate that children with HIA+CP are at much greater risk in terms of destructive outcomes than HIA-only and CP-only children. And their developmental pathway for this behavior pattern emerges early and is stable over time (Loeber, 1988; Lynam, 1996; Washbusch, 2002).

Causal Pathways.　Researchers have described three causal models to explain the development of HIA+CP behavior patterns: (1) the risk factor model, (2) the stepping-stone model, and (3) the subtype model. The risk factor model suggests that HIA is but one among several risk factors that leads to negative outcomes for children and that puts them on a pathway toward antisocial behavior patterns (Gresham et al., 2002; Lynam, 1996). Patterson, DeBaryshe, and Ramsey (1989) provided a model suggesting that disruptive child-rearing practices (e.g., harsh and inconsistent discipline, low levels of parental involvement, and poor supervision and monitoring) set the stage for the development of antisocial behavior problems.

Unskilled parents raising children with difficult temperaments unintentionally train their children to acquire aggressive and coercive forms of behavior via negative reinforcement. Patterson (2002) maintains that the contingent use of aversive strategies in parent–child interactions is central to the development of antisocial behavior patterns in young children. Later on, this same contingent use of coercive behavioral strategies is extended to teacher–child and peer–child interactions, thereby maintaining this behavior pattern over time and across settings. Patterson's (1982) Microsocial Coercive Family Process model indicates that parents attempt to use aggressive and coercive tactics to control their child's behavior. In turn, the child learns that arguing, escalation, confrontation, manipulation, and noncompliance often lead to escape from undesirable tasks or consequences (e.g., following parental directives, doing homework, or completing assigned chores).

This coercive cycle is repeated thousands of times throughout the child's early development. As a result, when the child enters school, he or she is equipped with oppositional-defiant behaviors that negatively impact child–adult relationships (Coie & Jacobs, 1993). Over time, the child's antisocial behavior increases in intensity and magnitude, and it ultimately results in extreme conduct problems. In this model, HIA is but one risk factor among several (e.g., poor parenting skills, lower verbal IQ, academic underachievement, and peer social rejection) that contribute to the development of HIA+CP.

The stepping-stone model, in contrast to the risk factor model, suggests that the presence of HIA early in children's development leads to oppositional-defiant behavior, which, in turn, escalates into CP. In this developmental model, the early onset of HIA problems, in conjunction with sustaining environmental factors, produces a chain of aversive and oppositional interactions between the child and parents, teachers, and peers. Moffitt (1993), like Patterson (1982), proposes that a difficult temperament at birth prompts an escalating chain of negative parent–child interactions that impede the child's social and academic development. This pattern of antisocial behavior becomes embedded in the child's daily routines and increases in frequency and intensity, eventually magnifying into severe CP. The stepping-stone model further suggests that early detection of and intervention with children with HIA can break the behavioral chain and therefore prevent early HIA problems from intensifying into oppositional-defiant disorder and conduct disorder (Gresham et al., 2002; Lynam, 1996).

The subtype model suggests that children with both HIA and CP constitute a unique subgroup (Lynam, 1996). Research reviewed by Lynam (1996) suggests that this subgroup of children has deficits in the ability to incorporate new information while engaging in goal-directed behavior. For instance, children with HIA+CP might struggle in social situations that shift between hostile, neutral, and positive interactions. This difficulty may result from failure to detect and respond to shifts in social cues. As such, these children are likely to continue engaging in confrontation even when peers behave more positively toward them in a particular social situation.

Further, these children are low in "constraint," which may explain why they tend to exhibit impulsive and sensation-seeking behaviors. Lynam (1996) speculates that children fitting the HIA+CP profile start out with low levels of constraint, which, in turn, makes it difficult for them to interpret feedback from the environment accurately. Early on, these children demonstrate signs of HIA that expands into oppositional-defiant disorder because parents unwittingly interfere with their children's goal-directed behavior. When they enter school, these children substantially deviate from the model behavior profile expected by most teachers (Walker et al., 1992) in that they have trouble staying quiet, remaining seated, complying with teacher directions, and transitioning between activities.

In summary, it appears that neither the risk factor nor the stepping-stone nor the subtype models fully explain the development of HIA+CP. Waschbush's (2002) meta-analysis concluded that the preponderance of evidence suggests that HIA+CP is a more serious disorder than HIA-only and CP-only that begins earlier in life and is more persistent over time. In addition, most of the research evidence suggests that the characteristics of this disorder (HIA and CP) combine synergistically rather than additively. That is, HIA and CP characteristics are more than simply an amalgam of behaviors that define HIA and CP. Waschbush (2002) concludes:

These findings imply that early and accurate identification of HIA may be important for preventing more serious disruptive behavior and that there may be multiple developmental pathways associated with HIA-CP, including a pathway in which HIA-CP emerges early and remains stable across development and a second pathway in which HIA-CP emerges after a history of HIA-only. (p. 134)

Early Detection and Assessment of HIA+CP. Early identification of children showing HIA+CP behavior patterns is essential because of the very poor prognosis for these children extending into adolescence and early adulthood. In light of the urgent need for the earliest possible identification of these children, Gresham and colleagues (2000, 2002) propose a multiple gating procedure that is a modification of the SSBD (Walker & Severson, 1990) described earlier.

This procedure, known as the early identification of antisocial behavior plus hyperactivity (EIABH), involves a set of assessment tools and procedures that increase in intensity, diagnostic precision, and costs. The EIABH consists of four stages—(1) teacher nomination, (2) multi-informant ratings, (3) intensive assessment, and (4) resistance to intervention—that are used in concert to identify children at risk for HIA+CP. Box 3.1 shows the four stages used in this screening process along with the operational definition of HIA+CP.

In Stage I (teacher nominations), it is possible for teachers to identify children at risk for HIA+CP. At this stage, teachers identify seven to eight children from their classes who most closely match the characteristics of this behavioral profile. This list of children is then rank ordered from most like (1) to least like (8) according to the operational definition of HIA+CP. The top three "most like" students pass though the first stage or gate.

In Stage II (multi-informant ratings), persons who are familiar with the children are asked to provide information regarding their behavior. We support using existing behavior rating scales with excellent psychometric properties to accomplish the assessments in this stage. These measures include the Child Behavior Checklist (CBCL) (Achenbach, 1991a), the Teacher Rating Form (TRF) (Achenbach, 1991b), and the Critical Events Index (CEI) (Walker & Severson, 1990). The TRF (completed by teachers) and the CBCL (completed by parents) both contain subscales relevant to HIA+CP—Delinquent Behavior, Aggressive Behavior, and Attention Problems. These subscales have been used to successfully differentiate the HIA+CP population from HIA-only and CP-only groups (Lynam, 1996; Waschbush, 2002). The CEI (completed by teachers and/or parents) contains 11 behaviors, out of a total of 33, that would be useful in identifying children at risk for HIA+CP: (1) steals, (2) sets fires, (3) has tantrums, (4) physically assaults an adult, (5) is physically aggressive toward other students, (6) damages others' property, (7) attempts to seriously injure others, (8) ignores teacher warnings or reprimands, (9) uses obscene language, (10) makes lewd or obscene gestures, and (11) exhibits cruelty to others. Students with high scores (98th percentile) on *two or more* of these instruments pass through the second gate.

In Stage III (intensive assessments), the assessments are characterized by more labor- and time-intensive procedures relative to those in Stages I and II. Procedures in this stage involve functional behavioral assessments using direct

Box 3.1

Early Identification of Hyperactivity-Impulsivity-Attention plus Conduct Problems (HIA+CP)

Definition: This behavior profile refers to aggressive, coercive, impulsive behaviors exhibited by children toward the social environment. Children fitting this behavior pattern show signs of hyperactivity, impulsivity, inattention, defiance, and aggressive behaviors that are frequently accompanied by a lack of remorse or empathy toward others.

Stage I: Teacher nominations

Stage II: Multi-informant ratings

Stage III: Intensive assessment

Stage IV: Resistance to intervention

and indirect methods (Gresham et al., 2001). The purpose of these assessments is to determine the specific function(s) that the problem behaviors are serving for students. These assessment procedures are described more fully in a subsequent section of this chapter.

The last stage of this multiple gating approach to early identification involves the notion of resistance to intervention as a marker for HIA+CP. That is, students are identified as being at risk for HIA+CP if they do not respond to evidence-based interventions that have been shown to be effective with other groups of students. Resistance to intervention refers to insufficient or unacceptable changes in a given behavior pattern as a function of intervention (Gresham, 1991, 2002; Gresham et al., 2001). Thus, children can be considered to be at risk for HIA+CP if their behavior patterns are unresponsive to our best interventions.

The goal of all interventions is to produce a discrepancy between baseline (preintervention) and postintervention levels of performance. The failure to produce an acceptable discrepancy between baseline and postintervention levels of performance within a reasonable time can be taken as partial evidence for HIA+CP. If an evidence-based intervention is implemented with integrity (i.e., as intended) and the target behavior does not change to desired levels, then modifications in the intervention may be necessary. It is possible that the intervention needs to be strengthened in a variety of ways:

◆ The intervention can be increased in *frequency* (e.g., implemented five rather than three times per week).

◆ The intervention can be increased in *intensity* (e.g., implemented three hours rather than one hour per day).

◆ The intervention can be increased in *duration* (e.g., implemented for three months rather than one month).

◆ The intervention can be supplemented or changed to an alternative, stronger intervention (e.g., implementing a more complex, time-consuming intervention with greater levels of expertise).

The literature on antisocial behavior, in general, indicates that these students have high rates of maladaptive behaviors and low rates of prosocial behaviors. As we have noted, their behavior can be extremely resistant to intervention, particularly if the interventions are not based on evidence-based practices and/or are implemented with poor integrity or fidelity (Gresham, 1999; Lane, 1999; Lipsey & Wilson, 1998). The term *best practices* suggests that a variety of interventions may be required to change maladaptive behavior patterns that have been well established. More detailed discussion of these types of interventions can be found in subsequent chapters of this book.

Functional Behavioral Assessment (FBA) and Antisocial Behavior

Researchers and practitioners increasingly are using functional behavioral assessment (FBA) methods to match intervention strategies to behavioral function in order to enhance the effectiveness of interventions. The use of FBA has been endorsed by organizations such as the National Association of State Directors of Special Education, the National Association of School Psychologists, and the National Institutes of Health (Reschly & Tilly, 1999). Recently, the journal *Behavioral Disorders* included a number of articles critiquing the use of FBA to meet the challenging behaviors of children and youths at risk for emotional and behavioral disorders. Research over the past 30 years in the field of applied behavior analysis indicates that FBA methods contribute to beneficial outcomes for children and youths (Sugai, Horner, & Sprague, 1999).

In 1997, amendments to the Individuals with Disabilities Education Act (IDEA) required the use of FBA and positive behavioral supports and interventions. Many behavior analysts had considered these methods to be best practices prior to this legislation, but the federal law originally did not require their use. Specifically, the IDEA now has the following mandated requirement:

> The team must address through a behavioral intervention plan any need for *positive behavioral strategies and supports.* In response to disciplinary actions by school personnel, the IEP [individual educational plan] team must, within 10 days, meet to develop a *functional behavioral assessment plan* to collect information. This information should be used in developing or reviewing and revising an existing behavior intervention plan to address such behaviors. In addition, states are required to address the inservice needs of personnel (including professionals and paraprofessionals who provide special education, general education, related services, or early intervention services) as they relate to *developing and implementing positive intervention strategies.* (*IDEA Amendments,* 1997; italics added)

Definition of FBA.   FBA can be defined as a systematic process for identifying events that *reliably* predict and maintain behavior. It uses a variety of methods for gathering information about antecedents (i.e., events that trigger the occurrence of behavior) and consequences (i.e., events that maintain behavior). Knowledge of the conditions maintaining problem behavior can be used to discontinue or control sources of reinforcement for it and to teach adaptive, functionally equivalent behaviors instead (Crone & Horner, 2003; O'Neill, Horner, Albin, Storey, & Sprague, 1997). It should be emphasized that FBA is not a single test or observation, but rather involves a collection of assessment methods to determine antecedents, behaviors, and consequences. The major goal of FBA is to identify environmental conditions that are associated with the occurrence and nonoccurrence of problem behaviors.

The function of behavior refers to the *purpose* that behavior serves for an individual in a particular setting or situation. Fundamentally, there are only *two* functions of behavior: (1) positive reinforcement, which involves anything that brings behavior in contact with a positive stimulus and (2) negative reinforcement, in which a behavior leads to escape, avoidance, delay, or reduction of an aversive stimulus. In other words, behaviors serving a positive reinforcement function allow the individual to "get something preferred," and behaviors serving a negative reinforcement function allow the individual to "get out of something nonpreferred." For example, if a student engages in disruptive classroom behavior and receives frequent peer attention for this behavior, this behavior is likely being positively reinforced. In contrast, if the student engages in disruptive behavior while he or she is supposed to be completing math work sheets, chances are that this behavior is being negatively reinforced by escape from math work sheet exercises.

The two functions of behavior just described have been further divided into five categories: (1) social attention/communication (positive social reinforcement), (2) access to tangible reinforcement or preferred activities (material or activity reinforcers), (3) escape, delay, reduction, or avoidance of aversive tasks or activities (negative reinforcement), (4) escape or avoidance of other individuals (negative social reinforcement), and (5) internal stimulation (automatic or sensory positive reinforcement) (Carr, 1994).

FBA Process and Procedures.   The FBA process takes place in the following sequence: (1) FBA interviews, which are used to guide direct observations of behavior; (2) observations of behavior, which can be done by teachers, behavior specialists, or school psychologists, to allow for the confirmation and refinement of hypotheses from initial FBA interviews; (3) formulation of formal behavioral hypothesis statements, which include the conditions likely to produce the problem behavior, delineation of the problem behaviors, and consequent events that appear to maintain the problem behaviors; and (4) specification of behavioral interventions based on this information. These interventions might involve changing the conditions that evoke problem behaviors, teaching new skills (appropriate behaviors), and altering the consequences that are maintaining the problem behaviors.

FBA methods can be either indirect or direct procedures for determining behavioral function. Indirect methods are removed in time and place from the actual occurrence of behavior (Cone, 1978; Gresham et al., 2001). Functional assessment interviews (with teachers, parents, and students), historical/archival records, and behavior rating scales or checklists are the most frequently used indirect FBA methods. Direct FBA methods assess problem behavior at the time and place of its actual occurrence and involve the direct observation of antecedents, behaviors, and consequences. Direct observation is used to confirm the information obtained by indirect methods. A useful method for conducting direct FBA is an antecedent-behavior-consequence analysis using an A-B-C recording form, as shown in Form 3.1 (Witt, Daly, & Noell, 2000). With this procedure, a student's behavior is observed in the classroom, playground, or other relevant setting, and

A-B-C Record Sheet for Use by Consultant

Student's Name: _____ Date: _____ Class: _____

Teacher: _____ Consultant: _____ Time: _____

In the Behavior column, note codes for the target behaviors as they occur. You can also record additional information about the behavior, such as the name of the student who was hit when the behavior "hitting" occurred.
In the Antecedent column, record the code for the classroom activity and any specific event that occurred just before the student exhibited the target behavior.
In the Consequence column, record what occurred just after the behavior using codes or brief narration.

Antecedent	Behavior	Consequence

List codes and their definitions here:

FORM 3.1 ◆

Antecedent-Behavior-Consequence Recording Form.

the events occurring immediately prior to and following the behavior are recorded. It should be noted that only immediate antecedent events can be assessed with this recording form.

Another important class of antecedent events, known as setting events, usually is obtained only through indirect assessment methods. Setting events are antecedents that are removed in time and place from the occurrence of behavior but are functionally related to that behavior (Wahler & Fox, 1981). Setting events can exert potentially powerful influences on behavior. Examples of setting events include confrontations on the school bus, physical abuse at home, sleep deprivation, and negative, coercive interactions with parents and siblings in the home.

Comprehensive descriptions of each FBA method are beyond the scope of this chapter. However, extensive and excellent descriptions of FBA methods and procedures can be found in other authoritative sources (see Knoster & McCurdy, 2002; O'Neill et al., 1997; Witt et al., 2000).

Behavioral Hypotheses and FBA. Behavioral hypotheses are testable statements regarding the function(s) of behavior that are based on FBA information. There may be several hypotheses for each problem behavior, and there can be several hypotheses for a single problem behavior. At a minimum, behavioral hypotheses should include the following: (1) setting events, (2) immediate antecedent events, (3) problem behavior, and (4) maintaining consequence(s). Behavioral hypotheses should be observable, testable, and capable of being accepted or rejected via data collection. The following are examples of testable behavioral hypotheses for a student:

◆ Frank is more likely to engage in disruptive and noncompliant behaviors when he comes to school without breakfast (setting event) and is asked to complete difficult math tasks (immediate antecedent). (Hypothesized function: escape from difficult, nonpreferred activities)

◆ Frank is more likely to engage in disruptive and noncompliant behaviors during group instruction activities (immediate antecedent) when he has had an altercation with peers before school (setting event). (Hypothesized function: peer social attention for disruptive and noncompliant behaviors)

◆ Frank is more likely to engage in disruptive and noncompliant behaviors when he has not had enough sleep the night before (setting event) and is asked to complete tasks within a cooperative learning situation (immediate antecedent). (Hypothesized function: avoidance of nonpreferred activities involving cooperation)

In summary, FBA is a useful model for identifying the proximal functions ("causes") of problem behaviors and the microvariables operating in specific situations that are sensitive to environmental contingencies (Walker & Sprague, 1999). FBA is extremely useful in understanding and intervening with problem behaviors in a particular setting. However, FBA has limited utility in understanding the variables that account for risk across multiple settings and in predicting students' futures. (We described these risk and protective factors earlier in the chapter.)

There are many reasons for using FBA with students with or at risk for antisocial behavior patterns. It has been shown to be useful in designing interventions for a number of problem behaviors. However, some of the behaviors exhibited by antisocial students are simply not amenable to FBA methods. For example, low-frequency and high-intensity behaviors such as physical assaults and arson are extremely difficult, if not impossible, to assess using FBA. Other behaviors that are more covert in nature (e.g., theft, vandalism, cruelty to animals, and illicit drug use) are also difficult to assess using FBA methods.

Office Discipline Referrals (ODRs)

Office discipline referrals (ODRs) are disciplinary contacts between students and the principal's office that result in written records of the incidents, in which the reasons for the referral and disposition of the cases are noted. Some schools computerize their recording procedures; others use a standard referral form for recording each ODR; still others document the incidents less formally (e.g., through narrative accounts).

The Collection and Analysis of ODRs

ODRs are nearly always initiated by classroom teachers and result from behavioral infractions of some type (e.g., teacher defiance, insubordination, aggression, property destruction, bullying, harassment, or violation of school rules). As a rule, teachers make these sorts of referrals either because they cannot deal with the discipline problem themselves within the classroom context or because they believe the infraction is of such severity that it warrants the involvement of school administrators and/or parents.

ODRs accumulate as part of the normal schooling process and reflect the school's accommodation of students' responses to the routine demands of schooling. They provide an archival record of the number and types of serious behavioral episodes occurring, on a student-by-student basis, for each school year. As such, they provide an interesting metric of school adjustment for individual students. ODRs can also be aggregated for groups of students within a school population by, for example, gender, grade level, or number of students receiving free or reduced-price lunches. Finally, they can be analyzed for the entire school population by year. There is an increasing trend for ODRs to be used by researchers and school personnel to identify behaviorally at-risk students and to assess the overall social climate of the school.

In some schools, it is not unusual for a majority of ODRs to be accounted for by less than 10% of the school's population. This finding parallels the common one in corrections research showing that approximately 65% of all juvenile crime is accounted for by 6–8% of the juvenile population (Loeber & Farrington, 1998). In some school settings, the pattern of ODRs is more randomly distributed. As a general rule, elementary school students average between zero and 1 ODRs each school year; the corresponding figure for middle school students is much higher—approximately 3.5 ODRs per student per year. It is not uncommon to find schools with substantially more ODRs than there are students in the school. ODRs have been used as a sensitive evaluative tool for schoolwide interventions and also for assessing intervention effects for small groups and individual students (Walker, Colvin, & Ramsey, 1995).

The typical antisocial student in the intermediate elementary grades will average 10 or more ODRs per school year (Sugai, Sprague, Horner, & Walker, 2000; Walker, Colvin, & Ramsey, 1995). The number for some of these students, however, can range up to 40 or more for the school year. Any student who has 10 or more ODRs per year is considered to be a chronic discipline problem and in need of intervention. Despite substantial differences in recording methods and annual changes in the makeup of the student population, ODRs show surprising levels of consistency across school years (Walker & McConnell, 1995).

Irvin, Tobin, Sprague, and Vincent (in press) conducted a thorough literature review and analysis of the validity of ODRs and their efficacy as measures of school climate and schoolwide interventions. In their review, these authors found a large number of studies on the use of ODRs by educational and psychological researchers. Across these studies, they found moderate correlations between ODRs and a wide range of variables relating to social-behavioral adjustment both within and outside the school setting (e.g., fighting, harassment and threats of violence, delinquency, aggression, social skills deficits, and classroom orderliness). However, in a recently published review of the ODR literature, Nelson, Gonzalez, Epstein, and Benner (2003) concluded that the predictive and concurrent validity of ODRs is relatively limited.

ODRs are an important tool for characterizing the school behavior of antisocial students and should be incorporated into any comprehensive assessment of them. ODRs represent an unobtrusive, nonreactive measure that is quite inexpensive to collect. Their use also extends well beyond that of the individual antisocial student and, as noted previously, allows school personnel to collect and analyze invaluable data that reveal the patterns of problem behavior occurring within the school setting. Thus, they empower school leaders to make important changes in the school's operations and to evaluate their effects at three levels: school, student group, and individual. In sum, their emergence is an important advance in the assessment of antisocial behavior patterns in school settings.

The School-Wide Information System (SWIS) for Recording and Analyzing ODRs

The School-Wide Information System (SWIS) is a Web-based software system for recording, entering, organizing, and reporting ODRs within schools. The system was developed by University of Oregon faculty in collaboration with elementary, middle, and high school personnel. SWIS can be used for the following purposes: (1) to assist schools in improving their disciplinary practices, (2) to design behavioral improvement and support plans for at-risk students and their families, (3) to report on school outcomes to district, state, and federal agencies, and (4) to collect aggregated ODR data across schools.

Once SWIS is installed in a school, the school's staff enter ODRs into a protected Web space as they occur. ODRs may then be summarized and analyzed for individual students, for groups of students who share certain characteristics, or for the entire student body over a given time. Printouts and graphic displays of data are produced by the SWIS software for use in the reporting process. Information about SWIS can be obtained by contacting Rob Horner, Ph.D. (College of Education, University of Oregon, Eugene, OR 97403). Use and adoption of SWIS can be negotiated through a licensure agreement with the system's authors and the University of Oregon.

The SWIS software has allowed the system's developers to build a normative database of ODRs via a large number of participating schools distributed across the nation. This database is rapidly expanding in both volume and diversity as SWIS continues to be adopted by a broad range of U.S. schools. This represents the first time that a national, normative database has been developed on school discipline referrals, and it provides an invaluable resource for future use by school personnel, online practitioners, policymakers, and researchers.

Conclusion

This chapter focused on how to become more knowledgeable regarding the role of reliable, valid, and accurate assessment in understanding and detecting antisocial behavior patterns. Valid assessment practices enable the making of correct decisions about individuals. There are a number of important decisions that should be based upon best practices in assessment (i.e., screening, classification, placement, intervention planning, and program evaluation).

We advocate using a problem-solving model to make decisions in which a problem is not an absolute concept, but rather a relative one, because different social agents (parents, teachers, students) may disagree on either the existence or the severity of the problem. In this model, current and desired levels of performance are specified from the perspective of different social agents. The four-stage problem-solving model includes problem identification, problem analysis, plan implementation, and problem evaluation.

This chapter placed a great deal of emphasis on early screening and identification of children at risk for antisocial behavior patterns. We cannot emphasize too strongly how important this is in deterring seriously at-risk children from the pernicious, long-term consequences of this behavior pattern. And there is a subset of children who are at even greater risk because of the co-occurrence of hyperactivity-impulsivity-inattention and conduct problems. Functional behavioral assessments and positive behavioral supports can inform intervention decisions children and youths. A subsequent chapter reviews and describes specific intervention programs that have proved effective in addressing the many problems that antisocial children and youths experience.

 InfoTrac College Edition Research Terms

Fledgling psychopath

Functional behavioral assessment

Office discipline referrals

References

Achenbach, T. (1991a). *Manual for the Child Behavior Checklist/4-18 and 1991 Profile*. Burlington: Department of Psychiatry, University of Vermont.

Achenbach, T. (1991b). *Manual for the Teacher's Rating Form and 1991 Profile*. Burlington: Department of Psychiatry, University of Vermont.

Baumeister, R., Smart, L., & Boden, J. (1996). Relation of threatened egotism to violence and aggression: The dark side of high self-esteem. *Psychological Review, 103,* 5–33.

Bennett, K. J., Lipman, E. L., Brown, S., Racine, Y., Boyle, M. H., & Offord, D. R. (1999). Predicting conduct problems: Can high-risk children be identified in kindergarten and Grade 1? *Journal of Consulting and Clinical Psychology, 67*(4), 470–480.

Bersoff, D. (1983). Social and legal influences on test development and usage. In B. Plake (Ed.), *Buros/Nebraska symposium on measurement and testing* (Vol. 1, pp. 126–161). Hillsdale, NJ: Lawrence Erlbaum.

Bocian, K., Beebe-Frankenberger, M., MacMillan, D., & Gresham, F. M. (1999). Competing paradigms in learning disabilities classification by schools and variations in the meaning of discrepant achievement. *Learning Disabilities Research & Practice, 14,* 1–14.

Broussard, C., & Northrup, J. (1995). An approach to functional assessment and analysis of disruptive behavior in regular education classrooms. *School Psychology Quarterly, 10,* 151–164.

Bullis, M., & Walker, H. (1994). *Comprehensive school-based systems for troubled youth.* Eugene: Center on Human Development, University of Oregon.

Carr, E. (1994). Emerging themes in functional analysis of problem behavior. *Journal of Applied Behavior Analysis, 27,* 393–400.

Cicchetti, D., & Nurcombe, B. (Eds.). (1993). Toward a developmental perspective on conduct disorder [Special issue]. *Development and Psychopathology, 5*(1/2).

Coie, J., & Jacobs, M. (1993). The role of social context in the prevention of conduct disorder [Special issue]. *Development and Psychopathology, 5*(1/2), 263–276.

Cone, J. (1978). The Behavioral Assessment Grid (BAG): A conceptual framework and taxonomy. *Behavior Therapy, 9,* 882–888.

Crone, D. A., & Horner, R. H. (2003). *Building positive behavior support systems in schools: Functional behavioral assessment.* New York: Guilford Press.

Del'Homme, M., Sinclair, E., & Kasari, C. (1994). Preschool children with behavioral problems: Observation in instructional and free play contexts. *Behavioral Disorders, 19,* 221–232.

Drummond, T. (1993). *The Student Risk Screening Scale (SRSS).* Grants Pass, OR: Josephine County Mental Health Program.

Eddy, J. (2001). *Aggressive and defiant behavior: The latest assessment and treatment strategies for conduct disorder.* Kansas City, MO: Compact Clinicals.

Eddy, J., Reid, J., & Curry, V. (2002). The etiology of youth antisocial behavior, delinquency, violence and a public health approach to prevention. In M. Shinn, H. Walker, & G. Stoner (Eds.), *Interventions for academic and behavior problems II: Preventive and remedial approaches* (pp. 27–52). Bethesda, MD: National Association of School Psychologists.

Elliott, D. (2001). *Youth violence: A report of the surgeon general.* Washington, DC. U.S. Department of Health and Human Services.

Feil, E. G., Walker, H. M., & Severson, H. H. (1995). The Early Screening Project for young children with behavior problems. *Journal of Emotional and Behavorial Disorders, 3*(4), 194–202, 213.

Forness, S., Kavale, K., MacMillan, D., Asarnow, J., & Duncan, B. (1996). Early detection and prevention of emotional or behavioral disorders: Developmental aspects of systems of care. *Behavioral Disorders, 21,* 226–240.

Gerber, M., & Semmel, M. (1984). Teacher as imperfect test: Reconceptualizing the referral process. *Educational Psychologist, 14,* 137–146.

Gresham, F. M. (1991). Conceptualizing behavior disorders in terms of resistance to intervention. *School Psychology Review, 20,* 23–36.

Gresham, F. M. (1999). Noncategorical approaches to K–12 emotional and behavioral difficulties. In D. Reschly, W. D. Tilly, & J. Grimes (Eds.), *Special education in transition: Functional assessment and noncategorical programming* (pp. 107–137). Longmont, CO: Sopris West.

Gresham, F. M. (2002). Responsiveness to intervention: An alternative approach to the identification of learning disabilities. In R. Bradley, L. Danielson, & D. Hallahan (Eds.), *Identification of learning disabilities: Research to practice* (pp. 467–520). Mahwah, NJ: Lawrence Erlbaum.

Gresham, F. M., & Lambros, K. (1998). Behavioral and functional assessment. In T. S. Watson & F. M. Gresham (Eds.), *Handbook of child behavior therapy* (pp. 3–22). New York: Plenum.

Gresham, F. M., Lane, K., & Lambros, K. (2000). Comorbidity of conduct and attention deficit hyperactivity problems: Issues of identification with "fledgling psychopaths." *Journal of Emotional and Behavioral Disorders, 8,* 83–93.

Gresham, F. M., Lane, K., & Lambros, K. (2002). Children with conduct and hyperactivity-attention problems: Identification, assessment, and intervention. In K. Lane, F. M. Gresham, & T. O'Shaughnessy (Eds.), *Children with or at-risk for emotional and behavioral disorders* (pp. 210–222). Boston: Allyn & Bacon.

Gresham, F. M., Lane, K., MacMillan, D., & Bocian, K. (1999). Social and academic profiles of externalizing and internalizing groups: Risk factors for emotional and behavioral disorders. *Behavioral Disorders, 24,* 231–241.

Gresham, F. M., Lane, K., MacMillan, D., Bocian, K., & Ward, S. (2000). Effects of positive and negative illusory biases: Comparisons across social and academic self-concept domains. *Journal of School Psychology, 38,* 151–175.

Gresham, F. M., MacMillan, D., Bocian, K., Ward, S., & Forness, S. (1998). Comorbidity of hyperactivity-impulsivity-inattention + conduct problems: Risk factors in social, affective, and academic domains. *Journal of Abnormal Child Psychology, 26,* 393–406.

Gresham, F. M., MacMillan, D., & Bocian, K. (1997). Teachers as "tests": Differential validity of teacher judgments in identifying students at-risk for learning difficulties. *School Psychology Review, 26,* 47–60.

Gresham, F. M., Watson, T. S., & Skinner, C. H. (2001). Functional behavioral assessment: Principles, procedures, and future directions. *School Psychology Review, 30,* 156–172.

Hawkins, J., VonCleve, E., & Catalano, R. (1991). Reducing early childhood aggression: Results of a primary prevention program. *Journal of the American Academy of Child and Adolescent Psychiatry, 30,* 208–217.

Hayes, S., Nelson, R., & Jarrett, R. (1987). The treatment utility of assessment: A functional approach to evaluating assessment quality. *American Psychologist, 42,* 963–974.

Hersh, R., & Walker, H. (1983). Great expectations: Making schools effective for all students. *Policy Studies Review, 2,* 147–188.

Hinshaw, S. (1987). On the distinction between attention deficit/hyperactivity and conduct problems/aggression in child psychopathology. *Psychological Bulletin, 101,* 443–463.

Hughes, J., Cavell, T., & Grossman, P. (1997). A positive view of self: Risk or protection for aggressive children. *Development and Psychopathology, 9,* 75–94.

Huizinga, D., & Jakob-Chien, C. (1998). The contemporaneous co-occurrence of serious and violent juvenile offending and other problem behaviors. In R. Loeber & D. Farrington (Eds.), *Serious and violent juvenile offending: Risk factors and successful interventions* (pp. 47–67). Thousand Oaks, CA: Sage.

Individuals with Disabilities Education Act Amendments of 1997. (PL 105-17). 20 USC Chapter 33, Sections 1400 et seq.

Irvin, L., Tobin, T., Sprague, J., & Vincent, C. (in press). Validity of office discipline referrals measures as indices of school-wide behavioral status and effects of school-wide behavioral interventions. *Journal of Positive Behavior Interventions.*

Kauffman, J. (1999). How we prevent emotional and behavioral disorders. *Exceptional Children, 65,* 448–468.

Kazdin, A. (1987a). *Conduct disorders in childhood and adolescence.* London: Sage.

Kazdin, A. (1987b). Treatment of antisocial behavior in childhood: Current status and future directions. *Psychological Bulletin, 102,* 187–203.

Knoster, T., & McCurdy, B. (2002). Best practices in functional behavioral assessment for designing individual student programs. In A. Thomas & J. Grimes (Eds.), *Best practices in school psychology* (4th ed., pp. 1007–1028). Bethesda, MD: National Association of School Psychologists.

Kratochwill, T., & Bergan, J. (1990). *Behavioral consultation and therapy.* New York: Plenum.

Lane, K. L. (1999). Young students at risk for antisocial behavior: The utility of academic and social skills interventions. *Journal of Emotional and Behavioral Disorders, 7,* 211–223.

Lipsey, M., & Derzon, J. (1998). Predictors of violent or serious delinquency in adolescence and early adulthood: A synthesis on longitudinal research. In R. Loeber & D. Farrington (Eds.), *Serious and violent juvenile offenders: Risk factors and successful interventions* (pp. 86–105). Thousand Oaks, CA: Sage.

Lipsey, M., & Wilson, D. (1998). Effective intervention for serious juvenile offenders: A synthesis of research. In R. Loeber & D. Farrington (Eds.), *Serious and violent juvenile offenders: Risk factors and successful interventions* (pp. 313–345). Thousand Oaks, CA: Sage.

Lloyd, J., Kauffman, J., Landrum, T., & Roe, D. (1991). Why do teachers refer pupils for special education: An analysis of referral records. *Exceptionality, 2,* 113–126.

Loeber, R. (1988). Natural histories of conduct problems, delinquency, and associated substance use: Evidence for developmental progressions. In B. Lahey & A. Kazdin (Eds.), *Advances in clinical child psychology* (Vol. 11, pp. 73–124). New York: Plenum.

Loeber, R. (1991). Antisocial behavior: More enduring than changeable? *Journal of the American Academy of Child and Adolescent Psychiatry, 30,* 393–397.

Loeber, R., Dishion, T., & Patterson, G. (1984). Multiple-gating: A multistage assessment procedure for identifying youths at risk for delinquency. *Journal of Research in Crime and Delinquency, 21,* 7–32.

Loeber, R., & Farrington, D. (Eds.). (1998). *Serious and violent juvenile offenders: Risk factors and successful interventions.* Thousand Oaks, CA: Sage.

Loeber, R., & Farrington, D. (Eds.). (2001). *Child delinquents*. Thousand Oaks, CA: Sage.

Loeber, R., & LeBlanc, M. (1990). Toward a developmental criminology. In M. Tonry & N. Morris (Eds.), *Crime and justice: A review of research* (Vol. 12, pp. 375–473). Chicago: University of Chicago Press.

Lynam, D. (1996). The early identification of chronic offenders: Who is the fledgling psychopath? *Psychological Bulletin, 120,* 209–234.

Messick, S. (1995). Validity of psychological assessment: Validation of inferences from persons' responses and performances as scientific inquiry into score meaning. *American Psychologist, 50,* 741–749.

Moffitt, T. (1993). Adolescence-limited and life-course-persistent antisocial behavior: A developmental taxonomy. *Psychological Review, 100,* 674–701.

Nelson, J. R., Gonzalez, J. E., Epstein, M. H., & Benner, G. J. (2003). Administrative discipline contacts: A review of the literature. *Behavorial Disorders, 28*(3), 249–281.

Office of Juvenile Justice and Delinquency Prevention. (1995). *Guide for implementing a comprehensive strategy for serious, violent and chronic juvenile offenders*. Washington, D.C.: Author.

O'Neill, R., Horner, R., Albin, R., Storey, K., & Sprague, J. (1997). *Functional assessment and program development for behavior problems*. Pacific Grove, CA: Brooks/Cole.

Olweus, D. (1979). Stability of aggressive reaction patterns in males: A review. *Psychological Bulletin, 86,* 852–875.

Patterson, G. (1982). *Coercive family process, Volume 3: A social learning approach*. Eugene: Castalia.

Patterson, G. (2002). The early development of coercive family process. In J. Reid, G. Patterson, & J. Synder (Eds.), *Antisocial behavior in children and adolescents: A developmental analysis and model for intervention* (pp. 25–44). Washington, DC: American Psychological Association.

Patterson, G., DeBaryshe, B., & Ramsey, E. (1989). A developmental perspective on antisocial behavior. *American Psychologist, 44,* 329–335.

Patterson, G., Reid, J., & Dishion, T. (1992). *Antisocial boys, Volume 4: A social interactional approach*. Eugene: Castalia.

Reschly, D. J., & Tilly, W. D. (1999). Reform trends and system design alternatives. In D. Reschly, W. D. Tilly, & J. Grimes (Eds.), *Special education in transition: Functional assessment and noncategorical programming* (pp. 19–48). Longmont, CO: Sopris West.

Salvia, J., & Ysseldyke, J. (1991). *Assessment* (4th ed.). Boston: Houghton Mifflin.

Schneider, M., & Leitenberg, H. (1989). A comparison of aggressive and withdrawn children's self-esteem, optimism, and pessimism, and causal attributions for success and failure. *Journal of Abnormal Child Psychology, 17,* 133–144.

Severson, H., & Walker, H. (2002). Proactive approaches for identifying children at risk for sociobehavioral problems. In K. Lane, F. M. Gresham, & T. O'Shaughnessy (Eds.), *Interventions for children with or at-risk for emotional and behavioral disorders* (pp. 33–53). Boston: Allyn & Bacon.

Sinclair, E. (1993). Early identification of preschoolers with special needs in Head Start. *Topics in Early Childhood Special Education, 13,* 12–18.

Sinclair, E., Del'Homme, M., & Gonzalez, M. (1993). Systematic screening for preschool behavioral disorders. *Behavioral Disorders, 18,* 177–188.

Sugai, G., Horner, R., & Sprague, J. (1999). Functional assessment-based behavior support planning research-to-practice-to research. *Behavioral Disorders, 24,* 253–257.

Sugai, G., Sprague, J., Horner, R., & Walker, H. (2000). Preventing school violence: The use of office discipline referrals to assess and monitor schoolwide discipline interventions. *Journal of emotional and behavioral disorders, 8(2),* 94–101.

Wahler, R., & Fox, J. (1981). Setting events in applied behavior analysis: Toward a conceptual and methodological expansion. *Journal of Applied Behavior Analysis, 14,* 327–338.

Walker, H., Colvin, G., & Ramsey, E. (1995). *Antisocial behavior in school: Strategies and best practices.* Pacific Grove, CA: Brooks/Cole.

Walker, H., Irvin, L., Noell, J., & Singer, G. (1992). A construct score approach to the assessment of social competence: Rationale, technological considerations, and anticipated outcomes. *Behavior Modification, 16,* 448–474.

Walker, H., & McConnell (1995). *The Walker-McConnell Scale of Social Competence and School Adjustment.* New York: Thomson Learning.

Walker, H. M., Nishioka, V. M., Zeller, R., Severson, H. H., & Feil, E. G. (2000). Causal factors and potential solutions for the persistent under-identification of students having emotional or behavioral disorders in the context of schooling. *Assessment for Effective Intervention, 26*(1), 29–40.

Walker, H., & Severson, H. (1990). *Systematic screening for behavior disorders.* Longmont, CO: Sopris West.

Walker, H., & Severson, H. (2002). Developmental prevention of at-risk outcomes for vulnerable antisocial children and youth. In K. Lane, F. M. Gresham, & T. O'Shaughnessy (Eds.), *Interventions for children with or at-risk for emotional and behavioral disorders* (pp. 177–194). Boston: Allyn & Bacon.

Walker, H., Severson, H., & Feil, E. (1995). *Early screening project: A proven child-find process.* Longmont, CO: Sopris West.

Walker, H., Severson, H., Nicholson, F., Kehle, T., Jenson, W., & Clark, E. (1994). Replication of the Systematic Screening for Behavior Disorders (SSBD) procedure for the identification of at-risk children. *Journal of Emotional and Behavioral Disorders, 2,* 66–77.

Walker, H., Severson, H., Todis, B., Block-Pedego, A., Williams, G., Haring, N., & Barckley, M. (1990). Systematic Screening for Behavior Disorders (SSBD): Further validation, replication, and normative data. *Remedial and Special Education, 11,* 32–46.

Walker, H., & Sprague, J. (1999). Longitudinal research and functional behavioral assessment issues. *Behavioral Disorders, 24,* 331–334.

Waschbush, D. (2002). A meta-analytic examination of comorbid hyperactive-impulsive-attention problems and conduct problems. *Psychological Bulletin, 128,* 118–150.

Witt, J. C., Daly, E., & Noell, G. H. (2000). *Functional assessments: A step-by-step guide to solving academic and behavior problems.* Longmont, CO: Sopris West.

Witt, J. C., Elliott, S. N., Daly, E., Gresham, F. M., & Kramer, J. (1998). *Assessment of at-risk and special needs children* (2nd ed.). Boston: McGraw-Hill.

Preventing Antisocial Behavior by Addressing Risk Factors Within Family, School, and Community Contexts

Introduction

This chapter focuses on best practices and proven intervention approaches in addressing the risk factors that propel vulnerable children and youths down a path toward destructive outcomes. Given that risk factors operate within and across different contexts (e.g., school, home, community) to produce these outcomes, it is essential that coordinated intervention approaches for preventing, eliminating, or reducing them be multicomponent, multi-agent, and multisetting in nature if they are to succeed. A single-component intervention, applied on a one-shot basis, that addresses only one setting-based constellation of risk factors (e.g., school) is unlikely to produce substantive or enduring changes in overall behavior. Whenever possible, it is crucial to involve parents, teachers, and peers in a coordinated intervention approach that not only targets the child's or youth's problematic behavior but also addresses the risk factors and systemic variables that cause or sustain the behavior over time (Kellam, 2002).

Prevention as an Overarching Goal of School-Based Intervention

The material in this chapter is referenced to the concept of prevention as defined in an earlier chapter of this book. That is, prevention is viewed not as a process or as an instrument for behavior change in and of itself, but rather as an end result or outcome of the behavior change process that is produced by the careful application of diverse intervention approaches applied within and across social contexts (i.e., the home, school, neighborhood, and community). We strongly agree with Greenberg, Domitrovich, and Bumbarger (2001) that earlier intervention is much more likely to be effective than later intervention in altering the developmental pathway of at-risk children toward problematic and destructive outcomes. Early intervention is a powerful tool when it is applied from day 1 in a child's life and school career, and especially when it interrupts the progression toward problematic behavior due to long-term risk exposure (Greenberg et al., 2001; Loeber & Farrington, 2001).

Shep Kellam, M.D., of the American Institutes for Research (AIR), is perhaps the foremost authority in this country on the topic of achieving high-quality prevention outcomes within applied social contexts. He has been studying barriers and obstacles to prevention over a distinguished 40-year research career focused on epidemiology (i.e., the study of disease) and the implementation of community- and school-based interventions within longitudinal field trials. Some of Kellam's key observations and lessons concerning prevention include these (see Kellam, 2002):

◆ The development of the field of preventive science over the past three decades has resulted in a growing body of prevention programs that have been rigorously tested for their efficacy and effectiveness within a range of community and other social contexts.

◆ Effective prevention requires addressing those specific features of social contexts that either help or hinder development of individuals and their capacities for meeting the demands of social adaptation (e.g., conforming with teacher expectations within an instructional setting).

◆ Effective prevention programs are often based in schools, and many of these programs also include family members as natural helpers or implementation agents.

◆ Prevention research and programming are best viewed from a public health perspective as (1) promoting social adaptation and psychological well-being and (2) reducing social maladaptation and the development of mental or behavioral disorders over the life course.

◆ Prevention is based on acquiring knowledge regarding risk factors and then directing appropriate intervention(s) resources at specific risk factors to promote positive outcomes and to forestall or deter adverse outcomes.

◆ Aside from their presence within and across social contexts, risk factors reside in the physical environment (e.g., an abusive home setting) and within the individual (e.g., destructive sensation seeking). They are also manifested in the interactive demand–response dynamics that come into play when individuals respond to the ordinary demands of the environment (e.g., behavioral escalation in response to a parental or teacher directive in order to escape from the demands of an unpleasant task).

These observations have considerable value in guiding the achievement of prevention outcomes for antisocial students within the context of schooling. They also point us in the direction of a social-ecological approach to account for all the dimensions necessary for achieving such outcomes (see Bronfenbrenner, 1979; Romer & Heller, 1983). In our view, social ecology is one of the few theoretical formulations that is adequate for conceptualizing the environmental, individual, and environmental-individual variables and dynamics involved in the complex process of intervening effectively with this population.

A central concept of social ecology is the notion of person–environment (P-E) fit. P-E fit or match occurs when the demands of the environment are consistent with the capabilities, skills, resources, and motivations of the individual. In other words, if that person is able and willing to respond appropriately to the task demands and requirements of the social environment (e.g., classroom, playground, home, or neighborhood) and the environmental demands are appropriate, then a P-E fit is likely to be in evidence along with its associated positive features (e.g., a satisfactory classroom adjustment). If anything universally characterizes the antisocial child, it is that he or she consistently either does not respond to these demands at all or responds to them inappropriately. Literally hundreds of studies conducted in school settings have shown that students with very challenging forms of behavior are more likely to (1) behave inappropriately in order to escape from teacher-imposed task demands and/or (2) engage in maladaptive behavior in order to seek attention (see Crone & Horner, 2003; O'Neill, Horner, Sprague, Albin, & Storey, 1997).

Using a social-ecological foundation in intervening with antisocial students in the context of schooling allows us to address simultaneously systemic problems within the school environment (e.g., chaotic classrooms, inadequate teacher support, poor administrative leadership, inappropriate or unclear expectations for academic performance or behavior, or weak instruction) and the skill deficits, motivational problems, and behavioral excesses of at-risk students who are *most* negatively affected by these conditions. By focusing on these two dimensions and the risk factors associated with each, it is possible to apply interventions selectively to bring them into alignment with each other and thus to achieve an improved person–environment fit and better social-academic adjustment.

As Kellam (2002) notes, in recent decades, a number of very effective, rigorously tested, and generalizable intervention approaches have been developed that have the potential to achieve true prevention goals and outcomes within the school setting (see Greenberg et al., 2001; Lane, Gresham, & O'Shaughnessy, 2002; Loeber & Farrington, 1998, 2001; Reid, Patterson, & Snyder, 2002; Shinn, Walker, & Stoner, 2002; Walker & Severson, 2002). Box 4.1 lists a series of critical reviews that profile many of these interventions. Their effects have been carefully monitored and evaluated across multiple school years, thus documenting the sustainability of gains produced by the interventions (see Greenberg et al., 2001). A comprehensive early-intervention program implemented by Hawkins, Catalano, Kosterman, Abbott, and Hill (1999), which involves child skills training, instruction in behavior management practices for participating teachers, and parent education, is an exemplar of such interventions. Unfortunately, for a variety of reasons, most of these proven or promising interventions, which constitute evidence-based and highly cost-effective practices, are typically not in evidence within most family, preschool, school, and community contexts.

Walker and Severson (2002) point out the urgent need to take a proactive long view in achieving substantive prevention outcomes, as opposed to merely reacting to the problems of youths when they become intractable or morph into serious conditions (e.g., school dropout, defiance of adults, adolescent offending and recidivism, drug and alcohol abuse, and violence). It is critical that these problems be dealt with before they exceed the tolerance limits of schools and communities and result in severe punitive sanctions. Policies and practices that will produce desirable outcomes in this regard are currently known. Unfortunately, the will to adopt them has been largely absent due to such factors as concerns about costs, skepticism about prevention outcomes, threats of redistribution of existing resources, reluctance to identify at-risk children and youths due to potentially stigmatizing effects, territorial imperatives and claims, and philosophical objections (see Kauffman, 1999). Unless we do indeed take the long view and proactively address these obstacles to the adoption and implementation of evidence-based, proven, and promising interventions, we will be unable to solve the myriad problems that children bring to the schooling process (see Walker & Severson, 2002).

To be successful and cost-effective in achieving prevention outcomes, an intervention must:

1. Address known risk factors and the precursors to destructive outcomes.
2. Be applied as early as possible in a child's life and school career.
3. Be carefully coordinated and delivered with integrity.
4. Be adequately funded.
5. Establish benchmarks and outcomes to gauge progress.

Box 4.1   Reviews of Effective Intervention Programs for Addressing Antisocial Behavior, Violence, and Risk Factors for Destructive Outcomes

- *Preventing Mental Disorders in School-Age Children: A Review of the Effectiveness of Prevention Programs.* Mark T. Greenberg, Ph.D., Director, Prevention Research Center for the Promotion of Human Development, College of Health and Human Development, Pennsylvania State University, University Park, PA 16802; phone 814-863-0112; fax 814-865-2530; Web site www.psu/edu/dept/prevention.

- *Effective Interventions for Children Having Conduct Disorders in the 0 to 8 Age Range.* Carolyn H. Webster-Stratton, Ph.D., Professor and Director, Parenting Research Clinic; Professor, Family and Child Nursing; Box 354801, 305 University District Bldg., School of Nursing, University of Washington, Seattle, WA; phone 206-543-6010; fax 206-543-6040; email cws@u.washington.edu.

- *Effective Programs and Strategies to Create Safe Schools.* Paul Kingery, Ph.D., Director, Hamilton Fish National Institute on School and Community Violence, National Office, 2121 K Street NW, Suite 200, Washington, DC 20037-1830; phone 202-496-2201; fax 202-496-6244; email kingery@gwu.edu; Web site www.hamfish.org.

- *Compilation of Early Violence Prevention Programs and Resources.* American Psychological Association. Julia M. Silva, Ph.D., APA Public Interest Directorate, 750 First Street NE, Washington, DC 20002-4242; phone 202-336-5817; fax 202-336-5723; email publicinterest@apa.org, Web site www.apa.org/pi.

- *Programs and Interventions to Make Schools Safer.* Video Series on Safe Schools, National Education Association, 1201 16th Street NW, Washington, DC 20036; phone 202-833-4000.

- *School-Based Aggression Prevention Programs for Young Children: Current Status and Implications for Violence Prevention.* Stephen Leff et al. (2001), *School Psychology Review, 30*(3), 344–362.

- "School Violence in Children and Adolescents: A Meta-Analysis of the Effectiveness of Current Interventions." *Journal of School Violence, 1*(2). Stacey Scheckner, fourth-year doctoral student, Florida State University, APA-approved Ph.D. Program in Counseling Psychology and School Psychology; Stephen A. Rollin, Professor, Combined Program in Counseling Psychology and School Psychology, Associate Dean for Graduate Studies and Research in Florida State University, College of Education, principal investigator on an OJJDP-sponsored grant on school violence prevention that is part of the Hamilton Fish Institute at George Washington University; Cheryl Kaiser-Ulrey, third-year doctoral student, Florida State University, APA-approved Ph.D. Program in Counseling Psychology and School Psychology; Richard Wagner, Professor, Department of Psychology, Florida State University, with a special interest

Box 4.1   *(Continued)*

in cognitive and behavioral science, reading, and the prevention of dyslexia. Web site www.haworthpressinc.com.

◆ *Youth Violence: A Report of the Surgeon General.* D. Satcher, Jan. 2001, Washington, DC: Office of the Surgeon General, U.S. Department of Health & Human Services.

◆ *Best Practices of Youth Violence Prevention: A Sourcebook for Community Action.* June 2002 (Revision). Timothy N. Thornton, M.P.A.; Carole A. Craft; Linda L. Dahlberg, Ph.D.; Barbara S. Lynch, Ph.D.; Katie Baer, M.P.H.; with contributions from Lloyd Potter, Ph.D., M.P.H.; James A. Mercy, Ph.D.; Erica A. Flowers, M.P.H.; Division of Violence Prevention, National Center for Injury Prevention and Control, Centers for Disease Control and Prevention, Atlanta, GA.

Obstacles and barriers to the adoption of proven-promising interventions can be grouped under four broad categories: (1) cost, (2) philosophical objections, (3) lack of awareness or knowledge about effective practices, and (4) excessive effort involved in implementing the intervention. Elliott, Witt, Kratochwill, and Stoiber (2002) have written extensively about this topic and the specifics of how interventions are chosen and evaluated by key school-based consumers (e.g., teachers, behavioral specialists, and administrators). Classroom teachers, for example, strongly prefer accelerative intervention approaches as compared to those with a reductive focus. In addition, they are quite sensitive to how much effort or work the intervention may require of them during implementation and how disruptive it may be of normal classroom routines.

Several options are possible when designing strategies to address complex, broad-based problems such as antisocial behavior or early delinquency. Option 1 involves investing in proven but previously untried approaches. Option 2 focuses on the expansion of existing, promising programs and providing additional resources and supports as needed. Option 3 seeks to improve outcomes and cost-effectiveness via better coordination of existing programs, resources, and services (Citizens Crime Commission, 2000). An amalgam of these options is often reflected in broad, school-based initiatives to address problem behavior, underachievement, school safety, and low-performing schools.

Reducing Risk Factors and Enhancing Protective Influences

The risk factors, influencing conditions, and larger societal forces that account for the struggles of youths today are pervasive but are infrequently addressed, in any systematic way, by prevention efforts. Of all these conditions of risk, perhaps the saddest and most unfortunate is society's diminished capacity to safely and effectively rear its children. The ramifications of this societal change are extremely destructive and will be a long time in reversing.

Walker and Severson (2002) describe some key findings regarding risk factors for destructive outcomes, along with promising strategies for addressing them, based on a synthesis of the empirical literature on this topic (see Loeber & Farrington, 2001). A summary of these findings follows:

- Risk factors are cumulative, and their negative impact increases with exposure to greater numbers of them.

- Both different and overlapping sets of risk factors are associated with certain negative, destructive outcomes.

- Risk factors can combine and interact in destructive ways with children and youths.

- Early-intervention approaches that also address key risk factors are highly effective in preventing subsequent delinquency.

- Long-term follow-up studies of early-intervention participants show superior prevention effects, compared with nonparticipating controls, on a broad range of outcomes including delinquency and violent acts.

- The savings from comprehensive early intervention in preschool settings lasting two school years, for disadvantaged children, can range up to approximately $11,000 per case depending on the number of outcomes assessed and the length of the follow-up period.

Realistically, many of these factors and conditions of risk are well beyond the reach of most social, educational, and judicial institutions. This is particularly true of schools. A number of these factors operate outside the realm of schooling, have their origins in the family, and have already begun to register their destructive effects on the developing child prior to school entry. As we have argued previously, it is critically important to enhance protective factors that can reduce the damaging effects of these risk factors over the long term.

The nonschool experiences of children and youths have everything to do with how they perform in school and how they react to the general experience of schooling (see Steinberg, 1996). The more risks they are exposed to outside of school and the longer such exposure lasts, the more damaging are their effects and the greater the negative impact on school performance (Reid, Patterson, & Snyder, 2002). Too often, these experiences and conditions impair school performance, contribute to school failure, and set the stage for destructive forms of behavior within and outside the school setting. Schools, as we have noted, can play important roles in buffering and offsetting the damaging effects of this kind of exposure to intractable risks. However, to do so, they must be adequately funded and be willing to enter into true collaborative partnerships with families, police, juvenile courts, and social service agencies (Walker & Severson, 2002; Walker & Shinn, 2002).

Coie and his colleagues (1993) have developed a conceptual framework governing the science of prevention in which they organize risk factors into seven broad categories. These include (1) constitutional handicapping conditions, (2) skill development delays and deficits, (3) emotional difficulties, (4) family circumstances, (5) interpersonal problems, (6) school problems, and (7) ecological risks. The focus of this book is on the role of schools in reducing and eliminating those risks that they are capable of impacting. In our view, schools can and should target skill development delays and deficits, emotional difficulties, interpersonal problems, and achievement-related problems. Effectively addressing the remaining categories of risk across family, neighborhood, and societal contexts requires working partnerships between schools and other agencies, as noted previously.

A little-known but powerful risk factor for children in general, and especially for students who are behaviorally challenging, has to do with the relative chaos or orderliness of the first-grade classrooms to which they are assigned. An intriguing longitudinal study dramatically illustrates the role of this variable in the development or prevention of aggressive behavior from first grade to middle school [see Kellam, Rebok, Ialongo, & Mayer (1994)]. After randomly assigning students to first-grade classrooms, these researchers found that these classrooms were approximately bimodal in their levels of disruption, with nearly half being chaotic and the remainder being reasonably well managed. Of the boys in the study who began schooling ranked in the top quartile of aggressive behavior by their teachers, those assigned to nonchaotic classrooms had odds of 3:1 for being highly aggressive in middle school. However, those boys assigned to chaotic classrooms had odds of 59:1 for being highly aggressive in middle school! This seminal finding suggests that poor classroom management by teachers in grade 1 is a huge, but preventable, risk factor for the development of antisocial behavior patterns among behaviorally at-risk children. Thus, working closely with first-grade teachers on their behavior management and instructional skills, as Hawkins and his colleagues (1999) have so effectively done, can yield substantial future benefits, offsetting destructive outcomes for at-risk students and establishing schooling as a key protective factor.

Target Domains for Preventing and Reducing Antisocial Behavior in School Settings

School readiness and school success (academic and social) should be the overarching goals of efforts to prevent school-based antisocial behavior. Solid longitudinal and developmental research efforts have established school engagement, bonding, and attachment as key correlates of school success (Hawkins et al., 1999; Kellam, Rebok, Ialongo, & Hawkins, 1994). School success, in turn, serves as a powerful protective factor against a host of adolescent risk factors including delinquency, violent offending, heavy drinking, sexually transmitted diseases, teenage pregnancy, multiple sex partners, school misbehavior, low achievement, and school failure and dropout. Similarly, Zigler, Taussig, and Black (1992) reviewed extensive evidence showing that the most effective prevention approach for adolescent delinquency consists of collaborative, early interventions involving parents, teachers, and community agencies delivered from preschool through grade 3. Thus, ensuring school success and assisting students to remain connected with schooling as long as possible are two of the best strategies available for preventing antisocial behavior, delinquency, and various health problems (e.g., drug use, teenage sex, and violence).

The most powerful, *school-based* risk factors to target for intervention to accomplish this important goal are those identified by Catalano, Loeber, and

McKinney (1999). These include (1) the early and persistent display of antisocial behavior, (2) academic failure in the elementary age range, and (3) lack of commitment to and full engagement with schooling. These authors have also identified some specific protective factors that can buffer, offset, and reduce the negative impact of these risks. In our view, schools are in an ideal position to participate in their development and enhancement. These protective factors include (1) participation in schools, peer groups, and communities that emphasize positive social norms, (2) the presence of warm, supportive relationships with adults, (3) opportunities to become involved in positive activities (e.g., sports and clubs), (4) recognition and support for participation in such activities, and (5) the development of cognitive, social, and emotional competence.

Recent research has demonstrated the interconnectedness of these social and academic outcomes of schooling in two ways: (1) as produced by interventions that target academic performance and the social dimensions of schooling and (2) via longitudinal analyses of prosocial and aggressive forms of behavior used as predictors of academic achievement and peer social relations over a five-year, follow-up period. Kellam and his colleagues (1994), for example, showed experimentally that gains in first-grade academic achievement, as measured by standardized achievement tests, resulted in substantially reduced levels of aggression as reflected in the subsequent behavioral ratings of classroom teachers.

These "crossover" or "spillover" effects are important in that they demonstrate the positive, collateral benefits that can accrue from well-designed interventions focused on one type of target behavior (e.g., academic performance). The results of this research suggest that by focusing on increasing academic performance it is likely that not only will academic achievement increase but aggression, as well as perhaps other forms of problem behavior, will show corresponding decreases.

In a similar vein, Caprara, Barbaranelli, Pastorelli, Bandura, and Zimbardo (2000) report longitudinal research demonstrating robust contributions of early prosocial behavior to children's later achievement in both academic and social domains. Prosocial behavior includes cooperating, helping others, sharing, and consoling or showing empathy. Caprara et al. (2000) argue convincingly that early prosocial behavior may positively contribute to later academic achievement *and* to other socially desirable outcomes. In further support of these findings, Malecki and Elliott (2002) report a longitudinal study of 139 elementary students in which (1) social skills were found to be positively predictive of concurrent levels of achievement and (2) problem behavior was negatively predictive of concurrent academic achievement. However, only social skills proved to be predictive of future academic performance, which replicates a key finding of the research reported by Caprara et al. (2000). Thus, a focus on improving social behavior will likely be reflected in positive changes in both social and academic outcomes, and vice versa.

These studies address target dimensions that are referred to as "academic enablers"; that is, they facilitate or enhance academic performance. DiPerna, Volpe, and Elliott (2002), in synthesizing the knowledge base on this topic, have shown that increasing academic enablers results in substantial improvements in academic performance. The intervention programs and models described next have the capacity to impact this broad class of academic enablers.

Promising Programs and Practices
for Preventing School-Based Antisocial Behavior

The best opportunities for preventing the development of antisocial behavior patterns exist in the prenatal-to-middle-school years. Walker and Severson (2002) have identified interventions for use within four sequential phases of this developmental continuum: prenatal, infancy, early childhood, and middle childhood. Similarly, the Oregon Citizens Crime Commission (2000), in its seminal report on preventing child delinquency, has identified interventions that fit into an early-childhood continuum (prenatal to age 5) and an elementary-age continuum (age 6–10). This report establishes developmental continua that at-risk children can move through seamlessly while simultaneously accessing developmentally appropriate interventions at each point along this pathway.

A variation of this organizing framework of the Citizens Crime Commission report is used herein to illustrate interventions in the prenatal-to-age-5 developmental period that address risk and protective factors and that also emphasize school readiness in academic and social skills domains. Interventions for use in the elementary and middle school grades are also described that (1) create positive school climates, (2) increase school bonding, engagement, and attachment, (3) teach violence prevention and school safety skills, (4) ensure that children get off to the best start possible in school, and (5) address the severest forms of antisocial behavior, predelinquent behavior, adolescent offending, and recidivism. The interventions profiled for use in the prenatal-to-age-5 period address secondary and/or tertiary prevention goals and outcomes; the interventions profiled for use in the elementary and middle school years span the full primary, secondary, and tertiary continuum.

Interventions in the Prenatal-to-Age-5 Developmental Period

Reid and his colleagues (2002) make the case that it is never too early to begin intervening to prevent antisocial and destructive forms of behavior that result from early and continuous exposure to multiple risks. This section focuses on four interventions that build sequentially upon each other within a continuum that spans the prenatal-to-age-5 developmental period. They include (1) the Olds Nurse Home Visitation Program, (2) the Regional Intervention Program, (3) the Perry Preschool Program, and (4) the First Step to Success early-intervention program. Strong evidence exists to support the effectiveness of each intervention in addressing risks, reducing aggressive and problematic behavior, contributing to positive long-term outcomes, and enhancing protective factors in the social domain.

The Olds Nurse Home Visitation Program. This program targets young, pregnant women who fit a certain risk profile (e.g., poverty, poor health, illegal drug use, cigarette smoking, alcohol consumption) that can result in prenatal damage to the infant. The Olds Nurse Home Visitation Program was developed over 25 years ago by psychologist David Olds to (1) address health risks to newborns, (2) reduce risk factors for later antisocial behavior, conduct disorder, and delinquency, and (3) teach caregivers the necessary skills to prevent the likeli-

© Rob Crandall/Stock Connection/PictureQuest

Visiting nurses provide at-risk mothers participating in the Olds Nurse Home Visitation Program with health instruction and parental training. Based on follow-up studies, this intervention program decreases the likelihood of child abuse and drug use by participating mothers, thus decreasing the liklihood of antisocial or delinquent behavior in their children.

hood of these outcomes. The program is staffed by registered public health nurses, who contact the mother-to-be during pregnancy and explain its services and benefits. Participation is voluntary, and program costs generally range from $4,000 to $7,000 for each year of the two-year intervention (see Olds et al., 1999). Olds program services are terminated on the child's second birthday.

The public health nurse provides the following services on a continuous basis from initial prenatal contact through the first two years of the infant's life: (1) social support and general advocacy, (2) instruction in wellness guidelines and healthy lifestyles, (3) training in effective parenting techniques, (4) transportation as needed, (5) respite care for parents who experience "affective burden" or burnout, and (6) training in how to access services for which the parent qualifies. Developing a sense of trust between the mother and the nurse is a high priority during the initial stages of the Olds program. The frequency of nurse visitation varies depending on the needs of the mother and stage of child development. For example, visits are scheduled weekly during the first month after contact during pregnancy and then biweekly until birth. Similarly, visits occur weekly for the first six weeks after the child's birth and then twice a month between age 2 and 21 months. For the last three months of the program, visits are scheduled monthly.

The Olds program is a research-based and theory-driven model that has been rigorously evaluated using scientific methods and replicated extensively in a number of states. The intervention addresses risk factors associated with a host of destructive child and family outcomes. Results of scientific studies of Olds program participants, as compared with untreated control groups, consistently yield impressive long-term outcomes for the experimental group. As a rule, follow-up studies over periods ranging up to 20 years show the following favorable outcomes for Olds participants:

◆ Reduction in substance abuse during pregnancy

◆ Reduction in child abuse and maltreatment

◆ Reduction in family size

◆ Reduction in chronic welfare dependence

◆ Improved caregiving and reduced frequency of child injuries during the first two years of life

The RAND Corporation has conducted a careful cost–benefit analysis of the Olds program. This analysis shows that the return on the initial cost of investment

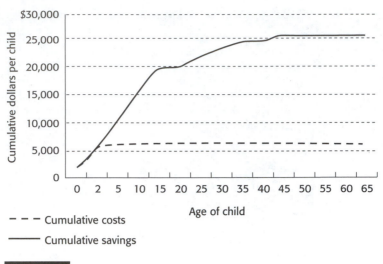

$----$ Cumulative costs

———— Cumulative savings

FIGURE 4.1

Costs and Savings for High-Risk Families in the Olds Program.
Source: Olds et al. (1999).

is realized, on average, well before the child's fourth birthday. The primary savings are in reduced welfare and criminal justice expenditures, as well as the generation of unanticipated tax revenues. Figure 4.1 illustrates the cumulative costs and savings for high-risk families in the Olds program in one locale (see Olds et al., 1999). The results show a highly favorable ratio of program costs to realized savings for Olds program participants.

The Olds program is an exemplar of the type of intervention, described by Kellam (2002), that simultaneously addresses risk factors and reduces or deters adverse events (i.e., destructive outcomes). In addition, it clearly results in the enhancement of key protective factors (e.g., self-advocacy, parenting skills, and overall competence) that contribute to a better quality of life for participants. The program's developer notes that intervention outcomes are more favorable for families at higher levels of risk and that beneficial effects on child abuse, neglect, and injuries during the first two years of life are more substantial for mothers who have little belief in their ability to control their life circumstances. In this sense, the program is clearly an indicated intervention for achieving tertiary prevention goals and outcomes. The Olds program is being considered for statewide adoption by a number of state departments of health. It is an exceptionally powerful and cost-effective intervention that holds great promise for reducing the prevalence of antisocial behavior and later delinquency among at-risk families.

The Regional Intervention Program (RIP). The Regional Intervention Program, established in 1969 at George Peabody College of Vanderbilt University, was designed originally to provide services to families with an autistic child under age 3. The program soon expanded its eligibility criteria to include all families of preschool children about whom behavioral or developmental problems were a concern. RIP families now include children with behavioral disorders, emotional disturbance, autism, and mental retardation, as well as multiple disabilities.

Many RIP parents are "held hostage" by the severe tantrums and out-of-control behavior of their young child. Most parents are at their wits' end by the time of their enrollment in RIP, and some have even been physically attacked by their child. Typically, RIP children engage in severe forms of oppositional-defiant behavior toward parents and other adults and display high levels of aggression toward siblings and other children. RIP is a selected-indicated intervention that addresses both secondary and tertiary prevention goals and outcomes.

RIP receives referrals from physicians, child care centers, social service agencies, and counselors, as well as relatives, neighbors, and friends of the family. The program requires a series of 24 two-hour visits distributed over approximately a seven-month treatment period. Parents receive skills training and exposure to the intervention in a cohort model wherein participants can support each other and share information as they move through the four treatment modules comprised in the RIP program: (1) behavioral skills training, (2) social skills training, (3) preschool classroom, and (4) child care/school intervention. Across these four modules, RIP parents receive instruction in and develop mastery of a broad range of generic parenting, monitoring, shaping, skills development, and behavior management strategies. Specific skills taught to parents include stating expectations in advance, "catching" the child being good, presenting limited and reasonable choices, ignoring problem behavior, helping the child establish self-management goals, staying in control, and waiting for neutral times to provide corrective feedback.

RIP has followed up on its graduates and profiled them in a series of medium- and long-term evaluation studies (see Strain & Timm, 2001). A sample of RIP graduates was evaluated when they were three to nine years beyond the end of the intervention. During home observations, these RIP participants complied with parental requests 82% of the time and interacted positively with their parents 97% of the time. During school observations, these same participants complied with teacher requests 89% of the time, were appropriately engaged during 90% of unstructured classroom time and 85% of structured academic periods, and generally behaved in a fashion indistinguishable from classroom peers with no problem history.

In addition, a sample of 40 RIP graduates was followed over a 25-year period and evaluated on a number of important, macro indicators of life adjustment and achievement. These participants were adults in their mid-20s and early 30s at the time of the follow-up. Key findings include these:

◆ All but one completed high school, and a large proportion went on to college and graduate school.

◆ All but one (the same one who dropped out of high school) were currently employed.

- During adolescence, one experimented with illegal drugs (marijuana), and one (the high school dropout) was involved with the criminal justice system (for theft).

- None were identified as in need of special education or as emotionally disturbed.

- There were no reports of their ever engaging in aggression toward parents, peers, or teachers after completing the program.

In addition, the parents reported that the program had transformed their lives.

RIP has been extensively replicated and has been adopted in a number of states and foreign countries. It is a highly effective program model that receives high consumer satisfaction ratings from participating parents and others (e.g., referral sources and school personnel). RIP empowers parents to regain control of their lives and to forge a healthy, positive family life. It produces outstanding results using educational and treatment procedures that are trustworthy and respectful.

The Perry Preschool Program.   This program was developed in the early 1960s in Ypsilanti, Michigan, by Dave Weikart and his associates. This exemplary preschool program for economically disadvantaged children and families stands as a classic demonstration of the power and lasting effects of early-intervention approaches that involve schools and families in meaningful partnerships. The Perry Preschool Program and its results through fourth grade have been described by Weikart, Bond, and McNeil (1978). In addition, this program has been the subject of numerous economic analysis studies of the long-term costs versus benefits of early intervention (see Barnett, 1985a, b).

Three- and 4-year-old children with no obvious handicapping conditions, along with their families, participated in the program and formed the experimental group. Control children were from the same population and shared largely identical characteristics with the experimental children. A majority of the children were of African American heritage, and all participants were randomly assigned to either experimental or control conditions. Graduates of the program have been followed up over three decades and evaluated on a host of important outcome variables, making the Perry Preschool Program one of the most important longitudinal follow-up studies of early-intervention effects ever conducted.

The program was delivered over one academic year and had three elements. The first was a center-based curriculum that operated for 2½ hours each morning, five days per week. The curriculum provided a mix of traditional nursery school activities and cognitively based instruction. The child-to-teacher ratio was 5:1, and teachers were trained in both early-childhood and special education areas. The second element of the program was home visiting by the preschool teaching staff, which occurred for 1½ hours, one afternoon per week. The final program element consisted of group meetings of the participating children's parents. The cost per child for one year of the program was $4,963.

Table 4.1 provides longitudinal follow-up assessment data for experimental group participants versus control group participants. The data show consis-

TABLE 4.1 ◆

Longitudinal Follow-Up Assessment Results for the Perry Preschool Program.

Category	Experimental	Control	p
Early childhood: IQ at age 5	95	83	<.01
Late childhood			
School years in special education	16%	28%	.04
Ever classified mentally retarded	15%	35%	.01
Adolescent/early adulthood			
Age 15 mean achievement test score	122.2	94.5	<.01
High school graduation	67%	49%	.03
Postsecondary education	38%	21%	.03
Arrested or detained	31%	51%	.02
Employed at age 19	50%	32%	.03
Receiving welfare at age 19	18%	32%	.04

Source: W. Bennett, *The Perry Preschool Program and Its Long Term Effects: A Benefit-Cost Analysis.* © 1985 High/Scope Press. Reprinted with permission.

tently clear effects favoring the experimental children over the others. Table 4.2 presents costs and benefits of the Perry Preschool Program calculated through age 19 and beyond age 19. After subtracting the costs of the program, the average per-child benefit through age 19 was an estimated $7,580 per case; the corresponding figure beyond age 19 was $12,126. These findings have important public policy implications in terms of providing access to high-quality early-childhood education—especially for those children who come from disadvantaged backgrounds, as many antisocial youths do.

Zigler and his colleagues (1992) analyzed the empirical evidence on effective approaches for preventing adolescent delinquency. After reviewing a number of commonly used approaches in the juvenile system (e.g., restitution), these authors have concluded that the most effective delinquency prevention approaches are collaborative, early-intervention programs, delivered from preschool to grade 3, involving school staff and parents in working partnership arrangements, that focus on preventing early school failure. Long-term outcomes of the Perry Preschool program provide strong support for this conclusion. In our view, all young children who are at risk for antisocial behavior should have access to such a preschool experience. However, achieving this outcome will require some major policy changes in our society.

The First Step to Success Early-Intervention Program. First Step to Success is a collaborative home and school intervention that addresses secondary prevention goals. This early-intervention program is designed to prevent and

TABLE 4.2 ◆

Costs and Benefits of the Perry Preschool Program Through Age 19 and Beyond.

Present Value of Costs and Benefits of the Perry Preschool Program Discounted at 5% (in 1986 dollars)

Benefits Through Age 19

	Child care	$ 714
	School cost savings	5,082
	Earnings increase	574
	Crime reduction	1,164
	Welfare reduction	46
	Total	$7,580

Benefits Beyond Age 19

	College costs	$ 621
	Earnings increase	14,403
	Crime reduction	1,386
	Welfare reduction	993
	Total	$16,160
	Total benefits	$23,740
	Total cost	$11,614
	Net benefits	$12,126

offset emerging antisocial behavior patterns among behaviorally at-risk K–2 students and to assist them in getting off to the best start possible in school (see Walker et al., 1997). The First Step program is coordinated and delivered by a behavioral coach (e.g., counselor, school psychologist, early interventionist, or resource specialist) who conducts screening procedures to identify qualified candidates, sets up the school-based part of the intervention, operates it initially, and then turns it over to the kindergarten or regular primary teacher after it is operating smoothly. The coach then works with the target child's parents and caregivers to teach them how to instruct their child at home in school success skills (e.g., cooperating, accepting limits, being ready for school, and completing work). A parent handbook, weekly training sessions in the parents' home, role-plays and discussion, and frequent telephone contact with occasional follow-up visits by the First Step coach are used to achieve caregiver mastery of this program component. At the same time, teachers recognize and reinforce these skills at school. Peers are also enlisted in the intervention as special helpers, and they tend to be very supportive of the target child's efforts to change as they share in all group activity rewards earned by the First Step student (Walker & Severson, 2002).

First Step consists of three interconnected modules: (1) screening and identification, (2) school intervention, and (3) home-based parent training. The program is applied to one target child at a time and requires an average of three months to implement. Although First Step can be implemented in specialized school settings, it is designed for and carefully adapted to the requirements and routines of regular classroom settings. The First Step program has been adopted in over 20 states and five Canadian provinces in addition to sites in Australia and New Zealand. The program also has been translated into Spanish and French, and it is currently being considered for adoption in Japanese schools. First Step is a popular program with educators and costs approximately $400 per case to implement in terms of professional time and materials.

First Step was developed through a four-year grant to the senior author from the U.S. Department of Education. A randomized trial involving 46 kindergartners and a wait-list control-group design was used to evaluate the First Step program's impact (see Walker et al., 1998). Across five pre- and postevaluation measures (four teacher rating measures and one direct observation measure), the average effect size for the intervention group changes, compared with wait-list participants, was .86, which is considered to be a robust magnitude of impact. The original cohorts 1 ($N = 24$) and 2 ($N = 22$) on whom the First Step program was first tested and evaluated were followed up into grades 6 and 5, respectively. The initial behavioral gains produced through exposure to the program beginning in kindergarten have proved to be surprisingly durable over this time span (see Epstein & Walker, 2002).

Box 4.2 summarizes important findings on the First Step to Success program's impact to date. Over the past four years, the First Step program's adoption by any Oregon school that wishes to do so has been supported by a $700,000 grant from the Oregon state legislature. Results of this statewide implementation were independently evaluated by the Human Services Research Institute of Salem, Oregon, and were very positive. Research is continuing on the program by its developers and by other investigators.

The First Step program has been included in a number of recent reviews of exemplary early-intervention programs for addressing aggressive, antisocial behavior. Perhaps the greatest value of the First Step program is that it bridges the transition from kindergarten to the primary grades and assists children in getting off to a good start in school. School success, especially early school success, represents one of the most powerful protective factors available against later destructive outcomes.

The foregoing interventions provide a continuum of exemplary programs that span the prenatal-to-age-5 period, which is one of the most important developmental stages in individuals' lives. If implemented in a sequenced, coordinated fashion, they address most of the risk factors that set vulnerable children up for antisocial behavior and subsequent destructive outcomes. The next section profiles two universal interventions and one indicated intervention that are proven approaches for use with at-risk and antisocial students in elementary and middle school.

Box 4.2   Major Findings to Date on the First Step to Success Program

- First Step produces effect sizes that are consistently in the 0.80 and above range.
- Long-term follow-up of kindergarten target children into grades 3 and 4 show acceptable persistence of behavioral gains in a majority of cases.
- Evaluation outcomes indicate that First Step produces child behavior change(s) despite less-than-optimal fidelity of implementation in the "real world."
- First Step has proved to work with diverse learners in rural, suburban, and urban school–community settings.
- The more severe the child's challenging behavior problems, the better First Step works.
- Research shows that First Step produces positive, collateral behavioral effects on the following outcome measures: (1) overall academic engaged time for the whole classroom, (2) teacher praise and criticism rates, (3) the problem behavior of other peers with challenging behavior patterns, and (4) positive and negative teacher student interactions.
- Consumer satisfaction results for the program are generally positive, although some teachers see the program as too much work, and others see it as too expensive.

Interventions in the Elementary and Middle School Grades

The context of public schooling provides one of the few opportunities for accessing the full range of children and youths who are in formative periods of their development. It allows for the screening and evaluation of children who bring with them the damaging effects of prior risk exposure and also makes it possible to deliver universal interventions that address the needs of *all* students.

As noted previously, it is critical that each child be evaluated at the point of school entry on two important dimensions that have everything to do with a successful school career: (1) the presence of challenging forms of behavior and (2) a lack of school readiness associated with learning to read. Children who manifest aggressive, coercive behavior patterns (e.g., antisocial children) suffer terribly in school and often victimize peers, teachers, and other adults in their reactions to the schooling experience. Frequently, they are pushed out of school in late middle school or beginning high school because their problems are so intractable and their overall behavior so aversive and noxious. Children who fail to learn to read or to read to the best of their abilities constantly receive the message that they are a failure in school. The cumulative effect of this negative feedback over time often results in their disengagement from schooling; they come to view it as a punishing experience, which eventually causes them to drop out. Further, those students who experience reading failure *and* challenging behavior are at very high risk of not finishing their K–12 schooling and are likely to have a low overall quality of life (Walker & Severson, 2002).

This section profiles the Second Step Violence Prevention Program and the Effective Behavior Support (EBS) program, which are universal interventions designed to impact school climates positively and to teach critical skills that help make all students competent, responsible, and caring. The Multisystemic Therapy (MST) program is described as well. MST is a tertiary-level intervention designed to meet the needs and problems of youths who have either begun offending or are at high risk for doing so. MST is an ecological intervention that focuses on family, school, peer, and community contexts. Collectively, these three interventions effectively address most of the behavioral priorities discussed immediately previously—provided they are implemented with care and integrity.

The two universal interventions address mainly, but not exclusively, primary prevention goals and outcomes. The EBS program, for example, uses a secondary prevention–intervention component, the Behavior Education Program (BEP) (see Crone, Horner, & Hawken, 2001), that provides daily monitoring and positive behavioral support for moderately-to-severely at-risk students for whom EBS proves insufficient. Target students are required to "check in" with an adult before school and to "check out" with an adult after school. The students also check in and out with teachers throughout the school day. Teachers provide feedback on the students' social behavior, via Likert ratings, at the end of each class period, and students take home daily report cards for their parents to sign. March and Horner (in press) have reported findings supporting the effectiveness of the BEP intervention to reduce problem behavior, particularly for those students whose problem behavior is maintained by teacher or peer attention.

The purpose of primary prevention approaches is to prevent the occurrence or onset of problems (i.e., to forestall harm) and/or to intercept such problems in their earliest stages of development. Implementing schoolwide discipline programs and fluoridating a community's water supply are two examples of universal interventions that are designed to prevent, respectively, school-based behavior problems and the development of tooth decay. Universal interventions are implemented so that all who are exposed to them receive the same intervention in the same manner and at the same dosage level. These interventions provide an important foundational context for implementing selected and indicated interventions for higher-risk students. These approaches are likely to be more effective when implemented in combination with a universal intervention than when implemented in isolation.

The Second Step Violence Prevention Curriculum. Second Step (Seattle Committee for Children, 1992) is a universal intervention designed to teach violence prevention skills from preschool through eighth grade. Taught as part of the regular school curriculum, it uses the same instructional methods as for language, math, science, social studies, and so forth. Second Step teaches four core skills known to be associated with violence prevention: (1) empathy, (2) impulse control, (3) anger management, and (4) conflict resolution. Teaching strategies used by Second Step include discussion, video representations of social scenarios, role-playing, debriefing, and feedback. Parents are also involved in the teaching and practice of target skills at home.

Typically, the Second Step curriculum is taught during three to four 45-minute instructional periods per week. It is instructionally sequenced so that more complex skill sets build upon less complex ones, and it is also arranged to take into account the growing maturity levels of students as they move through the elementary and middle school grades. Second Step is an evidence-based intervention program that is quite teacher-friendly. The program's developers also paid careful attention to multicultural issues in its development. The effectiveness of Second Step has been independently evaluated via a randomized control trial (see Grossman et al., 1997). Results of this investigation showed that, for intervention students as compared with nonintervention students, levels of aggression decreased and prosocial forms of adaptive behavior increased. In vivo behavioral observations recorded by professionally trained observers ($p < .03$ and $.04$, respectively) were used to document these outcomes. These effects were in evidence six months after the end of the Second Step intervention.

Second Step is currently used in approximately 15,000 U.S. schools. Further, it has been adopted extensively in Canada, Australia, New Zealand, and the United Kingdom, and has been translated into six languages—primarily Scandinavian languages but also Japanese. Second Step has received a number of awards from federal agencies, task forces, and interdisciplinary review committees in recognition of its excellence and exemplary features; these include the U.S. Department of Education; the U.S. Department of Health and Human Services; the Collaborative for Academic, Social, and Emotional Learning; the U.S. Department of Justice; and the U.S. Office of Safe and Drug-Free Schools. A recent review panel that recommended Second Step as a best practice concluded that "This well-organized, -structured, and -evaluated program has demonstrated effects on aggressive behaviors . . . and consists of beautiful, high-quality materials." Second Step is perhaps *the* most user-friendly violence prevention program available.

In summary, Second Step is a cost-effective intervention that contributes to establishing and maintaining a positive school climate and to addressing the precursors of violence. If all feeder elementary schools for middle schools taught Second Step systematically at each grade level, and if this process were replicated from middle through high school, there would be an enormous positive change in the social ecologies in the K–12 years. Second Step is strongly recommended as a best practice for making schools safer and violence-free and for creating optimal learning environments.

The Effective Behavior Support (EBS) Program.   Positive behavioral support (PBS) is a systemic intervention approach that has been enthusiastically received by school leaders in recent years as a means of creating disciplined, orderly, positive school environments that promote social competence among all students. PBS is defined as "consisting of a broad range of systemic and individualized strategies for achieving important social and learning outcomes while preventing problem behavior" (Anushko & Hunter, 2002). PBS approaches are systemwide in nature and require support from a majority of school staff in order to be effective. PBS principles and approaches have the potential to transform the overall culture and effectiveness of a school.

The key feature of PBS is that it creates a positive school environment in which all staff (administrative, classroom, lunchroom, playground, school bus, custodial, etc.) recognize and abide by the same set of behavioral expectations for students. George Sugai and Rob Horner of the University of Oregon are the principal developers of this approach. Their PBS model intervention has been broadly adopted in U.S. schools and is the most widely known and used program variation of its type (see Anushko & Hunter, 2002; Horner, Sugai, Lewis-Palmer, & Todd, 2001; Sugai & Horner, 1999). Full and complete installation of the EBS model requires two years.

Schoolwide, positive behavior support approaches address four behavioral challenges facing all schools: (1) intense behavior patterns of individual students, (2) group behavior patterns in classrooms, (3) group behavior patterns in nonclassroom settings, and (4) schoolwide behavior patterns that define the school culture (Horner et al., 2001). EBS provides a supportive, systemic context for addressing each of these challenges. The EBS developers recognized that, for schools to become more effective, (1) school leaders must adopt evidence-based, proven practices that are adapted to the school's characteristics and unique features, and (2) a strong support system must be developed to support and sustain them over the long term. The hallmark of an effective support-and-delivery system for PBS is a three-tiered model of prevention in which different intervention approaches are used to achieve primary, secondary, and tertiary prevention goals and outcomes. This prevention model was described and illustrated earlier.

The nine-step EBS approach systematically teaches mastery of key social competencies using effective instructional practices. The three core EBS skills that are commonly taught across school applications are (1) be safe, (2) be respectful, and (3) be responsible. Additional skills are sometimes taught by individual schools, but the total number of schoolwide competencies targeted usually does not exceed five. The nine steps for teaching schoolwide skills are as follows:

1. Define three to five schoolwide behavioral expectations.
2. Provide a "defining rule" for each expectation.
3. Build a culture of competence by teaching the schoolwide expectations to *all* students.
4. Teach behavioral expectations in an array of school settings.
5. Teach specific social behaviors that are examples of the behavioral expectations.
6. Teach behavioral expectations with "negative" examples.
7. Give students the opportunity to practice appropriate behaviors.
8. Reward appropriate behavior.
9. Acknowledge appropriate behavior on a regular basis after the skill is learned.

	Classroom	Gym	Hallway	Playground	Bus Area
Be safe	Follow directions	Follow directions	Walk	Go up ladders and down slides	Wait behind the red line
	Keep floors clear	Wait for turn	Open doors slowly		
Be respectful	Raise hand to talk	Follow rules of the game	Keep hands and feet to self	Use one-minute rule for sharing equipment	Keep hands and feet to self
	Keep hands and feet to self	Return equipment at bell	Talk quietly	Wait for your turn	Use appropriate language
Be responsible	Bring books and pencil to class	Participate	Keep books, belongings, and litter off floor	Stay within recess area	Keep books and belongings with you
	Do homework	Wear soft-soled shoes		Bring equipment back to class	Be on time

FIGURE 4.2

How EBS Social Skills Are Taught Across School Contexts.

Source: Horner et al. (2001).

Figure 4.2 illustrates how specific social skills are identified (and taught) within differing school contexts to achieve mastery of schoolwide behavioral expectations. In addition, Box 4.3 provides a sample teaching plan for teaching appropriate student behavior within the bus area. Replications of this basic strategy are used in all other school settings (classroom, playground, lunchroom, etc.) in teaching schoolwide behavioral expectations.

The primary tool for evaluating the efficacy of schoolwide PBS approaches has been disciplinary referrals to the principal's office (ODRs), which result in a written record of the incident(s) that prompt them and their disposition. This outcome variable has proved to have substantial value as a sensitive measure of schoolwide intervention effects. The School-Wide Information System (SWIS), which is a Web-based information system, is used for recording ODRs in EBS school applications. (This system was discussed in Chapter 3 on assessment.)

Figure 4.3 provides a longitudinal illustration of the impact of EBS on a middle school that initially had a very high annual level of ODRs. As the figure shows, the continuing implementation of EBS produced substantial, socially valid reductions in the school's overall frequency of ODRs across school years (Sugai, Sprague, Horner, & Walker, 2000). In addition, the culture and atmosphere of this middle school improved during this period, becoming a more orderly, manageable environment.

It is not uncommon to see a 40–50% reduction in ODRs within one school year in EBS schools (Horner et al., 2001; Taylor-Green et al., 1999). Currently, EBS has been adopted and implemented in over 400 schools nationally. There is a growing body of empirical studies that document its efficacy.

Box 4.3   **EBS Sample Teaching Plan**

If the instructional guidelines set out here were used by a team with the task of organizing a 20-minute instructional session for fourth- and fifth-graders in the bus area during the first week of school, the teaching plan might include the following features:

◆ Teaching would occur with 30–45 students at the bus area during a predefined time period.

◆ Teachers would begin the session by reviewing the schoolwide behavioral expectations and having students demonstrate that they knew the behavioral expectations.

◆ Teachers would provide positive examples (or have students provide examples) of the specific skills that exemplify the behavioral expectations in that area. "Being safe" in the bus area means standing behind the red line (separating the safe from the unsafe areas). "Being responsible" in the bus area means talking to friends without pushing or shoving. With each example of appropriate behavior, the teacher reviews the label of the behavioral expectation and how the behavior meets the rule that defines the expectation.

◆ Teachers would provide examples (or have students provide examples) of "doing it the wrong way." Being over the red line with one toe touching the line means not being behind the line. Giving a friend materials to hold means not keeping belongings together. Grabbing someone's cap or throwing pine cones at others means not keeping hands and feet to self. By providing examples of the most common behavioral errors, the instruction clarifies what is expected.

◆ If possible, a bus would be present, and every student in the group would have a chance to line up, get on the bus the "right way," and receive some form of recognition for correct behavior.

The instructional session would last 20 minutes, be fun, and result in every student not only demonstrating that he or she has a clear understanding of what is expected but also seeing that all the other students know what is expected. After students have been through similar experiences in the gym, cafeteria, hall, and class, they learn a small set of easy-to-remember behavioral concepts and a larger set of specific skills that exemplify these concepts. The most important specific skills are learned directly, and broader expectations are taught as concepts that help the children generalize to new, nontaught contexts.

The Multisystemic Therapy (MST) Program.   An outstanding example of an effective tertiary intervention is the Multisystemic Therapy (MST) program model developed by Scott Henggeler and his colleagues (Henggeler, 1998). MST is one of 11 "blueprint" violence prevention interventions validated as effective by Delbert Elliott, Ph.D., and his associates at the Center for the Study and Prevention

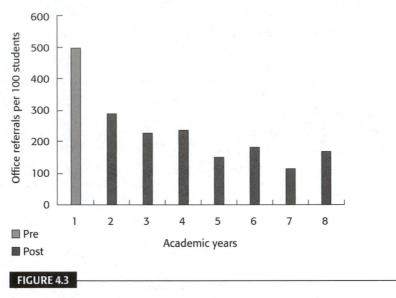

■ Pre
■ Post

FIGURE 4.3 ◆

Rate of Office Discipline Referrals per 100 Students at Fern Ridge Middle School Prior to and After Adoption of Schoolwide PBS.

of Violence at the University of Colorado. MST is highly effective with the most severely at-risk youths who have been or are about to be incarcerated for committing arrestable offenses, often of a violent nature. MST is a superb example of a complex intervention that (1) addresses key risk factors, (2) effects powerful behavior changes, and (3) coordinates multiple systems of care, support, and treatment. It has proven efficacy in preventing the recidivism of severely at-risk adolescents and also in reducing antisocial behavior (see Henggeler, Melton, & Smith, 1992; Schoenwald, Brown, & Henggeler, 2000). Steve Aos of the Washington Public Institute estimates that, for every act of recidivism that is prevented, a total of $30,000 is saved (Citizens Crime Commission, 2000). MST is highly recommended as a promising intervention for delinquent and potentially violent adolescents. The program works with adolescents who have other disorders as well, including those who are sex offenders, who have psychiatric disorders, and who suffer from neglect and abuse (see Brunk, Henggeler, & Whelan, 1987).

MST is based on the empirical knowledge bases that have emerged following the effective treatment of delinquency and adolescent drug abuse (Loeber & Farrington, 1998, 2001; Patterson, Reid, & Dishion, 1992; Reid et al., 2002). MST was designed to address the multiple problems that antisocial youths consistently experience in four contexts: family relations, peer relations, neighborhood/community, and schooling. MST is a family-focused intervention that teaches parents and caregivers the skills they need to assist their children to function more effectively across a range of social contexts. It rests upon a social-ecological foundation in which the individual is viewed as embedded within, interacting with, and influenced by environmental systems represented by family, school, work, peers, and community. Problem behavior may arise as a function of difficulty within any of these systems (e.g., parent–child, teacher–child, or peer–peer relationships) or between systems (e.g., home–school relationships).

The core focus of MST is on changing the social ecology of family dynamics in ways that promote positive adjustment and that reduce or buffer emotional and behavioral difficulties. MST has a strong emphasis on family preservation and improvement of family functioning as a means of addressing the problems of at-risk children and youths. The MST intervention is delivered by a trained therapist who is accessible to family members and who ensures that the intervention procedures are respectful of family values, beliefs, and culture. These therapists are available 24 hours per day, seven days per week. Each MST therapist works with four to five families at a time. Daily contact is common in the early stages of MST treatment and decreases to several times per week as the intervention progresses.

Like the Effective Behavioral Support program, MST is based on nine core principles that guide the intervention process; these principles are listed in Box 4.4. A detailed manual for practitioners is provided to ensure that intervention components are implemented according to a standard protocol. MST intervention procedures are individualized and carefully tailored to each family but are adapted from proven, problem-focused treatment approaches (e.g., behavioral parent training or cognitive behavior therapy). Interventions are selected, adapted, and delivered for each system or context in which the youth is experiencing problems and are coordinated so as to maximize the impact of the interventions within and between systems or contexts (see Schoenwald & Rowland, 2002). Therapist adherence to the core principles of MST is assessed according to a MST Adherence Scale completed by parents, youths, and therapists.

The evidence base for MST is described in elaborate detail in Schoenwald et al. (2000) and by Schoenwald and Rowland (2002). MST is highly regarded by experts as a powerful, cost-effective intervention that has proved successful for a youth population for whom the vast majority of interventions fail. If the MST intervention is delivered with solid treatment integrity and implementation protocols are carefully followed, there is a strong likelihood that it will produce documentable, positive effects. As noted previously, MST is included in the "blueprint" series of scientifically proven interventions, as validated by the Center for the Study and Prevention of Violence (see Henggeler, 1998), which provides the gold standard for documenting scientific approaches to preventing and reducing violence. According to Del Elliot, the leader of this seminal effort for translating research into effective practice(s), the intervention programs included in the blueprint series are so effective and well established that adopters need not evaluate them in terms of whether they work. However, the authors would qualify this statement as follows: *Any* intervention program, no matter how well established and proven, is only as good as the quality of its implementation.

As noted previously, the MST program has been successfully adapted for problems and youth populations for which it was not originally designed. For example, it has proved successful in treating adolescent drug abuse and in preventing the rehospitalization of youths with severe emotional problems (see Schoenwald et al., 2000; Schoenwald & Rowland, 2002). Most importantly, the MST program has been successfully adapted for families of very young children who are at risk for abuse, neglect, behavioral problems, or developmental delays (Pickrel & Henggeler, 1999; Schoenwald & Rowland, 2002). MST is being further evaluated with early-childhood target populations in several ongoing studies, one of which is a five-year effort by Michael Epstein and his colleagues at the University of Nebraska.

MST is one of the most carefully researched tertiary-level interventions currently available. The empirical knowledge base on the program continues to grow as more federal and state agencies make investments in it, which are then evaluated through ongoing research. The Washington State Institute for Public Policy recently reported a review and comparative evaluation of the cost-effectiveness of a series of programs for addressing delinquency including boot camps, MST, detention and incarceration, mentoring programs, intensive court probation, and intensive parole (Aos, 2002). This study found that MST was clearly superior to all other programs evaluated, and the study investigator(s) estimated that for every dollar invested in MST an average of $13.36 was returned in benefits. Thus, MST appears to be a very sound investment for community-based agencies searching for effective programs to reduce delinquency among severely at-risk youths.

In summary, as behaviorally at-risk youths move through schools in the absence of exposure to effective intervention services and supports, their problems are likely to become more intractable and more resistant to change. The three interventions described for use with youths in the elementary and middle school grades have the potential to offset this outcome and to positively impact both school and family functioning. They are all highly recommended.

Conclusion

This chapter focused on the prevention of antisocial behavior by addressing risk factors within family, school, and community contexts. In spite of huge advances in the treatment and prevention of the behavioral, social, and mental health problems of at-risk children in the past decade, the Surgeon General's Report on Youth Violence indicates that less than 10% of services delivered in schools and communities targeting antisocial behavior patterns are evidence-based (see Satcher, 2001). We have the knowledge and ability to substantively impact the problems of a majority of antisocial children and youths, but current practices show that we are seldom implementing what we know in this regard. Further, few studies to date have focused on coordinating evidence-based interventions among families, practitioners, and service providers in order to deliver comprehensive, unified approaches.

The programs reviewed in this chapter all qualify as effective and as evidence-based. They are exemplars of the kinds of interventions professionals should be adopting to meet the needs of the growing population of antisocial children and youths. They can make a real difference in the lives of these individuals and their families.

 ## InfoTrac College Edition Research Terms

David Olds

Olds Nurse Home Visitation Program

Positive behavior support

Positive school climate

References

Anushko, A. & Hunter, L. (2002). Implementing three-tiered intervention in schools. *Emotional & Behavioral Disorders in Youth, 2*(2), 27–31

Aos, S. (2002). *The juvenile justice system in Washington state: Recommendations to improve cost effectiveness*. Olympia: Washington State Institute for Public Policy.

Barnett, W. (1985a). Benefit-cost analysis of the Perry Preschool Program and its policy implications. *Educational Evaluation and Policy Analysis, 7*(4), 333–342.

Barnett, W. (1985b). *The Perry Preschool Program and its long term effects: A benefit-cost analysis*. Ypsilanti, MI: High/Scope Press.

Bronfenbrenner, U. (1979). *The ecology of human development*. Cambridge, MA: Harvard University Press.

Brunk, M., Henggeler, S., & Whelan, R. (1987). A comparison of multisystemic therapy and parent training in the brief treatment of child abuse and neglect. *Journal of Consulting and Clinical Psychology, 55,* 311–318.

Caprara, G., Barbaranelli, C., Pastorelli, C., Bandura, A., & Zimbardo, P. (2000). Prosocial foundations of children's academic achievement, *Psychological Science, 11*(4), 302–306.

Catalano, R., Loeber, R., & McKinney, K. (1999). School and community interventions to prevent serious and violent offending. *Juvenile Justice Bulletin,* U.S. Department of Justice, Office of Juvenile Justice and Delinquency Prevention, Washington, DC.

Citizens Crime Commission. (2000). *KIIDS: Kids intervention investment delinquency solutions.* Portland, OR: Author, Portland Metropolitan Chamber of Commerce.

Crone, D., & Horner, R. (2003). *Building the capacity to implement functional behavioral assessment in schools: A practical guide to function-based support.* New York: Guilford Press.

Crone, D., Horner, R., & Hawken, L. (2001). *The Behavior Education Program (BEP) handbook: A school's systematic guide to responding to chronic problem behavior.* Available from the Educational and Community Supports Program, University of Oregon, Eugene, OR.

DiPerna, J., Volpe, R., & Elliot, S. (2002). A model of academic enablers and elementary reading/language arts achievement. *School Psychology Review, 3*(93), 298–313.

Elliott, S., Witt, J., Kratochwill, T., & Stoiber, K. (2002). Selecting and evaluating classroom interventions. In M. Shinn, H. Walker, & G. Stoner (Eds.), *Interventions for academic and behavior problems II: Preventive and remedial approaches* (pp. 243–294), Bethesda, MD: National Association of School Psychologists.

Epstein, M., & Walker, H. (2002). Special education: Best practices and First Step to Success. In B. Burns & K. Hoagwood (Eds.), *Community treatment for youth: Evidence-based interventions for severe emotional and behavioral disorders* (pp. 177–197). New York: Oxford University Press.

Golly, A. M. (1994). *The use and effects of alpha and beta commands in elementary classroom settings.* Unpublished doctoral dissertation, University of Oregon.

Greenberg, M., Domitrovich, C., & Bumbarger, B. (2001). *Preventing mental disorders in school-age children: A review of the effectiveness of prevention programs.* Available from the Prevention Center for the Promotion of Human Development, College of Health and Human Development, Pennsylvania State University, State College, PA.

Grossman, D., Neckerman, H., Koepsell, T., Ping-Yu Liu, Asher, K., Beland, K., Frey, K., & Rivara, F. (1997). Effectiveness of a violence prevention curriculum among children in elementary school: A randomized control trial. *Journal of the American Medical Association, 277*(20), pp. 1605–1611.

Hawkins, D., Catalano, R., Kosterman, R., Abbott, R., & Hill, K. (1999). Preventing adolescent health-risk behaviors by strengthening protection during childhood. *Archives of Pediatric and Adolescent Medicine, 153,* 226–234.

Henggeler, S., (1998). Multisystemic therapy. In D. Elliott (Ed.), *Blueprints for violence prevention.* Boulder, CO: Center for the Study and Prevention of Violence.

Henggeler, S., Melton, G., & Smith, L. (1992). Family preservation using multisystemic therapy: An effective alternative to incarcerating serious juvenile offenders. *Journal of Consulting and Clinical Psychology, 60,* 953–961.

Horner, R., Sugai, G., Lewis-Palmer, T., & Todd, A. (2001). Teaching schoolwide behavioral expectations. *Emotional & Behavioral Disorders in Youth, 1*(4), 77–79, 93–96.

Horner, R. H., Sugai, G., Todd, A. W., & Lewis-Palmer, T. (in press). Schoolwide positive behavior support: An alternative approach to discipline in schools. In L. Bambara & L. Kern (Eds.), *Positive behavior support*. New York: Guilford Press.

Kauffman, J. (1999). How we prevent the prevention of emotional and behavioral disorders. *Exceptional Children, 65*(4), 448–468.

Kellam, S. (2002, October). Prevention science, aggression and destructive outcomes: Long term results of a series of prevention trials in school settings. Presentation to the National Press Club, Washington, DC.

Kellam, S., Rebok, G., Ialongo, N., & Mayer, L. (1994). The course and malleability of aggressive behavior from early first grade into middle school: Results of a developmental epidemiologically-based prevention trial. *Journal of Child Psychology and Psychiatry, 35*(2), 259–281.

Lane, K., Gresham, F., & O'Shaughnessy, T. (2002). *Interventions for children with or at risk for emotional and behavioral disorders*. Boston: Allyn & Bacon.

Loeber, D., & Farrington, D. (1998). *Serious and violent juvenile offenders: Risk factors and successful interventions*. Thousand Oaks, CA: Sage.

Loeber, D., & Farrington, D. (2001). *Child delinquents: Development, intervention and service needs*. Thousand Oaks, CA: Sage.

Malecki, C., & Elliot, S. (2002). Children's social behaviors as predictors of academic achievement: A longitudinal analysis. *School Psychology Quarterly, 17*(1), 1–23.

March, R, & Horner, R. (in press). Feasibility and contributions of functional behavioral assessment in schools. *Journal of Emotional and Behavioral Disorders*.

Olds, D., Henderson, C., Kitzman, H., Eckenrode, J., Cole, R., & Tatelbaum, R. (1999). Prenatal and infancy home visitation by nurses: Recent findings. *The Future of Children, 9*(1), 44–65. Monterey, CA: Packard Foundation.

O'Neill, R., Horner, R., Sprague, J., Albin, R., & Storey, K. (1997). *Functional analysis of problem behavior: A practical assessment guide* (2nd ed.). Pacific Grove, CA: Brooks/Cole.

Patterson, G., Reid, J., & Dishion, T. (1992). *Antisocial boys*. Eugene: Castalia.

Pickrel, S., & Henggeler, S. (1999). *Village early intervention program (VEIP) executive summary*. Unpublished document. Charleston: Medical University of South Carolina, Family Services Research Center.

Reid, J., Patterson, G., & Snyder, J. (2002). *Antisocial behavior in children and adolescents: A developmental analysis and model for intervention*. Washington, DC: American Psychological Association.

Romer, D., & Heller, T. (1983). Social adaptation of mentally retarded adults in community settings: A social-ecological approach. *Applied research in mental retardation, 4,* 303–314.

Satcher, D. (2001). *Youth violence: A report of the Surgeon General*. Washington, DC: U.S. Public Health Service, U.S. Department of Health and Human Services.

Schoenwald, S., Brown, T., & Henggeler, C. (2000). Inside multisystemic therapy: Therapist, supervisory, and program practices. In H. Walker & M. Epstein (Eds.), *Making schools safer and violence free: Critical issues, solutions and recommended practices* (pp. 99–113). Austin, TX: Pro-Ed.

Schoenwald, S., & Rowland, M. (2002). Multisystemic therapy. In B. Burns & K. Hoagwood (Eds.), *Community treatment for youth: Evidence-based interventions for severe emotional and behavioral disorders* (pp. 91–117). New York: Oxford University Press.

Seattle Committee for Children, (1992). *Second Step: A violence prevention curriculum*. Seattle: Author.

Shinn, M., Walker, H., & Stoner, G. (2002). *Interventions for academic and behavior problems II: Preventive and remedial approaches*. Bethesda, MD: National Association of School Psychologists.

Steinberg, L. (1996). *Why school reform has failed and what parents need to do*. New York: Simon & Schuster.

Strain, P., & Timm, M. (2001). Remediation and prevention of aggression: An evaluation of the regional intervention program over a quarter century. *Behavioral Disorders, 26*(4), 297–313.

Sugai, G., & Horner, R. (1999). Discipline and behavioral support: Preferred process and practices. *Effective school practices, 17*(4), 10–22.

Sugai, G., Sprague, J., Horner, R., & Walker, H. (2000). Preventing school violence: The use of office discipline referrals to assess and monitor school-wide discipline interventions. In H. Walker & M. Epstein (Eds.), *Making schools safer and violence free: Critical issues, solutions, and recommended practices* (pp. 50–57). Austin, TX: Pro-Ed.

Taylor-Green, S., Brown, D., Cohen, J., Dilworth, M., Doscher, S., Gassman, T., Hoag, L., Kartub, D., Langton, J., McCornack, L., Nelson, L., & Horner, R. (1999). *The High Five Program: A positive approach to school discipline*. Elmira, OR: Fern Ridge Middle School.

Walker, H., Kavanagh, K., Stiller, B., Golly, A., Severson, H., & Feil, E. (1997). *First Step to Success: An early intervention program for antisocial kindergartners*. Longmont, CO: Sopris West.

Walker, H., Kavanagh, K., Stiller, B., Golly, A., Severson, H., & Feil, E. (1998). First Step: An early intervention approach for preventing school antisocial behavior. *Journal of Emotional and Behavioral Disorders, 6*(2), 66–80.

Walker, H., & Severson, H. (2002). Developmental prevention of at-risk outcomes for vulnerable antisocial children and youth. In K. Lane, F. Gresham, & T. Shaughnessy (Eds.), *Interventions for children with or at risk for emotional and behavioral disorders* (177–191), Boston: Allyn & Bacon.

Walker, H., & Shinn, M. (2002). Structuring school-based interventions to achieve integrated primary, secondary, and tertiary prevention goals for safe and effective schools. In M. Shinn, H. Walker, & G. Stoner (Eds.), *Interventions for academic and behavior problems II: Preventive and remedial approaches* (pp. 1–26). Bethesda, MD: National Association of School Psychologists.

Weikart, D., Bond, J., & McNeil, J. (1978). The Ypsilanti Perry Preschool Project: Preschool years and longitudinal results through fourth grade. *Monographs of the High/Scope Educational Research Foundation, 3*.

Zigler, E., Taussig, C., & Black, K. (1992). Early childhood intervention: A promising preventative for juvenile delinquency. *American Psychologist, 47*(8), 997–1006.

Proven Principles and Practices for Managing Antisocial Behavior

CHAPTER

5

Introduction

In an earlier chapter, we described a variety of procedures for accomplishing screening and behavior classification tasks and for determining the functions that antisocial behavior patterns serve. Although assessment is an essential initial step in dealing with this behavior pattern, it is just that—a first step. For classroom teachers and administrators, the most important issue is coping with and managing this highly aversive and disruptive behavior pattern effectively (Sprick & Howard, 1998). However, much to the dismay of many classroom teachers who deal with antisocial students, they soon discover that the behavior management practices that work so well with typical students do not work with those displaying antisocial behavior. In fact, teachers find that their tried-and-true behavior management practices often make the behavior patterns of antisocial students much worse! The vast majority of teachers simply are not trained to cope effectively with such students.

How can it be that behavior management practices somehow work differently for students with antisocial behavior patterns? Do these students learn differently than typical students? Do they require interventions based on a completely different set of learning principles? As we shall see in this chapter, there is nothing all that different about how antisocial children learn to behave as they do. In fact, the contingencies and principles by which this behavior pattern is acquired are quite lawful and predictable.

This behavior pattern is learned primarily through the process of behavioral *coercion*. That is, antisocial children learn to control their environment and the individuals in it through the skillful use of coercive behavioral tactics that are very forceful in nature. Once learned, these tactics are highly resistant to change because they are powerfully reinforced and supported naturally by the social environment. Whereas typically developing children respond well to positive reinforcement and encouragement, children with antisocial tendencies learn primarily through the process of negative reinforcement. That is, by using coercive techniques, they learn to escape from or terminate situations and tasks they find unpleasant (e.g., responding to parental directives or completing teacher-assigned tasks). This chapter presents state-of-the-art information for effectively managing antisocial behavior patterns within the classroom setting.

Typical Environmental Responses to Antisocial Behavior

Children and youths exhibiting antisocial behavior patterns are characteristically dealt with in one of two ways: (1) via punishment-based strategies and (2) through clinical treatment (Eddy, Reid, & Curry, 2002; Sugai, Horner, & Gresham, 2002). Typically, these interventions are applied only after (reactively) the behavior pattern has evolved into a serious one for the family, school, and community. Further, by this point, these approaches have lost most of their already limited potential effectiveness. In spite of this fact, many schools continue to use punishment-based procedures as a first option in dealing with severe and well-developed antisocial behavior patterns. These punishment-based approaches are among the least effective responses to reducing antisocial behavior (Gottfredson,

1997; Tolan & Guerra, 1994). In addition, there is clear evidence that merely punishing problem behavior without providing a parallel system of positive behavioral support leads to increases in aggression, vandalism, truancy, tardiness, and school dropout (Mayer & Sulzer-Azaroff, 2002).

The other frequently used response to antisocial behavior is "clinical treatment," which is usually delivered in the context of counseling and psychotherapy within mental health clinics, the juvenile justice system, or the school setting (Eddy et al., 2002). However, there is very little evidence that either traditional counseling or psychotherapy (i.e., "talk therapies") are effective in dealing with antisocial behavior (Satcher, 2001). In fact, most counseling therapies are effective only in changing how antisocial children *talk about* and *perceive* their behavior. This is particularly true of counseling administered within a peer group context (Gottfredson, 1997). Unfortunately, these approaches are quite ineffective in changing how antisocial children *act* and *behave*. In short, counseling and psychotherapy far too often result in antisocial children learning how to "talk the talk" but not how to "walk the walk" in terms of lasting and meaningful behavior change (Gottfredson, 1997).

Neither sanctions nor clinical treatment(s) are effective interventions for antisocial children (see Loeber & Farrington, 1998, 2001; Reid, Patterson, & Snyder, 2000) primarily because these approaches do not address the core reasons for the development of antisocial behavior. Many professionals regard them as supplemental interventions at best. The causal factors underlying antisocial behavior patterns are described in the following sections.

Coercion in the Acquisition of Antisocial Behavior

Patterson and his colleagues (Patterson, 2002; Patterson, Reid, & Dishion, 1992) have contributed the most complete and detailed explanations of the causal events and processes that account for the development of antisocial behavior patterns. They present a causal model in which a host of family stressors (e.g., poverty, divorce, drug and alcohol problems, and abuse of family members) pressure family members severely. Under the influence of these stressors, normal parenting practices are disrupted, and family routines become chaotic, negative, and unpredictable. Disrupted parenting practices, in turn, lead to escalated social interactions among family members that involve the use of coercive techniques to force the submission of others. Over time, such conditions provide a fertile breeding ground for the development of antisocial behavior patterns. Children from these homes come to school with negative attitudes toward schooling, a limited repertoire of cooperative behavior skills, and a predilection to use coercive tactics to control and manipulate others.

The Role of Corporal Punishment

To what extent does the use of corporal punishment in the home contribute to the development of antisocial behavior patterns? Gershoff (2002) performed a meta-analysis of 88 studies involving over 36,000 participants in studies conducted between 1938 to 2000 to answer this question. Her findings suggest that,

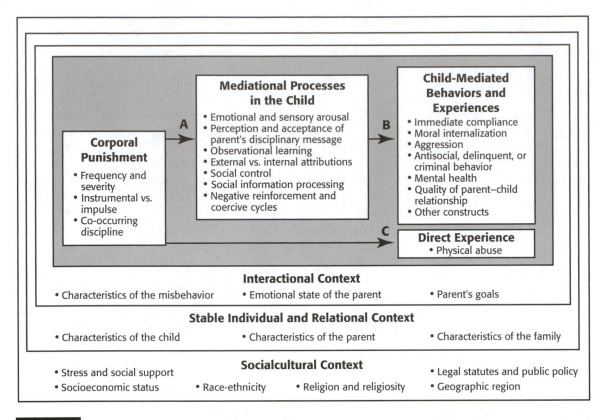

FIGURE 5.1

Conceptual Model of the Impact of Corporal Punishment on Later Destructive Outcomes.

although corporal punishment is associated with increased rates of immediate compliance, it is also associated with later childhood aggression, delinquent and antisocial behavior, and poor quality of parent–child relationships. Additionally, corporal punishment is a correlate of higher rates of aggression and criminal/antisocial behavior in adulthood.

Gershoff (2002) provides an instructive model for understanding the processes and contexts in which parental corporal punishment negatively affects young people's behavior. Figure 5.1 depicts this model, in which frequent and severe corporal punishment, delivered reactively (rather than planned), leads to aggression, mental health difficulties, and antisocial, delinquent, or criminal behavior. Of special interest here is the role of mediational processes that lead to negative child and adult outcomes.

Of particular relevance to the current chapter, Gershoff (2002) showed that parental corporal punishment sometimes initiates coercive cycles of parent and child behavior. As noted earlier, the key mechanism in the development of antisocial behavior patterns is coercion (Patterson, 2002), which involves the contin-

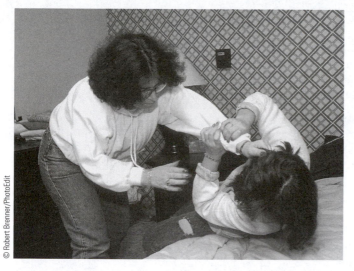

Corporal punishment and coercion correlates with higher rates of antisocial behavior in children. In childhood, these behaviors may include fighting, bullying, and noncompliance; in adolescence, the antisocial behaviors can escalate into criminal acts like assault.

gent use of aversive behaviors in a given social interaction. Coercive behavior, by definition, involves the process of negative reinforcement. Recall that negative reinforcement is defined by any behavior that allows for the avoidance, escape, or reduction of an aversive stimulus. In a given coercive social interaction, family members use aversive behaviors to exert short-term control over others within ongoing dyadic interactions (Patterson, 2002).

The above-mentioned, short-term control on the part of the child frequently results in the removal of task demands (i.e., escape for the child). For the parent, this situation involves termination of the child's aversive behavior, which reinforces the act of "giving in" (i.e., removing the task demands). Thus, the behavior of both parent and child is strongly reinforced by this type of situation.

Patterson and his associates have studied the ecology and dynamics of family interactions of antisocial children and youths more thoroughly than any group to date (see Reid et al., 2002). They find that many antisocial children progress from trivial to severe antisocial acts over time. Often, this process develops from a situation in which unskilled parents must care for an infant with a difficult temperament. Tense infant–caregiver interactions and negative relationships emerge and are damaged by the parents' limited ability to influence the child. Patterson (1982) conducted a sequential analysis showing that parental use of coercive procedures, which included corporal punishment intended to suppress hostile/aggressive behavior, actually increased their likelihood of occurrence by 50%. In a subsequent study, Patterson and his colleagues (1992) found that parental corporal punishment predicted children's antisocial behavior two years later.

As children develop their antisocial behavior patterns from preschool to mid-elementary school, their behavior changes in form and increases in intensity. For example, during the preschool years, these children often display aversive behaviors such as whining, noncompliance, and defiance. Later, during the elementary school years, these behaviors take the form of less frequent but higher-intensity acts such as hitting, fighting, bullying, and stealing. Finally, during adolescence, bullying and hitting may evolve into robbery, assault, lying, stealing, fraud, and burglary (Snyder & Stoolmiller, 2002).

What is clear in this progression is that, although the specific form of the behavior changes (e.g., from whining and noncompliance to hitting and bullying), its function remains the same. That is, coercive, negatively reinforced behavior remains at the heart of the development of antisocial behavior patterns. As children grow older, they gradually learn to escalate their aversive behavior in order to cause removal of parental task demands. This ability bestows enormous social control and power upon them. In short, they learn that, the more noxious and painful they can make their behavior to others, the more likely they are to accomplish their goals. Snyder and Stoolmiller (2002) eloquently describe this process:

> Coercion and escalation are bilateral processes. All members in families with aggressive antisocial children contribute to and reside in highly disputatious, hostile environments in which pain and coercion are primary strategies of social influence and control. Coercion is an insidious form of social influence. Because it is so powerful, its continued use often results in its transformation into a sharper and more caustic tool. Although powerful and effective in controlling other's behavior in the short run, it is self and relationship destructive in the long run. (p. 74)

The Matching Law and Coercive Behavior

One of the most conceptually powerful learning principles used to explain behavior is known formally as the Matching Law (Herrnstein, 1974). In his original formulation, Herrnstein (1961) stated that the rate of any given behavior matches the rate of reinforcement for that behavior. In other words, response rate matches reinforcement rate. Matching is studied in what are known as concurrent schedules of reinforcement. A concurrent schedule refers to the availability of reinforcement for two or more different behaviors related to two simultaneous, but different, available schedules of reinforcement (i.e., concurrently). For example, if aggressive behavior is reinforced every 3 times it occurs and prosocial behavior is reinforced every 15 times it occurs, then the Matching Law would predict that, on average, aggressive behavior will be chosen 5 times more frequently than prosocial behavior. Research has consistently shown that behavior under concurrent schedules of reinforcement closely follows or tracks the Matching Law (Nevin, 1988; Snyder, 2002).

With respect to antisocial behavior patterns, the Matching Law involves a choice between coercive behaviors maintained by negative reinforcement (e.g., threatening, hitting, bullying) and prosocial behaviors maintained by positive reinforcement (e.g., asking questions, negotiating conflicts, solving problems). Thus, the probability that a child will engage in either of these response patterns is directly dependent on the relative rate of reinforcement for each. Snyder and Stoolmiller (2002) suggest that the utility of a given behavior can be calculated by counting how often the behavior results in conflict termination divided by the frequency with which it occurs in conflict sequences. For instance, if defiant and aggressive behavior results in conflict termination 8 out of 10 times, then defiance/aggression has a utility index of 80%.

Prosocial behaviors for children with antisocial behavior patterns are relatively ineffective in terminating conflictive social interaction sequences. This means that teachers and parents dealing with such behavior have the odds stacked against them in trying to divert children from this well-established and highly effective pattern of coercion. The following sections describe how teachers and other social agents might deal with antisocial behavior patterns based on principles of reinforcement, precorrection, and matching.

Deviancy Training in Peer Relationships

Research has clearly shown that negative reinforcement (via coercive social interactions) is responsible for the acquisition of antisocial behavior. However, as children grow older, positive reinforcement appears to be the sole key mechanism for the maintenance and further refinement of antisocial behavior patterns (Snyder, 2002). Antisocial children tend to select peers as affiliates and friends who are primarily coercive and antisocial in both their verbal behavior and their actions. That is, they gravitate to "colleagues" or "associates" who reinforce their antisocial behavior. In their ongoing social interactions within these deviant peer affiliations, antisocial children model and positively reinforce each other's verbal reports of past antisocial behavior, as well as their future intentions to engage in antisocial behavior (Snyder, 2002).

For many young children, making the transition from home to school is often fraught with difficulty. Upon school entry, they must learn to share, negotiate disagreements, deal with conflicts, and participate in activities often involving competition. And they must do so in a manner that results in positive peer relationships, friendships, and social acceptance from peers (Coie, Dodge, & Kupersmidt, 1990; Snyder, 2002). Children with antisocial behavior patterns have enormous difficulty in accomplishing these social tasks. In fact, these children are more than twice as likely to initiate unprovoked verbal or physical aggression toward peers, to reciprocate peer aggression, and to continue aggressive behavior once it has been initiated (Snyder, 2002).

This unfortunate behavior pattern soon leads to peer rejection, which has a number of serious long-term negative outcomes. For instance, Kupersmidt (1983) found that the rate of delinquency and school dropout among rejected children was twice that of nonrejected peers. Other studies have shown peer rejection to be predictive of adult mental health difficulties, marital difficulties, and incarceration (Coie et al., 1990; Parker & Asher, 1987). Peer rejection therefore fuels the journey of antisocial children toward deviant peer affiliations and away from affiliation with normal peers. Once these deviant peer relationships coalesce into membership in a deviant peer group, the probability of a felony arrest within two years is .70 (Patterson et al., 1992).

Noncompliance in the Classroom

Like parents and peers, teachers frequently are inadvertently trapped in escalating social interactions with antisocial students that prove to be extremely disruptive and damaging to interpersonal relationships. Antisocial students are often highly agitated and bring to school a learning history based on noncompliance with parental instructions and commands (Walker, Colvin, & Ramsey, 1995). This pattern of oppositional behavior sustains a coercive behavioral process that can

Noncompliant behavior includes direct defiance, simple refusal, passive noncompliance, and negotiation. In passive noncompliance, a child refuses to comply by simply ignoring the adult's request.

be triggered by seemingly neutral events such as asking questions, making requests, or giving directions (Colvin & Sugai, 1989).

Noncompliance is an important first indicator of maladaptive behavior patterns such as aggression, antisocial behavior, chronic disobedience, oppositional behavior, social maladjustment, and conduct disorder (Patterson, 1982; Schoen, 1983). Patterson and his colleagues have shown that noncompliance within deviant family contexts often serves as the first behavioral response in a gradually escalating chain of ever more serious forms of challenging behavior (e.g., opposition/defiance, vandalism, stealing, and delinquency) (Patterson et al., 1992). Thus, noncompliance can function as a critical "gate key" behavior that not only triggers escalation within dyadic interactions involving parents, peers, and teachers but also serves as a port of entry into much more serious forms of antisocial behavior. By treating noncompliance effectively, it may be possible to prevent the development of these more destructive behaviors.

Noncompliance can be defined as a situation in which an adult (parent or teacher) issues a specific command or request to direct a child's behavior toward some end and the child actively or passively refuses to comply with the directive (Walker & Walker, 1991). The most common operational definition of noncompliance refers to a failure to comply with a specific directive and is noted if (1) no response is forthcoming, (2) no response is produced or initiated within a specified time (e.g., 5–10 seconds), or (3) some alternative, nonrequested behavior is performed instead (Schoen, 1983, 1986). Noncompliance can also refer to a failure to perform up to a prespecified performance standard when the child is fully capable of doing so (Morgan & Jenson, 1988).

Prompt compliance with teacher directives is a highly valued student attribute in the context of teaching, and resistance to them has long been a major teacher irritant. In a national survey of over 1,100 regular classroom K–12 teachers regarding forms of student behavior seen as most and least important to successful classroom adjustment, Hersh and Walker (1983) found that compliance with teacher commands was *the* most highly rated or preferred form of student behavior out of 56 behavioral descriptions listed. Walker and Sylwester (1998) note that noncompliance can also disrupt peer relationships and lead to social rejection.

In an important study on teachers' use of noncompliance strategies in teaching and managing their classrooms, Golly (1994) directly observed refusal responses of first- and second-graders to teacher directives. Forty elementary teachers, evenly divided between grades 1 and 2, participated in the study. Results of this study are summarized in Box 5.1.

Types of Noncompliance

Four types of noncompliance that commonly occur in parent–child and teacher–student social interactions have been identified: (1) passive noncompliance, (2) simple refusal, (3) direct defiance, and (4) negotiation (Kuczynski,

Kochanska, Radke-Yarrow, & Girnius-Brown, 1987). In passive noncompliance, the child chooses not to perform the requested behavior or task but doesn't *overtly* refuse to do so. In this type of noncompliance, the command or directive is simply ignored rather than acknowledged; however, the refusal is usually not accompanied by anger, hostility, or defiance.

Simple refusal, in contrast, means that the child acknowledges but does not comply with a request. Thus, the child may communicate, via words or gestures, that he or she does not intend to comply with an instruction or command (e.g., "No, I can't" or "Uh-huh"). In this type of noncompliance, refusal is usually communicated without anger or other negative emotion. However, if the person giving the command persists and attempts to force the issue, the child's subsequent noncompliance may be accompanied by anger and hostility.

Direct defiance refers to noncompliance accompanied by hostility, anger, negative affect, overt resistance, and even attempts at actual intimidation toward the person making the request. Defiance of this type, particularly within parent–child and teacher–student relationships, frequently is the end result of a series of progressively more emotional exchanges between the person giving the command and its recipient (Colvin, 1988; Patterson, 1982; Patterson & Bank, 1986). In this situation, the adult gives the command, often in an emotionally charged atmosphere in which the child may be in an agitated state, and the adult may also be angry or irritated. Under these conditions, the command is inevitably met with refusal, which may be accompanied by anger and hostility from the child. The adult then repeats the command in a more coercive and forceful manner, and the child again refuses, matching and even exceeding the adult's intensity and anger (i.e., the child ups the proverbial ante). As this process continues, it quickly escalates into direct defiance. Rarely are there satisfactory outcomes to these kinds of exchanges for either the adult or the child. At the very least, these coercive interactions damage adult–child relationships and set the stage for future episodes of this type.

A useful way of conceptualizing these escalating behavior patterns is in terms of a behavior chain. In a behavior chain, one response leads to another, which, in turn, leads to another response, and so on until the individual reaches the end of the chain. A behavior chain is simply a sequence of behavioral responses in which each response serves as a signal for the next one in the chain. And behavior chains are much easier to "break" or stop earlier rather than later in the behavioral sequence. In dealing with direct defiance, parents and teachers often make the cardinal mistake of issuing escalating prompts in an attempt to force the child to comply, which results in a lose-lose situation for both adult and child. Examples of escalating prompts are "You *will* do what I say!" and "I *insist* that you take out your books and finish your work now!" With antisocial children, such prompts are a veritable death knell for managing successfully an escalating pattern of highly agitated, noncompliant behavior (Colvin & Sugai, 1989).

Negotiation involves an attempt by the child to deflect the adult's commands essentially by reframing the nature or conditions of the directive. This is a common occurrence within parent–child interactions and is certainly not uncommon in the classroom. In this process, the child attempts to bargain with the giver of the command, proposes alternative solutions, attempts to redefine it, tries to compromise, and offers explanations and excuses. In short, the child continually makes counteroffers to the command, not unlike in legal or labor negotiations. Examples of negotiation attempts include these:

"Why do I have to do this now? I'd planned to do it later."

"Why can't I substitute extra-credit work in place of this assignment?"

"I can't do this in the time you have given me; it's too hard!"

"I can't concentrate on my work as long as Jan is tapping her pencil."

The use of negotiation is considered to be a rather sophisticated skill in a developmental sense. However, it can also be a trap for parents and teachers in that it provides a means for the child or student essentially to change the nature of the request, delay it, or escape it entirely.

In a study of command–compliance processes among parents and their preschool children, Kuczynski and his colleagues (1987) found that children's noncompliant responses represented attempts to influence parents to drop or modify their demands. These authors found that passive noncompliance and direct defiance decreased with age, whereas simple refusal and negotiation increased. These latter two forms of noncompliance are considered to be more sophisticated and competent forms of refusal. Very often, immature, antisocial children use passive noncompliance and direct defiance as strategies for coping with authority figures and for resisting their influence—and some are quite skilled in this regard.

As we have seen, young children are often inadvertently taught antisocial behavior patterns through the process of coercive social interactions with their parents, in which these maladaptive behaviors become negatively reinforced (Patterson, 2002). Teachers are then subsequently locked into dealing with highly noncompliant and difficult-to-manage children. Thus, attempts to change noncompliance at school should be accompanied, whenever possible, by attempts to get parents to alter their social interactions with their children at home.

School Approaches to Managing Problem Behavior

Schools are under intense pressures from the public to ensure that all students make adequate progress in their academic achievement. Although politically popular, these accountability pressures are somewhat unfair to educators for several reasons. First, schools can only do so much to educate children who come to school unprepared to learn because of abusive, coercive, and stressful home conditions. Second, schools are being asked to solve complex problems that children bring with them to the schooling experience (Walker, 1995). This section describes some typical approaches used by schools to cope with behaviorally challenging students.

Blaming

How do schools typically remediate or accommodate the problem behaviors of antisocial students? Usually, the first response has been to blame someone else (e.g., parents) for the child's maladaptive behavior. School personnel traditionally have tended to blame parents exclusively for their children's disruptive or aggressive behavior in school. This implies that family pathology and poor parenting are the exclusive causes of the child's problem behaviors. For students with antisocial behavior patterns, this view is not entirely incorrect. Recall that we described coercive family processes and negative reinforcement as the primary mechanisms through which antisocial children learn maladaptive behaviors at home, which then generalize to other settings (Patterson, 2002). However, it would be incorrect to assume that these factors account for *all* of children's behavior problems at school. Historically, schools have often referred parents to mental health clinics because of their children's behavior problems in school, the implication being that it is parents' exclusive responsibility to ensure that their children's problematic behavior is reduced to tolerable limits at school (Walker, 1995).

Parents are not always receptive to this point of view regarding their children's behavioral difficulties. Instead, they frequently blame the schools for being unable to control their children's school behavior. Students become sensitized to these parental views, which, if internalized, are likely to create negative attitudes toward teachers and schooling (Walker, 1995). Moreover, when teacher–student conflicts occur that spill over into the family–school relationship, the involved teacher often feels unsupported by school administrators, who must accommodate the interests of all parties to the dispute.

Assigning blame to the school or to parents for children's maladaptive behavior is a lose-lose situation. Parents are often not convinced of the school's point of view, and vice versa. For instance, mental health agency records indicate that the highest frequency of self-cancellations of family therapy sessions involve families who are referred by school systems because of their children's behavior problems at school. Clearly, these types of exchanges between parents and schools concerning problematic school behavior have not resulted in adaptive, positive responses, nor have they advanced the quality of family–school relationships.

Medication

The use of psychoactive drugs for problem behaviors at school is another popular school response to children's maladaptive behavior. This is particularly true for children who exhibit behaviors characterized by overactivity, impulsivity, and inattention, which are the main symptoms of attention deficit/hyperactivity disorder (ADHD) (American Psychiatric Association, 1994). Recall that in Chapter 3 we noted that behaviors characteristic of ADHD and antisocial behavior (conduct problems) often co-occur. Drug therapies such as Ritalin (methylphenidate) substantially reduce the overall rate of impulsive and disruptive behavior by lowering activity levels and increasing compliance with teacher or parental directives (Barkley, 1998; Jenson & Cooper, 2002).

Because drug therapy of this type typically makes children's behavior more compliant and thus easier to manage, it is not surprising that children experiencing behavior problems at school are often referred by schools, individual teachers, and/or parents to physicians for possible placement on drug therapy programs. In fact, some school districts are known to have placed intense pressures on parents to allow their children to participate in drug therapy programs in order to make their behavior more compliant and acceptable at school.

The goal of drug therapy with children is not to "cure" a given child's behavior problem(s) and/or disorder(s). Drug therapy does not produce enduring changes in a child's behavior, nor does it have an impact on a child's personality. Studies have shown that children's behavior quickly reverts to predrug levels of intensity and frequency when drug therapy programs are terminated (DuPaul & Stoner, 1994). Drug therapy may suppress the more undesirable features of a child's behavior, but it does not teach the child more adaptive strategies for achieving behavioral self-control and/or self-management. In addition, there is little convincing evidence that drug therapy has any substantial lasting effects on learning and academic achievement (Barkley, 1998; DuPaul & Stoner, 1994; Walker, 1995).

Recently, the largest controlled, clinical trial ever conducted on the treatment of ADHD was completed by the National Institute of Mental Health and the U.S. Office of Special Education Programs. Known as the MTA Study, this investigation sought to determine the long-term effects of medication management and behavior modification on ADHD symptoms (MTA Cooperative Group, 1999). Conducted at six sites across the United States and Canada over a 14-month period, the MTA Study compared the following four treatments for ADHD: (1) medication management (primarily Ritalin), (2) behavior modification (parent training, summer treatment program, paraprofessionals in general education classrooms), (3) combined medication management and behavior modification, and (4) usual community care (the control group). The MTA Study showed that the combined medication and behavior modification treatment and the medication management treatment were each more effective in reducing ADHD symptoms than either the behavior modification or the community care treatments. The combined and the medication management treatments did not differ significantly in reducing ADHD symptoms.

Specifically, the behavior modification treatment produced a reduction in ADHD symptoms for 34% of the children, the medication management treatment produced a 56% reduction, and the combined treatment produced a 68% reduction. Thus, by adding a behavior modification component to a medication management treatment, outcomes can be improved for an additional 12% of the children (from 56% to 68%). It should be noted that the outcomes of the MTA Study were observed 14 months after treatment. All treated children were also monitored at 24 and 36 months and will be tracked into early adulthood.

Counseling and Psychotherapy

Counseling and psychotherapy are among the most popular interventions for coping with acting-out, disruptive behavior patterns in classrooms. Surveys of teachers often indicate that counseling is the most preferred intervention for serious classroom problems (Walker, 1995). The appeal of counseling is understandable because it is expected that, through the counseling process, children will change by gaining insight into the reasons underlying their maladaptive behavior. With counseling, teachers do not have to assume responsibility for or play a role in the behavior change process.

Regrettably, counseling is among the *least effective* options available to us if the goal is to produce reliable, meaningful changes in student behavior. This is especially true for antisocial children and youths. The focus of counseling for antisocial children is generally on (1) helping them identify and understand the reasons for their disruptive, aggressive behavior and (2) helping them change their behavior accordingly. Usually, antisocial children are well aware of the appropriateness or inappropriateness of their behavior patterns and often are sensitive to the effects it has on others. Unfortunately, there is no empirical evidence to suggest that their awareness of the likely causes of their behavior has *any* effect on improving actual classroom behavior (Dryfoos, 1990). In short, to change the way antisocial children talk about and perceive the reasons for their misbehavior, counseling is a preferred intervention. However, to change actual misbehavior of these children, adopting evidence-based behavior change strategies is necessary (Elliott, Witt, Kratochwill, & Stoiber, 2002; Walker et al., 1995; Walker & Shinn, 2002).

Ineffective Teacher Attempts to Deal with Antisocial Behavior

Teachers typically try a number of management techniques in an attempt to control the behavior of antisocial students. Most of these techniques, unfortunately, are of limited effectiveness, and some may even strengthen the behaviors of concern. Examples of teacher strategies that can strengthen problem behaviors include reprimanding, arguing, escalating hostile interactions, and attempting to force compliance. These approaches are fruitless in dealing with students' antisocial behavior patterns because, as we have emphasized throughout this book, these children come to school well versed in the "science" of coercion, having had extensive practice in the family setting. In this context, the teacher is the amateur and the child is the professional. Thus, any attempts by the teacher to coerce or otherwise force compliance are likely to be met with escalation and more intense coercive behavior on the part of the student. This section describes several ineffective strategies used by teachers in general to deal with the noncompliant, acting-out behaviors of antisocial students.

Social Attention

Generally, teachers are very much alike in their approaches to managing antisocial behavior. Most often, they respond in ways designed to persuade or encourage the acting-out child to cease disruptive behavior and act more appropriately. Both positive social attention from peers and negative social attention from teachers function to strengthen the inappropriate behavior—thus making it much more likely in the future. Ironically, the teacher's direct efforts to stop the student from engaging in acting-out behavior is the very thing that strengthens and maintains it.

Teachers typically respond rapidly to the acting-out student's inappropriate behavior because it disrupts the classroom ecology and is highly aversive. In these cases, the student's problem behaviors might be considered "teacher-owned" in that the teacher has the responsibility for doing something about them. Teachers' efforts to manage problem behaviors are almost always directed toward making the student stop the inappropriate behavior as soon as possible. But their success in accomplishing this goal is highly variable (see Walker, 1995).

The antisocial student learns that it is much easier and more efficient to obtain peer and teacher social attention by engaging in disruptive, noncompliant behavior than by completing work, following classroom rules, and/or developing positive social relationships with peers. The antisocial student acquires a repertoire of behaviors and adopts a tactical strategy that force teachers and peers to respond to these highly aversive behaviors, often in a negative way (especially from teachers). Even though social attention from teachers is often negative, critical, and disapproving, it still functions to maintain the problem behavior. (See the discussion in Chapter 3 of functional behavioral assessment.) Many acting-out students appear to thrive on the hostile confrontations they have with teachers; their ability to confront, irritate, and otherwise make life miserable for teachers is rewarding.

Ignoring

Sometimes, teachers attempt to control the acting-out, disruptive behaviors of students by simply ignoring them. This strategy is based on the notion that the inappropriate behavior is maintained exclusively by teacher attention. However, this is often an ineffective intervention for at least three reasons. First, peer social attention (positive or negative) provides a huge amount of reinforcement for the student's continuation of acting-out behavior. As such, withholding teacher social attention for inappropriate student behavior that is maintained primarily by peer social attention will do nothing to change behavior.

Second, teachers find it extremely difficult, if not impossible, to ignore seriously disruptive behavior for any length of time because these students have learned to escalate their demands for attention in the face of teachers' limited ability to respond. The escalation of aversive behavior in these situations can be explained by the phenomenon of extinction burst. An "extinction burst" refers to a temporary increase in the frequency of some behavior after the removal of reinforcement for that behavior. Theoretically, if reinforcement is continually withheld, then the behavior will eventually decrease to zero levels, but total extinction can take a very long time and be quite aversive. Unfortunately, teachers eventually will be forced to respond to highly escalating behaviors (i.e., bursting) and thereby provide intermittent reinforcement for them—the end result of which is to further strengthen and maintain them.

Third, in some cases, the student's behavior is maintained by negative reinforcement in that it allows her or him to escape or avoid academic task demands in the classroom. If the student's escalation is serving this function (escape or avoidance), then simply ignoring the problem behavior will be ineffective in changing it.

Escalating Prompts

One of the most common mistakes teachers make in trying to control the inappropriate behavior of antisocial students is the use of escalating prompts that take the form of negative reprimands, disapproval, and/or criticism. Examples include statements such as "You will do what I say," "You won't talk to me that way," and "I told you to begin work now!" Sometimes, these techniques will result in a temporary reduction in inappropriate behavior; other times, they will produce no noticeable effect on behavior.

Studies of classroom interactions between teachers and disruptive children have shown that (1) such interactions are more likely to be negative than positive, (2) the teacher is more likely to reprimand inappropriate behavior than to praise appropriate behavior during these interactions, and (3) disruptive children tend to monopolize the teacher's time (Mayer & Sulzer-Azaroff, 2002; Sprick, Borgmeier, & Nolet, 2002; Walker et al., 1995). Such interactions reflect the experiences of most teachers in dealing with the highly aversive, inappropriate behaviors of antisocial children.

Teachers also differ in their interactions with disruptive and nondisruptive children. For example, the teacher who provides consequences (e.g., reprimands or terminating commands) for the inappropriate behavior of nondisruptive children tends to stop the behavioral infraction in question on the first or second occurrence. In contrast, disruptive children sometimes will not terminate their inappropriate behavior until the fourth, fifth, or even sixth attempt by the teacher (Walker, 1995). Consequently, the teacher's management behavior with disruptive children is placed on an intermittent schedule of reinforcement in which the students comply once for every four to five compliance requests. This contingency thus maintains the teacher's use of reprimands at a very high rate (Walker & Buckley, 1973).

Clearly, these teacher–student interaction sequences in the classroom are frustrating for teachers who have to deal with antisocial students. Frequently, the harder the teacher tries to control the student's behavior, the less effective these efforts are. This process can be physically and emotionally draining. To change the student's behavior, the teacher must apply proven and intense intervention procedures.

The application of these procedures (described in the next section) may initially require a fairly substantial investment of teacher time. However, as the child's behavior changes from inappropriate to appropriate, less and less teacher time will be required to effectively manage the behavior. If these procedures are implemented with integrity and consistency, teachers will soon notice a discernable positive effect on student behavior.

Proven Strategies for Preventing and Coping with Antisocial Behavior

This section focuses on three topics: (1) general principles for preventing and de-escalating oppositional, noncompliant behaviors, (2) procedures for managing student agitation levels that escalate into teacher–student confrontations, and (3) strategies for the effective use of teacher directives. Each of these topics has important implications for effectively intervening with antisocial students.

General Principles for Prevention and De-Escalation

There are several principles that, if implemented consistently, will lead to a decrease in the frequency and intensity of antisocial behavior patterns across situations and over time. The classroom ecology created by following these general principles will result in a more positive climate and set the tone for more positive teacher–student interactions. Practices derived from these principles (Walker,

1995) will communicate to low-performing and acting-out students that they have value and that the teacher cares about them. These practices or strategies include the following:

1. Establish a positive ecology for the classroom setting that is inclusive and supportive of *all* students, irrespective of their behavioral and academic characteristics.

2. Continually be aware that teachers and other adults can unknowingly form and express negative impressions of low-performing, uncooperative students to which such students are quite sensitive. Teachers should carefully monitor their impressions, keep them as neutral as possible, communicate a positive regard for students, and give students the benefit of the doubt whenever possible.

3. Establish and communicate high expectations in achievement and behavior for *all* students.

4. Create a structured learning environment in which students know what is expected of them and where they can access needed assistance in completing academic tasks.

5. Provide sharp demarcations between academic periods, but hold transition times between periods to a minimum.

6. Consider using cooperative learning strategies that allow diverse groups of students to interact, problem solve, collaborate, and develop skills in working together.

7. Systematically teach social skills that incorporate instruction in anger management and conflict resolution skills.

8. Keep academic programming and task difficulty commensurate with the skill levels of low-performing students. Antisocial students in particular tend to have weak academic skills and may react negatively to academic tasks or demands they perceive as being too difficult for them. These situations will often lead to hostile teacher–student interactions.

9. Teach students how to be appropriately assertive rather than aggressive (e.g., to disagree with or resist the demands of others without being hostile).

10. Use difficult situations as teaching opportunities ("teachable moments") for developing student skills in responding to such situations without being angry, aggressive, or coercive.

11. Find ways to praise and encourage acting-out students at the same or a higher rate than that for appropriately behaving students.

12. Communicate a genuine interest in the progress of acting-out students, and support them as they struggle to meet the complex demands of schooling.

13. Enhance the performance of acting-out students by using individualized instruction, cues, prompts, task analysis of academic tasks, debriefing, coaching, and positive incentives for task completion and accuracy (e.g., praise, free time, home privileges).

14. Avoid criticizing, ridiculing, verbally punishing, or arguing with any student, and especially acting-out students.

Another intervention strategy that has been shown to effectively reduce disruptive behavior in classrooms, and also prevent behavioral escalation, is class-wide curricular modification (Kern, Bambara, & Fogt, 2002; Kern, Mantegna, Vorndran, Bailin, & Hilt, 2001). Curricular modifications such as choice making, in which the student is given a choice of activities (e.g., reading or math), materials, task sequences (e.g., easy to difficult), and response requirements (e.g., responding orally rather than in writing), are quite effective in reducing rates of oppositional, noncompliant, and disruptive behaviors in the classroom (see Kern et al., 1998).

Teachers sometimes create their own difficulties with antisocial students through their attempts to "force" the curriculum on them without considering the possibility that modifying the task or allowing the student to choose between two alternatives may prevent behavioral escalation. Curricular modification can be a powerful, preemptive strategy to prevent the development of more intense and disruptive oppositional behaviors in classrooms.

The principles just discussed represent a *universal* intervention because they are applicable to all students and are designed to prevent many of the problems brought about by students' frustration with difficult task demands. Adherence to these principles will not, however, be sufficient to handle the problems that many antisocial students experience. Most antisocial children bring high levels of agitation and coercion skills to school and carry a perpetual "chip on their shoulders." These students are perceived as touchy and often "train" the social environment to handle them with kid gloves. This posturing behavior pattern allows them to escape or avoid the reasonable demands of parents, teachers, and peers.

Many antisocial students are highly successful with this coercive negative behavior pattern and find it an effective and efficient way of controlling the social environment and its accompanying demands and tasks. These students are likely to engage the teacher in difficult exchanges that often emerge from rather innocuous situations such as the teacher issuing commands, giving assignments, or providing corrective feedback. Knowing how to effectively deal with these exchanges is a critical teacher skill.

The same techniques of confrontation and escalation that antisocial children originally learn at home and then bring to the classroom are also frequently in evidence within the context of peer relations. Figure 5.2 illustrates this escalating, coercive process involving an interaction between an antisocial student and a peer who is accused of backbiting (i.e., saying negative things behind someone's back). The figure shows how the pressurized, attacking style of the antisocial student over this issue is reciprocated by the accused target peer, thus resulting in a rapid escalation of the intensity of the social exchange. In a matter of seconds, this kind of peer-to-peer interaction can spin out of control, resulting in potentially disastrous consequences. Law enforcement officers observe that this is the kind of situation they frequently must deal with in responding to a 911 call; all too often, such situations end in tragedy. This points up the importance of providing social skills training for antisocial students to teach them how to control and regulate their emotional, impulsive behavior. Equally important, peers need similar training in strategies that teach them how not to escalate the

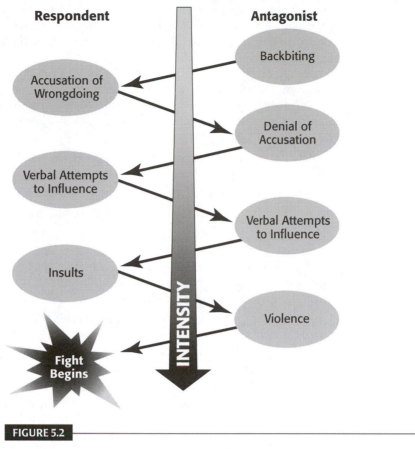

Respondent | **Antagonist**

Backbiting

Accusation of Wrongdoing

Denial of Accusation

Verbal Attempts to Influence

Verbal Attempts to Influence

Insults

Violence

Fight Begins

INTENSITY

FIGURE 5.2 ◆

Cycle of Escalated Interaction Among Peers.

Source: U.S. Office of Juvenile Justice and Delinquency Prevention (OJJDP) (1999).

situation and how to extricate themselves from such potentially dangerous interactions as early as possible in the chain of events.

We provide an illustration in the next section of principles and procedures for managing the student agitation that often lead to hostile teacher–student interactions. This information provides extremely valuable ammunition to teachers in avoiding, escaping from, and terminating escalated teacher–student interactions that often damage teacher–student relationships and threaten the teacher's ability to control the classroom.

Management of Student Agitation Levels

Antisocial students can be characterized as being grand masters of behavioral escalation. That is, when teachers issue a directive or command with which these students do not want to comply, they escalate their levels of noncompliance to ever-higher intensity levels until the command or directive is withdrawn. This is the behavioral escalation game, and it is a game teachers cannot win and should not play (Colvin & Sugai, 1989; Walker, 1995). The trick for teachers is to avoid getting caught up in these escalations and to get out of them as soon as they realize they are engaged in one. The following example of the behavior escalation game characterizes this process.

A teacher, Ms. Smith, instructs her class to take out their reading books and begin writing definitions of key words for the story on pages 25–33. The class begins organizing for the assignment—except Mike, who sits sulking at his desk. Ms. Smith approaches Mike, and the following exchange occurs:

MS. SMITH: Mike, I told the class to get ready for the assignment, but you aren't. Is there something the matter? [*Mike ignores Ms. Smith's question and avoids eye contact with her.*]

MS. JONES: Mike, I asked you a question, Now *what's* the problem here?

MIKE: There ain't no problem here, except you! I don't want to do this dumb work. Leave me alone.

MS. SMITH [*now angry*]: If you're going to be in my class, you will have to do your work like everyone else. Also, when I speak to you, I expect an answer. I don't like your attitude, and I will not tolerate it in my classroom. You better watch yourself or you'll be in the office.

[*This is not the first exchange of this type between Mike and Ms. Smith. Both carry residual anger from these prior episodes.*]

MIKE [laughs sarcastically]: Get off my case! I don't give a damn about you or this stupid class. Go ahead and write me up! [*Ms. Smith tells Mike to leave the room and report to the vice-principal. Mike goes ballistic, calls the teacher an obscene name, and pounds the wall as he strides out of the room. He continues to curse loudly as he leaves the classroom. Ms. Smith writes up the incident as insubordination and submits her report to the school office.*]

This aversive, escalating behavioral process between teacher and student occurs in thousands of classrooms daily, disrupting the classroom ecology and damaging teacher–student relationships. Teachers who respond "normally" to such situations (i.e., engage in escalation of the aversive interaction with the student) usually end up on the losing side of the confrontation. Walker (1995) notes that the behavioral process involved in this game progresses as follows:

1. The student is sitting in class in a highly agitated state, which may or may not be noticeably visible.

2. The teacher assigns a task or gives a direction, either individually or to a group of which the student is a member.

3. The student refuses to engage in the requested task.

4. The teacher confronts the student about his or her refusal.

5. The student questions, argues with, and/or defies the teacher.

6. The teacher reprimands the student and demands compliance.

7. The student explodes and confronts the teacher, and the situation escalates out of control.

This scenario is played out in front of 25–30 very interested observers (i.e., classmates) in the classroom. If the student "wins" the escalation game and forces the teacher to concede, then the teacher's ability to manage the classroom may be severely damaged. Other students may lose respect for the teacher and resent the fact that a single student, rather than the teacher, can essentially control the classroom. In contrast, if the teacher "wins" and is successful in establishing his or her authority over the student, this victory is likely to be short-lived and prove to be costly in the long run. The student may feel humiliated in front of his or her peers and will likely harbor feelings of long-term resentment toward the teacher. Typically, these students find ways to "get even" with the teacher. Thus, the teacher may "win the battle" but end up "losing the war."

What should teachers do instead of playing the behavioral escalation game with students? The key is to get out of these escalating interactions as quickly as possible. Of course, it is not always clear that students are in the agitated state that serves as a precursor to behavioral escalations, and teachers can involve themselves in the early stages of behavioral escalation before they realize what is happening. Strategies for dealing with this situation include avoidance and escape.

Avoidance Strategy. An important concept in dealing with escalating behavior cycles is to "pick one's battles" and to know when to leave students alone. If a student does not immediately engage an assignment, it is often best to wait and give him or her some leeway (i.e., the benefit of the doubt). Acting-out students quite often engage in delaying tactics as a way of (1) provoking parents and teachers, (2) engaging them in negative interactions, and (3) asserting their control and independence in certain situations.

The teacher who forces compliance to an instruction or command within a rigid, prescribed time frame will find that this strategy seldom produces a positive result with antisocial students. Waiting a reasonable time while not attending to students' passive noncompliance can be a reasonable alternative to direct confrontation. Many times, the students will engage in the assigned task if left alone and given sufficient time. It is vital, however, that the teacher not reinforce students' delaying tactics by either negative attention or signs of irritation and disapproval. Both of these types of teacher behavior will strengthen rather than weaken the student behaviors that produced them (i.e., students often are reinforced by "getting a rise" out of the teacher).

If it is obvious that the student is not going to engage in the assigned task and seeks to wait the teacher out, the teacher will have to address the situation. What the teacher obviously does not want to communicate is that the student does not have to play by the same rules as the rest of the class. In these cases, the teacher should approach the student quietly and inquire as to why he or she is not engaging in the assigned task. The teacher should speak in a low voice, remain calm, and try to keep the situation as private as possible. If the student begins to escalate by arguing or questioning, the teacher should *immediately* disengage and say something like the following: "If you need some time to yourself, go ahead and take it. You can sit quietly as long as you do not bother other students. Let me know if you need some help with the assignment or have questions."

At this point, the teacher should leave the student alone and allow him or her to deal with the situation without further assistance. In this way, it becomes the student's responsibility to cope with the situation. But the teacher should also make it abundantly clear that the student must complete the assigned task (either now or later) and that lost time will have to be made up. Neither the student nor his or her classmates should be left with the impression that delaying tactics will allow avoidance, escape, or reduction of assigned work. Walker (1995) suggests that teachers using this strategy communicate the following to the student:

◆ The student will not be able to control the situation by arguing with the teacher or asking questions. As long as the teacher is willing to answer the student's questions or to argue, the student, and not the teacher, is in control of the situation. This is a trap that must be avoided *at all costs*. In most cases, it leads to a worsening situation between the teacher and student.

◆ When the student is ready to work, the teacher will be there to provide any assistance and support required.

◆ The student will not be able to avoid, escape, or reduce the assigned work by showing signs of agitation, by sulking, or by using delaying tactics.

◆ The student will not be able to provoke or anger the teacher by using either verbal or physical means (e.g., being unresponsive, sulking, arguing).

Escape Strategy.   Inadvertently, teachers often find themselves in an escalating situation simply by answering questions, providing assistance, or clarifying instructions. As soon as teachers realize this, they should terminate (escape) the interaction and disengage with the student. A typical example is as follows:

TEACHER: Mike, you had a question about the assignment?

MIKE: I don't have a clue what you want me to do. [*The teacher repeats the directions given to the class for the assignment.*]

TEACHER: Does that help? Do you understand what I want you to do now?

MIKE: I guess, but I'm not going to do it because it's too hard for me. You know I hate math!

TEACHER: Mike, I have explained the assignment to you. You know what you have to do, and your job is to do it. If you want help, I'll give it to you. You have 15 minutes left to complete the assignment. [*The teacher disengages and walks away from Mike's desk. Mike sulks for a while and then gradually becomes more and more agitated. He raises his hand and the teacher approaches the desk.*]

TEACHER: Yes, Mike? [*Mike begins to hassle the teacher about the assignment and how his parents think it is unreasonable. The teacher says nothing to Mike in response and simply walks away. Mike goes ballistic, throws his math book across the room, and curses the teacher. The teacher sends Mike to the front office on a discipline referral.*]

Arguing or reasoning with Mike in his current emotional state would have gained nothing. In fact, it would have made the situation worse. Yet, many teachers fall into the trap of escalating negative social interactions in an attempt to establish control of their classrooms. It is likely that Mike would have become extremely aggressive with the teacher had she issued escalating prompts and attempted to force Mike to comply. In this sense, the situation resembles an earthquake in that it (1) comes out of nowhere, (2) does extensive damage in a matter of seconds, and (3) requires a long period of time for recovery. Indeed, these escalated behavioral events are often called "behavioral earthquakes," and they literally spiral out of control in a matter of seconds.

It is important to always keep in mind the issue of teacher safety. It is never a good idea to allow coercive teacher–student interactions to escalate out of control, particularly for older, more mature students, who are physically stronger than many teachers. Juvenile courts frequently place adjudicated youths in schools without informing teachers and administrators of their backgrounds. These students often have histories of assault and have committed other serious crimes. As such, escalating social interactions with these students often carry considerable risks to teachers and peers.

General Rules to Avoid Engagement in Escalated Interactions

Walker and Walker (1991) provide three general rules for teachers to avoid becoming engaged in these escalated interactions: These rules are as follows:

1. Do not make demands on or otherwise initiate contact with a student when he or she appears to be agitated.

2. Do not allow yourself to become "engaged" through a series of questions and answers initiated by the student.

3. Do not attempt to force the student's hand.

First, the teacher should wait until the student's agitated mood changes or passes before initiating an interaction that involves a direct request, command, or demand. When a student is agitated, a teacher's directive is likely to be perceived as an aversive, provocative event, especially when delivered in the presence of other students. In certain situations, the teacher can inquire about the student's problem but should not pair the inquiry with a command at that time if at all possible.

With regard to the second rule, the teacher should not respond to the student's questions or comments about the situation and, especially, should not argue with the student. If the student asks a question, the teacher should ignore it and/or simply restate what the student needs to do (i.e., repeat the command or instruction). The teacher should indicate that the question will be answered after the student does as instructed. If the student refuses, the teacher should leave him or her alone until the agitated state passes.

With regard to the third rule, if the student chooses not to comply or cooperate, the teacher should not try to coerce him or her through such tactics as hovering and waiting, using social punishment (e.g., glares, verbal reprimands, or social intimidation), or threatening future sanctions. The teacher should *never* touch, grab, or shake a student in any way, in this or other situations. If the situation calls a brief time-out, the loss of privileges or points, or some other consequence as part of the classroom rules/behavior management plan, the consequence should be applied promptly, with a minimum of verbalization. If the situation does not call for such action, the teacher should leave the student's presence and terminate the interaction.

Angry, escalating behavioral episodes are precipitated through the use of teacher directives such as requests, commands, or demands. Antisocial children tend to perceive adult directives as provocations rather than reasonable requests and are masterful at resisting them. Students' learning histories and behavioral inclinations have a great deal to do with how they react to teacher directives. Note, however, that the nature and timing of teacher commands and the context in which they are delivered have as much to do with student compliance as anything that occurs after a command has been issued. The following section reviews some critical issues related to teacher directives and provides guidelines for the delivery and use of this important technique for teaching and managing groups of students in the classroom and other settings.

Effective Delivery and Use of Teacher Directives and Commands

As described earlier in this chapter, noncompliance can assume different forms ranging from simple refusal to direct defiance of teacher directives or instructions. Often, student noncompliance is a direct function of the manner in which teachers issue these directives or instructions. Professionals have classified two main types of adult commands or directives given to children: (1) alpha commands and (2) beta commands (Forehand & McMahon, 1981; Williams & Forehand, 1984). Alpha commands involve clear, direct, and specific directives or instructions to students without additional verbalizations, and they allow for a reasonable period of time for a response. In contrast, beta commands are vague and/or multiple directives that are simultaneously given and that do not provide either a clear criterion for compliance or sufficient opportunity to comply. Beta commands are also accompanied by excess verbalizations from the person issuing the command. As such, the student receiving the beta command has no opportunity to demonstrate compliance and is often confused.

The use of alpha as opposed to beta commands has a long history in the military. Training in military leadership strongly emphasizes the use of clear, specific, and forceful commands to prevent misunderstanding and to increase compliance. Consider the first 10 minutes of the Academy Award–winning picture *Saving Private Ryan*. An analysis of the commands (orders) given by the Tom Hanks character (the sergeant in this sequence) reveals absolutely no beta commands in any form. Clearly, beta commands in this situation would lead to even more carnage and death than was experienced by the troops storming the beaches of Normandy.

The following are some examples of alpha commands:

"Matt, I want you to pick up your room as soon as you finish dinner."

"Luke, tell me what time you have to be at baseball practice today."

"Merilee, go see the vice-principal right now about yesterday's absence."

The following are some examples of beta commands:

"Matt, your room is always such a mess! Why don't you clean it up instead of waiting for me to do it for you? I get so tired of always picking up after you!"

"Lisa, stop talking to Laura unless you are discussing today's assignment. Besides, you are only supposed to be talking if you've finished all your work!"

"Mike, it's time for you to get to work. So get to it, and don't let me catch you loafing again or you'll have to stay in for recess!"

Alpha commands are more precise and specific than beta commands (i.e., simple, direct, and to the point). Most importantly, they provide both an opportunity and sufficient time for the student to demonstrate compliance (Walker & Walker, 1991). Alpha commands are associated with higher levels of compliance in both preschool and K–12. In contrast, beta commands are associated with lower rates of compliance and should be avoided whenever possible.

Sometimes, subtle distinctions are made among requests, commands, and demands. *Requests* are usually expressed in the form of a question and are often accompanied by social conventions such as "Would you please . . . ?" or "I'd like you to . . . ." Requests involve a solicitation, express a desire for something, and typically communicate that the person to whom they are directed has the option of refusing. *Commands* are more authoritative, do not involve the use of questions and social conventions, and usually do not allow the option of noncompliance. Further, commands may invoke social control or dominance by the person giving the command. Examples of such commands are "Take out your math books, turn to page 55, and begin work on the multiplication problems" and "Julie, it's time for you to help me take lunch count." Finally, *demands* involve authoritative commands or requests that do not allow for refusal. Demands are used by the persons issuing them to enforce compliance with ordinary commands. Commands typically escalate into demands by the teacher when they are refused by the student and may produce defiance. Defiance can be explosive, sometimes violent, and often highly damaging to the teacher–student relationship.

Teachers should consider the following guidelines in giving commands to maximize their effectiveness and to manage the classroom more effectively (Walker, 1995; Walker & Walker, 1991):

1. Use only as many commands as needed in order to teach and manage the classroom effectively. Research has shown that rates of noncompliance increase as the number of commands increase (Morgan & Jenson, 1988; Walker, 1995).

2. Try to limit the number of *terminating* commands given in favor of *initiating* commands. Terminating commands direct the student to stop doing something inappropriate (e.g., "Don, stop talking to Frank right now!"). Initiating commands direct the student to start doing something positive or productive (e.g., "Miguel, read this passage out of your book aloud to the class").

3. Give only one command at a time. If a series of separate tasks is involved, give distinct commands for each task.

4. Be specific and direct. Get the student's attention, establish eye contact, and describe what is wanted in a firm voice using alpha command language that is easily understood.

5. Allow a reasonable time (at least 10 seconds) for the student to respond to the command.

6. Do not repeat the command more than once if the student does not comply. Instead, use some other consequence or action to deal with the noncompliance.

7. Give commands in close proximity to the student instead of from a distance. This is particularly important with antisocial students.

The thoughtful and selective use of commands represents a best practice in teaching students and managing the classroom environment. Commands can be either effective or ineffective, depending on the nature of the command (alpha versus beta, or initiating versus terminating), the timing of the command, and the events subsequent to the command. Compliance with teacher commands and directives is typically a major problem with antisocial students and represents a key source of conflict between teacher and student. The skilled use of teacher commands will prevent many behavior problems and conflicts in the classroom and lead to a more productive classroom environment (Riegler & Baer, 1989; Vanderheyden & Witt, 2000).

Conclusion

Many antisocial children are inadvertently taught a pattern of oppositional, noncompliant behavior in the family context in which they are reared. This behavior pattern is highly destructive to family, teacher, and peer relationships. It also often serves as the first stage in an escalating cycle of ever more serious forms of negative behavior, as demonstrated by Patterson and his colleagues (see Patterson et al., 2002). It is important to change this behavior from negative to positive as early as possible in a child's life.

InfoTrac College Edition Research Terms

Corporal punishment

Deviancy training

MTA Study

Peer social attention

Ritalin

References

American Psychiatric Association (1994). *Diagnostic and statistical manual of mental disorders* (4th ed.). Washington, DC: Author.

Barkley, R. (Ed.) (1998). *Attention-deficit hyperactivity disorder: A handbook for diagnosis and treatment.* New York: Guilford Press.

Coie, J., Dodge, K., & Kupersmidt, J. (1990). Peer group behavior and social status. In S. Asher & J. Coie (Eds.), *Peer rejection in childhood* (pp. 17–59). New York: Cambridge University Press.

Colvin, G. (1988). *Lane School annual report.* Unpublished document. Eugene: Lane Educational Service District.

Colvin, G., & Sugai, G. (1989). *Managing escalating behavior.* Available from Behavior Associates, P.O. Box 5317, Eugene, OR 97405.

Dishion, T., Patterson, G., & Griesler, P. (1994). Peer adaptation in the development of antisocial behavior: A confluence model. In L. R. Huesmann (Ed.), *Current perspectives on aggressive behavior* (pp. 61–95). New York: Plenum Press.

Dryfoos, J. (1990). *Adolescents at risk.* New York: Oxford University Press.

DuPaul, G., & Stoner, G. (1994). *ADHD in the schools: Assessment and intervention strategies.* New York: Guilford Press.

Eddy, J. M., Reid, J., & Curry, V. (2002). The etiology of youth antisocial behavior, delinquency, and violence and a public health approach to prevention. In M. Shinn, H. Walker, & G. Stoner (Eds.), *Interventions for academic and behavior problems II: Preventive and remedial approaches* (pp. 27–52). Bethesda, MD: National Association of School Psychologists.

Elliott, S. N., Witt, J. C., Kratochwill, T., & Stoiber, K. (2002). Selecting and evaluation classroom interventions. In M. Shinn, H. Walker, & G. Stoner (Eds.), *Interventions for academic and behavior problems II: Preventive and remedial approaches* (pp. 243–294). Bethesda, MD: National Association of School Psychologists.

Forehand, R., & McMahon, R. (1981). *Helping the noncompliant child.* New York: Guilford Press.

Gershoff, E.T. (2002). Corporal punishment by parent and associated child behaviors and experiences: A meta-analytic and theoretical review. *Psychological Bulletin, 128,* 539–579.

Golly, A. M. (1994). *The use and effects of alpha and beta commands in elementary classroom settings.* Unpublished doctoral dissertation, University of Oregon.

Gottfredson, D.C. (1997). School-based crime prevention. In L. Sherman, D. Gottfredson, D. Mackenzie, J. Eck, P. Reuter, & S. Bushway (Eds.), *Preventing crime: What works, what doesn't, what's promising.* College Park: University of Maryland, Department of Criminology and Criminal Justice.

Guess, D., Helmstetter, E., Turnbull, H. R., & Knowlton, S. (1987). Use of aversive procedures with persons who are disabled: A historical review and critical analysis. *Monograph of the Association for Persons with Severe Handicaps* (Vol. 2). Washington, DC: Association for Persons with Severe Handicaps.

Harden, P., & Zoccollillo, M. (1997). Disruptive behavior disorders. *Current Opinions in Pediatrics, 9,* 339–345.

Herrnstein, R. (1961). Relative and absolute strength of response as a function of frequency of reinforcement. *Journal of the Experimental Analysis of Behavior, 4,* 267–272.

Herrnstein, R. (1974). Formal properties of the matching law. *Journal of the Experimental Analysis of Behavior, 21,* 486–495.

Hersh, R. & Walker, H. M. (1983). Great expectations: Making schools effective for all students. *Policy Studies Review, 2*(Special Issue No. 1), 147–188.

Jenson, P. & Cooper, J. (2002). *Attention deficit-hyperactivity disorder: State of the science—best practices.* New York: Civic Research Institute.

Kazdin, A. (1987). Treatment of antisocial behavior in children: Current status and future directions. *Psychological Bulletin, 102,* 187–203.

Kern, L., Bambara, L., & Fogt, J. (2002). Class-wide curricula modification to improve the behavior of students with emotional and behavioral disorders. *Behavioral Disorders, 27,* 317–326.

Kern, L., Mantegna, M., Vorndran, C., Bailin, D., & Hilt, A. (2001). Choice of task sequence to increase engagement and reduce problem behaviors. *Journal of Positive Behavioral Interventions, 3,* 3–10.

Kern, L., Vordran, C., Hilt, A., Ringdahl, J., Adelman, B., & Dunlap, G. (1998). Choice as an intervention to improve behavior: A review of the literature. *Journal of Behavioral Education,* 8, 151–169.

Kuczynski, L., Kochanska, G., Radke-Yarrow, M., & Girnius-Brown, O. (1987). A developmental interpretation of young children's noncompliance. *Developmental Psychology, 23,* 276–282.

Kupersmidt, J., Coie, J., & Dodge, K. (1990). The role of poor peer relationships in the development of disorder. In S. Asher & J. Coie (Eds.), *Peer rejection in childhood* (pp. 274–308). New York: Cambridge University Press.

Loeber, R., & Farrington, D. (Eds.) (1998). *Serious & violent juvenile offenders: Risk factors and successful interventions.* Thousand Oaks, CA: Sage.

Loeber, R., & Farrington, D. (Eds.) (2001). *Child delinquents: Development, intervention, and service needs.* Thousand Oaks, CA: Sage.

Mayer, G. R., & Sulzer-Azaroff, B. (2002). Interventions for vandalism and aggression. In M. Shinn, H. Walker, & G. Stoner (Eds.), *Interventions for academic and behavior problems II: Preventive and remedial approaches* (pp. 853–884). Bethesda, MD: National Association of School Psychologists.

Morgan, D., & Jenson, W. (1988). *Teaching behaviorally disordered students: Preferred practices.* Columbus, OH: Merrill.

MTA Cooperative Group. (1999). A 14-month randomized clinical trial of treatment strategies for attention-deficit/hyperactivity disorder. *Archives of General Psychiatry, 56,* 1073–1086.

Nevin, J. (1988). Behavioral momentum and the partial reinforcement effect. *Psychological Bulletin, 103,* 44–56.

Parker, J., & Asher, S. (1987). Peer relations and later personal adjustment: Are low-accepted children at-risk? *Psychological Bulletin, 102,* 357–389.

Patterson, G. (1982). *A social learning approach, Volume 3: Coercive family process.* Eugene: Castalia.

Patterson, G. (2002). The early development of coercive family process. In J. Reid, G. Patterson, & J. Snyder (Eds.), *Antisocial behavior in children and adolescents: A developmental analysis and model for intervention* (pp. 25–44). Washington, DC: American Psychological Association.

Patterson, G., & Bank, L. (1986). Bootstrapping your way in the nomological thicket. *Behavioral Assessment, 8,* 49–73.

Patterson, G., Reid, J., & Dishion, T. (1992). *A social interactional approach, Volume 4: Antisocial boys.* Eugene: Castalia.

Reid, J., & Eddy, J.M. (1997). The prevention of antisocial behavior: Some considerations in the search for effective interventions. In D. Stoff, J. Breiling, J., & J. Maser (Eds.), The handbook of antisocial behavior (pp. 343–356). New York: Wiley.

Reid, J., Paterson, G., & Snyder, J. (Eds.). (2002). *Antisocial behavior in children and adolescents: A developmental analysis and model for intervention*. Washington, DC: American Psychological Association.

Riegler, H., & Baer, D. (1989). A developmental analysis of rule-following. *Advances in Child Development and Behavior, 21,* 191–219.

Schoen, S. (1983). The status of compliance technology: Implications for programming. *Journal of Special Education, 17,* 483–496.

Schoen, S. (1986). Decreasing noncompliance in severely multihandicapped children. *Psychology in the Schools, 23,* 88–94.

Snyder, J. (2002). Reinforcement and coercion mechanisms in the development of antisocial behavior: Peer relationships. In J. Reid, G. Patterson, & J. Snyder (Eds.), *Antisocial behavior in children and adolescents: A developmental analysis and model for intervention* (pp. 101–122). Washington, DC: American Psychological Association.

Snyder, J., & Stoolmiller, M. (2002). Reinforcement and coercive mechanisms in the development of antisocial behavior: The family. In J. Reid, G. Patterson, & J. Snyder (Eds.), *Antisocial behavior in children and adolescents: A developmental analysis and model for intervention* (pp. 65–100). Washington, DC: American Psychological Association.

Sprick, R., & Howard, L., (1998). *The teacher's encyclopedia of behavior management: 100 problems/500 plans*. Longmont, CO: Sopris West.

Sugai, G., Horner, R., & Gresham, F.M. (2002). Behaviorally effective school environments. In M. Shinn, H. Walker, & G. Stoner (Eds.), *Interventions for academic and behavior problems II: Preventive and remedial approaches* (pp. 315–350). Bethesda, MD: National Association of School Psychologists.

Tolan, P., & Guerra, N. (1994). *What works in reducing adolescent violence: An empirical view of the field*. Boulder: University of Colorado, Center for the Study of Prevention of Violence.

U.S. Office of Juvenile Justice and Delinquency Prevention. (1999). *Research brief series*. Washington, D.C.: Department of Justice.

Walker, H., & Walker, J. (1991). *Coping with noncompliance in the classroom: A positive approach for teachers*. Austin, TX: Pro-Ed.

Walker, H. M. (1995). *The acting-out child: Coping with classroom disruption*. Longmont, CO: Sopris West.

Walker, H. M., & Buckley, N. (1973). Teacher attention to appropriate and inappropriate classroom behavior: An individual case study. *Focus on Exceptional Children, 5,* 5–11.

Walker, H. M., & Buckley, N. (1974). *Token reinforcement techniques: Classroom applications for the hard to teach child*. Eugene: E-B Press.

Walker, H. M., Colvin, G., & Ramsey, E. (1995). *Antisocial behavior in school: Strategies and best practices*. Pacific Grove, CA: Brooks/Cole, Inc.

Walker, H. M., & Gresham, F. M. (2002). School-related behavior disorders. In W. Reynolds & G. Miller (Eds.), *Handbook of psychology, Volume 7: Educational psychology* (pp. 511–532). Hoboken, NJ: Wiley.

Walker, H. M., Hops, H., & Fiegenbaum, E. (1976). Deviant classroom behavior as a function of combinations of social and token reinforcement and cost contingency. *Behavior Therapy, 7,* 76–88.

Walker, H. M., & Shinn, M. (2002). Structuring school-based interventions to achieve integrated primary, secondary, and tertiary prevention goals for safe and effective schools. In M. Shinn, H. Walker, & G. Stoner (Eds.), *Interventions for academic and behavior problems II: Preventive and remedial approaches* (pp. 1–26). Bethesda, MD: National Association of School Psychologists.

Walker, H. M., Sylwester, R. (1998). Reducing students' refusal and resistance. *Teaching Exceptional Children, 30*(6) 52–58.

Williams, C., & Forehand, R. (1984). An examination of predictor variables for child compliance and noncompliance. *Journal of Abnormal Child Psychology, 12,* 491–504.

Assessment and Classification of Social Competence Deficits Among Antisocial Youths

Introduction

A substantial majority of today's antisocial children and youths experience deficits in their social competence functioning. Earlier in this book, we defined antisocial behavior as the recurring violation of socially prescribed patterns of behavior across a range of contexts (home, school, community). As such, this definition captures the essence of the socially ineffective behavior that characterizes these children and youths to a significant degree. *Antisocial* behavior is the polar opposite of *prosocial* behavior, a behavior pattern involving cooperative forms of behavior and positive, reciprocal social exchanges. In contrast, antisocial behavior patterns are invariably hostile, aggressive, defiant, and sometimes violent; they severely challenge adult authority and consistently violate social norms.

A large body of research over the past 20 years demonstrates that antisocial students consistently fail in their social relations with the three most important social agents in their lives—peers, teachers, and parents (Patterson, Reid, & Dishion, 1992; Reid, Patterson, & Snyder, 2002). Antisocial students often do not display age-appropriate social behavior, and they tend to be extremely immature in nearly all their social interactions with peers and adults in school. As young children approaching school age become socialized to the norms and behavioral standards of society, they tend to gradually reduce their levels of aggressive behavior. In contrast, older students with antisocial behavior patterns display rates of aggression more typical of 3- and 4-year-olds (Patterson, 1982). These students often bring a contentious "chip on their shoulder" set of attitudes to many, if not most, social situations. Further, they tend to have poor adult models for positive, appropriate social behavior in the home and in other contexts. Parents of these children are likely to model negative attitudes toward school and toward authority figures in general, thus making parental cooperation in interventions difficult. Due to this dysfunctional learning history, antisocial students frequently display behavioral characteristics that cause them to be perceived as hostile and socially unskilled by peers and adults alike.

Gresham (2002a) notes that the current federal definition of emotional disturbance (ED), as specified in the Individuals with Disabilities Education Act (1997), includes two criteria that involve social competence difficulties: (1) an inability to build or maintain satisfactory interpersonal relationships with peers and teachers, and (2) the expression of inappropriate behavior or feelings under normal circumstances. Further, social competence deficits are commonly part of the diagnostic criteria applied to many of the psychological disorders described in the *Diagnostic and Statistical Manual of Mental Disorders* (*DSM-IV*), such as oppositional-defiant disorder, conduct disorder, and attention deficit/hyperactivity disorder (see American Psychiatric Association, 1994). Long-term personal and social adjustment status, in large measure, is based on individuals' ability to build and sustain satisfactory interpersonal relationships with others, be accepted by peers, build friendships, and terminate negative or destructive interactions and relationships with others (see Kupersmidt, Coie, & Dodge, 1990; Parker & Asher, 1987).

This chapter focuses on methods, procedures, guidelines, resources, and recommended best practices for screening and assessing the social competence deficits that antisocial students exhibit in school and home settings. The information in this chapter represents a comprehensive treatment of this topic because social skills and social competence are domains in which antisocial youths are often severely deficient. These social competence deficits, in turn, place their school and life adjustments at severe risk of failure.

Conceptualizations and Definitions of Social Skills

Social skills conceptualizations can be traced back to the 1930s. Moreno (1934), for example, developed sociometric assessment methods that yield information regarding peer relationships from members of students' peer groups. Sociometric assessment (described in detail later in this chapter) provides information on children's level of social acceptance, isolation, rejection, and popularity as judged by their peers. Moreno's work paved the way for the subspecialty of social competence based on a sociometric or peer popularity conceptualization. Many competing models of social competence have emerged in the years since Moreno's work was first published. Whereas Moreno's conceptualization focused on the outcomes or consequences of socially skilled behavior (e.g., social acceptance by others), the majority of other, competing models emphasize the specific competencies and behaviors that lead to socially skilled, effective functioning.

Subsequent to Moreno's groundbreaking work, a number of professional developments stimulated and maintained professional interest in the topic of social skills. These developments included (1) the work of behavior therapists and behavior analysts in isolating and teaching discrete forms of social behavior, (2) the assertion-training and affective-education movements in psychology and education, (3) the deinstitutionalization and mainstreaming movements, and (4) the regular education and full-inclusion initiatives. These rather diverse developments each independently highlighted the importance of social competence as a cornerstone for school and postschool success. In the past two decades, there has been an explosion of professional interest and investment in the development of children's social skills in general and those of at-risk students in particular (see Elksnin & Elksnin, 1995, 1998; Merrell, 1999, 2001)

A number of definitions of social skills have been used over the years by various professionals interested in children's social development. Merrell and Gimpel (1998) suggest that at least 15 definitions of social skills appeared in the professional literature. Despite these myriad definitions, social skills is perhaps best conceptualized as a *behavioral* construct because specific social behaviors are grouped or synthesized under the generic label "social skill." For example, discrete behavioral events such as complimenting others, cooperating, listening, greeting others, and gaining entry into ongoing play activities all would likely be seen as examples of socially skilled behaviors. Conceptually, we view social skills as a set of competencies that (1) facilitate the initiation and maintenance of positive social relationships, (2) that contribute to peer acceptance and friendship development, (3) that result in satisfactory school adjustment, and (4) that allow individuals to cope with and adapt to the demands of the social environment.

Peer acceptance and maintenance of friendships are socially important outcomes that antisocial students often lack. Antisocial students who aren't accepted by peers, teachers, or parents, and who are unable to adjust to school, may dropout.

Gresham (1986) indicated that there are three general approaches to defining social skills in the literature: (1) the peer acceptance definition, (2) the behavioral definition, and (3) the social validity definition. The peer acceptance definition suggests that socially skilled children and youths are those who are accepted by peers and who have many friendships. This definition relies heavily on sociometric assessment procedures, as developed by Moreno, to establish the extent to which children are popular with peers. Although relatively objective, the major drawback of the peer acceptance definition is that it fails to identify the specific forms of behavior that lead to social acceptance, popularity, and friendships. This book is concerned with students who likely fall at the opposite end of the peer acceptance continuum. Children who are rejected or neglected by peers, who behave in an atypical or unconventional manner, and who have few, if any, close friendships are at considerable risk for a host of later, destructive outcomes (Asher, 1990; Reid et al., 2002; Walker & Severson, 2002). In our view, any fully adequate definition of social skills should (1) address both social acceptance and popularity versus peer rejection and neglect, and (2) account for the behavioral correlates and outcomes of socially effective functioning.

Many respected researchers favor a behavioral definition in which social skills are those behaviors occurring in specific situations that increase the likelihood of being reinforced by others and/or that decrease the probability of being punished for one's social behavior (Foster & Ritchey, 1979; Strain, Cooke, &

Apolloni, 1976). This definition has several advantages over the peer acceptance definition. First, specific antecedents (e.g., situations, persons, or the behavior of others) of social behavior are identified that can give rise to social skills difficulties. Second, specific social behaviors that may be useful in remediating social skills deficits can be targeted for intervention. Third, the ecological contexts in which social skills difficulties take place can be clearly characterized using a behavioral definition and descriptions of the key social skills required for satisfactory performance within them.

Despite these advantages, a behavioral definition does not guarantee that the skills identified are, in fact, competent forms of social behavior. Members of society at large may not deem as important, for example, increasing the frequency of certain social behaviors (e.g., extending invitations) (Walker et al., 1998). As such, this calls for a much more comprehensive definition of social skills in order to capture the complexities of peer- and adult-related social competence (Walker, 1986).

Perhaps the most useful definition of social skills, for our purposes, is based on the concept of social validity. In this approach, social skills are defined as those identifiable behaviors occurring in specific situations that predict important social outcomes for children and youths (Gresham, 1983, 1986). Socially important outcomes are those that adults (e.g., teachers, parents, community members) consider important, adaptive, and functional within specific settings (Gresham, 2002b; Hawkins, 1991). Put differently, socially important outcomes are those that make a difference in individuals' adaptation both to societal expectations and to the behavioral demands of specific environments in which they function.

What are socially important outcomes? Research has shown that some of the most socially important outcomes for children and youths include peer acceptance (Newcomb, Bukowski, & Pattee, 1993; Parker & Asher, 1987), development and maintenance of friendships (Parker & Asher, 1987), successful school adjustment (Hersh & Walker, 1983; Walker, Irvin, Noell, & Singer, 1992), and teacher and parental acceptance (Gresham, 2002b; Gresham & Elliott, 1990; Walker & McConnell, 1995a, b). As noted previously, it is well established that children who are poorly accepted or rejected by peers, who have few friendships, and who adjust poorly to schooling are at much greater risk for lifelong maladaptive outcomes. Parker and Asher (1987), for example, showed that children having difficulties in peer relationships often demonstrate a behavior pattern that can be described as antisocial, aggressive, and characterized by school norm violations. Moreover, children who are overtly rejected by their peers are more likely to engage in adolescent delinquency than are those who are not rejected. In describing this developmental trajectory, Kupersmidt and her colleagues (1990) argued the following:

> Being actively rejected by one's peer group induces internal reactions in the child that then lead to psychopathological or antisocial outcomes. Feelings of personal inadequacy or . . . anger or resentment may lead to social orientations that give rise to more extremely maladaptive behavior. . . . those who turn against the peer group may be at risk for antisocial disorders. (p. 292)

A Taxonomy of Social Skills

Although we know a great deal about the dimensions underlying maladaptive behavior, much less research has focused on developing a taxonomy of social skills for the full range of children and youths. A taxonomy is useful because it allows for the classification of general dimensions of social skills that can be used for research and practice. Caldarella and Merrell (1997) synthesized 21 research investigations that used 19 social skills rating scales or inventories; the studies involved approximately 22,000 students age 3–18. Approximately 75% of the studies used teacher ratings of social skills, with about 19% also using parent ratings of social behavior. Peer sociometrics were used in only about 5% of the studies.

Table 6.1 depicts the social skills taxonomy that emerged from this study. It includes five broad domains or classes of social skills: (1) peer relationships, (2) self-management, (3) academic, (4) compliance, and (5) assertion. It should be noted that most of these domains have been incorporated into social skills curricula and intervention programs. (Examples of these programs are reviewed in Chapter 7.) The taxonomy is helpful because it provides a profile of social skills strengths and weaknesses; it also can be used to target domains of social skills deficits for intervention purposes and to assess the outcomes of interventions (Caldarella & Merrell, 1997).

Social Skills Versus Social Competence

McFall (1982) presented an extremely important theoretical conceptualization that distinguishes the concepts of social *skill* and social *competence*. In this view, social skills are the specific behaviors that an individual performs in order to successfully complete a social task (e.g., accomplishing peer group entry or making friends). *Social competence,* in contrast, is an evaluative term based on judgments by other social agents of an individual's social effectiveness.

Gresham (1986) suggested that evaluations of social competence should be based on at least three criteria: (1) relevant judgments of an individual's social behavior (e.g., by peers, teachers, and parents), (2) evaluations of social behavior relative to explicit, preestablished criteria (e.g., number of steps successfully completed in the performance of a social skill), and/or (3) behavioral performances relative to a normative standard (e.g., scores on social skills rating scales). It is important to note that social behaviors, in and of themselves, cannot be considered "socially skilled" apart from their impact on the judgments of significant others in a given social environment.

Classification of Social Skills Deficits

Determining the specific types of social skills deficits students may have is a crucial aspect of the social skills assessment process. The distinction between types of social skills deficits is important because, in each case, quite different intervention procedures are warranted. Gresham (1981) categorized social skills

TABLE 6.1 ◆

Social Skills Taxonomy.

Peer Relationships

Social interaction

Prosocial behavior

Peer-preferred social skills

Empathy

Social participation

Self-Management

Self-control

Social convention

Social independence

Responsibility

Compliance

Academic

School adjustment

Respect for social rules at school

Task orientation

Academic responsibility

Compliance

Social cooperation

Competence

Cooperation

Assertion

Assertive social skills

Social initiation

Social activator

deficits as representing either acquisition deficits or performance deficits. Later, Gresham (1995) identified a third type as a fluency deficit.

Social skills acquisition deficits can be described as either the absence of knowledge about how to perform a given social task or difficulty in knowing which social skills are appropriate in specific situations (Gresham, 2002a, b). Social skills acquisition deficits are perhaps best described as "can't do" problems

Social Skill Dimension

Competing Problem Behavior Dimension	Acquisition	Performance	Fluency
Present			
• Aggression • Oppositional behavior • Violent behavior • Noncompliance • Threats to others • Bullying behavior	Acquisition Deficit	Performance Deficit	Fluency Deficit
Absent	Acquisition Deficit	Performance Deficit	Fluency Deficit

FIGURE 6.1 ◆

Social Skills Classification Model.

(i.e., the student cannot perform the requisite social behavior even under optimal conditions). Social skills performance deficits can be characterized as the failure to perform a given social skill at acceptable levels even though the student may know how to perform the behavior. These types of deficits can be described as "won't do" problems. Students with fluency deficits exhibit awkward or otherwise unpolished performances of a given social skill despite knowing how to and wanting to perform it.

Another important aspect of this social skills classification model is the addition of a competing problem behaviors dimension (Gresham & Elliott, 1990). In this context, two dimensions of behavior are involved: (1) social skills /performance deficits (described previously) and (2) competing problem behaviors. For students with antisocial behavior patterns, these competing problem behaviors might include aggression, noncompliance, oppositional behavior, and/or violence. Most students with antisocial behavior patterns fail to either acquire or perform appropriate social skills because antisocial behaviors overwhelm and successfully compete with socially skilled behaviors. Figure 6.1 illustrates this two-dimensional classification model.

We consider this two-dimensional classification model to be crucial to linking assessment results to the intervention procedures as described in Chapter 7. Obviously, it is unnecessary to teach social skills to students who already have them in their repertoires. At the same time, interventions designed to increase the frequency of social skills performances (e.g., reinforcement-based procedures) are not a particularly efficient means of remediating social skills acquisition deficits, which are more effectively addressed using social learning methods (e.g., modeling, coaching, and behavioral rehearsal). Finally, students with fluency deficits require more practice, rehearsal, and performance feedback in order to develop fluent behavioral performances. Unfortunately, most social skills training studies and practices do not distinguish between the various types of social skills deficits and the intervention approaches that work best for each (Gresham, 1998a, b).

Criteria and Procedures for Targeting Specific Social Skills for Training

There are at least three criteria to consider in selecting specific social skills to target in social skills training efforts: (1) determining specific social skill deficits, (2) identifying competing problem behaviors, and (3) evaluating the social validity of targeted social skills.

Determining Specific Social Skills Deficits

Students receiving social skills training (SST) must be deficient (in terms of acquisition, performance, and/or fluency) in the target skills selected, and this deficiency must create problems either for the students or for key social agents (i.e., parents, teachers, and peers) who interact with them. On the face of it, this requirement may seem unnecessary. However, one of the factors contributing to the less-than-robust effects achieved from SST efforts is that students are often instructed in areas in which deficits do not create problems or in which they already perform at criterion levels. In such situations, incentives for behavior change are quite weak. It is essential to determine that a deficit in a particular skill or domain actually exists, that it creates problems, and that it is either an acquisition-, performance-, or fluency-based deficit. Finally, the importance of the skill to the student's daily functioning and the achievement of long-term, valued outcomes (e.g., social acceptance, effective adjustment, satisfactory mental health) must be carefully assessed.

Identifying Competing Problem Behaviors

Obviously, the goal of SST is for students to acquire and perform prosocial behaviors that are functional and adaptive across a variety of environments. For social skills acquisition deficits, competing problem behaviors may block or prevent the acquisition of socially skilled behaviors. For example, a student with a long history of noncompliant, oppositional, and coercive behavior may simply never learn prosocial behavioral alternatives such as cooperation, sharing, and self-control due to the absence of opportunities caused by the competing function of these aversive behaviors (Eddy, Reid, & Curry, 2002).

In the case of performance deficits, aggressive and violent behaviors might be performed instead of prosocial behaviors because they are more efficient, effective, and reliable in producing reinforcement from the environment. In most cases, the more frequent occurrence of antisocial behaviors relative to prosocial behaviors may be explained by the behavioral Matching Law (Hernstein, 1970). Recall that the Matching Law embodies the following rule: The rate of a given response will match the reinforcement rate for that response (see Chapter 5). Thus, if complimenting others is reinforced after every six occurrences and verbally abusing others is reinforced after every two occurrences, verbal abuse will be approximately *three times* more frequent than compliments. In many, if not most cases, the behavioral repertoires of students with antisocial behavior patterns follow the Matching Law.

Evaluating Social Validity

Social validity refers to consumer evaluations and reactions involving both the selection of social skills as training targets and the perceived value of achieved outcomes of the intervention. Consumer, as used here, refers to the recipients of social skills interventions or to the social agents (parents, teachers, and peers) who are affected by them and who are in a position to judge their social impact.

Based on Wolf's (1978) original conceptualization, Gresham (1986) viewed social validity as having three components: (1) social significance, (2) social acceptability, and (3) social importance. Social significance refers to consumers' perception of the goals or purposes of SST. We must be increasingly sensitive to contextual factors in establishing goals that (1) respect the rights of students and parents, (2) are culturally sensitive and appropriate, and (3) do not conflict with the values and preferences of parents, especially their moral and religious values. Educators who advocate for SST in school should have a clear rationale for why social skills are being taught, which social skills are being taught, and what the expected outcomes are.

It is important to recognize that the social significance of the behaviors targeted in SST is usually based on subjective evaluation. Subjective evaluations are judgments made by persons who interact with students or who are otherwise in a position to judge their behavior (Kazdin, 1977). Key social agents are likely candidates for subjectively evaluating the social significance of particular social skills targeted for intervention. Gresham and Elliott (1990) included a social significance component in their Social Skills Rating System (described later in this chapter) in which raters indicate how important a given social skill is for the student.

A useful, overarching rationale in this regard concerns the dual goals of schooling (i.e., the academic and social development of all children and youths). Schools are expected to develop students' potential to the maximum extent possible in these two areas, but they tend to emphasize academic development, often to

Indirect assessment methods are teacher or parent accounts of student behavior. Direct assessment methods, like structured observations, evaluate social skills as they occur in natural settings such as the playground or the classroom.

the exclusion of social development and competence. Socially effective behavior lays the groundwork for success not only in school but throughout life. In fact, recent empirical research clearly documents that *prosocial* student behavior provides an important foundation for later academic achievement outcomes (see Caprara, Barbaranelli, Pastorelli, Bandura, & Zimbardo, 2000). We have the ability to teach the social skills that underlie socially effective behavior in the same way that we teach the academic skills that are related to academic achievement. Additional research has shown that, the more socially competent students are in school, the greater will be their degree of *overall* school success and academic achievement (see Coie & Krehbiel, 1984; Gresham, Sugai, & Horner, 2001). Social skills are also directly related to the ability to develop friendships and support networks, both of which are important to individuals' quality of life.

Social acceptability refers to the degree to which treatment consumers find SST acceptable. Kazdin (1981) described treatment acceptability as a judgment that a given intervention (1) is fair in relation to a given problem, (2) is reasonable and nonintrusive, and (3) is consistent with professional standards about what a treatment should be. Acceptability is perhaps the first consideration in selecting an intervention because if treatment consumers perceive an intervention as acceptable then its subsequent use will be more likely. It should be noted, however, that acceptable treatments are not necessarily implemented with high integrity. Integrity refers to the extent to which a given intervention is implemented as intended by its developers or adopters (Gresham, 1989).

Consumer satisfaction or acceptability may not reflect the most effective interventions or even those that are necessarily in the best interests of target students. Gresham and Lopez (1996) suggest that some consumers (parents and teachers) may reject legitimate interventions because (1) they lack the necessary skills for implementation, or (2) they are philosophically opposed to the intervention. In each case, the end result may be that students do not receive the best available social skills interventions.

Social importance refers to the effects produced by SST and answers the following question: Does the quality and quantity of change in a student's social behavior make a difference in that student's functioning in school or society at large? That is, does it contribute to the achievement of valued social outcomes such as teacher and peer acceptance, school success, and improved friendships? We have previously stated that social skills are perhaps best conceptualized in terms of their social validity. Even the best social skills interventions will have only limited effects if they are applied to skills that have weak relationships to important social outcomes. Thus, in evaluating social skills curricula for use in such interventions, it is extremely important to carefully review the rationale and procedures used by the developers to select the target social skills included.

Assessment of Social Skills

Various methods have been used to identify and classify social skills deficits of children and youths. Social skills assessment methods, like other behavioral assessment procedures, can be coded as either direct or indirect (see Gresham &

Lambros, 1998). Indirect methods assess behavior that is removed in time and place from its actual occurrence. Examples of these procedures are Likert ratings by others (e.g., teachers, peers, or parents), interviews, and sociometric assessments. In contrast, direct methods assess behavior at the time and place of its actual occurrence. The most commonly used direct assessment method involves structured observation(s) of social behavior in the natural environment (e.g., classroom, playground, or cafeteria).

Gresham (2001) suggests that social skills assessments should involve five stages: (1) screening and selection of students for social skills interventions, (2) classification of specific types of social skills deficits, (3) selection of targeted skills and competing problem behaviors for intervention, (4) functional assessment, and (5) evaluation of the effects of the intervention. Box 6.1 presents 11 major goals of the social skills assessment process based on the recommendations of Gresham (2001). The following sections describe social skills assessment procedures that can be used to accomplish the 11 goals listed in the box.

Behavior Rating Scales

Behavior rating scales are one of the most common methods of quantifying teacher and parental judgments of children's behavior (Gresham & Elliott, 1990). Teacher judgments of students' school, social, and academic skills are among the primary bases of referrals for special education and related services. Gresham and Elliott (1990) and Merrell (1999) have noted that behavior rating scales have distinct advantages over other forms of assessment such as direct observations, interviews, or sociometric measures. First, they are less costly than individually administered tests and direct observations. Second, more objective, reliable, and valid information can be garnered from behavior rating scales than from other assessment methods such as projective personality tests. Finally, behavior rating scales may assist in identifying target behaviors for intervention purposes. Merrell (2001) summarizes the advantages of behavior rating scales as follows: "It is easy to see why they are widely used—they get at the 'big picture' of the assessment problem in a short amount of time, at moderate cost, and with a good deal of technical precision and practical utility" (p. 74).

Despite these significant advantages, several things should be considered when interpreting information derived from behavior rating scales. First, ratings by others represent summaries of *typical* rather than *actual* behavior in a particular setting. In this sense, behavior ratings reflect the relative rather than the absolute frequency of behavior. Second, behavior ratings are evaluative judgments that are influenced by a rater's social behavior standards, tolerance levels, and expectations for behavior (Hersh & Walker, 1983; Walker et al., 1992). Third, the social validity of the behaviors assessed should be considered. Recall that the social validity of behavior represents the *importance* that is attributed to the behavior by key social agents in the child's environment. Finally, multiple raters of a child's behavior within and across settings may agree only moderately with one another (Achenbach, McConaughy, & Howell, 1987; Gresham & Elliott, 1990).

Social Skills Rating Scales

A number of social skills rating scales are currently available; however, only four have sufficiently large and representative standardization samples, adequate psychometric properties, and customer-friendly availability from reputable test publishing companies.

The Social Skills Rating Scale (SSRS).   The SSRS (Gresham & Elliott, 1990) is a broad-based, multirater assessment of students' social behavior that affects teacher–student relations, peer acceptance, and academic performance. The SSRS is the only social skills rating scale that yields information from three key rating sources: teachers, parents, and students. The SSRS solicits information from these three sources in grades 3–12 and from parents and teachers for children age 3–5. The SSRS has three forms reflecting three developmental age ranges: preschool (age 3–5 years), elementary (grades K–6), and secondary (grades 7–12). The SSRS focuses on a comprehensive assessment of social skills; however, it also includes problem behaviors that compete with the acquisition and/or performance of socially skilled behaviors. Additionally, the teacher version of the SSRS includes a measure of academic competence because poor social skills, competing problem behaviors, and poor academic performance often co-occur.

Each item on the SSRS is rated on a 3-point frequency scale (0-Never, 1-Sometimes, 2-Very often) based on the rater's perception of the frequency of

Box 6.2 — Gresham and Elliott SSRS Rating Format and Examples of Items

	Frequency			Importance		
Helps others	0	1	2	0	1	2
Attends to instructions	0	1	2	0	1	2
Controls temper with peers	0	1	2	0	1	2
Responds appropriately to teasing	0	1	2	0	1	2
Gives compliments to others	0	1	2	0	1	2
Compromises in conflict situations	0	1	2	0	1	2

Frequency: 0-Never; 1-Sometimes; 2-Very often

Importance: 0-Not important; 1-Important; 2-Critical

the behavior. In addition, all SSRS forms (except the Student Elementary Form) use a 3-point Importance rating (0-Not important, 1-Important, 2-Critical). The importance ratings reflect the social validity of the social skill being assessed. Box 6.2 shows a sample of items and the rating format of the SSRS.

The SSRS includes five social skills domains: Cooperation, Assertion, Responsibility, Empathy, and Self-Control. Three of these domains are consistent across teacher, parent, and student forms (Cooperation, Assertion, and Self-Control). Responsibility is included only on the parent form, and Empathy is represented only on the student form. The SSRS also includes three problem behavior domains on the teacher and parent forms: Externalizing, Internalizing, and Hyperactivity. The Academic Competence scale is included only on the teacher form and reflects student performance in reading and mathematics, overall achievement, motivation, and parental encouragement. Scores on the three main scales (Total Social Skills, Total Problem Behaviors, and Total Academic Competence) are expressed as standard scores ($M = 100$, $SD = 15$). Table 6.2 lists the SSRS domain descriptions along with examples of items included in each domain.

The SSRS was standardized on over 4,000 students from preschool through high school, with equal numbers of boys and girls in the sample. The standardization sample was stratified by racial-ethnic group and was slightly overrepresented by Blacks and Whites and slightly underrepresented by Hispanics. The SSRS demonstrates excellent psychometric properties in terms of reliability and validity, and it has been used in numerous research studies in the 13-plus years since its publication. It has been translated into a number of languages including Spanish, Russian, Persian, Portuguese, and Hindi; the Student Form has also been adapted for administration using American Sign Language.

Walker-McConnell Scales of Social Competence and School Adjustment (SSCSA). The SSCSA (Walker & McConnell, 1995a, b) consists of two forms

TABLE 6.2

SSRS Subscale Domains and Problem Behavior Examples.

Subscale	Description	Examples
Cooperation	Behaviors facilitating academic performance	Follows class rules Pays attention Complies with instructions
Assertion	Behaviors involving initiation of social interactions or expression of opinions	Introduces self Questions unjust rules Refuses unreasonable requests
Responsibility	Behaviors involving following rules in home and community settings	Asks others for assistance Refuses unreasonable requests
Empathy	Behaviors expressing understanding of others' feelings	Listens to others Feels sorry when bad things happen to others
Self-Control	Behaviors involving inhibition of impulses or negative behavior	Controls temper in conflicts Responds appropriately to teasing
Externalizing	Behaviors representing undercontrolled or acting-out behavior pattern	Fights Bullies Gets angry
Internalizing	Behaviors representing overcontrolled behavior pattern	Is lonely Acts anxious Seems shy
Hyperactivity	Behaviors representing inattention, impulsivity, and hyperactivity	Is easily distracted Interrupts others Moves excessively

(Elementary and Adolescent) of a social skills rating scale designed to be completed by teachers and other school professionals. The Elementary version is designed for students in grades K–6, and the Adolescent version is for students in grades 7–12. Both forms were standardized on samples of approximately 2,000 students drawn from the four main geographic regions of the United States. Each item on the SSCSA is rated on a 5-point Likert scale reflecting the relative frequency of the behavior (from 1-Never occurs to 5-Frequently occurs). The elementary version has three subscales (Teacher-Preferred Social Skills, Peer-Preferred Social Skills, and School Adjustment), and the adolescent version has four subscales (Empathy, Self-Control, School Adjustment, and Peer Relations). Each subscale is expressed as a T-score ($M = 50$; $SD = 10$), and the total score is expressed as a standard score ($M = 100$, $SD = 15$). Box 6.3 shows a sample of items from each of the subscales and the rating format of the SSCSA.

The SSCSA has excellent psychometric characteristics in terms of reliability and validity. Further, the technical manual presents a series of validity studies showing that the scale accurately differentiates a number of at-risk groups from

Rating Format

	Never		Sometimes		Frequently
Makes friends easily	1	2	3	4	5
Shares laughter with peers	1	2	3	4	5
Controls temper	1	2	3	4	5
Expresses anger appropriately	1	2	3	4	5
Does seatwork as directed	1	2	3	4	5
Displays independent study skills	1	2	3	4	5

matched controls and correlates highly with other social skills measures such as the SSRS. Both versions of the SSCSA are relatively brief and, like the SSRS, cover a wide age range.

School Social Behavior Scales (SSBS).   The SSBS (Merrell, 1993) is a 65-item teacher rating scale measuring two domains of social behavior: Social Competence and Antisocial Behavior. Originally standardized on a sample of 1,858 children and adolescents in grades K–12, it was recently revised. As with the SSCSA, each item on the SSBS is rated on a 5-point Likert scale (from 1-Never to 5-Frequently). The total Social Competence and total Antisocial Behavior scores are expressed as standard scores ($M = 100$, $SD = 15$). Box 6.4 shows sample items and the rating format from the revised edition of the SSBS (Merrell, 2002).

The SSBS also has excellent psychometric properties in terms of reliability and validity. The technical manual presents a large number of studies demonstrating the criterion-related and construct validity of the scale. Like the SSRS and the SSCSA scales, the SSBS is relatively brief, user-friendly, and technically adequate.

Preschool and Kindergarten Behavior Scales (PKBS).   The PKBS (Merrell, 1994) is a 76-item behavior rating scale measuring the social skills and problem behaviors of children age 3–6. The PKBS was designed to be completed by teachers, parents, day-care providers, and others with sufficient exposure to children's behavior. It was standardized on a normative sample of 2,855 children from 16 states across the four geographic regions of the United States. Each item on the PKBS is rated on a 4-point Likert scale reflecting the perceived frequency of the behavior (from 0-Never to 3-Often).

Like the SSRS, the PKBS has two major scales—Social Skills and Problem Behavior—which are expressed as standard scores ($M = 100$, $SD = 15$). Extensive data regarding the technical adequacy of the PBKS are presented in the technical manual regarding its reliability and validity.

Box 6.4   Merrell SSBS Rating Format and Examples of Items

	Rating Format				
Scale A: Social Competence	Never	Sometimes		Frequently	
Cooperates with other students	1	2	3	4	5
Makes appropriate transitions between different activities	1	2	3	4	5
Completes school work without being reminded	1	2	3	4	5
Scale B: Antisocial Behavior					
Blames others for his/her problems	1	2	3	4	5
Takes things that are not his/hers	1	2	3	4	5
Is defiant to teachers or other school personnel	1	2	3	4	5

Sociometric Techniques

Sociometric assessment techniques differ from behavior ratings in that information regarding a student's social status is gathered directly from the student's peer group. As noted previously, sociometric assessment procedures were initially developed by Moreno (1934), who used peer nomination methods to evaluate children's friendship patterns. Although there are a host of sociometric assessment instruments available, they comprise two basic methods: (1) peer nominations and (2) peer ratings of others (Gresham, 1986). We review only peer nominations in this chapter because they have the longest history and the most extensive empirical support (see Newcomb et al., 1993).

With peer nominations, students are asked to rate peers according to certain nonbehavioral criteria. These criteria can be positive (e.g., best friends, preferred play or work partners, or liked most) or negative (e.g., liked least, nonpreferred play or work partners, or would not want as a friend). Peer nominations can also be indexed to behavioral criteria, such as students who best fit certain behavioral characteristics (e.g., talks least, fights with others, or is disruptive in class).

One of the most innovative and influential uses of peer nominations comes from Coie, Dodge, and Coppotelli (1982), who developed a sociometric classification system that identifies five status groups: (1) popular, (2) neglected, (3) rejected, (4) controversial, and (5) average. This classification system greatly increases the sensitivity and utility of sociometric assessment results. With this method, students are asked to select from a class roster the three peers they like most and the three peers they like least. For each student, the number of liked-most (LM) and liked-least (LL) choices received are summed, thereby creating an LM and an LL score for each student. These scores, in turn, are used to calculate social preference (LM − LL) and social impact (LM + LL) indices. All scores are standardized within each classroom, and sociometric status groups are created as follows: (1) popular (high social preference and social impact scores), (2) neglected (low social preference and social impact scores), (3) rejected (low social preference and high social impact scores), (4) controversial (mixed social preference and high social impact scores), and (5) average (average social preference and social impact scores).

One of the most consistent findings in the sociometric literature on peer acceptance and the lack thereof is that children who are classified as socially rejected tend to exhibit much higher levels of aggressive, oppositional, and noncompliant behaviors than members of any other sociometric status group (Coie & Kupersmidt, 1983; Dodge, 1983; Newcomb et al., 1993). These children are perceived by peers as being the least cooperative, most disruptive, most likely to start fights, and most likely to be disrespectful to school authorities. The overwhelming majority of students with antisocial behavior patterns are rejected by their peers, and few, if any, are considered popular, neglected, or average in sociometric status. Some students with antisocial behavior patterns might be considered controversial. Recall that controversial sociometric status identifies students who have a mixed social preference; that is, some peers like them and some dislike them. In certain settings, one might expect to find antisocial students having this type of sociometric status.

How should sociometric procedures be used in identifying the social competence functioning of antisocial students? One important use of sociometrics is in the early screening and identification of those students who are having difficulties with peers. Given the long-term predictive validity of rejected sociometric status, particularly for behaviorally at-risk children, this form of assessment should be considered in the comprehensive evaluation of the social functioning of students whose social behavior is of concern. Practical and ethical concerns in using sociometric procedures have been discussed extensively in the literature (see Landau & Milich, 1990; McConnell & Odom, 1986; Merrell, 1999). We recommend that the guidelines on their use from this literature be reviewed before administering them.

Functional Assessment Interviews (FAIs)

Interviews of key social agents involved with antisocial students are a key component of any comprehensive social skills assessment. The purpose of a functional assessment interview (FAI) is to identify the functions or causes of behavior based on the social agent's experiences with the student (O'Neill, Horner, Albin, Storey, & Newton, 1997). At the most basic level, student behavior may serve two primary functions: (1) a positive reinforcement function in which the behavior results in something desirable for the student (e.g., social attention, access to preferred activities, or use of material objects) and (2) a negative reinforcement function in which the behavior results in the avoidance, escape, delay, or reduction of something undesirable or aversive (e.g., difficult tasks, undesired social activities, or interruption of preferred activities) (Gresham, Watson, & Skinner, 2001).

An FAI has four essential goals: (1) to identify and define social skill(s) difficulties, (2) to assist in the differentiation of social skills acquisition, performance, and fluency deficits, (3) to identify competing problem behaviors that interfere with the acquisition, performance, and/or fluency of social skills, and (4) to obtain initial information regarding the possible functions of the target behavior. In some cases, an FAI might be one of the only ways available to assess social behavior (e.g., when the student has been suspended from school, placed in an alternative school, or arrested).

Individuals conducting an FAI should produce (1) a listing and precise description of social skills deficits and competing problem behaviors, (2) a tentative description of the possible functions the behavior(s) serves, and (3) an evaluation of the effects of a social skills intervention once it has been implemented. These steps can be described as problem identification, problem analysis, and problem evaluation (Gresham, 1998a). Box 6.5 shows an example of a semi-structured FAI that can be used to assess the social skills of students.

Systematic Observation of Social Behavior

The systematic observation of social behavior represents one of the most important social skills assessment methods. Observational data are sensitive to treatment effects and should be included in all social skills assessments and interventions (Gresham, 2001). Some approaches to systematic behavioral observation rely on elaborate and complex coding systems; however, we recommend that recording procedures be kept as simple as possible. Four factors should be considered in recording systematic behavioral observations: (1) operational definitions of behavior, (2) dimension(s) of the behavior to be assessed, (3) the number and types of behaviors assessed, and (4) the number of observation sessions.

Operational definitions of behavior describe the specific verbal, physical, temporal, and/or spatial aspects of the behavior and accompanying environmental events (Gresham, Gansle, & Noell, 1993). Operational definitions should have three characteristics: clarity, objectivity, and completeness (Kazdin, 1984). Walker and Severson (1990) provide a good example of an operational definition for the social skill of participation:

> This is coded when the target child is participating in a game or activity (with two or more children) that has a clearly specified and agreed upon set of rules. Examples would be: kickball, four-square, dodgeball, soccer, basketball, tetherball, hopscotch, and so forth. Nonexamples include tag, jump rope, follow the leader, and other unstructured games. (pp. 23–24)

One efficient way of creating an operational definition is by using the functional assessment interview (FAI) described earlier. The purpose of the FAI is to obtain clear and objective definitions of behaviors of concern to teachers and parents. Behavior rating scales can be used to identify general areas of concern and normative functioning levels of social skills and competing problem behaviors. Observations of behaviors in naturalistic settings (e.g., the classroom or playground) represent *direct* measures of social behavior and can be used to conduct

Box 6.5   Semistructured Functional Assessment Interview

PROBLEM IDENTIFICATION

◆ What social skills difficulties are of most concern to you? Please provide a clear, specific definition of the behaviors that concern you most.

◆ Are these behaviors acquisition (can't do) deficits, performance (won't do) deficits, or fluency (need more practice or refinement) deficits?

◆ About how often do you see these behaviors occurring? How often would you like them to occur?

◆ What, if any, competing problem behaviors interfere with the acquisition, performance, or fluency of desired social skills? Please provide a clear, specific definition of these behaviors?

◆ About how often do these behaviors occur?

◆ Are there activities or times of the day when the competing problem behaviors are more likely? Less likely?

◆ Is the desired social skill more likely to occur with some peers than others? Describe these typical social interactions.

◆ How does the student's failure to perform the desired social skill affect other students? How does it affect your teaching and discipline practices?

PROBLEM ANALYSIS

◆ When the student exhibits the social skill, what happens? What do you do? What do peers do?

◆ When the student exhibits competing problem behaviors, what happens? What do you do? What do peers do?

◆ What purposes (functions) do you think the competing problem behaviors serve for the student (social attention, task avoidance/escape, access to preferred activities)?

◆ Does the student engage in competing problem behaviors that achieve the same results as the socially skilled behavior? Are the competing problem behaviors equally or more functional in obtaining reinforcement?

◆ Are the competing problem behaviors associated with the presence of a specific person, place, thing, or time of day?

◆ What are some situations or activities in which the desired social skill could be taught or facilitated using incidental teaching (i.e., "teachable moments")? Describe how you might teach or facilitate the social skill in these situations or activities.

◆ Do you think the social skill might best be taught in a small group outside of the classroom? Why or why not?

◆ What types of strategies could you implement to decrease the competing problem behaviors? Describe how you might use them.

Box 6.5   *(Continued)*

PROBLEM EVALUATION

◆ Describe how you think the intervention worked?

◆ What behavior changes did you observe? Did these changes make a difference in the student's behavior in your classroom? How? In other settings? How?

◆ Is the student's behavior now similar to that of average or typical peers? If not, do you think continued use of the intervention would accomplish this goal? Why or why not? How long do you think this might take if you continued the intervention?

◆ How satisfied are you with the outcomes of the intervention? If you are not satisfied, what kinds of behavior changes would make you satisfied?

◆ Would you recommend this intervention to other teachers? Why or why not? What aspects of this intervention would you change before recommending this intervention to others?

a descriptive functional assessment. Collectively, these diverse measures provide a comprehensive picture of a student's social status, functioning, and effectiveness.

Social behavior occurs and can be assessed along the dimensions of frequency, temporality, and quality. Frequency (how often a social behavior occurs) is commonly used as an index of social competence. Some social skills may be considered problematic because they occur at low frequencies. For example, saying "please," "thank you," or "excuse me" or asking permission to leave one's seat in the classroom may be a problem because these behaviors occur at lower-than-expected levels.

Other social behaviors may be more appropriately measured by temporal dimensions of behavior such as duration, latency, or interresponse time (Gresham, 1985). Examples of social skills that can be measured by duration (how long a behavior lasts) include the length of social interactions with peers, the amount of time engaged in cooperative play, and the ratio of positive-to-negative social interactions. An easy way of using duration recording is to start a stopwatch when the student engages in the behavior, stop it when the student terminates the behavior, and restart it when the behavior is resumed. This process continues throughout the observation session. Duration is calculated by dividing the elapsed time on the stopwatch by the total time observed and multiplying by 100, which yields a percent duration or percent of observed time engaged in the target behavior.

The use of duration recording for alone and negative social behavior on the playground is strongly recommended for students with antisocial behavior patterns (Walker, Colvin, & Ramsey, 1995). "Alone" means a student is not within 10 feet of

Name: ___Jim_____   Date: ___1/1/02_____

Observer: ___Walker_____   Situation: ___Playground recess____

Behavioral Definition: Alone: The student is not within 10 feet of another child, is not socially engaged, and is not participating in a game or structured activity with other children. Examples include sitting, standing, shooting baskets, kicking balls off walls, and so forth.

Time Began	Time Ended	Elapsed Time

Percent Alone: Total Elapsed Time/ Total Time Observed x 100

FORM 6.1 ◆

Duration Recording Form.

another student, is not engaged in any organized activity, and is not exchanging social signals (verbal or nonverbal) with any other students. Negative social behavior is when a student is displaying hostile behavior or body language toward peers; attempting to tease, bully, or otherwise intimidate others; reacting with anger or rejection to the social bids of peers; or displaying aggressive behavior with the intent to harm or force the submission of peers.

Antisocial students spend more time alone (due primarily to the aversive nature of their behavior) and are more negative in their social interactions than are nonantisocial students. Based on playground recording, if a student spends 12–15% of the time observed in solitary activity ("alone") and engages in negative social interactions 10% or more of the time, he or she may be at risk for antisocial behavior. Form 6.1 provides an example of a playground duration recording for "alone."

A crucial feature of social behavior is its *quality*. Arguably, what truly makes a behavior socially skilled is its quality rather than its more objective features such as frequency or duration. Skilled musicians or artists are known by the creativity and quality of their performances, and so it is with children's social behavior. Quality of social behavior must be judged by others, and as such, it is closer to the notion of social competence described earlier.

An important decision in assessing social behavior involves selecting the total number of behaviors to assess and target for remediation. Some students will exhibit a relatively small number of social skills deficits and competing problem behaviors whereas other students will have a much larger number of these difficulties. The ultimate decision regarding which behaviors to target for intervention, and how many, should probably rest with the key social agents in the student's environment (e.g., teachers and parents).

Teachers and parents might be asked to list as many as 5–10 behaviors that they consider problematic. Although students may exhibit this many social behavioral excesses and deficits, not all of them are necessarily independent of one another. Target behaviors often can be organized into larger categories or dimensions that share certain similarities. These larger categories are known as response classes. For example, behaviors such as defying authority, ignoring instructions, failing to comply, and arguing might be part of a response class like oppositional behavior. Similarly, behaviors such as controlling one's temper, compromising, coping with teasing, and responding to peer pressure might be grouped under the response class of self-control. An important feature of response classes is that, in many cases, it may be possible to target just one or two members of a response class and effect a change in the remaining behaviors in that class (Gresham, 1985).

Another important issue in using direct observations of social behavior involves just how many observation occasions are needed to obtain a representative sample of behavior. The key question in this regard is: Are the observations representative of the student's *typical* behavior in the classroom, playground, or other setting? If one has an hour of time to invest in observing the social behavior of a target student, it is better to sample more occasions for a shorter period of time (e.g., four 15-minute observation occasions) than longer periods and fewer occasions (e.g., two 30-minute occasions or one 60-minute session). As a rule, the former strategy produces a more representative sampling of behavior.

Clearly, observers cannot be present in the classroom or on the playground every minute of every day. Given this practical constraint, observers must sample the behavior(s) of concern to obtain reasonable estimates of the baseline rates or durations of behavior. We suggest that observational data be collected for at least two or three sessions in the setting of concern. These sessions should reflect the setting(s) of most concern to those referring the student for social skills assessment and intervention.

Another issue in the use of observational data is that social behaviors do not typically have a normative database against which to compare or judge the severity of social skills deficits and competing behavioral excesses. One solution to this problem is to compare the target student's rates or durations of social behavior to that of selected nonreferred peers whose social behavior is considered typical or normative. This procedure allows for the development of a local "micronorm" that can be used for comparison purposes within the same setting.

Conclusion

Systematic attention to the careful assessment and development of socially competent performance within school settings is of paramount importance. Social competence is a key component of school success, which serves as a highly effective protective factor against a number of later destructive outcomes, including heavy drinking, delinquency, school failure and dropout, and sexually transmitted diseases (see Hawkins, Catalano, Kosterman, Abbott, & Hill, 1999). Antisocial students are regarded by teachers as among the least socially skilled, most socially rejected, and most problematic of all at-risk students, and they are often punished severely by school personnel (Walker & McConnell, 1995a, b). Careful screening and identification of their social skills acquisition and performance deficits, along with their competing problem behaviors, enables the delivery of cost-effective social skills instruction. Too often, systematic social skills training efforts are misguided and ineffective because these deficits are not carefully identified and tied directly to the instructional process.

 ## InfoTrac College Edition Research Terms

Behavior rating scales

Peer acceptance

Peer rejection

Sociometric assessment

References

Achenbach, T., McConaughy, S., & Howell, C. (1987). Child/adolescent behavioral and emotional problems: Implications of cross-informant correlations for situational specificity. *Psychological Bulletin, 101,* 213–232.

American Psychiatric Association (1994). *Diagnostic and statistical manual of mental disorders* (4th ed.). Washington, DC: Author.

Asher, S. (1990). Recent advances in the study of peer rejection. In S. Asher & J. Coie (Eds.), *Peer rejection in childhood* (pp. 3–16). New York: Cambridge University Press.

Caldarella, P., & Merrell, K. (1997). Common dimensions of social skills of children and adolescents: A taxonomy of positive social behaviors. *School Psychology Review, 26,* 265–279.

Caprara, G., Barbaranelli, C., Pastorelli, C., Bandura, A., & Zimbardo, P. (2000). Prosocial foundations of children's academic achievements. *Psychological Science, 11*(4), 302–306.

Coie, J., Dodge, K., & Coppotelli, H. (1982). Dimensions and types of social status: A cross-age perspective. *Developmental Psychology, 18,* 557–570.

Coie, J., & Krehbiel, G. (1984). Effects of academic tutoring on the social status of low-achieving, socially rejected children. *Child Development, 55,* 1465–1478.

Coie, J., & Kupersmidt, J. (1983). A behavioral analysis of emerging social status in boys' groups. *Child Development, 54,* 1400–1416.

Dodge, K. (1983). Behavioral antecedents of peer social status. *Child Development, 54,* 1386–1399.

Eddy, J. M., Reid, J., & Curry, V. (2002). The etiology of youth antisocial behavior, delinquency, and violence and a public health approach to prevention. In M. Shinn, H. Walker, & G. Stoner (Eds.), *Interventions for academic and behavior problems II: Preventive and remedial approaches* (pp. 27–52). Bethesda, MD: National Association of School Psychologists.

Elksnin, L. K., & Elksnin, N. (1995). *Assessment and instruction of social skills* (2nd ed.). San Diego: Singular.

Elksnin, L. K., & Elksnin, N. (1998). Teaching social skills to students with learning and behavior problems. *Intervention in school and clinic, 33,* 131–140.

Foster, S., & Ritchey, W. (1979). Issues in the assessment of social competence in children. *Journal of Applied Behavior Analysis, 12,* 625–638.

Gresham, F. M. (1981). Social skills training with handicapped children: A review. *Review of educational research, 51,* 139–176.

Gresham, F. M. (1983). Social validity in the assessment of children's social skills: Establishing standards for social competency. *Journal of Psychoeducational Assessment, 1,* 297–307.

Gresham, F. M. (1985). Behavior disorder assessment: Conceptual, definitional, and practical considerations. *School Psychology Review, 14,* 495–509.

Gresham, F. M. (1986). Conceptual issues in the assessment of social competence in children. In P. Strain, M. Guralnick, & H. Walker (Eds.), *Children's social behavior: Development, assessment, and modification* (pp. 143–179). New York: Academic Press.

Gresham, F. M. (1989). Assessment of treatment integrity in school consultation and prereferral intervention. *School Psychology Review, 18,* 37–50.

Gresham, F. M. (1995). Best practices in social skills training. In A. Thomas & J. Grimes (Eds.). *Best practices in social skills training* (3rd ed., pp. 1021–1031). Washington, DC: National Association of School Psychologists.

Gresham, F. M. (1998a). Social skills training with children: Social learning and applied behavior analytic approaches. In T. S. Watson & F. M. Gresham (Eds), *Handbook of child behavior therapy* (pp. 475–498). New York: Plenum.

Gresham, F. M. (1998b). Social skills training: Should we raze, remodel, or rebuild? *Behavioral Disorders, 24,* 19–25.

Gresham, F. M. (2001). Assessment of social skills in children and adolescents. In J. Andrews, D. Safloske, & H. Janzen (Eds.), *Handbook of psychoeducational assessment* (pp. 325–355). Orlando: Academic Press.

Gresham, F. M. (2002a). Best practices in social skills training. In A. Thomas & J. Grimes (Eds.), *Best practices in school psychology—IV* (pp. 1029–1040). Bethesda, MD: National Association of School Psychologists.

Gresham, F. M. (2002b). Teaching social skills to high-risk children and youth: Preventive and remedial strategies. In M. Shinn, H. Walker, & G. Stoner (Eds.), *Interventions for academic and behavior problems II: Preventive and remedial approaches* (pp. 403–432). Bethesda, MD: National Association of School Psychologists.

Gresham, F. M., & Elliott, S. N. (1990). *Social Skills Rating System*. Circle Pines, MN: American Guidance Service.

Gresham, F. M., Gansle, K., & Noell, G. (1993). Treatment integrity in applied behavior analysis with children. *Journal of Applied Behavior Analysis, 26,* 257–263.

Gresham, F. M., & Lambros, K. (1998). Behavioral and functional assessment. In T. S. Watson & F. M. Gresham (Eds.), *Handbook of child behavior therapy* (pp. 3–22). New York: Plenum.

Gresham, F. M., & Lopez, M. (1996). Social validation: A unifying concept for school-based consultation research and practice. *School Psychology Quarterly, 11*(3), 204–227.

Gresham, F. M., Sugai, G., & Horner, R. (2001). Interpreting outcomes of social skills training for students with high-risk disabilities. *Exceptional Children, 67,* 331–344.

Gresham, F. M., Watson, T. S., & Skinner, C. H. (2001). Functional behavioral assessment: Principles, procedures, and future directions. *School Psychology Review, 30,* 156–172.

Hawkins, R. (1991). Is social validity what we are interested in? Argument for a functional approach. *Journal of Applied Behavior Analysis, 24,* 205–213.

Hawkins, J. D., Catalano, R. F., Kosterman, R., Abbott, R., & Hill, K. G. (1999). Preventing adolescent health-risk behaviors by strengthening protection during childhood. *Archives of Pediatrics & Adolescent Medicine, 153,* 226–234.

Hernstein, R. (1970). On the law of effect. *Journal of the Experimental Analysis of Behavior, 13,* 243–266.

Hersh, R., & Walker, H. (1983). Great expectations: Making schools effective for all students. *Policy Studies Review, 2,* 147–188.

Individuals with Disabilities Education Act Amendments of 1997 (P.L. 105-17). 20 USC Chapter 33, Sections 1400 et seq.

Kazdin, A. (1977). Assessing the clinical or applied significance of behavior change through social validation. *Behavior Modification, 1,* 427–452.

Kazdin, A. (1981). Acceptability of child treatment techniques: The influence of treatment efficacy and adverse side effects. *Behavior Therapy, 12,* 493–506.

Kazdin, A. (1984). *Behavior modification in applied settings* (3rd ed.). Homewood, IL: Dorsey Press.

Kupersmidt, J., Coie, J., & Dodge, K. (1990). The role of peer relationships in the development of disorder. In S. Asher & J. Coie (Eds.), *Peer rejection in childhood* (pp. 274–308). New York: Cambridge University Press.

Landau, S., & Milich, R. (1990). Assessment of children's social status and peer relations. In A. M. LaGreca (Ed.), *Through the eyes of the child* (pp. 259–291). Boston: Allyn & Bacon.

McConnell, S., & Odom, S. (1986). Sociometrics: Peer-referenced measures and the assessment of social competence. In P. Strain, M. Guralnick, & H. Walker (Eds.), *Children's social behavior: Development, assessment, and modification* (pp. 215–286). New York: Academic Press.

McFall, R. (1982). A review and reformulation of the concept of social skills. *Behavioral Assessment, 4,* 1–35.

Merrell, K. (1993). *School Social Behavior Scales*. Austin, TX: Pro-Ed.

Merrell, K. (1994). *Preschool and Kindergarten Behavior Scales*. Austin, TX: Pro-Ed.

Merrell, K., & Gimpel, G. (1998). *Social skills of children and adolescents: Conceptualization, assessment, and treatment*. Mahwah, NJ: Lawrence Erlbaum.

Merrell, K. W. (1999). *Behavioral, social, and emotional assessment of children and adolescents*. Mahwah, NJ: Lawrence Erlbaum.

Merrell, K. W. (2001). Assessment of children's social skills: Recent developments, best practices, and new directions. *Exceptionality, 9*(1/2), 3–18.

Merrell, K. W. (2002). *School Social Behavior Scales* (2nd ed.), Eugene: Assessment Intervention Resources.

Moreno, J. (1934). *Who shall survive? A new approach to the problem of human interrelations*. Washington, DC: Nervous and Mental Disease Publishing.

Newcomb, A., Bukowski, W., & Pattee, L. (1993). Children's peer relations: A meta-analytic review of popular, rejected, neglected, controversial, and average sociometric status. *Psychological Bulletin, 113,* 306–347.

O'Neill, R. E., Horner, R. H., Albin, R. W., Storey, K., & Newton, S. (1997). *Functional analysis of problem behavior: A practical assessment guide.* Pacific Grove, CA: Brooks/Cole.

Parker, J., & Asher, S. (1987). Peer relations and later personal adjustment: Are low-accepted children at-risk? *Psychological Bulletin, 102,* 357–389.

Patterson, G. R. (1982). *Coercive family process, Vol. 3: A social learning approach*. Eugene: Castalia.

Patterson, G. R., Reid, J., & Dishion, T. (1992). *Antisocial boys*. Eugene: Castalia.

Reid, J. B., Patterson, G. R., & Snyder, J. J. (Eds.). (2002). *Antisocial behavior in children and adolescents: A developmental analysis and the Oregon Model for Intervention.* Washington, DC: American Psychological Association.

Strain, P., Cooke, R., & Apolloni, T. (1976). *Teaching exceptional children: Assessing and modifying social behavior.* New York: Academic Press.

Walker, H.. (1986). The Assessments for Integration into Mainstream Settings (AIMS) assessment system: Rationale, instruments, procedures, and outcomes. *Journal of Clinical Child Psychology, 15*(1), 55–63.

Walker, H., Colvin, G., & Ramsay, E. (1995). *Antisocial behavior in school: Strategies and best practices.* Pacific Grove, CA: Brooks/Cole.

Walker, H., Irvin, L., Noell, J., & Singer, G. (1992). A construct score approach to the assessment of social competence: Rationale, technological considerations, and anticipated outcomes. *Behavior Modification, 16,* 448–474.

Walker, H., & McConnell, S. (1995a). *Walker-McConnell Scale of Social Competence and School Adjustment: Elementary Version.* Florence, KY: Thomson Learning.

Walker, H., & McConnell, S. (1995b). *Walker-McConnell Scale of Social Competence and School Adjustment: Secondary Version.* Florence, KY: Thomson Learning.

Walker, H., & Severson, H. (1990). *Systematic Screening for Behavior Disorders.* Longmont, CO: Sopris West.

Walker, H. M., Forness, S. R., Kauffman, J. M., Epstein, M. H., Gresham, F. M., Nelson, C. M., & Strain, P. S. (1998). Macro-social validation: Referencing outcomes in behavioral disorders to societal issues and problems. *Behavioral Disorders, 24*(1), 7–18.

Walker, H. M., & Severson, H. H. (2002). Developmental prevention of at-risk outcomes for vulnerable antisocial children and youth. In K. L. Lane, F. M. Gresham, & T. E. O'Shaughnessy (Eds.), *Interventions for children with or at risk for emotional and behavioral disorders.* Boston: Allyn & Bacon.

Wolf, M. M. (1978). Social validity: The case for subjective judgment, or how applied behavior analysis is finding its heart. *Journal of Applied Behavior Analysis, 11,* 211–226.

Principles and Procedures of Social Skills Instruction and Generalization Programming for Antisocial Children and Youths

CHAPTER
7

Introduction

In the previous chapter, we discussed how the construct of social competence differentiates children and youths with antisocial behavior from those who do not exhibit this behavior pattern. We also indicated that children and youths who have low social competence levels are often rejected and/or poorly accepted by their peers. As a result, they have immense difficulties in establishing and maintaining meaningful friendships throughout their lifetimes. In fact, by the upper elementary grades, most antisocial children have "burned their bridges" to healthy affiliations with peers who behave in a conventional manner. Thus, they are left to choose their affiliates from pools of other students who share their characteristics.

The work of Patterson and his colleagues shows that when these at-risk students band together into a deviant peer group their collective risk status for delinquency and other forms of antisocial behavior escalates dramatically (see Patterson, Reid, & Dishion, 1992; Reid, Patterson, & Snyder, 2002). In Chapter 6, we also emphasized that an antisocial behavior pattern involves diverse forms of behavior (e.g., vandalism, aggression, theft) and exposure to risk factors (e.g., antisocial parents, chaotic parent–child relationships, poor parenting practices). Based on these findings, it is reasonable to provide many of these children and youths with ongoing, thorough, and carefully structured social skills training (SST) to strengthen their social competence (Bullis, Walker, & Sprague, 2001). This type of instruction, combined with coaching and incentive systems for using newly acquired social skills, increases the likelihood that at-risk children on a path to destructive outcomes will be able to forge healthy relationships with a wide range of peers and teachers. These relationships, in turn, will contribute both to school success and to bonding and attachment to the process of schooling. These have been established as important protective factors against later negative outcomes in adolescence including delinquent violent acts, aggression and bullying, heavy drinking, and sexually transmitted diseases (see Hawkins, Catalano, Kosterman, Abbott, & Hill, 1999).

Before embarking on an SST program, keep two issues clearly in mind. First, not all antisocial children and youths are necessaily socially incompetent within all the contexts in which they function. Although the behavior of antisocial students is almost universally considered obnoxious by their teachers and peers, many antisocial individuals are extremely socially adept at achieving their goals, albeit often inappropriate ones, and they use their interpersonal skills to achieve antisocial ends (Bullis et al., 2001). Obviously, these individuals do not need SST in the same manner as do those antisocial children and youths demonstrating social skills acquisition and/or performance deficits. For this reason, a comprehensive and accurate social skills assessment, as described in Chapter 6, is essential to an SST intervention that will effectively and accurately target the student's *specific* problems.

Second, at-risk children and youths who are antisocial can be extremely resistant to even our most intense and powerful interventions (Bullis et al., 2001; Gresham, 2002a; Reid, Patterson, & Snyder, 2002). Students exhibiting antisocial behavior patterns in the school setting typically are characterized by aggression, hostility, and persistent violation of social norms. They have a history of successfully resisting tactics of adult social influence. To make matters worse, they are often resistant to well-implemented, evidence-based interventions delivered within the school setting. When they do not change their behavior in response to these often expensive school interventions, they are blamed and socially punished by the school personnel involved—which often leads them to drop out. Failing that, they become candidates for assignment to alternative educational settings in which the possibility exists that they will be socialized by other deviant peers to ever more diverse and higher levels of deviance (see Dishion & Andrews, 1995).

These outcomes are especially likely unless good-faith intervention attempts are applied very early in the students' educational careers with solid implementation fidelity—beginning in preschool is none too soon! In fact, Kazdin (1987) has suggested that after age 8 a well-established antisocial behavior pattern should be viewed more as a chronic condition, such as diabetes, that cannot be "cured" in the medical sense but that can be managed effectively over the long term with appropriate interventions and supports. This notion will be developed further in our discussion of a continuum of behavioral supports and generalization programming. Having said this, it is important to note that at-risk children and youths should be given every opportunity to succeed during their *entire* school careers. It is never too late to intervene effectively even though the impact of the intervention may be attenuated somewhat among older students who have a long history of involvement with antisocial behavior or disruptive behavior patterns. Such older students can especially benefit from systematic social skills instruction and coaching as they prepare to enter the adult world of independent living and work.

This chapter describes best-practice procedures and recommended guidelines for implementing SST, focusing on two levels of social skills interventions: (1) universal interventions and (2) individualized interventions. Before implementing a social skills intervention, it is also recommended that the reader consider the list of 10 cardinal rules for conducting social skills training listed in Box 7.1.

A Continuum of Behavioral Supports for Teaching Social Skills

All students do not require the same level and intensity of intervention for mastering prosocial behavior in schools. Some are candidates for intensive intervention of a remedial nature due to their prior risk factor exposure; others will benefit from less intensive efforts designed to achieve broad-based prevention outcomes through the application of universal intervention approaches. Walker and Severson (2002) distinguish between prevention of and intervention with antisocial behavior patterns. *Prevention* refers to an outcome (the end result) that is accomplished via various types of intervention strategies. For example, vaccines in the 1950s prevented (and virtually eradicated) the disease of polio. *Intervention,* in contrast, is a collection of approaches or processes that allow for the achievement of prevention outcomes; that is, intervention becomes a means to an end.

Three levels of prevention have been identified in the public health literature—primary, secondary, and tertiary—and each level has a different goal. This conceptual model of prevention, as described and illustrated in Chapter 2, is particularly well suited for school settings. The goal in primary prevention is to *prevent* negative outcomes; the goal in secondary prevention is to *reverse* the impact of negative outcomes; and the goal in tertiary prevention is to *reduce* negative outcomes (O'Shaughnessy, Lane, Gresham, & Beebe-Frankenberger, 2002).

A comprehensive approach to teaching social skills in schools entails the following: (1) teaching appropriate behaviors rather than merely punishing inappropriate ones, (2) matching the level of intervention resources to the level of behavioral challenges presented by students, and (3) designing and integrating multiple systems dealing with the full range of behavioral challenges (Sugai, Horner, & Gresham, 2002). These principles and their careful application are extremely important in achieving the prevention goals noted previously.

Primary prevention efforts utilize universal interventions designed to impact *all* students in the same manner under the same conditions. Examples of universal interventions are classwide social skills training programs, schoolwide discipline plans, and districtwide reading curricula. In a classwide or schoolwide social skills program, for example, all students receive instruction on the same basic social skills taught in exactly the same way. Approximately 80–90% of all students will respond successfully to this type of universal intervention (Sugai et al., 2002). For this large group of typical students, the goal is to enhance and maintain their current level of social skills, prevent alienation from teachers and peers, and reduce or eliminate norm-violating behaviors that could eventually lead to adoption of an antisocial lifestyle. In other words, primary prevention approaches seek to keep problems from developing or emerging. Schoolwide social skills intervention programs have the potential for developing a positive social culture within the school where everyone endorses and responds to a common set of shared values such as safety, responsibility, and respect (Sugai et al., 2002).

Students who do not respond adequately to such universal interventions will likely require secondary prevention efforts using either small-group or individualized, selected interventions. That is, a relatively small number of students typically "select" themselves out as needing more powerful interventions due to their inadequate response(s) to the universal intervention. These interventions incorporate much more expensive and labor-intensive strategies. An estimated 5–10% of all students will require selected SST programs designed for a subset of the target student population, and the procedures will be individually tailored and fine-tuned to fit the specific needs of these target students. The goal here is to decrease the occasions or situations in which their high-risk behaviors are likely to occur and to instill an effective prosocial behavioral repertoire that may also facilitate their responsiveness to universal interventions (Sugai et al., 2002).

A still smaller subset of a school's student population (e.g., 1–5%) will typically require even more intensive, tertiary prevention efforts, because their problem behaviors and social competence deficits prove to be resistant to selected interventions. These more intensive interventions are referred to as "indicated" in the psychological literature. Behavioral supports provided for these students must be both intense and individualized in nature, and they frequently require systems of coordination and integration in which school personnel must collaborate with other social service agencies (e.g., mental health, juvenile justice, and social services) (Sugai et al., 2002; Walker & Severson, 2002). These students must be exposed to very powerful interventions to reduce the frequency, intensity, and complexity of severe problem behaviors and to provide effective, alternative prosocial replacements for them. Sugai and his colleagues (2002) suggest that the central goal underlying these indicated interventions is to find and teach prosocial behaviors that will successfully compete with interfering problem behaviors—an important but difficult task.

Universal interventions are particularly useful within prevention contexts, whereas selected and intensive interventions are more applicable to the remediation of well-established behavior patterns that have proved resistant to previous behavioral-change efforts. Because universal SST interventions are less difficult to implement and because all students are exposed to them in the same manner, they are more likely to be acceptable to teachers. Selected and intensive interventions have the disadvantage of appearing to treat individual students in a way qualitatively different from that accorded other students. However, it's important to note that some students will require these more intensive interventions, based on their inadequate responsiveness to universal interventions, and it

©Cleve Bryant/PhotoEdit

Tertiary prevention is essential for behaviors resistant to primary and secondary approaches. This level of prevention requires powerful actions designed to reduce inappropriate, problem behaviors, and often calls on social service agencies for collaboration and support.

is a mistake to deny them access to these more specialized treatments. Further, as we have noted elsewhere, selected and indicated interventions are likely to be more efficient and to have a greater impact if they are applied in the context of a prior well-implemented, universal intervention.

Universal SST interventions are obviously less powerful than either selected or indicated interventions, and different standards are used to judge their effectiveness. Universal interventions have their greatest impact among students who are "on the margins"—who are mildly at risk or who are just beginning to show the early signs of an emerging antisocial behavior pattern. On many occasions, systematic exposure to universal intervention approaches might be sufficient to tip these students in the right direction and divert them from a destructive path leading to antisocial behavior. The best way to judge the effectiveness of a universal intervention is to assess the extent to which it reduces the expected base rate of problem behaviors among groups of students (i.e., at classroom, school, or district levels). Selected and indicated interventions, in contrast, must be evaluated in terms of how effective they are in changing the behavior of individual students in the desired directions. As such, judgments about the efficacy of selected and indicated interventions are usually made on a case-by-case basis.

Proven Approaches for Accomplishing Social Skills Instruction

Social skills training (SST) has four primary goals: (1) promote skills acquisition, (2) enhance skill performance, (3) remove or reduce competing problem behaviors, and (4) facilitate generalization and maintenance of skills. Many students who qualify for individualized, selected, and indicated interventions display a combination of acquisition, performance, and fluency deficits and thus will require differing social skills instructional strategies. Universal interventions, as described next, do not require such differentiation and classification of students' specific social skills deficits.

A Universal Approach: The LIFT Program

As discussed previously, with universal approaches the focus is on the entire classroom, and all students are targeted to the same degree and in the same manner. Regular classroom teachers and playground supervisors typically play critical roles in the implementation of universal interventions. The classroom is an ideal setting for interventions that either prevent or decrease antisocial school behavior. Classroom-level interventions enable equal and simultaneous access to all students under identical conditions.

Classrooms and playgrounds are two of the main contexts for delivering social skills and interaction training involving peers and adults. The classroom makes it possible to provide instruction in social skills using the same procedures and guidelines as in teaching academic content. The playground provides many occasions and opportunities (1) to prompt and coach students to apply the peer interaction skills they've been taught and (2) to recognize, praise, and reward their attempts to display the target skills.

There is tremendous potential for students to learn and practice new social skills at school. In fact, the school is a more "natural" venue for teaching social behavior using naturally occurring behavioral incidents to develop social skills (via incidental teaching strategies). And teachers and students generally feel comfortable with this approach, particularly when it is integrated into the ongoing academic program.

The following universal intervention, developed by John Reid and his colleagues at the Oregon Social Learning Center (OSLC), is a relatively low-cost and brief intervention that can be implemented with existing school personnel in home, classroom, and playground settings (Reid & Eddy, 2002). These three settings allow the direct participation of the three social agents who are most important in children's lives and whose involvement is critical to the successful outcome of any behavioral intervention. This program is titled "Linking the Interests of Families and Teachers" (LIFT), which highlights the importance of close collaboration between home and school in any prevention and intervention efforts. The goal of LIFT is to prevent antisocial behavior patterns from leading to more and greater problems later on (e.g., conduct disorder in elementary school children). LIFT is a multifaceted approach that combines parent education with social skills training for all students. The social skills program and parent education components run simultaneously in order for information and procedures to be replicated for target children in both school and at home, thus increasing the likelihood of achieving behavioral consistency across settings. It should be noted, however, that conducting classroom social skills instruction *without* the parent education component is still a viable option for students whose parents refuse participation. Access to a social skills program or other treatment(s) should *never* be denied to students whose parents choose not to implement or support home intervention procedures. As a rule, in most cases, substantial benefits can be derived from the school intervention alone.

Home Intervention. The parent education component of LIFT teaches parents to use consistent and effective positive reinforcement strategies, discipline, and monitoring skills at home (Reid & Eddy, 2002). This component is delivered during six weekly sessions lasting 1½ hours per session for a total of 9 contact hours. Like most parent-training programs, LIFT uses a variety of presentation formats including lectures, videotaped examples and nonexamples, and role-playing. The parent education component is delivered in a group format to facilitate group teaching-learning, networking, and communication among parents who share similar interests, concerns, and/or challenges with their children.

In the LIFT program, first-grade parents receive instruction emphasizing how to coach their children in developing positive peer relationships, and fifth-grade parents are taught problem-solving skills that will prepare and assist their children in negotiating the perils and challenges of adolescence. Additionally, a phone-message/answering machine (i.e., the "LIFT Line") allows teachers to record messages to parents about classroom and homework activities and to provide information regarding their children. A more detailed description of LIFT can be found in other publications (see e.g., Eddy, Reid, & Fetrow, 2000).

Classroom Intervention. The LIFT classroom intervention is designed around 20 lessons lasting one hour each. Many components of the intervention can be easily integrated in the regular academic curriculum and thus be reinforced throughout the school year. Generalization and maintenance of social skills is the primary focus of this approach. All children are included so nonproblem students can learn ways of including and supporting their peers. The classroom teacher is the primary instructor, which means that skills such as cooperation and listening can be practiced and reinforced throughout the school day.

Teaching social skills in a normative peer group context has one main advantage: Students can observe each other's behavior during skills practice sessions. Also, less successful individuals and groups can observe the interactions and end products of more successful individuals and groups. Cooperative peer groups have been shown to support and motivate change in both academic achievement and social competence areas (Johnson & Johnson, 1986; Slavin, 1984). The simple act of pairing unpopular children with popular children will significantly improve the social interaction skills of both and can also lead to the increased social acceptance of the unpopular children (Bierman, 1986; Bierman & Furman, 1984).

In cooperative learning arrangements, students have the opportunity to pool their knowledge and skills while completing a project or assignment together. For example, during a "Dealing with Anger" lesson in the LIFT program, student teams are instructed to create a 5-minute video depicting positive ways of dealing with an anger-provoking situation. Students take different roles (director, actor, camera person) and work on developing a script as a group. Participating students share their skills and knowledge and learn from each other in completing a problem-solving or production task.

Many of the whole-class, LIFT social skills lessons are based on teaching those competencies in which antisocial children are traditionally weak. Students spend 45–60 minutes each week engaged in role-plays, dramatizations, and other cooperative activities that address the following topics:

◆ Following rules

◆ Listening

◆ Developing study skills

◆ Listening and asking questions

◆ Identifying feelings

◆ Complimenting others (giving and receiving)

◆ Cooperating

◆ Joining groups

◆ Including new people

◆ Dealing with anger

Almost all social skills curricula can be adapted to meet the needs of an entire classroom. Lessons were developed for the LIFT whole-class approach by examining several curricula and adapting activities so that all students could participate in them.

In addition to traditional social skills lessons, this whole-class approach calls for students to gather in a classroom meeting once each week. There are two goals for these meetings. One is to give each student the opportunity to speak to the rest of the class while the other students listen. This is an especially useful activity for both antisocial and neglected students. The second goal is to provide an opportunity to learn problem-solving skills. Once the problem-solving procedure has been taught and the students and classroom teacher feel comfortable with all the steps involved, the class meeting becomes a forum for solving student problems. Relevant problems generally involve such issues as social-interactional ones or rule-following compliance difficulties.

Students begin each class meeting with a review of the social skills introduced up to that point. For example, during the sixth week of class meetings, the teacher starts with a quick review in the form of a question-and-answer game about following rules, listening, pinpointing feelings, and asking appropriate questions. After this review, each student "checks in." That is, students are invited to share examples from their own lives in which they used a particular social skill, briefly describing the situation and then identifing the skill involved (more review and practice).

Over time, students use the check-in procedure to identify problems that can then be worked through using the problem-solving strategy. After check-in, students either engage in learning one of the following four problem-solving steps or use the entire sequence to actually solve problems. These steps cover the basic strategies usually employed when teaching problem solving:

◆ Clearly state the problem.

◆ Brainstorm alternative solutions.

◆ Evaluate the feasibility of solutions.

◆ Try out a solution.

Most antisocial students have no idea how to solve problems effectively. They devote little time to thinking through problems, tend to jump in impulsively, and often end up doing something inappropriate (e.g., yelling, fighting, or giving up). Not only are these students provided with an opportunity to learn more effective problem-solving strategies, but they can practice again and again and observe how their peers use these same problem-solving strategies. For their part, nonproblem students learn effective ways of working through problems with aggressive and antisocial students, as well as techniques for examining issues in their own lives.

Playground Intervention: The Playground Behavior Game.   The LIFT playground intervention provides the context for facilitating ongoing generalization training efforts. This intervention component is a variation of the Good Behavior Game (Barrish, Sanders, & Wolfe, 1969) and is conducted immediately after each of the 20 classroom sessions described previously. (The Good Behavior Game divides the classroom in half and awards points and privileges to the team of students that most closely adheres to class rules.) The goal of this intervention is to ensure continual practice of newly acquired skills within natural settings in which coaching (cuing, prompting, debriefing) is available. It targets inappropriate behaviors as well. We strongly recommend using an additional incentive (or reward) system when first implementing a social skills program of this type in order to motivate student mastery of the skills.

Before starting this program, assign students to teams of four to six members each. Teams should have roughly equivalent numbers of boys and girls and be composed of both popular and rejected or neglected children. Friends can be occasionally paired in teams, especially if one of the students feels comfortable participating with the other. If possible, desks for each team should be placed together. But group selection and membership does not have to remain fixed. If a particular group seems to be having difficulty, then the groups should be reconfigured to achieve more even performance among them. If a group-based or cooperative approach of this type is used throughout the school year for academic subjects, consider reconfiguring the groups every two or three months.

The Playground Behavior Game is substantially more difficult to describe than it is to implement. It has been our experience that, once in place, the game has a tremendous positive impact on the social behavior of most students, including those who are antisocial. Adult playground supervisors are also positively affected by this activity. Without the Playground Behavior Game or some other free-play incentive system, generalization and maintenance of newly learned skills to and within natural settings are highly unlikely. Without providing for achievement of these critical outcomes, teaching social skills is not really a good investment of teachers' and students' time in terms of cost–benefit ratios.

Component I: Positive Behavior. Although positive behavior on the playground is acknowledged for individual students in LIFT, the actual rewards are earned for *all* students. When a predetermined criterion is met, the entire class qualifies for a valuable group reward. This is known as an interdependent group contingency because the reward for the group depends upon the behavior(s) of each group member. The playground supervisors circulate among students during recess looking for examples of positive, prosocial behaviors such as interacting nicely with peers, following directions, playing properly with playground equipment, and staying within designated boundaries.

The playground supervisors must move around a great deal in order to observe, monitor, coach, and reinforce positive student behavior. When the supervisors observe a student engaged in an appropriate form of behavior, they call attention to it and present the student with an armband.

The supervisors might distribute anywhere from 20 to 50 armbands per period to recognize instances of positive student behavior. The classroom teacher can assist the playground supervisors by focusing on certain target social skills for adult recognition and reinforcement. For example, some classes may have problems in quietly or quickly lining up after recess. The supervisors can be instructed to make a special effort to acknowledge positive "line behavior." Or, if the social skill lesson that week involves accepting new people into games, the playground supervisors can make this the primary target behavior for which students receive armbands.

Another LIFT variation for distributing positive incentives involves student representatives. Two or three students in the class are enlisted as special helpers to distribute armbands to their classmates for performing positive behaviors and demonstrating target social skills. This should not be attempted, however, until all students are thoroughly familiar with the Playground Behavior Game. Also, the selected students should be rotated so that everyone has a chance to distribute positive incentives to their classmates. This technique works well with the full range of elementary school students. It relieves the playground supervisors of some of the monitoring burdens and makes students more responsible for their own behavior. The armbands are collected at the end of the recess period.

Component II: Negative Behavior. Negative social behavior in LIFT is addressed in a group format although student behavior is tracked individually. Monitoring student behavior on the playground requires a score sheet for each class, with student names listed by team (see "Component IV: Materials"). The playground supervisors use this score sheet to track occurrences of negative behavior.

All teams start recess with the same number of points. The class should be told that all groups have been given all of the possible points because you (the classroom teacher) trust that they will not engage in negative behaviors or break playground rules during recess. Explain that, any time a student engages in negative behavior with other students or breaks a playground rule, he or she will lose one of the team's preawarded points. If, at the end of recess, the total points remaining for a group is greater than a predetermined criterion, each group member earns a sticker, and the group's success is recorded on a large progress chart displayed in the classroom. Over the course of the year, the criteria for earning a reward become more and more difficult as students increase their social skill levels.

Students can lose points for behaviors such as teasing, arguing, name-calling, bullying, leaving the boundary area, entering the building, fighting, not coming at the signal, not using playground equipment properly, and not following directions. It is important to mark off points even for small infractions. The LIFT playground supervisors, for example, should not ignore lower-level infractions and wait for a physical fight to occur. Rather, they should intervene early in the behavioral chain of escalating events and mark off points for name-calling, arguing, and teasing, because these behaviors are often precursors to more serious "behavioral earthquakes" such as fighting or other forms of physical aggression.

Participating LIFT classroom teachers should work closely with playground supervisors in creating a list of social behaviors and skills that will prompt the loss of points. In implementing the LIFT program, let students know that not all negative behaviors, rule infractions, or even attempts to use the positive behavior(s) taught during social skills lessons will be observed every time but that, on average and over time, many of these behaviors will be noted and recorded. These intermittent schedules of reinforcement tend to produce steady, moderate increases in positive social behavior and corresponding decreases in negative behavior.

Component III: Debriefing. As recess is ending, the playground supervisors should hand the score sheet to the classroom teacher. This sheet serves as the mechanism for communication between supervisors and participating classroom teachers. A few examples of both positive and negative recess behavior are noted on it.

As students enter the classroom following recess, they can drop their armbands into a large jar. A short class discussion should take place in which students are praised for specific positive behaviors on the playground. During this discussion, it may be appropriate to refer to a student by name, especially if it is an antisocial student displaying positive social behavior on the playground. Or a more general statement can be made to a group, such as "I heard that the Green Team did an excellent job of including someone else in their game."

It is also important to point to specific examples of negative behavior and to describe or review them. Students should *not* be referred to individually for their negative behavior, as others may tend to focus blame on them. For example, avoid saying, "The Red Team lost two points; one point for Frank leaving the boundary area and one when Laura teased Matt." For one or two of the incidents, it is important to ask students how a negative situation might have been handled in a more positive way.

Students can earn small rewards for good performance in a number of ways in the LIFT program. First, the entire class can earn a prize of some type when the jar of armbands is full. Second, group members can earn stickers for meeting the daily criteria. Vary the order and choice for prizes, stickers, and progress charts in order to keep student motivation high.

Component IV: Materials. The following materials are needed in implementing the Playground Behavior Game:

- ◆ Large poster displayed in the classroom listing playground rules
- ◆ Nylon armbands (or any tangible reward that can be distributed easily on an individual basis)
- ◆ Jar for collecting armbands (or other tokens)
- ◆ Classwide prizes for distribution when the jar is full (e.g., plastic animals, lunch coupons, stickers, extra free time, and snacks)

◆ Score sheet divided by team and listing all students—for example:

RED TEAM	GREEN TEAM	BLUE TEAM
Frank	Luke	Pat
Laura	Jose	June
Matt	Judy	Seth
Jill	Gabrielle	Jan
Julie	Audrey	Marty

◆ Clipboard and pencil

◆ Progress chart for tracking group progress

Getting a Universal Social Skills Program Going in Your Classroom

The aims or goals of any social skills program are to change students' interpersonal behaviors with peers and adults and to improve the effectiveness of their social behavior. Valued outcomes include friendship making and social acceptance within peer groups, acceptance by significant adults, good school adjustment, better mental health, improved academic performance, and lack of contact with the juvenile court. The universal (whole-class) approach to teaching social skills illustrated by LIFT and the accompanying incentive system via the Playground Behavior Game to ensure generalization and maintenance is an ideal way of reaching these goals. As we have noted, this universal approach may not work for the most seriously antisocial students, but it is a logical and natural starting point for intervening with such students. Box 7.2 lists the key steps and time line for implementing LIFT.

Selected Approaches to Social Skills Training

Whenever possible, social skills interventions should be delivered within the context of natural school settings and be embedded within target students' peer groups. The LIFT universal social skills intervention described previously is an excellent means of doing so. The rule to remember is this: Isolated, pullout approaches divorced from the peer group are to be avoided whenever possible because they are unlikely to be effective. However, it is also important to remember that a certain percentage of students (e.g., 10–15%) typically will not respond to a universal-intervention program and may need a more intense, selected-intervention approach (Sugai et al., 2002).

In reviewing the intervention literature on the state of pullout social skills programs, Gresham (1998b) argues that social skills interventions can be made more effective by attending to three key issues. First, social skills interventions should be matched to the specific types of social skills deficits and competing behavioral excesses students exhibit. These deficits and target behaviors were described in detail in Chapter 6. As we shall see, interventions for remediating acquisition deficits require different approaches than interventions for performance or fluency deficits. Second, social skills interventions should be conducted primarily using informal or incidental teaching strategies that take

Box 7.2

Box 7.2 Key Steps and Time Lines for Implementing LIFT

One Month Prior

1. Review age-appropriate social skills curricula.
2. Make a list of students for each team (remember four to six students, equal mix of males and females, and only one or two rejected students per team).
3. Prepare materials for the Playground Behavior Game (or other free-play incentive system).
4. Meet with playground supervisors to review playground rules and the incentive system.
5. Make one to two hours available during the weeks of social skills instruction.

One Week Prior

1. Order relevant lessons.
2. Prepare a 1- to 2-minute description of the lesson's skill.
3. Prepare a short demonstration or role-play of the lesson's skill (3–5 minutes).
4. Let students and parents know what is coming.

Day 1

1. Move desks.
2. Introduce the social skills program.
3. Begin the first lesson.

Ongoing

1. Continue to plan new group activities.
2. Monitor the Playground Behavior Game.
3. Provide rewards earned during the Playground Behavior Game.
4. Reconfigure groups as necessary.

Source: Reid and Eddy (2002).

advantage of naturally occurring behavioral incidents or events. Teaching social skills using these naturalistic behavioral processes is more likely to facilitate the generalization and maintenance of prosocial behavior. Third, social skills interventions should consider the functional aspects of generalization by conceptualizing the generalization process within a competing behaviors model (Horner & Billingsley, 1988). That is, the goal of programming for functional generalization is to make socially skilled behaviors more efficient and reliable relative to competing problem behaviors (Gresham, 1998b, 2002a). For example, the advantages and incentives for complying with a rule or behaving appropriately should at least equal (and hopefully exceed) those for not doing so.

Example of a Selected-Intervention Approach

A number of selected social skills intervention approaches can be used to teach prosocial behavior and social skills. Many of these are referenced at the end of this chapter. For purposes of illustration, we have chosen an example from the *Social Skills Intervention Guide* (SSIG) (Elliott & Gresham, 1991), which teaches 43 social skills that teachers and parents broadly agree are important to the development and effective functioning of children and youths. As a selected intervention, the SSIG focuses on those students within a classroom who need additional and more intensive instruction in order to master the target skills. Generally, small-group instruction formats and individualized tutoring, instruction, coaching, and debriefing are used to deliver curricular content in this manner. The SSIG is tied directly to the Social Skills Rating System (SSRS) (Gresham & Elliott, 1990), described in Chapter 6. Recall that the SSRS assesses social skills across five domains of interpersonal functioning: (1) cooperation (e.g., helping others, sharing materials, complying with rules and instructions), (2) assertion (e.g., asking others for information, introducing oneself, responding to the actions of others), (3) responsibility (e.g., communicating with adults, caring for property or work), (4) empathy (e.g., showing concern and respect for others' feelings and viewpoints), and (5) self-control (e.g., responding appropriately to teasing and name-calling, taking turns, compromising).

Selected social skills interventions have four fundamental objectives: (1) promoting skill acquisition, (2) enhancing skill performance, (3) removing or reducing competing problem behaviors, and (4) facilitating generalization and maintenance of acquired social skills (Gresham, 2002a). It is common for students to experience a combination of acquisition, performance, and fluency deficits that coexist with competing problem behaviors. As described in Chapter 6, an accurate assessment and classification of these deficits should be conducted *prior to* initiating a social skills intervention. Box 7.3 presents a number of specific social skills intervention strategies that are used in the SSIG.

Procedures for Promoting Skills Acquisition

The decision to implement an intervention to promote the acquisition of social skills depends on whether (1) a student does not have a particular social skill in his or her behavioral repertoire and/or (2) the student does not know a specific step in the performance of a behavioral sequence (Gresham, 2002a). The three key procedures used to remediate social skills acquisition deficits are coaching, modeling, and behavioral rehearsal. Elliott and Gresham's (1991) SSIG recommends that these procedures be implemented in a tell-show-do sequence corresponding to coaching, modeling, and behavioral rehearsal, respectively. Box 7.4 provides guidelines for using coaching, modeling, and behavioral rehearsal for remediating social skills acquisition deficits.

Coaching involves verbal instruction to teach social skills and utilizes students' receptive language skills. Coaching takes place in a sequence of three fundamental steps: (1) presenting social rules or concepts, (2) providing opportunities for practice or rehearsal of the target social skills, and (3) providing specific informational feedback regarding the student's performance of the social

Box 7.3   Social Skills Intervention Strategies

Promoting Skill Acquisition

- Modeling
- Coaching
- Behavioral rehearsal

Enhancing Skill Performance

- Manipulation of antecedents
  Peer initiation strategies
  Proactive classroom management strategies
  Peer tutoring
  Incidental teaching
- Manipulation of consequences
  Contingency contracting
  Group-oriented contingency systems
  School–home notes
  Verbal praise
  Preferred activity reinforcers
  Token/point systems

Removing Competing Problem Behaviors

- Differential reinforcement
  Differential reinforcement of other behavior (DRO)
  Differential reinforcement of low rates of behavior (DRL)
  Differential reinforcement of incompatible behavior (DRI)
  Differential reinforcement of decreasing rates of behavior (DRD)
- Overcorrection
- Time-out
- Systematic desensitization (for anxiety-based competing behaviors)
- Flooding/exposure (for anxiety-based competing behaviors)

Facilitating Generalization and Maintenance

- Topographical generalization
  Training diversely
  Exploiting functional contingencies
  Incorporating functional mediators
- Functional generalization
  Identifying strong competing stimuli in specific situations
  Identifying strong competing problem behaviors in specific situations
  Identifying functionally equivalent socially skilled replacement behaviors
  Increasing the reliability and efficiency of socially skilled behaviors
     (building fluency)
  Decreasing the reliability and efficiency of competing problem behaviors

| Box 7.4 | **General Guidelines for Modeling, Coaching, and Behavioral Rehearsal** |

Modeling

Benefits of Learning the Skill

1. Ask why the social skill might be important.

2. Identify potential consequences for using the social skill.

3. Use examples from movies, television, books, and so forth in which characters use the social skill.

4. Identify settings and situations in which the skill could be and should be used.

Task Analysis of Skill Components

1. Select a social skill to be discussed (e.g., compromising in conflict situations).

2. Brainstorm behaviors a person would have to perform to compromise in a conflict situation.

3. Write students' ideas on a flip chart or the chalkboard.

4. Discuss the relevance of each idea and decide which behaviors would be important in compromising in conflict situations.

5. Decide with the group which behaviors would be most important in compromising in conflict situations.

6. Decide with the group the order or sequence in which the behaviors should be performed.

7. Identify with the group potential problems that might occur when performing the skill (e.g., taunting, verbal aggression).

Demonstration of Skills Using Modeled Instruction

1. Decide whether you or another student in the group will model the skill.

2. Point out the necessary behaviors for performing the skill. Write these on the board before modeling the skill.

3. Tell students to watch and see if each behavioral step is performed and if it was performed in the proper sequence.

4. Model the skill or have another child model the skill.

5. After modeling, solicit feedback from students in evaluating the modeling sequence. Discuss comments offered.

Rehearsal of Skills

1. Have students practice the skill with each other.

2. Provide specific feedback regarding behavioral rehearsals.

3. Offer suggestions for how performances might be improved.

4. Remodel the skill and require repeated behavioral rehearsals to build fluency.

Box 7.4 *(Continued)*

Program for Generalization.

1. Role-play a number of situations in which the skill could be used.
2. Vary the situations in which the skill could be used (e.g., number and type of persons present, type of conflict situation, location of the conflict situation).
3. Teach a number of variations in performing the skill in the same situation.
4. Show students how there are numerous ways of accomplishing the same goal in a social interaction (e.g., multiple ways of resolving conflict).

Coaching

1. Present a social concept (e.g., ask the group what compromise means).
2. Ask for definitions of the social concept.
3. Sharpen the group's definition of the social concept (e.g., "Compromise could also mean . . . as well as . . .").
4. Ask for specific behavioral examples of the social concept (e.g.,"What are some things kids would do to show that they are compromising?").
5. Elicit from the group potential consequences for using and not using the skill.
6. Generate settings and situations in which the social skill would be appropriate and inappropriate.
7. Use behavioral rehearsal to practice the skill.
8. Elicit specific performance feedback about the behavioral rehearsals.
9. Build fluency with repeated rehearsals of the skill.

Behavioral Rehearsal

Covert Rehearsal

1. Have students close their eyes. Present a scene involving a social interaction.
2. Have students imagine themselves performing the social skill in the scene.
3. Have students imagine how other people in the scene would respond to their behavior.
4. Have students imagine alternative behaviors they could perform in the scene and the consequences associated with each.

Verbal Rehearsal

1. Present a social situation involving a social interaction.
2. Have students identify each step in performing the social skill.
3. Have student orally arrange these steps in a proper sequence.
4. Have students describe situations in which the skill would be appropriate.
5. Have students describe potential consequences of performing the social skill.
6. For each situation, have students describe alternative social behaviors and the consequences associated with each behavior.

Box 7.4 *(Continued)*

Overt Rehearsal

1. Describe a role-play situation, select participants, and assign roles for each participant.

2. Have participants role-play the social situation. Instruct observers to watch the performances of each participant closely.

3. Discuss and evaluate performances in the role-play, and provide suggestions for improved performances.

4. Ask participants to incorporate feedback suggestions as they replay the scene.

5. Select new participants to role-play the same scene.

6. Build fluency with repeated rehearsals of the social skill.

skill. As such, coaching means "telling" the student how to perform a social skill and "telling" the student about his or her effectiveness in using the skill.

Coaching transmits general principles of social interaction, allows for the integration of behavioral sequences in performing a social skill, sets appropriate goals for accomplishing social interactions, and enhances students' awareness of the impact of their social behavior on others (Renshaw & Asher, 1983). One key assumption in coaching is that students can use general principles of social interaction to guide and regulate their behavior across a variety of social situations. As such, coaching might be considered a means of teaching rule-governed behavior because one does not have to teach to each and every social situation students are likely to encounter. Rule-governed behavior stands in contrast to contingency-shaped behaviors, which require that specific behavioral contingencies be taught for every situation that students might encounter in the natural environment (Elliott & Gresham, 1991).

Modeling is based on the principle of observational learning and vicarious reinforcement as described by Bandura (1977) in his classic work. Learning a behavioral skill through modeling does not require the observer to actually perform the behavior, nor does the observer have to directly experience the consequences of performing the behavior. Modeled instruction allows for the presentation of the entire behavioral sequence involved in a given social skill and teaches the observer how to integrate specific behavioral actions into a composite behavior pattern.

Modeling is based, in part, on the principle of vicarious reinforcement, whereby observers learn a behavior by being indirectly reinforced for observing a model receiving reinforcement for social skill performances. In contrast, the goal of direct reinforcement procedures, as used to remediate social performance deficits, is to increase the frequency or rate of application of already-learned social skills. Modeling is one of the most efficient and effective means of teaching

Social skills training that incorporates peer modeling improves and enhances appropriate social skills and prosocial behaviors, including cooperation, responsibility, and empathy.

© David Young-Wolff/PhotoEdit

social skills because it does not involve teaching each and every behavioral component in a social skill sequence (Elliott & Gresham, 1991).

Behavioral rehearsal refers to practice of a newly learned social skill within a structured and controlled role-play situation. Behavioral rehearsal also allows students to improve their proficiency with a given social skill without experiencing negative or adverse consequences. From a social learning perspective, Bandura (1977) has argued that behavioral rehearsal is critical for the acquisition of social behavior.

Behavioral rehearsal can be used in three ways: covert, verbal, and overt. In covert rehearsal, the student uses visual imagery to imagine the performance of a given social skill in a specific situation. Verbal rehearsal requires that the student recite out loud the steps and correct sequence of usage for a particular social skill. Overt rehearsal requires that the student actually perform the social skill being taught. These three forms of behavioral rehearsal can be used in various combinations or steps to rehearse a given social skill. Box 7.5 provides an example of how to teach the social skill of compromising in conflict situations via coaching, modeling, and behavioral rehearsal.

Procedures for Enhancing Skills Performance

The majority of social skills interventions involve procedures designed to increase the frequency of prosocial behavior, and not to teach specifically how to perform a social behavior per se. In other words, most social skill(s) difficulties are *performance* rather than *acquisition* deficits. This implies that the majority of social skills interventions should occur in naturalistic settings such as the classroom and playground rather than in small-group situations. Procedures for doing so were described earlier in this chapter.

Social skills may not be performed at sufficiently high or desirable frequencies due to two factors: (1) inappropriately arranged antecedents and (2) inappropriately arranged consequences. A number of specific interventions can be classified as antecedent- and consequence-based strategies.

Box 7.5   **Example of Teaching Compromising in Conflict Situations Using Coaching, Modeling, and Behavioral Rehearsal**

Objective: The student will compromise in conflict situations with others by changing an opinion, modifying actions, and/or offering alternative solutions.

Coaching

1. Introduce the skill and ask questions about it.
   When was the last time you had an argument with one of your class-mates? What was the argument about and what did you do? What happened?
   What does the word *compromise* mean?
   What are some things people would do to show that they are compromising?
   How do people show that they are not willing to compromise?
   What are some good things that might happen if you compromise in an argument or disagreement with your classmates, friends, teachers, or parents?
   What are some bad things that might happen if you do not compromise with classmates, friends, teachers, or parents?

2. Define the skill and discuss key terms.
   Compromising is ending disagreements or arguments with others by offering alternative ideas, actions, or suggestions. Key terms: *compromise, negotiate, alternatives, listening, opinions, give and take.*

3. Discuss why the skill is important.
   Sometimes you can avoid arguments or disagreements by compromising.
   Many times you can come up with a better solution to a disagreement by compromising or listening to another person's opinions.
   A lot of times people will think better of you if you calmly end dis-agreements rather than yelling, screaming, or fighting.
   In a compromise, everybody involved gets some of what they want (i.e., everybody involved gets something and gives something up).

4. Identify skill steps and have students repeat them.
   Recognize that you are in a situation that has the potential for conflict.
   Identify the main source of disagreement and the reason the person or other people is/are upset.
   Listen to what other person or people is/are saying.
   Calmly present your side and see how others react.
   Offer a compromise.
   If others accept the compromise, enact it.
   If others do not accept the compromise, offer another solution or ask for alternatives.

Box 7.5 *(Continued)*

Modeling

1. Using one of the following situations, model and role-play the situation with students.

   You are at a friend's house on Saturday, and the two of you want to watch TV. Your friend wants to watch cartoons, but you want to watch a movie on another channel. Your friend says that it's his house and you will watch what he wants to. You start to argue.

   Your parents tell you to clean your room, but you want to go to a friend's house. You get mad, yell at them, and start to get into a huge fight.

   On the playground, another kids grabs the basketball you are playing with and won't give it back. You grab it back, and the other kid starts yelling at you and wants to fight with you.

Behavioral Rehearsal

1. Choose two participants to role-play the first situation.

2. Have students state how they are going to compromise.

3. Role-play the situation.

4. Instruct others to watch what goes on.

5. Give feedback on compromising skills.

6. Ask the group to critique compromising behaviors.

7. Select new participants and role-play the other situations.

Antecedent-based interventions focus on arranging the social environment so that appropriate social behavior is more probable. For example, the use of prompts, cues, cooperative games, and environmental rearrangements can make prosocial behavior more likely to occur. Many readers may be familiar with cooperative learning strategies and classwide peer tutoring as a means of increasing academic performance. An additional advantage of these strategies is that they often facilitate prosocial behaviors. Both of these intervention approaches are based, in part, on the notion of antecedent control of behavior.

Two basic strategies falling under the rubric of antecedent-based interventions are peer-mediated interventions and cuing/prompting. Kohler and Strain (1990) classified peer-mediated interventions into three types: peer initiations, peer tutoring, and peer modeling. Peer initiation strategies involve having students' peers initiate and maintain prosocial social interactions. This approach has been used primarily with socially isolated students who have low rates of positive social interactions. Peer tutoring has been used mainly to remediate academic deficiencies; however, it may produce benefits in the social realm as well. Finally, peer modeling is used in most universal and selected social skills training approaches as a means of enhancing the performance of appropriate behavior.

Cuing and prompting procedures utilize verbal and nonverbal cues or prompts to signal and facilitate prosocial behaviors. Often, a simple prompt is all that may be needed to cue students to engage in appropriate social behavior. Cuing and prompting are among the easiest and most efficient means of social skills intervention (Elliott & Gresham, 1991; Walker, Colvin, & Ramsey, 1995).

Consequence-based interventions involve either presenting or removing events contingent upon student behavior that makes these events more likely. The process of presenting and removing events or conditions contingent on behavior that will increase that behavior's frequency is known as reinforcement. Reinforcement can be either positive or negative. Positive reinforcement involves the presentation of positive events (e.g., praise, tokens, access to preferred activities), and negative reinforcement involves the removal, reduction, or avoidance of aversive events (e.g., poor grades, loss of recess privileges, verbal reprimands). The majority of social skills interventions rely on positive rather than negative reinforcement principles.

Delivery of positive reinforcement strategies typically include (1) reinforcement-based strategies (social praise, access to preferred activities, token or point systems), (2) behavioral contracts, and (3) school–home notes. Reinforcement-based approaches may also include group contingency systems such as the Playground Behavior Game described earlier.

Behavioral contracts are formal written agreements between the student and intervention agents (teachers and/or parents). These contracts specify the relation between behavior and its consequences and should follow the guidelines specified in Box 7.6. Behavioral contracts are effective in enhancing the performance or quality of prosocial behaviors and decreasing the occurrence of competing problem behaviors (Elliott & Gresham, 1991).

School–home notes are an effective means of communicating between teachers and parents regarding students' social behavior. Teachers can easily use school–home notes within the context of social skills instruction programs. An efficient approach to delivering social skills interventions is to incorporate school–home notes into behavioral contracts, thereby taking advantage of each strategy. Box 7.7 presents some practical guidelines for designing school–home note systems for use in social skills interventions.

Procedures for Reducing or Removing Competing Problem Behaviors

Most antisocial students display destructive forms of behavior that compete successfully with either the acquisition or performance of essential social skills. The developmental trajectory for these competing forms of behavior often proceeds from overt to more covert antisocial behavior patterns over time. Longitudinal research also demonstrates that the nature of antisocial behavior patterns evolves from preschool to adolescence (Snyder & Stoolmiller, 2002). In the preschool years, this behavior pattern may take the form of whining, compliance, and opposition/defiance. During the elementary years, it typically escalates into less frequent but more serious behavioral events such as bullying, unprovoked aggression, and severe defiance of adults. Finally, during adolescence, an already well-developed pattern of destructive behavior is sometimes accompanied by

Box 7.6   Guidelines for Writing Behavioral Contracts

1. Clearly specify in the contract what you and the student expect to gain from agreeing to participate in the contract. For instance, you might want a student to increase the frequency of cooperating with peers without prompting; in return, the student may desire access to more free time on the computer. You can also write a behavioral contract for an entire class. In return, the class can gain access to a group-preferred reinforcer (free time, reduction in certain class assignments, and the like).

2. Specify in the contract only observable behaviors that can be easily monitored. A behavioral contract deals with *behavior,* not attitudes, opinions, or other unobservable events.

3. Specify in the contract the negative consequences for failing to meet the stated terms.

4. Add a bonus clause to reinforce consistent compliance with the contract over an extended time.

5. Have all parties sign and date the contract.

6. Monitor the degree of compliance with the contract.

7. Keep contracts simple and clear, because elaborate, complex contracts only confuse students.

8. If the contract does not change student behavior or if you want to change the target behaviors or reinforcers, renegotiate.

new forms of covert antisocial behavior such as stealing, vandalism, arson, and burglary (Patterson & Yoerger, 2002).

What causes this evolution of antisocial behavior over time? A key vehicle for understanding the development of this behavior pattern involves coercion theory. According to this theory, antisocial behaviors are acquired because they are functional in helping children either avoid or escape aversive events in their environment (Patterson et al., 1992). For example, the whining and noncompliance behaviors of a preschool child are often functional in removing adult-imposed demands on the child's behavior. Similarly, lying may be functional in avoiding punishment from school authorities. In such situations, these behaviors will be negatively reinforced because they allow the child to avoid or escape aversive events.

Not all antisocial behavior, however, is controlled by negative reinforcement. Behaviors such as bullying, being verbally aggressive toward authority figures, and stealing may be positively reinforced through social attention, material rewards, peer status, or access to preferred activities. Given that competing problem behaviors often are under the control of either negative or positive reinforcement contingencies, steps must be taken to reduce or remove these forms of maladaptive behavior as part of any social skills training program.

Box 7.7   Guidelines for Designing School–Home Notes

1. Schedule a conference with the parents to discuss target behaviors and goals of the social skills intervention. This may be done via telephone.

2. At this conference, discuss and define target behaviors that will be on the school–home note. Define these behaviors as specifically as possible so that everyone knows what behaviors are expected.

3. Design the note to include room for the student's name, teacher's signature, and target behaviors, and space for the teacher to check whether the behaviors were performed. Keep the note simple, including space for not more than three target behaviors.

4. Use the following guidelines to establish the responsibilities of the parties involved:

Parents will be responsible
> For providing the note to their child each day before school.
> For providing or withholding reinforcers based on results of the child's behavior at school that day as indicated on the note when the child brings it home.

The child will be responsible
> For taking the note to school each day.
> For having the note signed by the appropriate persons at school.
> For bringing the note home each day from school.

The teacher will be responsible
> For checking appropriate spaces on the note.
> For signing the note.

5. At a meeting between the teacher, parents, and child, decide what level of behavioral performance will constitute a "good note."

6. Assist parents and child in determining what reinforcers and privileges will follow the reception of a "good note." Provide parents with a list of possibilities.

7. Emphasize to parents the importance of following through consistently with specified consequences for the child who brings home a "good note."

8. Caution parents not to ridicule or scold their child for not having a "good note." Stress that they should simply withhold reinforcers and privileges. At the same time, instruct parents to praise the child when he or she brings home a "good note."

9. Arrange contingencies for the child's failure to meet his or her responsibilities with respect to the note system (e.g., lost note, didn't take note to school, didn't bring note home, didn't get note signed). Stress to parents that forgotten responsibilities should result in the same consequences as not having a "good note."

Box 7.7   *(Continued)*

10. As child's behavior improves, gradually phase out the use of notes. For example, send weekly notes instead of daily ones. But do not abruptly drop the note system.

Source: Adapted with permission from S. N. Elliott and F. M. Gresham, *Social Skills Intervention Guide: Practical Strategies for Social Training.* © 1991 American Guidance Service.

A number of techniques are useful in reducing the occurrence of these competing problem behaviors (see Box 7.3). A useful way of conceptualizing interventions to reduce competing behaviors and to increase the occurrence of prosocial behaviors is through the Matching Law (Hernstein, 1974). Succinctly stated, the Matching Law means that the relative rate of any behavior depends on the relative rate of reinforcement for that behavior (i.e., response rate tends to match reinforcement rate). For example, if verbal aggression is reinforced by social attention each time it occurs and appropriate verbal behavior is reinforced only every 10 times it occurs, then verbal aggression will be 10 times more likely to occur than appropriate verbal behavior. Given these principles of matching, a child will typically select behaviors to perform that are the most functional in producing reinforcement and avoiding punishment.

One way to reduce antisocial behavior and to increase prosocial behavior is through the use of differential reinforcement. Differential reinforcement, as the name implies, involves the provision of different rates of reinforcement for different behaviors. The goal here is to provide a relatively higher rate of reinforcement for prosocial behavior and a relatively lower rate of reinforcement for antisocial behaviors. Three types of differential reinforcement are commonly used: (1) differential reinforcement of other behavior (DRO), (2) differential reinforcement of low rates of behavior (DRL), and (3) differential reinforcement of incompatible behavior (DRI).

DRO involves the delivery of a reinforcer after any behavior *except* the target behavior. DRO is usually delivered on the basis of timed intervals in which the first behavior that occurs after a given period is reinforced. For instance, if the target behavior of verbal aggression does not occur in a 1-minute interval, then the first behavior that occurs after a minute is reinforced. The behavior could be simply sitting quietly, working on assignments, or performing any other behavior except verbal aggression. The overall effect of DRO is to decrease the relative rate of the target behavior and to increase the relative rates of all other appropriate forms of behavior.

DRL involves reducing the occurrence of target problem behaviors but not increasing the rates of prosocial behaviors. One way of using DRL in the classroom is to provide reinforcement when the overall frequency of a target problem behavior is reduced in a prespecified time interval. For example, a teacher may set a criterion of three or fewer occurrences of verbal aggression in a 30-minute math lesson. If the target child meets this criterion, then he or she will receive reinforcement. This criterion can be gradually reduced to fewer and fewer occurrences of verbal aggression over time. A variation of DRL is to apply it within the context of a group contingency system, as in the Playground Behavior Game. Teachers can create a classroom version of this in which teams are formed and reinforcement depends on team reductions in problem behaviors.

DRI refers to the reinforcement of behaviors that are incompatible with the target behavior. In DRI, the frequency of competing problem behaviors is reduced, and the frequency of prosocial behaviors is increased. The key difference between DRO and DRI is that the former does not require the incompatibility of behaviors to be reinforced whereas the latter does. For example, complimenting others is incompatible with insulting others; sharing is incompatible with being stingy; and compromising with others in conflict situations is incompatible with arguing with others. Using DRI, a child's behavior should follow the Matching Law, so that incompatible problem behaviors decrease and prosocial behaviors increase.

Facilitating Generalization and Maintenance

A major problem in SST involves generalizing trained social skills across settings and situations and maintaining them over time. Getting social skills to generalize is often more difficult than teaching such skills to students in the first place. That is, it is easier to get some social skills to occur in one place for a limited time than it is to get them to occur in multiple settings for an extended time (Gresham, 2002a). Generalization of behavior change is related to the notion of resistance to intervention. That is, if social skills deficits occur at low frequencies and competing problem behaviors occur at high frequencies, then the generalization of social skills will be more difficult to achieve (Gresham, 1991).

Generalization can be viewed from two perspectives. One perspective emphasizes the form or *topography* of behavior, the other its behavioral *function* (Stokes & Osnes, 1989). In a topographical description of generalization, prosocial behaviors generalize across situations or settings (setting generalization) and behaviors (response generalization) and over time (maintenance). Box 7.3 summarizes these categories of generalization.

We believe that a more useful approach is based on the concept of behavioral function as opposed to topography. Functional generalization consists of two types: stimulus and response. Stimulus generalization refers to the occurrence of the same behavior under variations of the original stimulus: The greater the difference between training conditions and subsequent conditions under which the skill will be performed, the less generalization there is likely to be. Response generalization refers to the occurrence of multiple social behaviors in the presence of or under the influence of the same stimulus. This is known as a functional response class.

It is helpful to understand the concept of functional generalization within the context of competing behaviors as described previously. For example, suppose a student has acquired a new prosocial skill that demonstrates good generalization across multiple settings. However, a new situation occurs that contains a strong competing stimulus (e.g., a disliked peer), which immediately prompts the occurrence of previously displayed maladaptive behaviors. The net effect or outcome of this scenario is that the new prosocial skill or behavior will not generalize to situations in which the strong competing stimulus is present (i.e., the disliked peer).

A major reason that many social skills fail to generalize to new settings and situations is that newly taught prosocial behaviors are overpowered by strong competing stimuli and behaviors. At school, a student may behave appropriately until he or she encounters a peer group that engages in and encourages rule violations or norm violations, which sets the occasion and provides incentives for the student to engage in inappropriate behaviors. This is an important concept for understanding why some behaviors generalize to new situations but others do not and why a skill or behavioral competency that has been maintained for a long time may suddenly deteriorate (Gresham, 2002a; Horner & Billingsley, 1988).

Evaluating Social Skills Curricula for Use in Conducting Social Skills Training

Alberg, Petry, and Eller (1994) conducted an extensive review and analysis of available social skills curricula and developed decision-making tools, as well as individual profiles of these curricula, to assist consumers and potential adopters in making informed, comparative judgments when selecting programs for conducting SST. This work was supported by a three-year federal grant from the U.S. Department of Education and resulted in the commercial publication of the *Social Skills Planning Guide* (see Alberg et al., 1994).

This guide is inexpensive and easy to use and contains software that provides instant access to 76 different social skills programs ranging from preschool to high school levels; the software is available for both the Macintosh and PCs. The *Planning Guide* contains a Comparison Summary Checklist, which is a functional tool that aids educators in comparing the advantages and disadvantages of each of the social skills programs included in the software. The guide addresses such key topics as (1) why social skills should be taught systematically, (2) what the key components of social skills programs are, (3) how to select a social skills program, and (4) how to work with others in the selection process. This resource is highly recommended for educators both as an important source of information on a diverse range of social skills curricular programs and as a guide for comparatively evaluating available programs in terms of their key features and components.

Conclusion

This chapter examined specific school-based principles and procedures for intervening with antisocial children and youths. The literature on antisocial behavior among children and youths provides ample confirmation that they tend to affiliate with others like them who behave in an unconventional manner. This is especially true as they mature and the risks escalate that they will become members of a deviant peer group, which, in turn, is associated with dramatic increases in delinquent behavior (Patterson et al., 1992; Reid et al., 2002). Behaviorally at-risk children, who are on a path to antisocial behavior with its attendant negative outcomes, are especially in need of the social skills and behavioral competencies that will allow them to establish and maintain friendships with peers who behave in a conventional manner. If social networks of this type are successfully developed for antisocial children or youths, they can serve as a long-term protective factor in buffering or attenuating the risk exposure to which antisocial youths are characteristically subjected (Elliott, 1998; Hawkins et al., 1999). Developing such social skills repertoires may be one of the most important services that schools can provide antisocial students.

Infotrac College Edition Research Terms

Oregon Social Learning Program

Peer-mediated interventions

Social skills instruction

Teaching social skills

References

Alberg, J., Petry, C., & Eller, S. (1994). *The social skills planning guide*, Longmont, CO: Sopris West.

Bandura, A. (1977). *Social learning theory*. Englewood Cliffs, NJ: Prentice-Hall.

Barrish, H., Sanders, M., & Wolf, M. M. (1969). Good behavior game: Effects of individual contingencies for group consequences on disruptive behavior in a classroom. *Journal of Applied Behavior Analysis, 2,* 119–124.

Bierman, K. (1986). Process of change during social skills training with preadolescents and its relation to treatment outcome. *Child Development, 57,* 230–240.

Bierman, K., & Furman, W. (1984). The effects of social skills training and peer involvement on the social adjustment of preadolescents. *Child Development, 55,* 151–162.

Bullis, M., Walker, H. M., & Sprague, J. (2001). A promise unfulfilled: Social skills training with at-risk and antisocial children and youth. *Exceptionality, 9,* 67–90.

Dishion, T., & Andrews, D. (1994). *A multicomponent intervention for families of young adolescents at risk: An analysis of short term outcomes.* Eugene: Oregon Social Learning Center.

Eddy, J., Reid, J., & Fetrow, R. (2000). An elementary school-based prevention program targeting modifiable antecedents of youth delinquency and violence: Linking the interests of families and teachers (LIFT). *Journal of Emotional and Behavioral Disorders, 8,* 165–176.

Elliott, D. S. (Ed). (1998). *Blueprints for violence prevention.* Boulder, CO: Center for the Study and Prevention of Violence.

Elliott, S. N., & Gresham, F. M., (1991). *Social skills intervention guide: Practical strategies for social skills training.* Circle Pines, MN: American Guidance Service.

Gresham, F. M. (1986). Conceptual issues in the assessment of social competence in children. In P. Strain, M. Guralnick, & H. Walker (Eds.), *Children's social behavior: Development, assessment, and modification* (pp. 143–179). New York: Academic Press.

Gresham, F. M. (1991). Conceptualizing behavior disorders in terms of resistance to intervention. *School Psychology Review, 20,* 37–50.

Gresham, F. M. (1998a). Social skills training with children: Social learning and applied behavior analytic approaches. In T. S. Watson & F. M. Gresham (Eds.), *Handbook of child behavior therapy* (pp. 475–497). New York: Plenum.

Gresham, F. M. (1998b). Social skills training: Should we raze, remodel, or rebuild? *Behavioral Disorders, 24,* 19–25.

Gresham, F. M. (2002). Social skills assessment and instruction for students with emotional and behavioral disorders. In K. Lane, F. M. Gresham, & T. O'Shaughnessy (Eds.), *Interventions for children with or at risk for emotional and behavioral disorders* (pp. 242–258). Boston: Allyn & Bacon.

Gresham, F. M. (2002b). Teaching social skills to high-risk children and youth: Preventive and remedial approaches. In M. Shinn, H. Walker, & G. Stoner (Eds.), *Interventions for academic and behavior problems II: Preventive and remedial approaches* (pp. 403–432). Bethesda, MD: National Association of School Psychologists.

Gresham, F. M., & Elliott, S. N. (1990). *Social skills rating system.* Circle Pines, MN: American Guidance Service.

Hawkins, D., Catalano, R., Kosterman, R., Abbott, R., & Hill, K. (1999). Preventing adolescent health risk behaviors by strengthening protection during childhood. *Archives of Pediatrics and Adolescent Medicine, 153,* 226–234.

Hernstein, R. J. (1974). Formal properties of the matching law. *Journal of the Experimental Analysis of Behavior, 21,* 486–495.

Horner, R., & Billingsley, F. (1988). The effects of competing behavior on the generalization and maintenance of adaptive behavior in applied settings. In R. Horner, G. Dunlap, & R. Koegel (Eds.), *Generalization and maintenance: Lifestyle changes in applied settings* (pp. 197–220). Baltimore: Brookes.

Johnson, D. W., & Johnson, R. T. (1986). Mainstreaming and cooperative learning strategies. *Exceptional children, 52*(6), 553–561.

Kazdin, A. (1987). Treatment of antisocial behavior in children: Current status and future directions. *Psychological Bulletin, 102,* 187–203.

Kohler, F., & Strain, P. (1990). Peer-assisted interventions: Early promises, notable achievements, and future aspirations. *Clinical Psychology Review, 10,* 441–452.

Patterson, G., Reid, J., & Dishion, J. (1992). *Antisocial boys, Vol. 4: A social interactional approach.* Eugene: Castalia.

O'Shaughnessy, T., Lane, K., Gresham, F. M., & Beebe-Frankenberger, M. (2002). Students with or at-risk for learning and emotional-behavioral difficulties: An integrated system of prevention and intervention. In K. Lane, F. M. Gresham, & T. O'Shaughnessy (Eds.), *Interventions for children with or at-risk for emotional and behavioral disorders* (pp. 3–17). Boston: Allyn & Bacon.

Patterson, G., & Reid, J. (1970). Reciprocity and coercion: Two facets of social systems. In C. Neuringer & J. Michael (Eds.), *Behavior modification in clinical psychology* (pp. 133–177). New York: Appleton-Century-Crofts.

Patterson, G., & Reid, J., & Dishion, J. (1992). *Antisocial boys, Vol. 4: A social interactional approach.* Eugene: Castalia.

Patterson, G., & Yoerger, K. (2002). A developmental model for early- and late-onset delinquency. In J. Reid, G. Patterson, & J. Snyder (Eds.), *Antisocial behavior in children and adolescents: A developmental analysis and model for intervention* (pp. 147–194). Washington, DC: American Psychological Association.

Reid, J., & Eddy, J. M. (2002). Interventions for antisocial behavior: Overview. In J. Reid, G. Patterson, & J. Snyder (Eds.), *Antisocial behavior in children and adolescents: A developmental analysis and model for intervention* (pp. 195–202). Washington, DC: American Psychological Association.

Reid, J., Patterson, G., & Snyder, J. (Eds.). (2002). *Antisocial behavior in children and adolescents: A developmental analysis and model for intervention.* Washington, DC: American Psychological Association.

Renshaw, P., & Asher, S. (1983). Children's goals and strategies for social interaction. *Merrill-Palmer Quarterly, 29,* 353–374.

Slavin, R. (1984). Team assisted individualization: Cooperative learning and individualized instruction in the mainstreamed classroom. *Remedial and Special Education, 5,* 33–42.

Snyder, J., & Stoolmiller, M. (2002). Reinforcement and coercion mechanisms in the development of antisocial behavior: The family. In J. Reid, G. Patterson, & J. Synder (Eds.), *Antisocial behavior in children and adolescents: A developmental analysis and model for intervention* (pp. 65–100). Washington, DC: American Psychological Association.

Stokes, T., & Osnes, P. (1989). An operant pursuit of generalization. *Behavior Therapy, 20,* 337–355.

Sugai, G., Horner, R., & Gresham, F. M. (2002). Behaviorally effective school environments. In M. Shinn, H. Walker, & G. Stoner (Eds.), *Interventions for academic and behavior problems II: Preventive and remedial approaches* (pp. 315–350). Bethesda, MD: National Association of School Psychologists.

Walker, H. M., & Severson, H. (2002). Developmental prevention of at-risk outcomes for vulnerable antisocial children and youth. In K. Lane, F. M. Gresham, & T. O'Shaughnessy (Eds.), *Interventions for children with or at-risk for emotional and behavioral disorders* (pp. 177–194). Boston: Allyn & Bacon.

Walker, H. M., Colvin, G., & Ramsey, E. (1995). *Antisocial behavior in school: Strategies and best practices.* Pacific Grove, CA: Brooks/Cole.

CHAPTER 8

Bullying, Harassment, Peer-Related Aggression, and Mean-Spirited Teasing in School

Introduction

This chapter focuses on the playground social behavior of antisocial, highly aggressive students, especially in the elementary grades. Particular attention is given to the problem of bullying, the role of antisocial students in its perpetuation, and its impact on peer social relations and friendship making. The good news is that various strategies and intervention programs are available for addressing this problem in our schools; the bad news is that the incidence of bullying is increasing. The chapter also addresses the negative-aggressive forms of playground behavior that are so characteristic of antisocial students.

The Bullying Phenomenon in U.S. Society

Bullying, mean-spirited teasing, and harassment have existed among children and youths since society first began aggregating them as part of the schooling process. However, these destructive social forces seem to have increased and become much more damaging and toxic in their social impact. Until fairly recently, the social impact on victims resulting from students' engagement in these forms of behavior was regarded as a rite of passage, with only limited intervention by school personnel. Nearly everyone can recall from childhood either directly experiencing or witnessing ugly situations involving bullying. The psychological scarring and emotional impact of bullying episodes has been well documented in the research literature. We suspect that these experiences do not fade easily from victims' memories.

This country has been slow to recognize the damaging effects of bullying at school and to take responsibility for doing something about it. In contrast, European countries (e.g., Norway and Britain) have been more proactive in this regard and have a much longer history of investment in developing solutions to bullying and harassment. To date, the best and most widely cited work on bullying prevention is that of Olweus and his colleagues in Norway (see Olweus, 1978, 1993, 1994).

Our lack of investment in dealing proactively with school bullying does not stem from its being a less severe problem in U.S. than in European schools. Lee (1993) suggests that approximately 160,000 U.S. students miss school each day due to fear of victimization by bullies, and the rates of bullying in European and U.S. schools appear to be nearly comparable. Sampson (2002), however, cites evidence from U.S. surveys of bullying showing higher rates in U.S. schools. Suffice it to say that the phenomenon of bullying in U.S. schools is at least as problematic as it is in European schools.

What accounts for all the media and societal attention now being focused on bullying and harassment in our schools? Two developments likely account for a substantial part of it. One relates to the huge surge of public concern over the school shooting tragedies that occurred in the 1990s; in that decade, the number of school shootings per year did not change appreciably, but the number of killed and wounded per episode increased substantially. The careful planning and conspiratorial features of these shootings provided a chilling addendum to the shock of these events, particularly among parents of school-age children and youths. Further, a majority of these school shooters apparently were motivated by a desire to get even with peers, and in some cases with adults, and to extract revenge for the bullying, harassment, and ridicule they had suffered at the hands of their schoolmates. This was especially true of Eric Harris and Dylan Klebold at Columbine High School in Colorado.

The second development relates to a 1999 U.S. Supreme Court decision in which the Court found in favor of the plaintiffs, who sued a school district for its failure to address the victimization of a female student who was repeatedly bullied, harassed, and severely emotionally victimized by other students in the school. The impact of this decision has been far-reaching, putting schools on notice that they must do something about bullying and harassment or face the possibility of unpleasant legal consequences. It is indeed unfortunate that a court decision was necessary to galvanize school efforts to address this severe social problem, which clearly merits attention in its own right. However, this phenomenon replicates a pattern of school-related social changes mandated by court decisions in the second half of the 20th century due to the failure of schools to act on them.

Box 8.1 provides some facts about bullying, as well as statistics from surveys of students and school personnel, that document the current extent of this problem in U.S. schools. These data are representative of what has been happening in U.S. schools over the past decade. Bullying is something that we *must* effectively address in the future, because it is one of the worst things that can happen to students during their schooling.

Definitions, Types, and Effects of Bullying, and Roles of Students

Snell, MacKenzie, and Frey (2002) identify three critical features common to most definitions of bullying: (1) a clear power imbalance between victim and bully involving factors such as physical size, age, maturity, social status, social resilience, and peer support; (2) an intent to cause harm or injury; and (3) repeated and chronic instances of aggression and intimidation that target a specific individual. Walker, Colvin, and Ramsey (1995) define bullying as a form of peer-related aggressive behavior that involves coercion, intimidation, and threats to another's personal safety or well-being. This definition includes relational aggression in which threats to withdraw friendship or to divulge secrets are used as levers of manipulation to gain power or control in relationships. Olweus (1996) has developed the most comprehensive definition of bullying; he characterizes it as recurring exposure over time to negative actions by one or more others. These negative actions include intentionally inflicting, or attempting to inflict, injury or discomfort upon another and can be expressed physically (hitting, kicking, choking) or verbally (name-calling, taunting, teasing, spreading rumors). Other professionals do not include teasing as a form of bullying (see

Box 8.1   Statistics and Facts on Bullying in U.S. Schools

◆ Bullying among school-age children is quite common. Surveys of bullying indicate that 1 in 4 students in grades 4–6 are bullied regularly, and 1 in 10 are bullied weekly.

◆ Nearly 90% of middle and high school students report having observed bullying, and nearly 80% say they have been victimized by bullying themselves.

◆ Of school-age children, 6–10% are chronically bullied; there are more chronic victims of bullying among elementary than middle or high school students.

◆ Six percent of students are bullied and also bully others.

◆ A recent survey of over 15,000 U.S. students reported that 30% of children said they had been involved in bullying. Of the 30%, 13% said they had bullied other children and 10% said they had been bullied.

◆ Repeated bullying has been cited as a factor in suicide, weapons carrying, truancy, school dropout, and extreme acts of hostility and aggression toward others.

◆ Both boys and girls engage in bullying of their peers but in different ways—boys are more overtly aggressive whereas girls are more passive and covert in their bullying behavior.

◆ Youths who bully others are more likely to have children who are bullies.

◆ Children who have few or no friends are more likely to be bullied than those who have many friends.

◆ Peers tend to have a "blame the victim" view of students who are frequently the target of bullying.

◆ The courts are increasingly open to hearing arguments from the chronic victims of bullying regarding the school's duty to stop chronic victimization.

◆ Intervention studies of bullying in European countries (e.g., Norway) show that school bullying can be reduced by 30–50%.

Sources: School Safety News Service (2001); U.S. Department of Education (1998).

Sampson, 2002). However, if the teasing is demeaning, mean-spirited, and intended to degrade an individual, either in private or public contexts, we believe it should be defined as a form of bullying.

It is important to distinguish harassment from bullying. Harassment is an illegal act and occurs when an individual is verbally or nonverbally taunted and demeaned in relation to certain attributes such as gender, race or ethnicity, religion, and/or sexual orientation. Harassment in the workplace was originally defined as an illegal act, and this definition has been extended to other settings including schools. Now, legal sanctions can result from the persistent harassment of students, even on the playground! However, criminalizing the playground behavior of young boys and girls is something that requires great circumspection as it may lead to some undesirable social consequences. Particularly among younger children, there seem to be far better ways of dealing with these problems than through legal sanctions. At the same time, however, girls of middle and high school age are frequent victims of harassment by boys, and it is important for schools and parents to have the option of pursuing legal recourse for these actions when they persist.

Currently, there are enormous pressures to extend the force of law to the more extreme and egregious forms of bullying. A number of states have considered or are considering this option. These laws, statutes, regulations, and policies provide the following potential benefits for educators: (1) They define specific forms of objectionable behavior in legal terms; (2) they outline and delineate the legal requirements for complying with the law; and (3) they provide guidelines for the indemnification of injured parties. Table 8.1 provides a review of law, statute, and policy developments across a series of representative states concerning bullying and harassment in school settings and reveals some of their common features (see Sprague, Walker, Nishioka, & Smith, in press).

The U.S. Department of Education has identified four types of bullying: physical, verbal, emotional, and sexual. Examples of each type include the following:

- Physical bullying—punching, poking, strangling, hair pulling, beating, biting
- Verbal bullying—hurtful name-calling, teasing, and gossiping about others
- Emotional bullying—defaming, humiliating, blackmailing, extorting, ostracizing, manipulating friendships and social affiliations
- Sexual bullying—propositioning, exhibitionism, voyeurism, abuse

Bullying is also differentiated in terms of direct versus indirect forms. *Direct* bullying refers to confrontative, open attacks on an individual involving physical contact, threats, and intimidation. In contrast, *indirect* bullying is more subtle in nature and consists of verbal and gestural forms such as spreading rumors, name-calling, ostracizing, excluding from peer controlled activities, and damaging another's reputation.

Boys bully at higher rates than do girls. Both boys (80%) and girls (60%) report being bullied more often at the hands of boys than girls (Snell et al., 2002). Further, boys are more likely to engage in direct bullying and girls in indirect bullying. Bullies are usually physically stronger than their victims, tend to be average in peer popularity, are slightly below average in intelligence, and are typically surrounded by several passive bullies who provide social support for their acts of bullying (Olweus, 1996; Smith & Sprague, 2002).

Peers are divided into four groupings in relation to the roles they assume regarding bullying: perpetrator, victim, bystander, and nonparticipant. The perpetrator, of course, is the bully; the victim is the target of the bully's attack; bystanders are peer observers who do not actively engage in the bullying episode but lend tactical support to it through observation of the situation; nonparticipants are

TABLE 8.1

Features of Representative State Anti-Bullying and Anti-Harassment Policies, Statutes, and Laws

Critical School-Related Elements/Features	CO	MI	CA	OR	WA	OK	WV	NH	U.S. Department of Education*	National Association of Attorneys General*
Mandates "safe, secure, peaceful" school environment	Yes**	***	Yes					Yes		
Specifically mentions bullying?	Yes	Yes	Yes	Yes	Yes	Yes	Yes	Yes		
Specifically mentions harassment?		Yes	Yes	Yes	Yes	Yes	Yes	Yes	Yes	Yes
Specifically mentions intimidation?		Yes		Yes	Yes	Yes	Yes			
Specifically prohibits bullying, harassment, or intimidation?	Yes	Yes		Yes	Yes	Yes	Yes			
Defines bullying?	Yes	Yes		Yes	Yes	Yes	Yes		Yes	
Defines harassment?		Yes	Yes	Yes	Yes	Yes	Yes			Yes
Defines intimidation?		Yes		Yes	Yes	Yes	Yes			
Is school-site specific?		Yes	Yes			Yes				
Mandates a statewide policy?										
Mandates a county- or district-level policy?	Yes			Yes	Yes	Yes	Yes			
Mandates a school-by-school policy?		Yes	Yes						Yes	
Mandates oversight by representative panel, task force, team, etc.?		Yes	Yes	Yes	Yes	Yes	Yes		Yes	
Mandates needs assessment?						Yes			Yes	
Mandates policy training for staff?		Yes			Yes		Yes		Yes	
Mandates clinical training for staff?					Yes				Yes	

(continued)

TABLE 8.1

(Continued)

Critical School-Related Elements/Features	CO	MI	CA	OR	WA	OK	WV	NH	U.S. Department of Education*	National Association of Attorneys General*
Mandates a school plan?			Yes						Yes	
Mandates investigative procedures?		Yes		Yes			Yes		Yes	
Mandates or outlines specific adult responses?				Yes			Yes		Yes	
Mandates anonymity for reporting students?		Yes		Yes			Yes		Yes	
Addresses reprisal, retaliation, or false accusation?		Yes		Yes	Yes		Yes		Yes	
Sets out student consequences?	Yes	Yes		Yes		Yes				
Sets out adult responsibilities?				Yes	Yes		Yes		Yes	
Sets out conditions for school/employee indemnification or immunity?	Yes	Yes		Yes	Yes		Yes	Yes		
Critical Behavioral Elements/Features										
Involves										
Gestures	Yes	Yes				Yes				
Written	Yes	Yes			Yes	Yes	Yes			
Verbal	Yes	Yes			Yes	Yes	Yes	Yes	Yes	
Physical	Yes	Yes			Yes	Yes	Yes	Yes	Yes	
Harm to student		Yes		Yes	Yes	Yes	Yes	Yes	Yes	
Harm to student's property		Yes		Yes	Yes	Yes	Yes			
Reasonable fear of harm to person or their property		Yes		Yes	Yes	Yes	Yes			

(continued)

TABLE 8.1

(Continued)

Critical School-Related Elements/Features	CO	MI	CA	OR	WA	OK	WV	NH	U.S. Department of Education*	National Association of Attorneys General*
Based on race, ethnicity?		Yes	Yes		Yes				Yes	Yes
Based on gender?		Yes	Yes		Yes				Yes	Yes
Based on religion or creed?		Yes			Yes				Yes	Yes
Based on sexual orientation?		Yes			Yes				Yes	Yes
Based on disability or physical attributes?		Yes			Yes				Yes	Yes
Based on socioeconomic or other distinguishing features?		Yes	Yes							
Disruption of education or educational mission by any of the above		Yes		Yes	Yes		Yes	Yes		

*Not rule- or policy-making bodies and as such can't promulgate or enforce law or policy. In cases where the item indicates "Mandates" the reader should substitute "Suggests" or "Recommends."

**A "Yes" response indicates that documents available at the time of publication addressed the item in some form. Some items were more fully addressed by some state documents than by others.

***A blank response indicates that the item was not addressed by the documents available at the time of publication.

peers who play none of these roles. A successful strategy for addressing bullying, based on the role dynamics of bullying, requires the following:

1. Discourage the bully from attacking peers.

2. Teach the victim strategies for avoiding and escaping from situations that involve bullying.

3. Make bystanders aware of the supportive nature of their role in the bullying, and discourage them from observing and remaining present when bullying occurs.

4. Teach nonparticipants to discourage bullying among their peers and to not show approval in any form for bullying when they see or hear of it.

Frequent victims of bullying tend to be of two types: passive-submissive or provocative. Passive-submissive victims are likely to be insecure, anxious, fearful, cautious, and withdrawn, and the act of bullying is powerfully reinforced through their submissive and avoidant responses to it. In contrast, provocative victims display annoying and aggressive reactions to bullying and thereby inadvertently reinforce it through their intense emotional reactions (Smith & Sprague, 2002). Effective solutions to bullying require that systematic and coordinated attention be given to students in each of the four student roles, with the most direct intervention focusing on the bully and the victim.

Male bullies tend to have positive attitudes toward the use of violence and coercion in their social interactions. Typically, they are impulsive, have a need to socially dominate others, display little empathy, and manifest aggressive, emotional reactions when *they* are taunted or teased. Female bullies, in contrast, tend to assume the role of leader among a core group of female peers, are socially cruel and manipulative of peers' feelings and behavior, and attempt to socially ostracize victims through engaging in backbiting, spreading rumors, trashing reputations, and rewarding peers for isolating the target of bullying (Olweus, 1996; Smith & Sprague, 2002; Snell et al., 2002).

Criminal behavior is a well-known correlate of persistent bullying. Olweus (1991) has shown that adolescent bullies have a 60% chance of having at least one criminal conviction by age 24 with 40% having three or more arrests (see Snell et al., 2002). Bullies and chronic offenders also have an elevated risk of committing later violent acts (Reid, Patterson, & Snyder, 2002; Satcher, 2001).

The effects of bullying on victims have been well documented. Victims tend to avoid school and have negative attitudes about the schooling experience. Frequent victimization often leads to social neglect and rejection and to emotional problems including lower self-esteem (see Hodges & Perry, 1999; Kochenderfer & Ladd, 1996; Olweus, 1978, 1993, 1996; Smith & Sprague, 2002; Snell et al., 2002). Epstein, Plog, and Porter (2002) have reviewed empirical evidence showing that victims of bullying also tend to have poorer physical health, depressive reactions, feelings of loneliness and anxiety, and psychological distress.

Bullying has clear negative consequences for both perpetrator and victim that ultimately lead to a lower quality of life for both. Interrupting and redirecting this cycle of aggression and victimization is a major step toward creating a positive school climate that is supportive, nurturing, and psychologically healthy.

Male bullies are often socially dominating and aggressive. Female bullies, however, are more likely to be socially manipulative and cruel, which is demonstrated in behaviors like gossiping and teasing.

It is unlikely that bullies are born fully formed. This socially destructive pattern of behavior is usually learned, developing out of long-term exposure to unfortunate social contexts in which violence and coercion are modeled as effective ways of relating to others and achieving social goals. It is also possible that severe bullying follows a developing pathway of gradual escalation that begins with mean-spirited teasing and provocation in which bullying skills are practiced and refined. If such is the case, then it is very important to address chronic, mean-spirited teasers early on in this trajectory.

Bullying by Antisocial Students and Peer Reactions

A majority of U.S. elementary and middle school students report that they have been bullied at some point in their school careers, with rates of bullying showing substantial increases as students move from elementary to middle school settings (Sampson, 2002). One of the behavioral tendencies that characterizes many antisocial students is mean-spirited teasing, harassment, and bullying of others.

These highly aggressive forms of behavior include intimidation, humiliation, coercion, demeaning acts, and threats to the safety and psychological well-being of others, usually peers.

Antisocial students can generally be expected to receive the same kind of treatment they administer to others and also to be socially avoided by normal peers whenever possible. Both the short- and long-term costs of such social reciprocity are severe for antisocial students. Our observations of antisocial students and their interactions with nonantisocial peers in free-play settings, such as recess, indicate that (1) their levels of positive social behavior are approximately equal to or slightly below those of peers, (2) their levels of negative-aggressive social behavior are substantially higher than those of peers, and (3) the levels of positive and negative social behavior directed toward peers by antisocial students are perfectly matched by the behavioral reactions and social behavior directed toward them by peers (i.e., peers tend to be just as negative with the antisocial student as that student is with them).

Walker and his colleagues investigated this phenomenon in a behavioral observation study in recess settings. They systematically observed the playground social behavior of a sample of antisocial ($N = 39$) and at-risk control ($N = 41$) fifth-graders. The two groups of students differed in terms of their relative risk status for antisocial behavior and for the development of conduct disorder and delinquency (from extreme to minimal) (see Shinn, Ramsey, Walker, Stieber, & O'Neill, 1987; Walker, Shinn, O'Neill, & Ramsey, 1987). Table 8.2 contains means and standard deviations for positive and negative playground behavior of the antisocial and at-risk control students, as well as their respective, interacting peer partners. In terms of overall percentage or level, there was a relatively small difference in positive social behavior directed toward peers by the antisocial and

---

TABLE 8.2

A Comparison of Means ($\overline{X}$) and Standard Deviations (SD) of Students' Percentage of Time Observed for Playground Coded Variables

Variable	Antisocial (N = 39)		At-Risk Control (N = 41)	
	($\overline{X}$)	SD	($\overline{X}$)	SD
Total positive behavior by target toward peers	38.36	13.5	44.06	17.8
Total negative behavior by target toward peers	9.92	10.7	4.05	5.2
Total positive behavior by peers toward target	31.26	12.8	33.83	15.0
Total negative behavior by peers toward target	8.10	8.0	3.42	3.4

Source: Shinn et al. (1987).

at-risk students. In contrast, the negative behavior of the antisocial students was more than double that of the at-risk students. Interestingly, the interacting peers (partners) of the antisocial and the at-risk students in these observations directed similar levels of positive social behavior toward them. However, they displayed almost the same level of negative social behavior toward antisocial students as those students had directed at them (i.e., 8.10 versus 9.92). A similar effect was noted for the at-risk control students (that is, 3.42 versus 4.05). Thus, nonantisocial peers appear to reciprocate or match *both* the positive and the negative social behavior of antisocial and at-risk students, even though the levels of negative behavior displayed by the antisocial students are more than double those for the at-risk control students.

These findings suggest that nonantisocial peers are strongly oriented toward social reciprocity and the matching of negative-aggressive initiations and social responses occurring during their social exchanges with antisocial students. Nonantisocial peers are often drawn into hostile social exchanges with antisocial youths and can display substantial negative behavior in extricating themselves from such situations. In our coding systems, we record this behavior in a discrete category we call "adaptive negative." Both peers and antisocial students are often quick to escalate initially negative situations of a mild nature into hostile exchanges involving anger and physical aggression. The residual social costs of such exchanges are reflected in social avoidance, tainted reputations, biased responses to their behavior, and negative interpretations of the behavioral intentions of antisocial students. Hollinger (1987) argues that normal peers regard even the neutral social behavior of antisocial students as hostile. This reputational bias is one of the reasons it is so difficult to change the behavior of antisocial, bullying students in a way that reduces social rejection by peers.

Thus, we strongly recommend that nonantisocial peers be involved, as supportive agents and natural therapists, in any attempts to remediate the behavior problems of antisocial students. Peers must be trained in some of the same social skills as antisocial students, be provided with opportunities to rotate through the role of special helper or behavioral support monitor on the playground, and share equally in activity rewards earned for the whole group by antisocial students for engaging in positive, cooperative behavior. The RECESS program for aggressive behavior, profiled later in this chapter, incorporates these critical features and was designed for use with this aggressive target population in grades K–3.

Generic Principles for Coping with School-Based Bullying

High rates of bullying in school can be a precursor to violence and should be a red-flag indicator that immediate and drastic actions need to be taken to reduce them. A schoolwide approach, involving parents whenever possible, is perhaps the best way to cope with this problem. It has been said that sunlight (that is, public exposure) is the best remedy for bullying. The student body must also be involved in developing workable solutions to this problem. Perhaps the most important ingredient in effective interventions for bullying is to directly involve all parties in the solution as supportive agents (i.e., teachers, students, parents, and neighborhood or community members, as appropriate) (Smith & Sprague, 2002). A positive school climate in which mutual respect exists between students and staff and a sense of cohesion, inclusion, and fairness is present can be an effective force against bullying. Creating a schoolwide awareness of the problem of bullying and developing and enforcing rules, limits, and sanctions against it are also extremely important measures.

Olweus (1991, 1993, 1996) has conducted the seminal work to date in developing effective interventions against bullying in schools. His Bullying Prevention Program (Olweus, 2000), also profiled later in this chapter, is one of the 11 Blueprint Programs that have been scientifically validated by the Center for the Study and Prevention of Violence at the University of Colorado. Olweus's universal intervention has produced substantial reductions in rates of being bullied and of bullying others. Further, these results have been replicated for boys and girls and across school sites. His interventions for bullying are based on several key principles:

◆ It is important to create a school (and home) environment that is characterized by warmth and involvement from adults but that sets firm limits for unacceptable behavior.

◆ When violations of these limits occur, then nonhostile, nonphysical sanctions should be consistently applied.

◆ Careful monitoring and surveillance of student activities should occur within and outside the school.

◆ Adults should act as responsible authorities during all adult–child interactions, and especially when bullying occurs.

Olweus used these general principles to develop specific intervention techniques for addressing bullying in school, classroom, and individual contexts. He argues that two important prerequisites for determining the effectiveness of these intervention components are *awareness* and *involvement;* that is, all parties (teachers, parents, students) must assume ownership of the problem of bullying and commit themselves to developing workable solutions to it.

Table 8.3 presents the key intervention components developed by Olweus for use at the school, classroom, and individual levels. This universal intervention for bullying requires the involvement of the entire school and the development of working relationships with parents. However, it is likely that some antisocial, aggressive students will also require intensive, selected interventions in order to bring their negative behavior into the normal range of expected behavior. Some highly recommended resources for preventing and intervening with bullying are profiled later in this chapter. Box 8.2 lists some principles and strategies for use by teachers and other school personnel in dealing effectively with teasing, harassment, and bullying.

Antisocial students, particularly those in middle school and high school, are perpetrators of actions that can threaten the safety of peers and adults in school. However, this behavior pattern usually begins much earlier, prior to school entry, and escalates through negative social behavior, teasing, and bullying to high levels of intensity. When this occurs, antisocial students are at risk for suspension and permanent expulsion from school, placement on home-tutoring regimens, and as-

TABLE 8.3 ◆

Olweus Program Components for Bullying at School, Class, and Individual Levels

School Level	Class Level	Individual Level
• School conference day on bully/victim problems	• Class rules against bullying: clarification, praise, and sanctions	• Serious talks with bullies and victims
• Better supervision of recess	• Regular class meetings	• Serious talks with parents of involved children
• More attractive school playground	• Cooperative learning	• Teacher use of imagination
• Contact telephone	• Meeting teacher—parents/children	• Help from neutral students
• Meeting staff—parents	• Common, positive activities	• Advice to parents (parent brochure)
• Teacher groups for the development of the "school climate"	• Role playing	• Discussion groups with parents of bullies and victims
• Parent circles (study and discussion groups)	• Literature	• Change of class or school

Source: From "Bully/Victim Problems Among School Children: Basic Facts and Effects of a School-Based Intervention Program," by D. Olweus. In D. J. Pepler & K. H. Rubin (Eds.), *The Development of Childhood Aggression,* pp. 411–446. Copyright © 1991 Lawrence Erlbaum. Reprinted by permission.

signment to specialized settings such as day treatment, alternative schools, or residential care facilities. Much can be done to prevent the development of these unfortunate outcomes early on in a child's preschool and early school experiences.

The Social Behavior of Antisocial Students in Free-Play Settings

Antisocial students have their most difficult adjustment problems on the playground, where adult supervision and monitoring are weakest. Traditionally, adults have had little to say or do about what happens among peers in this setting. Only the most obvious and egregious episodes of psychological abuse, bullying, harassment, and hostile social exchanges come to the attention of playground supervisors and other adults in the school setting. Mean-spirited teasing and provocation, physical and emotional intimidation, and even humiliation are daily occurrences in most school settings. These events are most likely to occur in low-traffic areas of the school, where supervision tends to be lax, and on the playground, where the ratio of supervisors to students tends to be especially thin. Antisocial students are often at the core of these unpleasant and unfortunate circumstances. To make matters worse, many teachers avoid playground duty, thus leaving the important tasks of playground supervision and mediation to untrained personnel ill equipped to deal with the severe behavioral challenges that commonly occur in this setting.

Box 8.2   Recommended Strategies for Teachers in Coping with Bullying

1. Provide students with opportunities to talk about bullying and enlist their support in defining bullying as unacceptable behavior.

2. Involve students in establishing classroom rules against bullying. Such rules may include a commitment from the teacher to not "look the other way" when incidents involving bullying occur.

3. Provide classroom activities and discussions related to bullying and violence including the harm that they cause and strategies to reduce them.

4. Develop a classroom action plan to ensure that students know what to do when they observe a bully–victim confrontation.

5. Teach cooperation by assigning projects that require collaboration. Such co-operation teaches students how to compromise and how to assert without demanding. Take care to vary the grouping of participants and to monitor the treatment of participants in each group.

6. Take immediate action when bullying is observed. All teachers and school staff must let children know that they care and will not allow anyone to be mistreated. By taking immediate action and dealing directly with the bully, adults support both the victim and the witnesses.

7. Confront bullies in private. Challenging a bully in front of peers may actually enhance his or her status and lead to further aggression.

8. Notify the parents of both victims and bullies when a confrontation occurs, and seek to resolve the problem expeditiously at school.

9. Refer both victims and aggressors to counseling whenever appropriate.

10. Provide protection for victims whenever necessary. Such protection may include creating a buddy system whereby students have a particular friend on whom they can depend and with whom they share class schedule information and plans for the school day.

11. Listen receptively to parents who report bullying and investigate reported circumstances so that immediate and appropriate school action may be taken.

12. Avoid attempts to mediate a bullying situation. The difference in power between victims and bullies may cause victims to feel further victimized by the process or to believe that they are somehow at fault.

Source: U.S. Department of Education (1998).

The authors of this book have spent hundreds of hours observing the playground behavior of antisocial, aggressive students and supervising implementation of intervention programs designed to change or improve it. The relatively unstructured nature of this setting, combined with low levels of adult monitoring and supervision, provide numerous opportunities for peer conflict(s), and

TABLE 8.4 ◆

Playground Social Behavior: Means ($\overline{X}$) and Standard Deviations (*SD*) for Playground-Code Categories by Student Group

Playground Social Behavior Dependent Variable	Externalizers (*N* = 73)		Internalizers (*N* = 76)		Normal Students (*N* = 52)	
	($\overline{X}$)	(*SD*)	($\overline{X}$)	(*SD*)	($\overline{X}$)	(*SD*)
1. Social engagement	30.1	16.8	27.4	13.1	35.1	15.3
2. Social involvement	32.9	15.6	43.9	15.3	40.9	16.2
3. Participation	22.6	28.7	7.4	16.1	14.2	22.6
4. Parallel play	5.8	7.5	10.7	10.6	4.9	7.5
5. Alone	6.1	8.3	8.6	10.0	3.5	5.5
6. No codable response	1.5	1.7	1.7	3.6	1.3	2.0
7. Total negative behavior	6.0	7.9	1.8	4.2	1.9	5.6

simple interventions are usually insufficient to prevent and/or resolve them. As a rule, antisocial students require formal structures, carefully monitored by adults, in order for the aversive and impulsive characteristics of their behavior to be managed and controlled effectively. Thus, the playground represents an especially difficult challenge for antisocial students in terms of regulating their emotions and displaying positive behavior. At the same time, it is an important setting for teaching these students positive alternatives to the coercive and aggressive strategies they commonly use to achieve their social goals.

The behavioral profile that emerges from studies of antisocial students' social behavior on the playground is characterized by coercion, conflict, rule infractions, and engagement in instrumental and reactive forms of aggression. Table 8.4 illustrates the playground social behavior of elementary school students who represent three types of behavior patterns: externalizing, internalizing, and "normal."

These behavioral profiles were generated through the national standardization process for development of the Systematic Screening for Behavior Disorders (SSBD) early-identification procedure (see Walker & Severson, 1990). Playground observations were recorded for a large sample of students in the primary and intermediate grades, representing 20 school districts in 10 states. Teacher rankings and ratings were used to assign students in regular classrooms to externalizing, internalizing, and normal groups based on standardized behavioral definitions and descriptions provided to each participating teacher. Externalizers exhibited acting-out, aggressive, and antisocial behavior patterns; internalizers were socially isolated, avoidant of social contact, fearful, and depressed; normal (average) students were those judged not to have either externalizing or internalizing problems and who represented the average behavioral characteristics of the entire class.

These student groups were observed during regular playground activities in the absence of any intervention(s). The professionally trained observers who recorded observations were blind as to the group assignment of the target students. During each successive 10-second interval, the observer coded one of the following six categories that best represented the student's behavior during that interval: social engagement, social involvement, participation, parallel play; alone, and no codable response. The first three categories could be coded as either positive (+) or negative (−), and the remaining three with a slash (/) if they occurred. Social engagement was coded to capture free-play exchanges among peers in which the target student engaged in verbal behavior, and social involvement was coded when the target student exhibited nonverbal, peer-related social behavior. Participation refers to involvement in structured games and activities with identifiable rules; parallel play means that two students engaged in the same activity within close proximity of each other but did not communicate or interact; alone means the target student was socially isolated and not interacting with anyone. Finally, no code means the student was doing something (e.g., talking with an adult) that could not be recorded with the coding system being used.

As Table 8.4 shows, externalizers had a far less favorable social-behavioral profile than either internalizers or normals. For example, they had higher rates of negative social behavior directed toward peers, and they spent less time socially engaged than did normals due primarily to their aversive behavioral characteristics. Internalizers, in contrast, had very low levels of negative social behavior but spent substantially more time alone and in parallel play than did either externalizers or normals. Across these code categories, the normal students appeared to have relatively positive and adaptive behavioral profiles on the playground.

It is remarkable to note just how positive the social behavior of so-called normal peers is at recess (see the behavioral profile for normal students in Table 8.4). In spite of the lack of structured playground settings, most children are, as a rule, quite positive with each other; the exception is those who are antisocial or aggressive. The social behavior of antisocial students has great salience in free-play settings because it stands in stark contrast to what is normative for this setting.

Peer-related social adjustment is determined primarily by the social exchanges among peers within unstructured, free-play settings at school. Antisocial students are severely at risk in this regard. Empirical research indicates that antisocial students have high rates of aggressive behavior at recess, as well as in other unstructured school and nonschool settings (see Pettit & Dodge, 2003; Reid, Patterson, & Snyder, 2002). Further, this evidence indicates that they develop negative reputations among their peers that persist long after their antisocial behavior has improved; this fact helps explain why it is so difficult to change the social status of antisocial children and youths and to reverse patterns of social rejection.

Teasing and Provocation in Playground Situations

Antisocial, aggressive children and youths experience great difficulty in joining ongoing peer groups and with teasing and provocation. They tend to be unskilled in their attempts at accessing ongoing (already formed) peer groups

Box 8.3

General Observations About Peer Group Entry Resulting from Focus Groups and Scoring of Video Scenes

- Eight- to 10-year-olds are far more sensitive to subtle social cues and nuances of social situations than expected.

- The researchers' choices of when it is appropriate to join peer group activities are uncorrelated with those of 8- to 10-year-olds.

- Eight- to 10-year-olds believe it is OK to interrupt a peer-controlled activity and ask to be involved if:
  Peers are organizing for or setting up the activity.
  The ongoing activity involves parallel play (e.g., a puzzle).
  The activity involves two persons and turn taking.

- Eight- to 10-year-olds display considerable resilience and persistence in the face of rejection of their social bids.

- Opposite-sex social bids appear to be more likely to be rejected than same-sex bids.

that have come together around an activity, and they respond to teasing and provocation by others with intense anger, which may be accompanied by threats and tantrums.

Walker and his colleagues conducted a series of focus groups to gather information on how students generally respond to teasing and provocations, as well as the strategies they use to join ongoing peer groups (see Irvin et al., 1992; Irvin & Walker, 1993; Walker, Irvin, Noell, & Singer, 1992). As part of the focus group procedure, groups of primary- and intermediate-level students, both boys and girls, were interviewed about their knowledge and impressions regarding these social tasks. The focus group participants were asked to code video scenes illustrating some of the social dynamics within each of these tasks. The researchers also independently coded the video scenes to provide a comparative basis for evaluation. The results of these activities were most instructive and are reported in Boxes 8.3 and 8.4 and Tables 8.5 and 8.6. These findings shed light on the beliefs, attitudes, and normative standards that children hold about responding to teasing and provocation and about joining ongoing peer groups. Boxes 8.3 and 8.4 report the researchers' general conclusions and impressions regarding these difficult and complex tasks that children must face on a daily basis.

Overall, the focus group children were quite sensitive to the nuances and subtle features of the social-situational dynamics involved in joining peer groups and dealing with teasing and provocation. Surprisingly, when coding the video scenes of play groups, the social judgments of the senior author and his colleagues turned out to be essentially *unrelated* to those of focus group members regarding the most appropriate time to attempt joining the peer-controlled activity. There was considerably more agreement between adults and children on which approach strategies were adaptive and which were maladaptive.

Box 8.4   **General Observations About Teasing and Provocation Resulting from Focus Groups and Scoring of Video Scenes**

◆ Some teasing is friendly and some is mean and provocative. Most teasing among 8- to 10-year-olds seem to be of the mean, provocative type. This appears true for boys and girls.

◆ Friendly, acceptable teasing appears more characteristic of adolescents.

◆ Teasing among boys involves themes of intimidation, power, domination, control, humiliation, and threats to one's safety. In contrast, teasing among girls involves themes of social cruelty, deception, hurt feelings, subtle rejection, manipulation, and being left out.

◆ Some teasing appears to be deliberate; other teasing is primarily prompted by circumstances or the situation and is largely spontaneous or accidental.

◆ Everyone is teased at some point, but there are children who are heavy-duty targets of teasing and those who are high-rate teasers of others.

◆ Factors that increase one's probability of being teased include:
Overreacting (tantrums)
Being atypical or not fitting in with social norms or dress codes
Having atypical physical or behavioral attributes (being short, wearing glasses, needing a hearing aid, or having strange habits)
Being socially and athletically unskilled

◆ Most teasing is done by groups to an individual who is selected as a target.

◆ Teasing among friends is sometimes OK while teasing among strangers or acquaintances is often not OK.

◆ Size is a major factor in teasing among boys.

◆ Eight- to 10-year-olds are not analytical or reflective about teasing; their responses to it and attitudes about it are mostly emotional.

◆ Adaptive responses to teasing seem to be ignoring, asking the persons to stop, and leaving the situation.

◆ Maladaptive responses to teasing seem to include teasing back, name-calling, getting mad or crying, hitting or having tantrums, and threatening harm.

◆ Eight- to 10-year-olds have firm beliefs in the effectiveness of strategies for stopping teasing that have no effect or actually make it worse.

The information contributed by focus group participants regarding their reactions to and beliefs about teasing and provocation line up well with the extensive literature that has developed on teasing, bullying, harassment, and hazing over the past decade (Epstein, Plog, & Porter, 2002; Georgesen, Harris, Milich, & Young, 1999; Olweus, 1996). A clear majority of the focus group members felt

TABLE 8.5 ◆

Peer Group Entry Dos and Don'ts Resulting from Analysis of the Literature and Focus Groups

Dos	Don'ts
• Hover and wait.	• Ask informational questions.
• Help others, be of assistance.	• Talk about yourself.
• Make group-oriented, positive statements.	• Disagree with those in the group.
• Initiate only during natural breaks.	• Interrupt the group.
• Respond promptly to invitations.	• Seek attention.
• Say, "Can I play?" If not, act disappointed.	• Brag.
• Take any offer—even for partial involvement (e.g., referee).	• Instruct those in the game.
• Tell your name, say you're new or visiting, and ask to play. If refused, ask others to play.	• Barge in and say, "I'm playing!"
• Select a game that is fun. If refused, look for someone who has no friends.	• Make threats—"Let me play or I'll tell someone you hit me!"
• Play by yourself as an alternative.	• Be persistent—tag along and persist until you finally get to play.
• Take whatever is offered to you.	
• Know the game you select and know the rules; don't play unless you do.	
• Get someone to teach you the rules quickly.	

that there was very little "friendly" teasing—that most teasing was mean and hurtful. And girls consistently reported that they were often hurt and embarrassed by teasing from boys.

Table 8.5 contains a list of dos and don'ts about peer group entry gleaned from an analysis of the professional literature and from the focus groups. Table 8.6 contains a similar list about teasing and provocation. Some of the strategies contributed by the focus groups appear to be ingenious and potentially effective; others would appear to have no effect or to actually make the situation worse (e.g., walk away and get a friend to scream at the teasers).

Focus group interviews with randomly selected boys and girls in grades 3–5 indicated that (1) all viewed themselves as having been victims of teasing by others; (2) concern about teasing was a major social constraint in their lives, especially for girls; (3) they would go to great lengths to avoid situations in which they were likely to be teased; and (4) none would admit to teasing others. Apparently, we need additional information from *teasers* about their beliefs, motivations, and actions regarding teasing.

TABLE 8.6 ◆

Teasing and Provocation Dos and Don'ts Resulting from Analysis of the Literature and Focus Groups

Dos	Don'ts
• Ignore.	• Cry.
• Leave the situation.	• Get visibly angry or lose temper.
• Protect self.	• Escalate (move up a notch).
• Rebuff in a firm manner.	• Counteraggress (match).
• Get help (call teacher or supervisor).	• Say, "Get out of here!"
• Tell the teacher.	• Walk away and get a friend to scream at them.
• Request that the teasers stop; if it doesn't work, then tell the teacher.	• Gang up on them; spread the word, and get them to isolate the teaser or provoker.
• Request that the teasers stop; walk away; if it doesn't work, go tell someone.	• Tease back.
• Walk toward the teacher, but don't tell unless the teasers follow.	• Call the teasers names.
• Give warnings, but stop after two.	• Act hurt or serious.

In order to gain the perspectives of teasers, the researchers asked teachers to nominate children in the primary and intermediate grades who were frequent teasers of others. Focus group sessions were scheduled with the six children who were nominated (all boys in grades 3 and 4). The comments and body language of these boys were most interesting and strongly suggested that self-disclosure of numerous incidents of mean-spirited teasing was a marker for these children. It may be a marker for antisocial children as well. Box 8.5 provides a first-person account, by the senior author, of the initial encounter between these boys and the three adults who were conducting the focus group. It is important to note that none of the boys or adults involved had seen each other before and were meeting for the first time.

In recent years, some interesting research has been reported on teasing that reveals how adults and children perceive it and what strategies they think are most appropriate for coping with it. For example, Scambler, Harris, and Milich (1998) reported a study in which they prepared a videotaped scene in which two students are seen teasing another child about being held back in school for one year. The scene was arranged so the child being teased provides three different reactions: (1) an ignore reaction (in which the victim crossed his arms and remained silent), (2) a humorous reaction (in which the victim made a joke about being held back), and (3) a hostile reaction (in which the victim made an angry comment). Children who viewed the scenes preferred the reactions in the following order: humorous, ignore, and hostile. And

Box 8.5   Case: The Teaser Terrorists

The six boys, displaying aggressive body language, entered the room in which the focus group activity was to be held. It was as though the James Boys, Ike Clanton, and the Cole Younger Gang had all walked into a room at once. Within a few minutes, I thought we would need more than just three adults to handle the situation. Each of the six boys looked like a behavioral escalation waiting to happen.

The focus group leader stated that we were here to talk about teasing and provocation. Immediately, two hands shot up—those of two boys who were eager to tell their stories. One commented that he teased a lot and was *really* good at it! The focus group leader said that we would get to each boy but asked that we first go around the table, tell our names, and state where we were from; she began by introducing herself. Two boys introduced themselves as Jason and Jeremiah; they were from two local elementary schools. I was next in line and introduced myself as Hill Walker from the University of Oregon. Immediately, they all looked at me, and one of the boys said, "Hill Walker? What kind of stupid name is that?"

I was stunned at the boldness of the question because I was an adult and they'd never seen me before. I was also momentarily speechless and had no response to the query. However, it made a lasting impression.

These boys went on to relate a litany of cruel stories about how they had victimized others. They seemed to be competing among themselves to see who had committed the most outrageous acts of teaser terrorism. Although it was impossible to verify the truth or accuracy of their accounts, it was clear that they had not the slightest remorse about the acts they described.

---

both teasers and frequent victims of teasing most preferred the humorous reaction to the teasing situation.

A related study by Landau, Milich, Harris, and Larson (2001) provided a replication and extension of the Scambler et al. (1998) teasing study. These researchers examined the reactions of 164 preservice teachers and 184 elementary children to the three videotaped responses. After viewing the tape, the teachers and children completed a series of questions designed to elicit their judgments about the teasing situation. Specifically, participants were asked to rate how effective the target child's responses to the teasing were, how likely the child was to be teased in the future, how angry the target child would be, how angry they would be if they were in the target child's position, and whether the teasers in the video scene were teasing in a fun or hurtful way. Participating teachers were asked to frame their responses to the questions so as to estimate how the target child would be viewed by classmates in order to assess how well teachers are able to anticipate children's reactions and feelings.

This study produced the following outcomes: (1) Preservice teachers predicted that the participating children would rate both the victim and the teaser more positively than was actually the case; (2) teachers overestimated how the children would rate the effectiveness of the victim's response; (3) teachers over-estimated how hurtful the children would rate the teasing; and (4) teachers underestimated how angry the children would rate the victim as being. Children and teachers both agreed that the target child's becoming upset at the teasing was not an effective method for stopping it and that ignoring would be a more effective strategy. In contrast, the teachers predicted that the children would find the humorous reaction to be more effective than the children perceived it to be. There were minimal gender differences in children's reactions to the teasing scenarios; it was not possible to test for sex differences among the teachers due to the imbalance of females and males in the sample.

These two studies are important contributions to the emerging knowledge base on teasing and its destructive effects. A key recommendation of Landau et al. (2001) concerns the need to develop greater sensitivity among teachers and other school personnel regarding the emotional impact of teasing on victims, as well as on those peers who observe it happening. Their results show that teasing is a source of considerable anger, stress, and anxiety for children and that teachers may underestimate its emotional impact on them. Our experience is certainly consistent with these findings. We think mean-spirited teasing should become a priority for schools not only because of the emotional and reputational damage it causes but also because of the real possibility that it can escalate into patterns of harassment and bullying over time.

Generic Strategies and Procedures for Addressing Negative-Aggressive Behavior and Rule Infractions on the Playground

We recommend four general approaches for preventing negative-aggressive behavior and rule infractions on the playground: (1) teaching antisocial students and their peers normative standards regarding social relations with peers and playground rules; (2) teaching adaptive strategies regarding joining already-formed peer groups and dealing with teasing, provocations, and bullying, as well as complying with adult commands and requests; (3) teaching generic social skills that will improve students' chances for social acceptance and social engagement; and (4) teaching anger management and conflict resolution strategies. Each of these approaches is discussed in this section.

Teaching Normative Standards

Walker, Hops, and Greenwood (1984, 1993) found that the behavioral standards which extremely aggressive children hold for peer relations and rule-governed behavior are often quite divergent from those of other children. It is likely that these aggressive children come from home environments in which the behavioral standards they are exposed to are not normative and in which they are not taught to respect systems of authority and established rules of conduct. In implementing intervention programs to improve the quality, or positive valence, of aggressive children's social behavior, it is necessary to preteach normative standards and behavioral expectations, because their ability to meet the minimal criteria for reinforceable responses during the intervention is much too limited.

Walker and his associates developed a social skills training (SST) procedure in which they used direct instruction procedures to teach awareness and understanding of playground rules and normative standards governing peer relations. Lists of playground expectations were solicited from a series of elementary schools, and a generic set of rules was developed that would apply to most recess periods. For each target student, these rules were reviewed with teachers and playground supervisors and fine-tuned to fit the idiosyncratic requirements of the particular school. The target student was then instructed in each rule on the list via the use of discussion, role-plays, coaching, and debriefing. Sometimes, peers were used as instructional assistants in this teaching process; other times, only the teacher or behavioral specialist and the target student were involved.

A similar procedure was used to teach target students to distinguish between positive and negative forms of verbal, physical, and gestural social behavior. This instructional procedure proved to be highly effective in facilitating the necessary discriminations in the role-playing situation. For both playground rules and peer-related social behavior, this training procedure was followed by an incentive-based, behavior management system on the playground. This general approach of preteaching rules and social behavior, combined with a behavior management procedure to support their applications, was highly effective. It dramatically reduced the amount of time required for aggressive children to acquire a much more adaptive and prosocial pattern of behavior.

Teaching Adaptive Strategies for Specific Social Situations

Figures 8.1–8.3 provide schematic representations of the critical features involved in joining play groups, teasing and provocation, and compliance, respectively. They provide useful conceptual road maps for structuring instruction/intervention efforts that are geared toward improving the social skills and competence of antisocial students.

For example, in Figure 8.1, three different scenarios are used to teach discriminations between interruptive and noninterruptive ways of approaching and seeking to join ongoing peer groups. As the figure shows, there are some general prerequisites for successfully joining already-formed groups of peers engaged in an ongoing activity. For example, the student should (1) know the rules of the target game or activity and have the necessary skills to participate in it, (2) not ask questions of group members that require an answer, (3) try hovering around the activity and waiting for an invitation, and (4) time a request to coincide with natural breaks in the activity. Bragging and instructing members of the group should be avoided at all costs! In the instructional procedure, positive, neutral, and negative examples of interruptive strategies are contrasted with noninterruptive strategies, and the distinguishing features of each are illustrated. The probable reactions of peers to these strategies are also addressed.

Figure 8.2 illustrates the instructional approach as applied to typical situations involving teasing and provocation. Examples of strategies for coping with teasing

Scenarios

1. Group game ("Drop the Flag")
2. Group or dyadic/cooperative (puzzle)
3. Dyadic/competitive (darts)

Times and ways to join in

	Positive	Neutral	Negative
Interruptive	Polite request	Positive verbalization	Physical aggression
Noninterruptive	Polite request	Wait	Threaten or brag

Response options

1. *Externalizing:* brag, instruct, barge in
2. *Internalizing:* hover, ask questions
3. *Appropriate:* ask to join in

How others might react

1. Ignore
2. Invite
3. Reject
4. Defer

FIGURE 8.1 ————————————————————————◆

Joining-In Overview.

and provocation are provided for five situations ranging from ambiguous, to accidental, to hostile. The strategies for coping with teasing and provocation involve two critical dimensions: engagement and quality. Responses to teasing and provocation can be either positive or negative and can either engage or disengage the teaser.

As a rule, disengagement with the teaser terminates the teasing episode and so is a desirable strategy. Positive techniques for dealing with teasing and provocation include (1) ignoring the teasing (if possible), (2) counterteasing (but only under certain conditions that do not prompt escalation of the teasing into bullying), (3) walking away from the situation, (4) asking the teaser to stop in a direct manner, and (5) threatening to or actually seeking assistance from an adult if the teasing persists, becomes severe, or escalates into bullying or into a threat to one's safety and well-being. Undesirable responses to teasing include getting mad and crying, giving chase to the teaser, having a tantrum, fighting and threatening to fight.

The adaptive and maladaptive features of each strategy are discussed in considerable detail with target students. Aggressive, antisocial students are

Scenarios*

1. Ambiguous
2. Ambiguous/accidental
3. Accidental
4. Friendly
5. Hostile

Response options

	Engaged	Disengaged
Positive	• Countertease • Don't take too seriously	• Leave situation • Ignore completely
Negative	• Fight and chase • Get angry and cry	• Threaten to summon adult authority • Ask person to stop teasing

*Girls' and boys' scenarios vary in thematic content.

FIGURE 8.2

Teasing and Provocation Overview.
Source: Walker et al. (1987).

---

taught to resist their urges to engage in spontaneous teasing as part of this instructional process. However, because of the powerful situational triggers associated with teasing, the emotional arousal that the process of teasing can generate, and the social rewards that accrue to the teaser (e.g., dominance, attention, and submissive behavior by the target of teasing), it can be very difficult to get many children and youths to voluntarily refrain from this form of abusive playground behavior.

Figure 8.3 presents a template for compliance in relation to adult and peer directives. Here, situational determinants that mediate compliance with teacher and peer directives include (1) clear versus unclear statements, (2) distinctions between requests, commands, and demands, (3) directives applied to individuals versus members of groups, and (4) commands given within the context of orderly versus disorderly environments. Strategies reviewed and discussed during the instructional procedure range from immediate, direct compliance to outright defiance. Target students are urged to adopt the strategies of direct compliance, requests for clarification, negotiation around the command or request, and simple

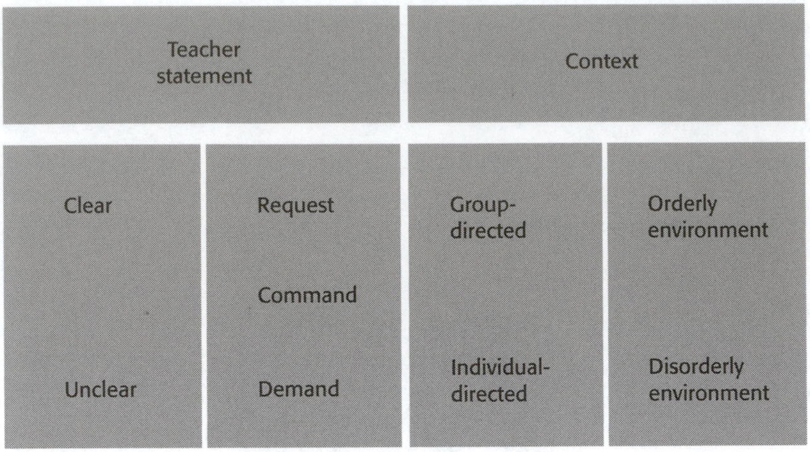

Teacher statement			Context	
Clear	Request	Group-directed	Orderly environment
	Command		
Unclear	Demand	Individual-directed	Disorderly environment

Response options*

Compliance	1. Compliance
	2. Request for clarification
	3. Negotiation
	4. Simple refusal (with reason)
	5. Not meet expected standards
	6. Passive noncompliance
Noncompliance	7. Defiance

*Response options sample 3 alternatives from list: 2 inappropriate and 1 appropriate for each item.

FIGURE 8.3 ◆

Compliance Overview.

refusal (but with a reason given for the refusal). These students are also urged to avoid the responses of passive noncompliance (i.e., partial compliance) and outright defiance.

In sum, systematic instruction in these three domains, combined with coaching, debriefing, and incentive systems applied within natural settings, can have a positive impact on the teacher- and peer-related adjustments of antisocial students. In some schools, the necessary resources and expertise may not be available to systematically teach adaptive strategies in this manner. In such cases, playground supervisors should, at a minimum, use cuing/prompting, debriefing, and behavior-specific praise to help antisocial students improve their coping skills.

Teaching Generic Social Skills

Antisocial students are often deficient in the generic social skills that promote teacher and peer acceptance and that contribute to school success. These core skills are particularly important for peer relations and mediate these students' ability to

Anger control and management skills, when taught by a teacher or parent, can help antisocial students recognize and control their anger before it escalates.

gain access to peer-controlled social networks and to recruit and maintain friends. Chapters 6 and 7 provide detailed information and recommended guidelines on assessment strategies and the development of social competence through systematic SST.

For elementary school students, it is essential to directly teach the social skills that support both teacher- and peer-related adjustment. For middle and high school students, it is also important to teach social skills that support self-related forms of adjustment. Peer- and self-related forms of adjustment (e.g., controlling emotions and impulses and self-regulating behavior) have the most direct relevance for free-play settings involving peer relations.

Teaching Anger Management and Conflict Resolution Strategies

One of the characteristic features of an antisocial behavior pattern is a high level of agitation that often leads to conflicts with peers and adults. These children and youths carry intense levels of anger, frustration, and even rage due to the social and environmental conditions of abuse to which they have been exposed. Antisocial children and youths also experience feelings of alienation. Many have great difficulty controlling and managing their anger effectively, and most have not been taught appropriate methods of expressing anger and dissatisfaction.

For antisocial students, the expression of anger and the initiation of conflict with others can have powerful instrumental effects that are personally rewarding. Tantrums, sulking, and direct confrontations are generally effective means of controlling the behavior of others. Antisocial children are masters at escalating these emotional conditions to a point at which the social exchange becomes so aversive that peers, teachers, and parents give in and/or withdraw from the situation. Thus, these emotional states come to have a powerful value for antisocial students, allowing them to shape the social environment to their liking. For example, if a student chooses to resist a demand, the sudden escalation of anger often causes the demand to be withdrawn, deferred, or renegotiated.

It is important to the long-term development of antisocial students that they learn how to recognize and control their anger and to avoid the initiation of spontaneous and unnecessary conflicts with others. They must also learn to resolve conflicts without resorting to the use of coercion, threats, and physical force. Highly aggressive children and youths tend to view the world as a more dangerous and hostile place than do other children; they are also more easily provoked into responding physically as a means of resolving perceived problems. Thus, anger management and anger control, as well as conflict resolution, are ideal subject matter for systematic SST with antisocial students.

In the area of anger management and control, it is important to teach antisocial students how to (1) recognize their own anger and the emotional psychological arousal that accompanies intense anger, (2) identify the situations and events that seem to trigger this anger, (3) recognize the unpleasant consequences that can result from intense expressions of anger, and (4) learn appropriate methods of expressing anger and frustration. Many aggressive children resort to coercive tactics and strategies because they do not have the necessary social skills to cope with important social tasks and demands. Thus, anger management training should always be accompanied by systematic SST.

Coie, Underwood, and Lochman (1991) reported a comprehensive intervention for improving antisocial students' social relations with peers and reducing their aggressive behavior in schools. Their intervention consists of four major components: (1) social problem-solving skills, (2) positive-play training, (3) group-entry skill training, and (4) ways to deal with strong negative feelings. This is a now classic and very well conceptualized approach for improving the social adjustment of antisocial, aggressive children. The social problem-solving component of this intervention is designed to teach and assist aggressive children to generate alternatives to difficult situations that are adaptive but that still *efficiently* produce valued outcomes. Positive-play training is designed to strengthen target students' repertoires of positive, prosocial behavior (e.g., turn taking, following the rules of games and activities, sharing, and cooperating). Group-entry skill training is extremely important in that it provides a vehicle for accessing peer-controlled activities in an acceptable manner. Finally, strategies for controlling emotions are taught in order to assist students in managing anger and coping with intensely negative feelings.

Anger control strategies typically consist of self-talk, cognitive mediation, relaxation training, behavioral rehearsal, and opportunities to control emotions and manage negative feelings in a range of social situations, including difficult ones. Coie and his colleagues (1991) cite evidence that emotional control techniques of this type can be effective in coping with negative feelings and reducing aggression. The investment of time and effort in anger management and control strategies for antisocial students is highly recommended.

Antisocial students are in dire need of strategies for dealing with their frequent conflicts involving peers and adults. Social problem-solving strategies in which students are taught to generate alternatives for solving conflicts are invaluable. These students also need process skills for effective conflict resolution; these include negotiation, cooperation, listening, turn taking, the ability to assume the other person's perspective, and a positive attitude (Pettit & Dodge, 2003; Reid, Patterson, & Snyder, 2002).

RECESS: A Comprehensive Intervention for Aggressive Behavior

The Reprogramming Environmental Contingencies for Effective Social Skills (RECESS) program is a comprehensive behavior management intervention for aggressive children in grades K–3 who tease, harass, and bully others (Walker et al., 1993). RECESS teaches prosocial forms of peer-related behavior and applies sanctions (e.g., loss of points, time-out) for negative-aggressive behavior, rule infractions, teasing, and bullying.

RECESS has four major program components: (1) systematic training in cooperative, positive social behavior via prepared scripts, discussion, and role-playing for the aggressive child and all other class members; (2) a response cost point system in which points are awarded at the beginning of each recess period and then subtracted for inappropriate social behavior and rule infractions; (3) praise by the RECESS program consultant, teacher, and playground supervisor for positive, cooperative, interactive behavior; and (4) concurrent group and individual reinforcement contingencies with the group activity rewards available at school and the individual rewards (privileges) available at home. RECESS focuses on the aggressive child's peer-related social behavior with the goals of decreasing negative-aggressive social initiations and responses to within normal limits and teaching a positive, constructive pattern of relating to others.

RECESS consists of four sequential phases: (1) recess only, (2) classroom extension, (3) fading, and (4) maintenance. During the recess-only phase, which lasts for 10 days, the consultant has the responsibility of monitoring the target child's behavior and interactions with peers. In the last three days of this phase, the RECESS consultant teaches the playground supervisor to operate the program, closely monitoring the supervisor while doing so. In the classroom extension phase, which lasts approximately 15 days, the program is extended to the classroom if necessary; if not, the program is continued during recess as in phase 1. During the fading phase, which lasts about 15 days, the major components of the program are eliminated, with the goals of making the program easier to manage and reducing the target child's dependence on external support procedures. The first three phases thus last approximately 40 days. The final phase, maintenance, continues indefinitely and consists of a low-cost variation of the intervention procedures in which praise and a surprise group activity reward are made available if covert monitoring of the aggressive child at recess indicates that his or her social behavior falls within the normal range.

RECESS can have a substantive impact on the social behavior of aggressive children in grades K–3. It is a complex behavior management program based on a reduce-and-replace strategy. That is, the target child's negative-aggressive behavioral repertoire is reduced or eliminated and replaced with an adaptive, prosocial behavior pattern. The RECESS referral graph in Figure 8.4 illustrates why RECESS is framed in this manner. That is, the negative-aggressive rate of most antisocial children is eight to nine times higher than that of their peers while their positive social behavior is typically very close to the average level for normal peers.

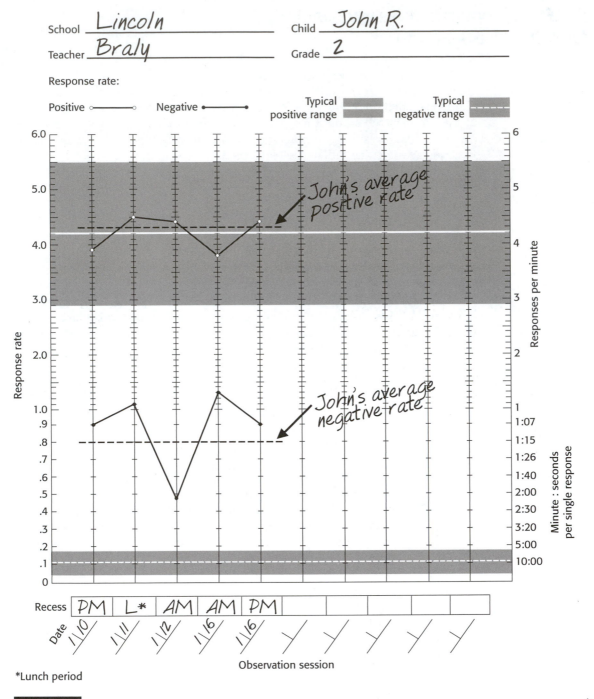

School _Lincoln_   Child _John R._

Teacher _Braly_   Grade _2_

Response rate:

Positive o——o   Negative •——•   Typical positive range   Typical negative range

FIGURE 8.4

RECESS Referral Graph.

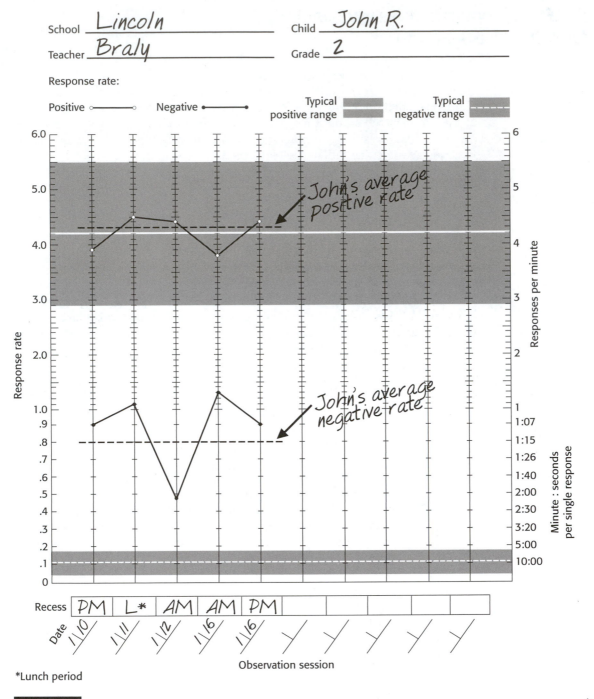

*Lunch period

The information in this figure is based on in vivo playground observations of 19 negative-aggressive primary grade students and 21 socially "normal" students as nominated by their teachers. The shaded area at the top of the graph defines the normal range of positive social responses displayed by the 21 normal students; the average of this group is indicated by the white line. The average rate of positive social responses for the 19 aggressive students is indicated by the dotted line at the top, which shows that the positive response rate was nearly identical for the two groups.

Similarly, the shaded area at the bottom of the graph defines the range of negative social responses for normal students, with the white line indicating the average rate for this group (i.e., 0.11 per minute, or about one negative-aggressive social response every 9 minutes). In contrast, the average rate for aggressive students was eight to nine times higher than for normal students. The data plotted for John (shown by the solid lines) are typical for aggressive, antisocial students in this range.

These results indicate that the most important task in dealing with such children is to reduce their rate of negative-aggressive social responses to within-normal limits, as defined by the social behavior of nonantisocial peers. Once the aversive, antisocial features of their behavior are under control, they are in a position to learn and practice an adaptive, prosocial behavior pattern. RECESS accomplishes this goal efficiently for most negative-aggressive students to whom it is applied in grades K–3, which represents an ideal developmental window in which to intervene effectively with these students.

Form 8.1 is a sample of a completed RECESS point record form; Form 8.2 is a blank copy for the reader's use. This form contains the core elements of the RECESS program's implementation and also provides for the delivery of behavior-specific praise and bonus points and the subtraction of previously awarded points for negative-aggressive behavior and rule infractions. It can be attached to a clipboard and used throughout recess periods on the playground. One point for each 5 minutes of recess is awarded on the form *prior to* the beginning of the recess period. The target student's task is to keep these points by behaving appropriately, interacting positively with peers, and avoiding playground rule infractions. For each instance in which a point is subtracted, it is important to inform the student, in a matter-of-fact way, of the point loss and the reason for it.

Tables 8.7–8.9 display results of the RECESS program's actual application for 10 highly aggressive students in grades K–3. These tables illustrate the target students' performance across program phases on three measures: (1) rate per minute of negative-aggressive social responses, (2) rate per minute of positive social responses, and (3) rate per minute of playground and classroom rule infractions.

Table 8.7 shows that RECESS had a substantial effect in reducing the target students' rates of negative-aggressive social behavior from the preintervention phase to the recess-only phase. These rates increased only slightly during the period when the playground supervisor was being trained to assume operation of the program. And over the long term, the negative rates of these aggressive students stayed in the normal range, as defined by the negative-response rates of nonaggressive peers (i.e., 0.11 per minute). In contrast, as Table 8.8 shows, RECESS had no discernible or predictable effect on the positive-response rates

INSTRUCTIONS FOR RECESS SUPERVISORS

A. **Praise:** Give praise frequently during each recess (at least once every 5 minutes). Keep tally in circle provided. Initial tally at end of each recess. (During days 1–7, the consultant should praise every 2 or 3 minutes.)

B. **Bonus points:** If child is extra-thoughtful or handles a difficult situation admirably, give a bonus point, tell the child, and, if possible, jot down a brief description.

C. **Point losing:** Cross out one point for every rule broken. Tell child as soon as possible (see rules on clipboard).

D. **Timeout:** If all the *regular* points are lost during a given recess, have the child sit out for the duration of that recess (bonus points are not lost). If child doesn't cooperate with this, inform the teacher or consultant.

FORM 8.1 ◆

Completed Point Record Form.

Source: From *RECESS: A Program for Reducing Negative-Aggressive Behavior,* by H. Walker, H. Hops, and C. Greenwood. Copyright © 1993 by Educational Achievement Systems, Seattle, WA. Reprinted by permission.

RECESS

Name _____   Date _____

	Regular points	Bonus points and description	
Morning recess			COUNT PRAISE INITIAL
Lunch recess			COUNT PRAISE INITIAL
Afternoon recess			COUNT PRAISE INITIAL

INSTRUCTIONS FOR RECESS SUPERVISORS

A. Praise: Give praise frequently during each recess (at least once every 5 minutes). Keep tally in circle provided. Initial tally at end of each recess. (During days 1–7, the consultant should praise every 2 or 3 minutes.)

B. Bonus points: If child is extra-thoughtful or handles a difficult situation admirably, give a bonus point, tell the child, and, if possible, jot down a brief description.

C. Point losing: Cross out one point for every rule broken. Tell child as soon as possible (see rules on clipboard).

D. Timeout: If all the *regular* points are lost during a given recess, have the child sit out for the duration of that recess (bonus points are not lost). If child doesn't cooperate with this, inform the teacher or consultant.

FORM 8.2 ◆

Blank Point Record Form.

Source: From *RECESS: A Program for Reducing Negative-Aggressive Behavior,* by H. Walker, H. Hops, and C. Greenwood. Copyright © 1993 by Educational Achievement Systems, Seattle, WA. Reprinted by permission.

TABLE 8.7

Negative-Response Rates During Preintervention and Intervention Phases of RECESS for 10 Socially Negative-Aggressive Children During Recess and Classroom Periods

Phases	Subjects										Total Group	
	1	2	3	4	5	6	7	8	9	10	($\overline{X}$)	SD
Recess												
Baseline	.91	.99	.85	.97	.105	.34	.55	.22	.47	.11	.69	.35
1a Consultant-operated	.01	.07	.06	.02	.01	.11	.01	.04	.03	.03	.04	.03
1b Recess-supervisor-operated—consultant present	.17	.04	.03	.05	.06	.02	.02	.02	.01	.00	.05	.04
2 Recess-supervisor-operated—extended to classroom	.02	.05	.11	.24	.32	.09	.07	.01	.18	.14	.14	.09
3 Fading	.08	.12	.13	—	.38	.13	.10	.02	—	—	.12	.11
Classroom												
B1 Prerecess program	.00	—	.28	.11	.22	.25	.00	.46	.41	.10	.26	.16
B2 Postrecess program	.02	.19	.15	.25	.07	.28	.00	.15	.26	.07	.15	.10
2 Class extension	.00	.06	.04	.18	.09	.08	.00	.05	.06	.05	.07	.05
3 Fading	.01	.00	.01	—	.04	.13	.00	.12	—	—	.05	.05

Source: From *RECESS: A Program for Reducing Negative-Aggressive Behavior,* by H. Walker, H. Hops, and C. Greenwood. Copyright © 1993 by Educational Achievement Systems, Seattle, WA. Reprinted by permission.

of these students. This is likely a result of their already having been within normal limits on this behavioral dimension. Finally, Table 8.9 shows that the RECESS program had a strong positive impact in reducing the frequency of playground and classroom rule violations.

It is unusual to find a consultant-based, selected-intervention program that is more effective than RECESS in altering the playground behavior of antisocial, aggressive students in grades K–3. This program was developed, systematically tested, and revised over a five-year period (see Walker, Hops, & Greenwood, 1984, 1993), and it has been applied successfully to the behavior of hundreds of antisocial, aggressive students.

If implemented correctly, RECESS will have a powerful impact on the social behavior of these students. And only the most aggressive, antisocial students in grades K–3 qualify for RECESS, due to the power of the intervention program and the time and effort required to implement it (i.e., 40–45 hours of program consultant time over a two- to three-month intervention period). In spite of these positive effects, our experience is that long-term maintenance procedures must be built into the RECESS program in order to preserve be-

TABLE 8.8

Positive-Response Rates Across Program Phases for 10 Socially Negative-Aggressive Children in RECESS

Phases		1	2	3	4	5	6	7	8	9	10	$\overline{X}$	SD
						Subjects						Total Group	
Recess													
Baseline		3.07	3.91	5.30	5.23	3.18	4.08	1.56	1.91	5.00	3.50	3.92	1.30
1a	Consultant-operated	2.37	5.70	5.98	5.31	2.53	4.47	1.90	1.60	5.10	2.89	3.88	1.69
1b	Recess-supervisor-operated—consultant present	2.91	5.73	6.15	6.12	3.65	3.95	2.32	1.22	4.65	2.43	4.12	1.72
2	Recess-supervisor-operated—extended to classroom	3.03	3.79	5.64	4.63	2.44	4.54	1.80	1.88	5.13	3.88	3.83	1.34
3	Fading	3.17	3.81	5.61	—	2.90	3.77	2.00	2.01	—	—	3.26	1.24
Classroom													
B1	Prerecess program	.29	—	3.04	3.14	1.30	2.98	.18	2.98	3.51	1.82	2.46	1.28
B2	Postrecess program	1.89	1.31	2.85	2.02	1.42	2.40	.43	1.98	3.67	1.80	2.09	.88
2	Class extension	.57	1.27	2.66	2.13	2.18	1.77	.18	1.68	1.96	.74	1.75	.79
3	Fading	.75	1.10	1.10	—	2.36	2.49	.55	2.48	—	—	2.35	.86

Source: From *RECESS: A Program for Reducing Negative-Aggressive Behavior,* by H. Walker, H. Hops, and C. Greenwood. Copyright © 1993 by Educational Achievement Systems, Seattle, WA. Reprinted by permission.

havioral gains achieved during the intervention. It is very important that the maintenance phase of RECESS be implemented over the long term, following completion of the first three program phases. Maintenance procedures should stay in effect for at least the remainder of the school year in which RECESS is implemented.

Children who are at serious risk for developing antisocial behavior patterns in the K–3 years are often expected by school personnel to "grow out of it." That is, maturity and the growth process are somehow supposed to work a magical transformation in diverting the aggressive child from a path leading to antisocial behavior, conduct disorder, and delinquency. However, the evidence shows that young bullies often get worse and that, instead of growing out of it, they actually grow into it (Loeber & Farrington, 2001). The best course thus seems to involve attacking this problem as early as possible in its developmental trajectory. This means identifying it immediately, recognizing it for what it is, and intervening comprehensively and consistently. There is no better place to start than on the playground, where this behavior pattern develops in a most unfortunate manner, but which affords numerous opportunities for teaching prosocial behavior patterns with peers and adults.

TABLE 8.9

Playground and Classroom Rule Breaking Rate Across Program Phases for 10 Socially Negative-Aggressive Children in RECESS

Phases		1	2	3	4	5	6	7	8	9	10	$(\overline{X})$	SD
						Subjects						Total Group	
Recess													
Baseline		.20	.88	.52	.66	.21	.06	.07	.17	.19	.31	.30	.27
1a	Consultant-operated	.02	.04	.02	.01	.01	.05	.02	.09	.02	.20	.03	.02
1b	Recess-supervisor-operated—consultant present	.05	.03	.02	.10	.03	.02	.00	.17	.00	.05	.04	.05
2	Recess-supervisor-operated—extended to classroom	.08	.04	.16	.16	.07	.03	.01	.01	.02	.06	.07	.05
3	Fading	.02	.04	.04	—	.19	.01	.01	.04	—	—	.04	.06
Classroom													
B1	Prerecess program	.00	—	.03	.05	.01	.00	.00	.10	.05	.00	.03	.03
B2	Postrecess program	.19	.08	.00	.13	.09	.01	.00	.15	.00	.00	.06	.07
2	Class extension	.00	.02	.04	.03	.12	.03	.00	.02	.00	.01	.03	.03
3	Fading	.00	.00	.01	—	.46	.02	.00	.01	—	—	.04	.17

Source: From *RECESS: A Program for Reducing Negative-Aggressive Behavior,* by H. Walker, H. Hops, and C. Greenwood. Copyright © 1993 by Educational Achievement Systems, Seattle, WA. Reprinted by permission.

Profiles of Recommended Bullying Prevention Programs in Schools

There are three well-conceptualized and empirically developed bullying prevention programs for use in school settings: (1) the Bullying Prevention Program, by Olweus (2000), (2) Steps to Respect, by the Committee for Children (2001), and (3) Bully-Proofing Your School, by Garrity, Jens, Porter, Sager, and Short-Camilli (1994). Each of these intervention programs is described here.

The Bullying Prevention Program

The Bullying Prevention Program is the gold standard for programs dealing with school-based bullying. It rests upon a solid foundation of outstanding scientific research on bullying in Norway and the United States. As noted previously, the Bullying Prevention Program is one of the 11 Blueprint Programs scientifically validated by the Center for the Study and Prevention of Violence. It is a multi-level, multicomponent program designed to reduce and prevent bully–victim problems in school settings. Implemented by school staff, the program's overall goal is to restructure the existing school environment in order to reduce the opportunities and the social rewards for bullying behavior.

The program targets students in elementary, middle, and junior high school. All students participate in the universal-intervention aspects of the program, with bullies and victims exposed to additional, individualized interventions. The core components of the program are implemented at the school, classroom, and individual levels. Extensive empirical evidence points to the effectiveness of the Bullying Prevention Program.

The program costs approximately $200 per school and $65 per participating teacher to cover the costs of classroom materials. In addition, the program requires an on-site coordinator. Information about this and other Blueprint Programs can be obtained by contacting the Center for the Study and Prevention of Violence, Institute of Behavioral Science, University of Colorado at Boulder, Box 442, Boulder, CO 80309-0442; phone 303-492-8465; fax 303-443-3297.

Steps to Respect

Steps to Respect was developed by the Committee for Children, a nonprofit agency in Seattle, Washington, that designs and distributes intervention programs, based on social learning principles, for use in school settings. The program's twin goals are to reduce bullying and to promote healthy peer relationships. A universal intervention designed to achieve primary prevention goals and outcomes, it targets intermediate-grade-level students in elementary schools. Steps to Respect is based on research related to the core elements that are essential in the prevention and reduction of bullying (see Snell, MacKenzie, & Frey, 2002).

The major components of the Steps to Respect program include a program guide, staff training, a student curriculum, and telephone-based consultation services. These components address bullying problems and issues at the following levels: schoolwide, adult, peer group, and individual. The content of the student lessons focuses on skills for coping with bullying, general friendship skills, and emotion management skills. Steps to Respect also teaches empathy and methods of assisting the victims of bullying. To its great credit, the program pays considerable attention to the role of bystanders in the perpetuation of the act of bullying.

The Steps to Respect curriculum is taught by regular elementary teachers as subject matter content. Specific topics include recognition of bullying, safe and effective responses to bullying, emotional competence, supportive peer group behaviors, friendship skills, self-management skills, and positive social values. This curricular content was designed to be integrated within other academic areas. The curricular materials consist of scripted lesson cards, handouts, overhead transparencies, and videotaped scenarios. Steps to Respect also includes a program overview component for parents and information on how parents can support the program at home.

The program requires staff training for high-quality implementation. Staff training consists of a core training session and two specialty training sessions that take place over a two- to three-day period. The core training involves all school staff; the specialty training is targeted at the classroom instructors of Steps to Respect.

Steps to Respect is published by and available from the Committee for Children. For more information about the program, its components, and its costs, contact the Committee for Children at 568 First Avenue South, Suite 600, Seattle, WA 98104-2804; phone 206-343-1223, toll-free 800-634-4449; fax 206-438-6765; Web site www.cfchildren.org.

Bully-Proofing Your School

Bully-Proofing Your School is based on the principles for addressing bullying developed by Olweus. The program has three major components: (1) development of a heightened awareness that a bullying problem exists in a school, (2) instruction in protective skills and techniques, and (3) creation of a positive school climate through promotion of a "caring majority" in the school. Bully-Proofing was designed to reduce bullying in school and to increase students' sense of personal safety through staff and parent education about bullying dynamics and implementation of interventions to prevent it.

One of the most widely used bullying programs available, Bully-Proofing has been featured in a number of national media venues. A comprehensive longitudinal evaluation of the program is reported in Epstein, Plog, and Porter (2002). The program features 10 sessions that deliver its content and specific procedures. The Bully-Proofing series consists of (1) the Bully-Proofing Comprehensive Approach for Elementary Schools, (2) the Bully-Proofing Comprehensive Approach for Middle Schools, (3) Bully-Proofing Your Child: A Parent's Guide, and (4) Bully-Proofing Your Child: First Aid for Hurt Feelings. The series is published by Sopris West Educational Services, 4093 Specialty Place, Longmont, CO 80504-5400 or P.O. Box 1809, Longmont, CO 80502; phone 303-651-2829, toll-free 800-547-6747; fax 888-819-7767; Web site: www.sopriswest.com.

Recommended Resources for Addressing Teasing, Bullying, and Negative-Aggressive Student Behavior

Materials describing the RECESS program include detailed procedural manuals for program consultants, teachers, and playground supervisors, plus a packet of program consumables (forms, charts, and posters). Information about the RECESS program can be accessed by contacting the senior author at the Institute on Violence and Destructive Behavior, College of Education, 1265 University of Oregon, Eugene, OR 97403; phone 541-346-3591; fax 541-346-2594; email hwalker@oregon.uoregon.edu. Once purchased, RECESS can be used for repeated program applications.

Valerie Besay, a British school psychologist and expert on school bullying, has written an outstanding book on bullying in schools and has also developed a school-based staff development program for use in coping with bullying. The book *Bullies and Victims in Schools: A Guide to Understanding and Management* provides both a comprehensive treatment of the topic and numerous suggestions for coping with bullying. The book is divided into two parts: Part One focuses on understanding bullying, and Part Two on what to do about it. The U.S. distributor for the book is Taylor and Francis, 1900 Frost

Road, Suite 101, Philadelphia, PA 19007; phone 215-785-5800. Besay's staff development training program for controlling bullying in school, We Don't Have Bullies Here, is structured around a typical school day and explains how daily procedures can be organized and coordinated for reducing bullying. The program is a universal intervention that involves a whole-school approach. It is available from V. E. Besay, 57 Manor House Road, Jesmond, Newcastle upon Tyne, NE2 2LY, England.

The National Center for School Safety has published an 18-minute film, *Set Straight on Bullies,* to assist school administrators in educating teachers, parents, and students about the severity and implications of schoolyard bullying. This award-winning film tells the story of a bullying victim and the adverse effects on his life, as well as the lives of the bully, other students, and his parents and teachers. The film is especially suitable for raising awareness of and sensitivity toward bullying and its damaging effects among students, parents, teachers, and other school personnel. The National School Safety Center also maintains an extensive inventory of resource materials on bullying and its prevention. *Set Straight on Bullies* and these additional resource materials are available for purchase from the National School Safety Center, 4165 Thousand Oaks Boulevard, Suite 290, Westlake Village, CA 91362.

The U.S. Department of Education maintains an excellent Web site on the topic of bullying. Resource materials include the *Manual for Schools and Communities on Bullying,* which offers information on school-level interventions for bullying, user-friendly classroom activities for teachers, individual interventions for bullying students, suggested community activities, and recommended action steps for school administrators. Specific bullying prevention and coping strategies are included for classroom teachers, students, and parents. Finally, an extensive list of resources is provided consisting of bullying programs, innovative approaches to bullying prevention, and books and reports on bullying and related topics. This Web site is a highly recommended resource on bullying for educators, mental health professionals, and related services personnel. The address is www.cde.ca.gov/spbranch/ssp/bullymanual.htm.

Conclusion

The chapter focused on bullying, teasing, and related behavior, especially on the playground. The social behavior of antisocial students on the playground can be extremely problematic for peers and a most intractable behavior management problem for school staff. Mean-spirited teasing, bullying, and negative-aggressive forms of behavior violate social norms and can lead to social rejection by peers and adults alike. Well-developed patterns of aggressive behavior, expressed in the form of mean-spirited teasing, harassment, and bullying, have a destructive effect on both victim and victimizer. One of the best approaches to preventing these unfortunate behavioral outcomes is to teach antisocial students alternatives to aggressive behavior as early as possible in their lives and school careers.

Social skills training that emphasizes cooperation, empathy, referential communication, acceptance, responsible decision making, and positive regard for others is an important tool for teaching adaptive, prosocial behavior patterns to all students. Significant advances have been made in this area in the past decade through research and the development of best practices (Bullis, Walker, & Sprague, 2001; Elksnin & Elksnin, 2001). More than any other group, antisocial students are in need of systematic exposure to such training.

 ## InfoTrac College Edition Research Terms

Bullying prevention

Physical bullying

School-based bullying

References

Bullis, M., Walker, H. M., & Sprague, J. R. (2001). A promise unfulfilled: Social skills training with at-risk children and youth. *Exceptionality, 9*(1, 2), 67–90.

Coie, J., Underwood, M., & Lochman, J. (1991). Programmatic intervention with aggressive children in the school setting. In D. Pepler & K. Rubin (Eds.), *The development and treatment of childhood aggression* (pp. 389–407). Hillsdale, NJ: Erlbaum.

Committee for Children. (2001). *Steps to Respect: A special issue on bullying prevention program.* Seattle: Author.

Elksnin, L., & Elksnin, N. (Eds.). (2001). Adolescents with disabilities: The need for occupational social skills training [Special issue]. *Exceptionality, 9*(1, 2), 91–105.

Epstein, L., Plog, A., & Porter, W. (2002). Bully-proofing your school: Results of a four-year intervention. *Emotional and Behavioral Disorders in Youth*, Summer, 55–56, 73–78.

Garrity, C., Jens, K., Porter, W., Sager, N., & Short-Camilli, C. (1994). *Bully-proofing your school.* Longmont, CO: Sopris West.

Georgesen, J., Harris, M., Milich, R., & Young, J. (1999). "Just teasing . . .": Personality effects on perceptions and life narratives of childhood teasing. *Personality and Social Psychology Bulletin, 25*, 1254–1267.

Hodges, E. V. E., & Perry, D. (1999). Personal and interpersonal antecedents and consequences of victimization by peers. *Journal of Social and Personality Psychology, 76*, 677–685.

Hollinger, J. (1987). Social skills for behaviorally disordered children as preparation for mainstreaming: Theory, practice and new directions. *Remedial and Special Education, 8*(4), 17–27.

Irvin, L. K., & Walker, H. M. (1993). Improving social skills assessment of children with disabilities: Construct development and applications of technology [Special issue]. *Journal of Special Education Technology, 12*(1), 63–70.

Irvin, L. K., Walker, H. M., Noell, J., Singer, G. H. S., Irvine, A. B., Marquez, K., & Britz, B. (1992). Measuring children's social skills using microcomputer-based videodisc assessment. *Behavior Modification, 16*, 475–503.

Kochenderfer, B., & Ladd, G. (1996). Peer victimization: Cause or consequence of school maladjustment? *Child Development, 67*, 1305–1317.

Landau, S., Milich, R., Harris, M., & Larson, S. (2001). "You really don't know how much it hurts": Children's and preservice teachers' reactions to childhood teasing. *School Psychology Review, 30*(3), 329–343.

Lee, J. (1993). *Facing the fire: Experiencing and expressing anger appropriately.* New York: Bantam Books.

Loeber, R., & Farrington, D. P. (2001). *Serious and violent juvenile offenders: Risk factors and successful interventions.* Thousand Oaks, CA: Sage.

Olweus, D. (1978). *Aggression in the schools: Bullies and whipping boys.* New York: Wiley.

Olweus, D. (1991). Bully/victim problems among school children: Basic facts and effects of a school-based intervention program. In D. Pepler & K. Rubin (Eds.), *The development and treatment of childhood aggression* (pp. 411–446). London: Erlbaum

Olweus, D. (1993). *Bullying at school: What we know and what we can do.* Cambridge: Blackwell.

Olweus, D. (1994). Annotation: Bullying at school: Basic facts and effects of a school–based intervention program. *Journal of Child Psychology and Psychiatry, 35*, 1171–1190.

Olweus, D. (1996). *The revised Olweus Bully/Victim Questionnaire.* Unpublished material. Bergen, Norway: Research Center for Health Promotion.

Olweus, D. (2000). *Bullying prevention program.* Boulder, CO: Center for the Study and Prevention of Violence.

Pettit, G., & Dodge, K. (Eds.). (2003). Violent children [Special issue]. *Developmental Psychology, 39*(2).

Reid, J. B., Patterson, G. R., & Snyder, J. J. (Eds.). (2002). *Antisocial behavior in children and adolescents: A developmental analysis and the Oregon Model for Intervention.* Washington, DC: American Psychological Association.

Sampson, R. (2002). *Bullying in schools.* Problem-oriented guides for police series. Washington, DC: U.S. Department of Justice.

Satcher, D. (2001). *Youth violence: A report of the Surgeon General.* Washington, DC: U.S. Public Health Service, U.S. Department of Health and Human Services.

Scambler, D. J., Harris, M. J., & Milich, R. (1998). Sticks and stone: Evaluations of responses to childhood teasing. *Social Development, 7*, 234–249.

School Safety News Service. (2001). *School Safety Update: The Newsletter of the National School Safety Network*, May.

Shinn, M. R., Ramsey, E., Walker, H. M., Stieber, S., & O'Neill, R. E. (1987). Antisocial behavior in school settings: Initial differences in an at-risk and normal population. *The Journal of Special Education, 21*(2), 69–84.

Smith, S. G., & Sprague, J. R. (2002). The mean kid: An overview of bully/victim problems and research-based solutions for schools. *Oregon School Study Council Bulletin, 44*(2) [whole issue].

Snell, J. L., MacKenzie, E. P., & Frey, K. S. (2002). Bullying prevention in elementary schools: The importance of adult leadership, peer group support, and student social-emotional skills. In M. R. Shinn, H. M. Walker, & G. Stoner (Eds.), *Interventions for academic and behavior problems II: Preventive and remedial approaches* (pp. 351–372). Bethesda, MD: National Association for School Psychologists.

Sprague, J. R., Walker, H. M., Nishioka, V., & Smith, S. G. (in press). *School safety and prevention strategies: Proven and practical solutions for educators.* New York: Guilford.

U.S. Department of Education. (1998). *Preventing bullying: A manual for schools and communities.* Washington, DC: U.S. Department of Education.

Walker, H. M., Colvin, G., & Ramsey, E. (1995). *Antisocial behavior in schools: Strategies and best practices.* Pacific Grove, CA: Brooks/Cole.

Walker, H. M., Hops, H., & Greenwood, C. R. (l984). The CORBEH research and development model: Programmatic issues and strategies. In S. Paine, G. T. Bellamy, & B. Wilcox (Eds.), *Human services that work* (pp. 57–78). Baltimore: Paul H. Brookes.

Walker, H., Hops, H., & Greenwood, C. (1993). *RECESS: A program for reducing negative-aggressive behavior.* Seattle: Educational Achievement Systems.

Walker, H. M., Irvin, L. K., Noell, J., & Singer, G. H. S. (1992). A construct score approach to the assessment of social competence: Rationale, technological considerations, and anticipated outcomes. *Behavior Modification, 16,* 448–474.

Walker, H. M., & Severson, H. H. (1990). *Systematic Screening for Behavior Disorders (SSBD): User's guide and technical manual.* Longmont, CO: Sopris West.

Walker, H. M., Shinn, M., O'Neill, R., & Ramsey, E. (1987). A longitudinal assessment of the development of antisocial behavior in boys: Rationale, methodology and first year results. *Remedial and Special Education, 8*(4), 7–16, 27.

Parent Involvement in the Schooling of Antisocial Students: Critical Issues and Best Practices

CHAPTER

9

Introduction

The origins of antisocial behavior patterns in school are usually embedded in the family conditions to which these children are exposed. Although evidence suggests that antisocial behavior patterns are causally related, in varying degrees, to such constitutional factors as neurobiology, temperament, and hormonal levels, there is considerable documentation that antisocial behavior is often strongly associated with pathological family conditions (Kazdin, 1985; Loeber & Farrington, 2001; Patterson, 1982; Patterson, Reid, & Dishion, 1992; Reid, Patterson, & Snyder, 2002). This is particularly true of children for whom signs of antisocial behavior begin to emerge early in their lives—that is, well before they start formal schooling. Evidence indicates that these youngsters are (1) socialized to antisocial behavior patterns by the toxic family conditions and incompetent parenting styles to which they are exposed from earliest infancy and (2) are often at severe risk for later destructive outcomes (Patterson, 2002; Synder & Stoolmiller, 2002).

Because of the central role that family and home conditions play in the etiology of many antisocial behavior patterns, families must become partners with schools and other social institutions and agencies if satisfactory solutions to this problem are to be found. For reasons to be described in this chapter, it is *extremely* important that effective parent involvement be a central feature of any school-based attempt to address antisocial student behavior (Reid, 1993). Although it is possible to achieve positive behavioral changes in the school setting without involving parents in the intervention, any behavioral gains achieved in a school-only intervention run the risk of being specific to that setting. Whenever possible, parents of antisocial students should participate in the planning and implementation of school interventions, for several reasons. First, many of the adjustment problems that antisocial students experience at school have their origins in the home. Second, the more settings there are in which interventions for antisocial behavior can be implemented, the more likely there is to be a substantive, overall impact on students' total behavior. Third, parental support in coordinating the school and home components of an intervention (e.g., monitoring, praising, debriefing, delivering home rewards) can significantly increase the effectiveness of any school intervention. Finally, parent involvement sometimes opens the door for parent education that can lead to more effective parenting practices, more positive parent–child interactions, and improved student self-esteem. Parents have been shown to be key natural helpers and therapists whose participation significantly enhances an intervention's overall impact with challenging offspring—especially if they are invested in its planning and implementation (Strain & Timm, 2001).

As discussesd in previous chapters, normal parenting practices are severely disrupted in families that are stressed by such external and internal factors as divorce, poverty, abuse (physical, sexual, psychological, drug and alcohol), conflict, and unemployment. Disrupted parenting practices, in turn, provide a nurturing context for the development of antisocial behavior patterns in young children (Loeber & Dishion, 1983; Loeber & Farrington, 2001; Patterson, 1983; Patterson et al., 1992; Reid et al., 2002). Five parenting practices are critical to the development of adaptive, positive, and cooperative patterns of behavior among children and youths in general.

They are (1) appropriate, fair discipline that is predictable but not harsh or punitive; (2) monitoring and careful supervision of the child's whereabouts, activities, and peer affiliations; (3) parent involvement in the child's life, and investment of time and energy in his or her development; (4) use of positive family management techniques of encouragement, support, praise, positive regard and valuing, and appropriate structure and consequences governing the child's daily activities; and (5) the ability to resolve conflicts among family members and to manage crises.

Family environments that lack these critical parenting practices are often chaotic and unhealthy settings in which to rear children (Wahler & Dumas, 1986). Children emerging from these homes typically are ill prepared for the normal demands of schooling (e.g., taking instruction, sharing, cooperating, working independently, complying promptly with commands). Because of the aversive nature of their behavioral characteristics, they face social rejection by both peers and teachers within just a few years of entering school. The best window for diverting these children from an antisocial path in the school setting is upon school entry (i.e., K–3), at which point systematic efforts can be made to ensure that they get off to an optimal start in their school careers (Eddy, Reid, & Curry, 2002; Walker & Shinn, 2002). This involves, among other things, learning to read as well as possible by the end of third grade and acquiring an adaptive, prosocial behavior pattern that contributes to school success and the development of friendships.

Professionals increasingly believe that successful treatment of antisocial behavior among children and youths requires comprehensive interventions coordinated across home and school settings (Patterson et al., 1992). Reid (1993) has argued persuasively that intervention efforts for antisocial behavior must address the three social agents who have the greatest-impact on the child's behavior (i.e., parents, teachers, and peers). If intervention occurs early in a child's school career and involves a family–school partnership, there is a much greater likelihood of achieving a positive result. The experience of the authors is completely in accord with this view.

This chapter presents information and guidelines on two important topics: (1) how to involve parents in supporting their child's behavioral adjustment to teachers and peers and (2) how to achieve positive teacher–parent interactions on an ongoing basis. These are important outcomes for school personnel to strive for, not just for antisocial students but for all students. The first section focuses on the role of parents in forging effective parent–teacher communication; the second presents and illustrates specific techniques and guidelines for achieving this goal.

© Amy Etra/PhotoEdit

Parental participation in school-based intervention efforts is essential. Most often, the results of parent involvement includes enhanced parent-child interactions, as well as improved relations with teachers and peers.

The Role of Parents in Developing Healthy Children

What would you say is the number-one way to raise students' achievement at school: (1) lengthen the school day, (2) decrease class size, or (3) increase parent involvement? If you chose item 3, "increase parent involvement," you are not alone in your thinking. Results of national surveys consistently indicate that most educators view more parent involvement as one of the best ways to improve student achievement. We do not know of a single teacher, school administrator, counselor, or school psychologist who does not believe that a student's parents can make a huge contribution to that child's positive emotional and academic development. Further, these professionals generally agree that parent support and involvement in their child's schooling can have a significant impact on their school success. Many teachers depend heavily on parent involvement to support their students in completing homework assignments and class extras, such as special projects. One of the key elements of effective schooling is regularly assigned and completed homework. The teacher's ability to call on parents for their support in coping with student behavior problems at school is equally important. In a *Phi Delta Kappa* poll representing over 20,000 students and their teachers, the number-one intervention strategy teachers reported using when dealing with students at risk for behavior problems was notifying and conferring with parents (Lombardi, Odel, & Novotny, 1990).

Families can contribute, albeit often unknowingly, to a student's development in a most negative fashion. The nature of young children's behavior at home usually typifies what can be expected as they progress through schooling. Research has shown, for example, that a preschooler's noncompliance with parental directives is the cornerstone or "gatekey" behavior for the further development of antisocial behavior (McMahon & Forehand, in press; Patterson, 2002). The failure of parents to teach reasonable compliance in this regard can be extremely serious. Noncompliance often serves as the first step in a chain of increasingly aversive behavioral events that ultimately place the child at severe developmental risk. Although the great majority of young children's interactions with their parents are affectionate and positive, studies have shown that even nonproblem boys demonstrate an aversive act of some type about once every 2 minutes (Patterson, 1982). As young children approach school age, however, most will reduce their rates of aversive behavior by approximately half through the socialization efforts of parents. Unfortunately, this is not true for antisocial children, whose rates actually accelerate over the course of their school careers. Thus, children with high rates of negative, coercive social behavior upon entering school are likely to start their educational careers off on the wrong foot— and they often go downhill from there (Patterson, 2002).

Many researchers have characterized the family as providing one of the main early training grounds for delinquency, and there appears to be considerable truth to this assertion. Wahler and Dumas (1986) cite extensive evidence that parents who have criminal records produce children who have a much greater chance of becoming delinquents in adolescence. For example, in a follow-up study of 350 children through age 18, West and Farrington (1977) found that 37% of sons whose fathers had criminal records became delinquent; the equivalent

Box 9.1   Case: Sam, the Cookie Monster

By age 4, Sam Jackson's parents already knew he was "difficult." His almost constant whining and arguing had his parents feeling overwhelmed and depressed. A typical example of an interaction with his parents begins with Sam asking for a snack. His mother says, "No." Next, Sam climbs onto the counter, and his mother says in a louder and firmer voice, "No, get down now." Sam continues to badger his mother. His mother then goes on to explain that dinner is coming, that she is saving the cookies, and that he has already had three. Finally, she reaches the point of being unable to stand the nagging and screams at Sam. "You are a terrible whiner! I am so sick of this! Go ahead and get a cookie. Your dad will deal with you later." Sam almost always gets his cookie; and in this particular example, it took only about 10 minutes of nagging, badgering, and tantrum throwing. After hundreds of these types of interactions, Sam has learned that he needs only to escalate quickly to extreme forms of negative behavior to get what he wants. Sam's parents give in to him, not understanding that there are other options for dealing with the situation.

figure for sons of fathers who had no criminal record was 8%. These authors cite further evidence that if one or both parents are arrested prior to or during a child's life then his or her chances of becoming delinquent in adolescence are 12 times greater than normal! An early pattern of well-developed antisocial behavior is one of the best predictors of later delinquency, which, in turn, is a strong predictor of adult criminality (Patterson et al., 1992).

As already noted, parents of antisocial children tend to use harsh and inconsistent disciplinary practices, are usually not involved in a positive manner in their children's lives, and are weak at monitoring and supervising their children's daily activities (Loeber & Dishion, 1983; Patterson, 2002; Patterson et al., 1992). In addition to these negative parenting factors, what seems to further differentiate nonantisocial from antisocial children is how parents respond to their aversive behavior. Parents of antisocial children are more inconsistent and noncontingent in both their praise for and their punishment of their children's behavior. That is, their use of praise and punishment bears no logical relationship to the child's actual behavior. Such parents often give in to their child's coercive, demanding behavior, which usually escalates the negative behavior they were trying to stop in the first place. Box 9.1 recounts a typical incident in the home of a somewhat troublesome preschooler that exemplifies this process.

Sadly, many children learn to control their family members through similarly aggressive and aversive means. To make matters worse, these antisocial children get little, if any, instruction in *prosocial* behavior—that is, in how to be positive, empathic, and cooperative in their interactions with others. Observations of distressed families show that, when it does occur, the positive behavior of antisocial children often goes unnoticed or is responded to inappropriately (e.g., with

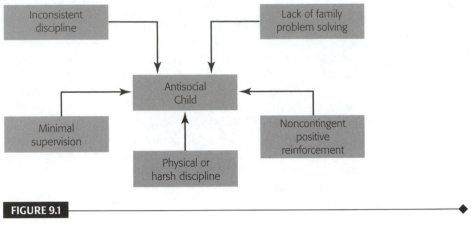

FIGURE 9.1

Typical Parenting Practices Used by Parents of Antisocial Children.

criticism such as "You picked up your room but you never do it when I ask you"). Apparently, parents of these children often lack many of the key management skills for dealing with challenging child behavior. Figure 9.1 summarizes researchers' findings regarding the parenting practices typically used by parents of antisocial children.

To make matters worse, antisocial children often live in families in which unemployment, poverty, and stress are common. Of course, it is important to remember that many children who live in poverty or come from divorced families do *not* become chronic delinquents and often do relatively well in school and in their peer relations. Such children and youths are called "resilient" because they succeed in life despite being exposed to substantial risk factors that seem to negatively influence many others. (See Katz [1997] for a thorough discussion of this important topic.) Still, children who live in disadvantaged conditions and whose parents are marginal in their ability to discipline, monitor, and provide positive support for their children are at high risk for developing antisocial behavior and eventual delinquency in adolescence.

Where does this leave you as Sam Jackson's teacher? Should you simply blame his mother and father, decide there is nothing you can do, and give up? If you do these things, Sam will most certainly fail at school. Fortunately, there are a number of positive things you can do for Sam by engaging his parents in his schooling, even if he comes from a highly stressed home environment. The next section outlines specific and practical steps for improving school and teacher interactions with all parents, especially those like Sam's.

Improving Ongoing Interactions with Parents

Few would deny that, over the course of children's development, their parents are the most consistent and important caregivers in their lives. Parents generally have a strong impact on their children's social and academic growth. They are obviously in a position to exert a tremendous influence on their children's development. Teachers need to do everything possible to involve parents in the schooling process and to assist them in using this influence to motivate their children's school performance. To the maximum extent possible, teachers and schools should use parental resources in fostering children's development in school. Most parents seem to be willing to invest the necessary time and effort to foster their children's school success.

Schools tend to resist offering special educational services to most at-risk, antisocial students in the elementary years (see Walker, Nishioka, Zeller, Severson, & Feil, 2000). Yet these students' parents tend to be available and willing to be involved in their children's schooling. And for those families for which prospects of parent involvement might appear hopeless, remember that even the smallest changes in unhealthy parenting can produce momentous changes down the road. This section provides guidelines and easy-to-follow techniques for involving *all* parents in their children's schooling.

Developing a Positive Attitude Toward Parents

The importance of approaching parents in a positive manner seems almost too obvious to merit discussion. However, our observations of parent–teacher interactions tell us that far too many teachers are frustrated in their interactions with parents and their efforts to involve them in their children's schooling. Old "baggage" in the form of previous experiences with difficult parents often negatively colors these new interactions.

It is well known that schools are not necessarily parent-friendly places for the parents of problematic students. Many of these parents were themselves difficult students and may have negative memories of their school experiences. Thus, they are distrustful of the school setting and often expect the worst when they are required to have contact with school personnel. Indeed, parents are not necessarily supportive of schooling and may actually foster negative attitudes toward school among their children.

Unnecessary conflicts sometimes arise between school and home. A teacher, for example, can quickly become impatient with or discouraged by parents who are unavailable for classroom volunteering, who fail to respond to notes or forms that are sent home, or who don't find the time to attend parent–teacher conferences. Often, these parents are labeled as "uncooperative" by educators, which leads teachers to become even more frustrated with their misbehaving children. This, in turn, leads the school to complain and the parents to feel as if they are being falsely blamed for their children's difficulties at school. A vicious cycle quickly ensues.

Positive parent involvement must begin early in children's school life. Those first interactions between parents and the kindergarten teacher, school principal, and even school secretary are extremely important. From then on, parent contacts with teachers, counselor, principal, and other school personnel should be respectful, helpful, and friendly. As a first step, every effort should be made to create a school atmosphere in which all parents are respected, valued, and made to feel welcome. This task should be a priority of the principal and fully supported by teachers.

Teacher–parent communication must be proactive, positive, and timely.

Whenever possible, school contacts with parents should begin with discussion of children's strengths. In fact, strength-based assessment of children's and youths' assets has gained popularity in the educational and mental health fields (see Epstein & Sharma, 1998). Too often, school professionals let personal beliefs about parents (e.g., that they are uncooperative, hostile, or demanding) get in the way of effective interactions and functional parent–teacher relationships. Parents deserve to be treated at least as well as you would want to be treated if your child were in the classroom. If your child were a student, which of the following would you want from her or his teacher?

◆ To hear from that person at the beginning of the year
◆ To know specific expectations of the child
◆ To learn about problems before things get out of hand
◆ To have a general idea of what is happening in the classroom
◆ To know when the child is doing well

Positive communication with parents can quickly demonstrate a teacher's competence, professionalism, and concern for students. Most importantly, it can also lay the foundation for an effective working relationship between schools and families—one that can yield enormous benefits for both.

Establishing Regular Communication

Positive communication with parents needs to begin on the first day of school. Schools should always make the first move; they should never wait until something goes wrong to establish school–home communication with parents. Regular communication does not always entail individual letters or phone calls to parents. Rather, simple letters, short memos, and general newsletters that all students take home work well. Also consider mailing notes home—it costs a minimal amount to mail a note to 30 households. A quick, positive note expressing enthusiasm about the upcoming year is all that is needed to establish a person's reputation as a teacher who communicates positively with parents. A sample letter of introduction is provided in Box 9.2.

Classroom Calendars.   In addition to short letters or memos sent to all parents throughout the year, a useful technique of communication is a monthly, bi-monthly, or weekly newsletter or classroom calendar. Calendars are easily created from teachers' planning books. They are especially useful to parents because the specific information contained therein enables them to ask their children specific questions about school and classroom activities. No longer need parents be faced with blank looks because all they can ask their children is, "What did you do in school today?" For instance, if the calendar shows that, on Wednesday, students reviewed a spelling test, practiced using a compass, and were introduced to their new science component, the rain forest, parents are armed with much more specific information about what is happening in school.

The other advantage of an up-to-date calendar is that it gives parents information about school tasks that students need to prepare for. For example, it is most helpful if parents know in advance about homework assignments, upcoming tests or quizzes, field trips, and other special classroom or schoolwide activities. Box 9.3 provides a sample calendar.

Newsletters.   Newsletters work in much the same way as calendars. Many teachers already use this technique and even involve their students in helping to write items. Box 9.4 shows a sample newsletter.

Good-News Notes.   Sometimes called "school–home notes," good-news notes are another great way to provide positive information to parents. Parents and students like to see special accomplishments and contributions acknowledged in this way.

Box 9.3 Sample Calendar

NOVEMBER

Monday	Tuesday	Wednesday	Thursday	Friday
6	7	8	9	10
PE Computer lab Homework: Read chapters 8 & 9 Math fact sheet	Homework: Study for spelling test	Begin section on Japan Spelling test Homework: None	Library Homework: Math—do review questions	Homework: Finish reading *Charlotte's Web*

Once a teacher creates a supply of good-news notes, it takes mere seconds to jot down a few positive words about a student's school behavior or academic performance. Attendance records are a good way of tracking who has had a good-news note sent home recently. Form 9.1 shows a sample form for a good-news note.

These notes have been used extensively to improve the academic and behavioral functioning of students and the communication process between parents and schools. Aside from their positive communication value, perhaps the greatest benefit of school–home notes is that they enable parents to deliver appropriate rewards at home for successful school performance. A wide range of home-based incentives can be accessed to support students' school behavior and performance.

Phone Calls. One of the most effective, yet underutilized, parent communication techniques is the quick phone call. These phone calls consist not of long conversations, but rather brief updates on how each child is doing in the classroom. Getting in the habit of phoning parents with positive comments about their child leads to big payoffs down the line and makes subsequent phone calls about problem behavior a lot easier. If teachers make just 2 calls each afternoon, they will have made 10 calls in a week. Thus, a teacher can cover an entire classroom in just two or three weeks. At regular intervals, teachers should set a goal for themselves of reaching two to three parents by phone each day.

Early in the year, a good way to start a phone call to a new parent might be to ask how her or his child is responding to school. This enables each parent to talk about the child without the teacher leading the parent one way or the other. These calls also let parents know that the teacher will use the phone to touch base with them every once in a while so they can work together to create the most positive school experience for their children.

4th Grade News: February 1–15, 2004

Editor: Mr. Rodriguez

Assistant Editors: Ashley Clien, Jason Smith, and Steven Johnson

Letter from the Editor

Dear Parents,

Happy Valentine's Day. We will be exchanging valentines on Friday, February 13. If you would like to volunteer to help at our party, please drop me a note.

Students finished *The Celery Stalks at Midnight* and have book reports due next Wednesday.

Everyone is enjoying our new time in the computer lab.

Sincerely,

Don Rodriguez

Upcoming Trip

Seattle Art Museum
March 2, 2004
Permission Slip Attached—
Return by February 25, 2004

New Activity

Computer lab began last Monday. We will have computer lab every Monday.

Book Report

By: Laura Ringsmann
Book: *Little House in the Big Woods*
Author: Laura Ingalls Wilder

This was a book about a little girl named Laura and her sisters, Mary and Carrie. Everything happened a long time ago. Laura's father had to shoot animals for food and her mother had a large vegetable garden. I liked this book because it had lots of intersting stories about the olden days and because the girl's name was Laura.

A good way to start a parent phone call is by briefly describing some recent positive behavior or achievement by the student. An open-ended question about the parent's perception of a recent classroom assignment or activity is another good approach. Occasionally, these phone conversations can lead to effective problem solving, particularly if there is a concern or problem at school for which parental input is important.

As discussed in Chapter 7, Reid and his colleagues (Reid, Eddy, Fetrow, & Stoolmiller, 1999) have developed a collaborative home–school intervention program with universal and selected components called LIFT (Linking the Interests of Families and Teachers). Teacher–parent communication is a key feature of the LIFT program. Teachers provide daily information regarding classroom activities and take-home assignments via recorded phone messages for parents. Parents, in turn, access the message by phone and then leave specific questions or concerns as messages for their child's teacher. It is not necessary for the parent and teacher to talk directly in order for this procedure to work. The procedure gives

GOOD NEWS

Name: _____

Date: _____

_____

_____

_____

_____

_____

Sincerely: _____

_____

Sample Blank Good-News Note.

the teacher a quick and easy avenue for communicating with parents on an individual, personalized basis.

In the LIFT program, each teacher was provided with a phone in their classroom for their exclusive use, which proved to be a very popular option. Once the phone was installed in the classroom, teachers sent letters to all parents letting them know about the new answering machine. To avoid the problem of misplaced phone numbers, a sticker or refrigerator magnet with the teacher's name and number printed on it was included. These teachers greatly appreciated the ease and convenience of this communication technique. Most found that it increased their frequency of parent contacts two- or threefold.

This program costs less than $60 per month per classroom in most areas. If the school lacks funds for this purpose, there are alternatives. Some teachers secure outside funding, apply for funds from the school district or local school–parent group, or initiate their own fund-raising program to get the program started. This investment is well worth the effort, and the program represents a significant procedural advance in the quality and effectiveness of parent–teacher communication.

Using a Problem-Solving Approach

Antisocial children and youths pose many obstacles to effective classroom management. Sometimes, no matter how hard teachers try to prevent problems, they have a student who constantly challenges them and disrupts the classroom. In such cases, they should not wait too long to call on the student's parents for assistance. Waiting until a student needs to be removed from school before contacting the parents is clearly not an example of effective parent involvement. We recommend a structured teacher–parent problem-solving approach when it becomes necessary to involve parents because of the child's antisocial behavior in the classroom or on the playground.

School personnel may have been exposed to problem-solving techniques through their preservice or continuing education, and some may use problem-solving strategies in their professional interactions. However, relatively few teachers or school administrators use this simple approach when working with parents.

The problem-solving worksheet in Form 9.2 is useful whenever the need to communicate with parents arises due to a student's problem behavior. The worksheet helps keep the focus on finding solutions, rather than reviewing the problem behavior and possible causes. The latter approach is usually not productive and can lead to pejorative labeling and blaming of the parents—both of which are poisonous to positive parent–teacher relations. Parents who get a call from an overwhelmed or agitated teacher tend to feel as if the teacher is blaming them or somehow expecting them to magically solve their child's behavior problems at school. In contrast, parents who receive a solution-focused call from the teacher are much more apt to participate in finding a workable answer to the problem. The key lies not in blaming parents but in searching for solutions while keeping reviews of the problem(s) to a minimum.

Each component of the worksheet comes with its own set of "Dos and Don'ts," as shown in Box 9.5. This problem-solving form provides a useful structure for conducting parent–teacher meetings. Its use helps parents and teachers maintain a focus on seeking solutions and keeps the process positive.

Managing Home–School Interventions

A problem-solving meeting or phone call often culminates in some type of home–school intervention. Many parents want to be actively involved in a partnership and to provide more structure at home; however, they may need a teacher's guidance to do so. The home is a potential resource for developing positive child behavioral outcomes. Social skills training to improve students' social competence and school adjustment is an excellent area in which to conduct joint school–home interventions. Students can be taught specific social skills at school (e.g., eye contact, turn taking, cooperativeness, sharing, and negotiation), and parents can prompt and reinforce the appropriate display of these skills in the home and community. (See the case study of the First Steps program in Chapter 10.) Home rewards can also be delivered if students' school and home performance meet preestablished standards or criteria. This can be an extremely effective way to conduct systematic social skills training, but it requires (1) careful monitoring and supervision, (2) frequent communication between teachers

STEP 1: STATE THE PROBLEM

_____

_____

STEP 2: BRAINSTORM SOLUTIONS

1. _____   5. _____

2. _____   6. _____

3. _____   7. _____

4. _____   8. _____

STEP 3: EVALUATE SOLUTIONS

a. Can we agree to cross any solutions off the list?
b. What are the advantages and disadvantages of each solution?

Solution: _____

Advantages   **Disadvantages**

_____   _____

_____   _____

Solution: _____

Advantages   **Disadvantages**

_____   _____

_____   _____

FORM 9.2 ◆

Problem-Solving Worksheet.

Solution: _____

Advantages   **Disadvantages**

_____   _____

_____   _____

_____   _____

STEP 4: PICK A SOLUTION

_____

_____

STEP 5: WRITE AN AGREEMENT

(Include who will do what by when.)

_____

_____

_____

_____

FORM 9.2 ◆

Problem-Solving Worksheet *(continued)*.

and parents, and (3) joint planning and implementation. Procedures and guidelines for conducting social skills training are presented in Chapters 6 and 7.

Home–School Cards.   An excellent way for parents to stay informed about their child's school performance is the home–school card. The student is responsible for carrying the card between school and home on a daily basis. Form 9.3 is one example of a home–school card, but teachers and parents should work together to create a card that works for individual students.

At first, parents should be encouraged to reinforce (praise) their child simply for bringing the card home. Eventually, they may want to reinforce, with praise or privileges, improved school performance. Teachers can also provide

Box 9.5   Dos and Don'ts of Problem Solving

Step 1: State the Problem

DO

◆ Stay calm.
◆ State the problem using clear and specific words.
◆ Start by taking some resonsibility.

DON'T

◆ Blame the parent.
◆ Go on and on.
◆ Use jargon.

Step 2: Brainstorm Solutions

DO

◆ Stay calm.
◆ Be specific.
◆ Generate many possible solutions.

DON'T

◆ Evaluate too soon.
◆ Be defensive.
◆ Lecture.
◆ Bring up the past.
◆ Stop thinking of new solutions just because one sounds good.

Step 3: Evaluate Solutions

DO

◆ Stay calm.
◆ Talk about the future.
◆ Allow each person an equal say.
◆ Start small.

DON'T

◆ Ask parents to do things they cannot.
◆ Skip advantages or disadvantages.

Step 4: Pick a Solution

DO

◆ Stay calm.
◆ Combine solutions.

DON'T

◆ Leave without a solution to try.
◆ Give up.

Step 5: Write an Agreemennt

DO

◆ Stay calm.
◆ Make a time to follow up.
◆ Take responsibility for the success of the intervention.
◆ Be ready to try problem solving again.

DON'T

◆ Blame parents for failures.

	Monday	Tuesday	Wednesday	Thursday	Friday
Paid attention					
Turned in assignments					
Worked independently					
Raised hand					
Had materials					

Name: _____ Date: _____

Comments:

Code:
4 = excellent
3 = satisfactory
2 = needs improvement
1 = unacceptable

_____   _____
Teacher's Name   Parent's Initials

FORM 9.3

Home–School Card.

support, praise, or privileges for antisocial students who return the card to school and who improve their school performance. In each case, parents initial the card to indicate that it has been reviewed and discussed.

Teachers should use their own judgment when meeting with parents to plan a home–school intervention involving the use of home–school cards. Not all parents are ready or willing to provide tangible rewards to their children for appropriate school performance. When a parent is open to doing so, the teacher should be prepared with a list of ideas for home incentives, as well as estimates of how much each is worth in terms of the student's school performance. Based on the parents' knowledge of their child and the teacher's observations at school, an appropriate list of individualized home rewards should be relatively easy to create. As part of this process, however, it is important to establish the cost of each reward option on the list in terms of points earned at school or the number of good home–school cards brought home. Low-value items should be relatively easy to earn (e.g., 15 extra minutes of TV time), but higher-value items (e.g., having a friend over, going to a movie, or going on a family outing) should require much greater amounts of acceptable performance.

A sample list of home rewards and incentives (reinforcers) is provided in Box 9.6.

Home–School Contracts.   A more formal home–school contractual arrangement may result from a problem-solving meeting with parents, especially when the student is included in developing solutions. A school contract is simply a formal, written agreement among the student, parent or parents, and teacher. The contract can focus on almost any student behavior appropriate to the context of school (e.g., paying attention, doing assignments, getting along with peers, and complying with teacher requests and commands). The contract should also include an agreement about specific student, parent, and teacher behavioral responsibilities necessary to make it work. A simple contract that meets these specifications is shown in Box 9.7.

Contractual arrangements of this type are an excellent way to precisely define behavioral expectations and standards. They represent a public commitment to a solution that has been cooperatively derived by all parties to the agreement; as such, they can serve as strong motivation for students to change their behavior.

Providing Encouragement at Home

Parents sometimes turn to their child's classroom teacher for assistance with behavior problems at home. Teachers are viewed by many parents as child development experts and as highly skilled in the management of child behavior. Although a teacher may feel comfortable dealing with students' classroom behavior, giving advice to parents may be a different matter. Probably the most important message a teacher can give to parents in this situation is that the confidence they show in and the encouragement they give to their child can be a powerful tool for developing positive behavior. Parents and teachers need to encourage children's efforts and achievements, no matter how small. As adults, we tend to overlook children's positive behavior and to focus on the things they do wrong. Children need and want their parents' vote of confidence; it helps build their self-esteem and makes them feel valued.

Too often, parents withhold their encouraging words until their child meets some absolute standard of achievement or accomplishment (e.g., a better grade in math, a tidy room at home, or a week with no arguing). When parents hold out for high achievement in this manner, some children conclude that they can never be good enough, that they can never achieve perfection. For example, the child who has difficulty in math may never learn to multiply if the parent fails to acknowledge his or her efforts to improve. Encouragement implies reasonable expectations, and recognition of small goals or steps is *very* important in this regard.

Teachers can help parents focus their encouragement on a single child behavior at a time by teaching them how to set up behavioral contracts with their children—whether the contract be for getting along with others, following directions, or cleaning up the bedroom. Some parents may resist the idea of contracting with their children. In these cases, it helps to point out how they already use informal contracts on an everyday basis with their children—for example, "Help

Box 9.6   Sample List of Home Reinforcers

Food

Having dried fruit as snack

Eating popcorn in the evening

Choosing dinner one night

Getting to take a special lunch to school

Having a small cookie, gum, cake, pie, etc.

Going out for pizza with the family

Choosing dessert for the evening meal

Baking (brownies) or cooking with parent(s)

Parent Time

Playing one 5-minute game with parent(s)

Having a story read

Taking a walk with parent(s)

Being taken out to a movie

Going out with parent(s) for ice cream

Having special night out with one parent

Going to the park with parent(s)

Baking (brownies) or cooking with parent(s)

Shopping with parent(s)

Using special "grown up" toy that requires parental supervision for
_____ (specified time limit)

Riding a motorcycle with parent or other adult

Resources

Playing Nintendo or other video game

Choosing a special TV program

Taking bottles and cans back to the store and keeping or splitting the refund

Using special "grown up" toy that requires parental supervision for
_____ (specified time limit)

Using Mom's makeup

Using a parent's tools

Privileges

Choosing a special TV program

Having shared bedroom to self for one hour a day

Having first dibs on bathroom in the morning for _____ (specified time)

Box 9.6   *(Continued)*

Privileges *(Continued)*

Playing Nintendo or other video game

Earning telephone time

Getting permission to go to a special event (party, dance, etc.)

Having privacy time

Staying up half an hour later

Choosing from a grab bag of small items all wrapped up

Going swimming

Going out to play

Having a friend over for the evening

Having a friend spend the night

Watching cartoons

Visiting grandparents, uncle, aunt, etc.

Making a craft project (woodwork, weaving, etc.) (work on it for 15 minutes a night with one parent)

Looking at a book in bed before lights-out

Helping cook or bake

Riding a bike

Pushing the grocery cart

Going fishing

Going hiking

Going to a friend's house to play

Using parent's tools

Earning lottery tickets that can be drawn for larger prize

Going on a scavenger hunt

Costs Money

Renting a video

Renting Nintendo or other video game

Choosing from a grab bag of small items all wrapped up

Going out to a movie

Getting a comic book

Going out for ice cream with parent(s)

Earning articles of clothing for self

Shopping with parent(s)

Earning money (allowance)

Going ice skating or roller skating

me with the groceries, and then you can play," or "When you finish your homework, you can watch TV."

Formal contracts or charts are a means of providing children with recognition for their positive behavior. Many parents find these techniques helpful for teaching new skills or familiarizing children with new routines. Other parents use contracts to help children get back on track when they are having a hard time with something they already know how to do, such as doing schoolwork or chores without being asked. Box 9.8 lists guidelines to help parents in the use of contracts and point charts at home. In addition, setting up a formal contract or chart involves at least six steps: (1) selecting a target behavior, (2) making a point-reward chart, (3) writing a reward menu, (4) keeping track of the points earned, (5) adjusting the contract or chart, and (6) discontinuing the program.

Selecting a Target Behavior.   Parents should start by choosing one target behavior for the child to work on. The selected behavior needs to be observable and countable. For example, "Show respect" might actually be "Follow directions within 10 seconds without arguing." The target behavior or task should be described in positive rather than negative terms and should be broken down into easy-to-accomplish steps. For example, cleaning the child's room might include five steps: (1) putting trash in the wastebasket, (2) pulling up the comforter, (3) putting the pillow on the bed, (4) putting dirty clothes in the hamper, and (5) folding or hanging up clean clothes.

Making a Point-Reward Chart.   The parent should write down the target behavior on a chart and ensure that the child understands all the components of the chart. They should also write down the time(s) when they will check to see whether the behavior has been performed. Next to each behavior, they should list the number of points (e.g., checks or stars) the child can earn for that behavior. The number of points for a particular behavior will depend on its difficulty. Forms 9.4 and 9.5 provide examples of easy-to-understand charts and contracts.

Preparing a Reward Menu.   Parents should sit down with their child and discuss the reward menu. Box 9.6 contains many ideas for home rewards that are inexpensive or that require only the parents' time. Some parents will be

Point Chart

_____
(Name)

_____ Tasks

Week of _____

	Mon	Tues	Wed	Thur	Fri	Sat	Sun

I, _____ , will earn a point for each of the tasks noted above. At the end of the day, if I have earned 4 of the 6 points, I will receive a star for the day. If I have earned 5 stars by Sunday, I can choose one of the rewards from the list.

I, _____ , will check each day at 7 P.M. to record _____ 's points on each task. I will give rewards as specified above, offering the weekly reward by Sunday at 10 A.M. if 5 stars have been earned for the week.

Reward list: _____   _____

_____   _____

_____   _____

_____   _____

_____   _____

FORM 9.4 ◆

Sample Point-Reward Chart.

MY CONTRACT

I, _____ , agree to do the following chore: _____

Step 1: _____

Step 2: _____

Step 3: _____

Step 4: _____

Step 5: _____

For each step completed, I can earn _____ .

This chore needs to be completed by _____ (time)

If I can do it without being reminded, I can earn _____ .

_____
Child's signature

I, _____ (parent), agree to check the chore by _____

(time), and will reward each step completed with _____ .
This can be exchanged for items in the grab bag.

_____
Parent's signature

FORM 9.5 ◆

Sample Point-Reward Contract.

uncomfortable rewarding their child's behavior. These parents should be encouraged to give the system a try and to pick only rewards with which they feel comfortable. Consistently recognizing and noting the child's behavior is the most important component of this system. The rewards simply serve to get the child going; eventually, these new behaviors will become part of the child's own repertoire of behaviors. Teachers can point out to resistant parents that many adults also work for extra incentives or rewards (e.g., bonuses, commissions, recognition, or extra privileges).

Keeping Track of the Points Earned.   When a child earns a point, parents should record it on the chart with lots of enthusiasm. And when the child has enough points for a reward, the parents should be sure to make it available. For example, they shouldn't offer 30 minutes of time with a parent who usually has to work late.

Adjusting the Contract or Chart.   Parents should keep the old charts and look at them from time to time to see how much progress their child has made. To improve the program, they can make the behavioral definitions clearer, add new rewards to the menu, or make the reward slightly more difficult to attain.

Discontinuing the Program.   Parents need not keep a point chart or contract indefinitely—only until the child's behavior improves sufficiently or until he or she has learned the new routine. They can let the child know that the chart helped her or him to make improvements and that he or she has added a new skill or behavior to his or her repertoire. Parents should continue to praise improved behavior and newly acquired skills, but they can phase out the chart as the child's behavior warrants. They might consider having a family party, special dinner, or extra treat to celebrate the child's "graduation" from the chart or contract.

Providing Discipline at Home

Parents also look to their child's classroom teacher for assistance with discipline at home. Three noncorporal disciplinary strategies that have proved easy to learn and use by parents are time-out, removal of privileges, and work chores.

Box 9.9　　The Time-Out Procedure

One of the most important things to remember about time-out is to *use it;* do not simply threaten to use it. Once you have decided to use time-out, follow these simple steps:

1. *Label the problem* with a simple statement such as "You didn't stop arguing—that's a time-out."
2. *Wait 10 seconds* for the child to go.
3. *Set a timer* for 5 minutes, or check your watch.
4. *Remove yourself* and do not talk to or check on the child during the time-out period.
5. *Stay neutral* when time-out is up, and avoid discussion of the event causing the time-out.
6. *Carry on* with regular activities with the child when time-out is over.

Time-Out.　Time-out is a commonly used discipline technique that works well at home for children ages 2 through about beginning middle school age. Often, teachers use brief, in-class time-out procedures at school, so teaching the parents of difficult-to-manage children to use this technique at home makes sense. Teachers can go over the following simple instructions with parents *and their child* prior to implementing the time-out procedure at home:

1. Stay calm when asking a child to go to time-out.
2. Start with a 5-minute time-out.
3. Add 1 minute each time a child does not comply with time-out up to a limit of 10 minutes.
4. After 10 minutes, if the child still will not go to time-out, take away a privilege (see the privilege removal section).
5. Do not lecture a child once time-out is over.

It is a good idea to observe and closely monitor the child's behavior following time-out to identify an instance of adaptive behavior that is reinforceable (with praise) as soon after the return from time-out as possible. In this way, the child learns that it's his or her actual behavior that results in positive and negative consequences and that adults will not have "holdover" anger. Because of residual anger, children are sometimes ignored for long periods by parents and teachers following time-out. If this occurs too often, children learn that inappropriate behavior is more likely than appropriate behavior to produce adult attention (even though negative in tone). This is an unfortunate lesson indeed, and one that should be avoided at all costs.

Box 9.9 reviews the time-out procedure, and Box 9.10 provides general guidelines for administering time-out. Teachers can share this material with parents as they deem appropriate; however, they should be sure to discuss it and answer any questions parents have prior to, during, or following its use.

Privilege Removal.   If children fail to comply with time-out, then parents need to be prepared to use privilege removal as a backup consequence to the time-out. The following scenario serves as an example:

> Justin's mother Sarah asks him to clean up his Legos and set the table for dinner. Justin continues sitting and playing, ignoring his mother's direction. Sarah says, "That's not minding, Justin. Take a time-out." Justin continues to ignore her, so Sarah says, "Justin, you now have 6 minutes in time-out." Justin starts to pound the floor and accuses his mother of picking on him. Sarah adds another minute to time-out. This continues until Sarah gets to 10 minutes. Sarah gives Justin one last chance: "Justin, that's 10 minutes; either you pick up your Legos now and set the table or go to time-out." Justin continues to act out, so Sarah says, "OK, Justin, you just lost TV time after dinner."

Box 9.11 lists guidelines for implementing privilege removal should children refuse to go to time-out. Parents can create a list of possible privileges to remove before they begin using time-out. Common privileges to remove include watching TV, playing with a favorite toy or piece of sports equipment (e.g., bike, skateboard, soccer ball), playing with a friend, using the stereo or radio, snack-

---

Box 9.11   Guidelines for Privilege Removal

1. Decide which privileges to use as backups when children refuse to go to time-out.

2. Keep the privileges under your control by making sure that you can monitor the ones you remove. For example, if you take away a bike for an hour, know where the bike is, and lock it up if necessary.

3. Remove the privilege for no more than an hour or two. Lengthy privilege removal only serves to foster resentment.

4. Follow through. When you say that a privilege has been lost, remove it that same day.

5. Remove the privilege as soon as possible. The sooner the discipline issue is over, the easier it will be to restore a harmonious atmosphere.

---

ing, going to a planned activity, using the phone, and going out to play. The critical thing to remember about time-out is staying calm! In addition, parents should be sure to take away or limit something they can actually control. For example, taking away Justin's TV time will not be a good idea if Sarah must go to work that evening and cannot be present to supervise her son.

Work Chores.   The work chore is usually one of the more effective discipline strategies for use with older children. Work chores function in much the same way as time-out; instead of going to time-out, however, children do some kind of "job" around the house. Work chores should be short, requiring 5–10 minutes to complete. Work chores should also involve some household (or outside) chore that the child is not usually required to do. The list of possible work chores must be individualized by child and household. In one family, cleaning the tub might be a job the child never does, so using it as a work chore would be a good idea. In another home, cleaning the tub might be a regular child-assigned chore, so another task would be needed as a work chore. A sample list of chores is provided in Box 9.12 to help parents start thinking about ideas for chores. However, the best way to generate a list is for parents to walk around the house with a pad of paper and jot down the little jobs that take 5–10 minutes to complete. Parents should have the list ready and refer to it if the child misbehaves (e.g., does not follow directions, talks back, or fights with a brother or sister). If the child does not complete work chores, then parents need to remove a privilege (see the previous section).

Parents of difficult children are often deficient in basic parenting practices such as discipline monitoring, positive family management, involvement, problem solving, and conflict resolution. If anything, they tend to overuse punishment. It is always important to encourage parents to use positive strategies when there is a problem, although this does not come naturally for even the most skilled parents. However, many behavior problems can be addressed effectively using such a positive approach. The case in Box 9.13 illustrates this point.

Box 9.12   Examples of Short and Long Work Chores

Short Chores

1. Clean the kitchen or bathroom sink
2. Sweep a floor
3. Clean a bathroom mirror
4. Empty the dishwasher
5. Fold one load of laundry
6. Vacuum the carpet in one room
7. Dust one room
8. Wipe down one wall
9. Sweep the front or back sidewalk
10. Clean a tub or shower
11. Clean out a kitchen cabinet
12. Clean out the refrigerator
13. Scrub a floor
14. Polish some furniture
15. Water plants
16. Clean out the garbage can
17. Pick up litter in the yard
18. Take out the garbage
19. Wipe down the kitchen cabinets
20. Wash the dishes
21. Bring firewood in
22. Wash the car
23. Clean up dog "dirt" in the yard
24. Clean a toilet
25. _____
26. _____
27. _____

Long Chores

1. Wash windows
2. Clean mold off tiles in shower
3. Clean mold off windows
4. Scrub the outside of pots and pans
5. Rake leaves
6. Vacuum house
7. Pull weeds
8. Chop wood and/or stack it
9. Mow the lawn
10. Clean the oven
11. _____
12. _____
13. _____

Box 9.14 is a handout for parents on how to perform key parenting skills correctly and effectively. If possible, all parents should receive a copy of the handout, but it is critical that parents and primary caregivers of antisocial students be exposed to this information. Ideally, the teacher should schedule an appointment to discuss these practices and the handout. If parents are receptive to learning more about effective parenting, the resources listed at the end of this chapter can be recommended to them.

Box 9.13   Case: How Michael Got the Hang of It

Michael is 7. His mother wants him to hang up his coat when he gets home from school each day. She has tried talking, yelling, and even not letting him watch TV at night when he forgets. Now she is ready to try a more positive approach. She first puts in a new hook right at his level. Michael really likes charts with stars, so she decides to give him a star each time he remembers to hang up his coat. The next time Michael comes in, his mom is on the phone. She excuses herself and gets a star out of the box. Michael kind of throws his coat at the hook. His mother says, "I'm glad you tried to hang your coat up. Here is a star for your chart. Let's pick up your coat together this time." Later that evening when Michael comes in, he drops his coat in the hallway. His mother ignores this. The next afternoon he does hang his coat on the new hook, and his mother gives him the star. Several days later, when Michael is remembering well, his mother lets him hang up his coat without the star. She is careful, though, to praise him for hanging up his coat without being told; she says, "Michael, I'm glad you hung up your coat. I don't have to give you a star each time. I think you're really becoming more responsible."

Coping with Noncompliance

As discussed briefly earlier in this chapter, noncompliance with adult requests, commands, and demands is one of the more frustrating child behaviors with which parents and teachers must cope. Further, as we also noted previously, noncompliance frequently serves as a gatekey behavior for the development of far more serious behavioral tendencies. Patterson and his associates (Patterson, 1983, 2002) and Loeber and Farrington (2001) have clearly shown that one path to an antisocial behavior pattern involves progression from trivial, maladaptive forms of behavior to more disruptive and deviant forms. Thus, persistent noncompliance, for example, can lead to tantrums, to oppositional-defiant behavior, to verbal and physical aggression, to stealing and other forms of covert deviance (e.g., shoplifting), and, finally, to delinquency. This is a most destructive and costly progression. In some instances, it is possible to prevent these outcomes by dealing effectively with the noncompliance at the outset so that the more serious forms of maladaptive behavior do not come into play later on.

Antisocial children are particularly vulnerable to having problems complying with adult directives. They are inadvertently taught a pattern of noncompliance through the manner in which their parents frame and deliver such directives to them and the manner in which they respond if the child refuses to comply. Essentially, these children learn that they often do not have to comply because parental follow-through rarely occurs; however, they intermittently comply—just often enough so that the parents' frequency of giving such directives is maintained at high levels. Children who have been taught such a behavior pattern bring it to school and try it out on teachers and other school personnel. Unfortunately, teachers, who are busy instructing large groups of students, have the same problems as parents in correctly framing, delivering, and following through on their directives.

Box 9.14   Tips for Parents on Effective Family Management Techniques

Research on parenting has identified five key parenting practices that are important in the upbringing of well-adjusted children.

1. *Discipline.* Parental discipline needs to be fair, consistent, and predictable. It should *never* be harsh or punitive. There should be a logical relationship between your children's behavior and the consequences that are applied to it.

2. *Monitoring.* Careful monitoring of children's activities, whereabouts, and friendships and peer associations is one of the most important things that you can do to ensure that your children grow up healthy, well adjusted, and safe.

3. *Parental involvement.* This practice involves simply spending time with your children, in either structured or unstructured activities. The parent–child contact is the important thing, and the activity chosen is usually incidental to the time spent together and the positive interactions that occur.

4. *Positive parenting techniques.* Positive parenting means being supportive of and encouraging to your children. It is important to establish a warm, caring relationship that involves mutual respect and affection. In this way, you will be better able to influence your children in the right direction using techniques such as social interest, praise and approval, persuasion, and logical thinking—without resorting to punishment and other negative methods of behavioral control.

5. *Problem solving, conflict resolution, and crisis intervention.* During their upbringing, children experience many minor crises that, nevertheless, loom very large in their lives. When they bring problems to you for assistance, it is extremely important that you respond immediately and completely. Alternatives should be developed for them to consider in solving the problem, and you should encourage them to choose one that is acceptable and that works for them. Children should always have the confidence that such problems will receive a fair hearing and that they will have access to your assistance as needed.

Adherence to these simple, yet critically important, practices in your parenting efforts will have a positive impact on your children and your relationship with them. Further, they will contribute to a much more positive set of family dynamics. The following rules are offered for your consideration in parenting your children. They can be helpful in the prevention of adjustment problems later.

1. Set up a daily debriefing time in which you review your children's day. Questions like "Tell me what you did today?" "What did you do that was fun or interesting?" "Who did you play or talk with?" and "Did anything happen that was a problem or that you didn't like?" are excellent ways to conduct such a debriefing. Why should you debrief? First, it tells your children that you care for them and are concerned about what happens in their lives. It is also an excellent method for screening to detect problems that you might not discover otherwise. Once children start school, it is extremely important to conduct a daily debriefing of this type on an ongoing basis.

Box 9.14   *(Continued)*

2. Monitor your children's activities, behavior, schedules, whereabouts, friendships, and associations carefully. It is important to provide such monitoring in a positive, caring manner, but to do so in a way that is neither smothering nor unnpleasant. Careful monitoring of this type can be a powerful protective factor. As children grow and mature, such monitoring may have to change form and become more subtle and less direct; however, it is extremely important that it occur, especially as they enter adolescence, when the risks of problems are so much greater.

3. Teach your children positive attitudes toward school. School should be perceived as a highly valued activity. A pattern of cooperative, prosocial behavior will do a great deal to foster a good start in school and ensure both academic achievement and social development over the long term.

4. Teach your children, prior to entering school, to listen as you read to them. Your children should see the material you are reading and associate the sounds of the words with the symbols on the page. This activity is an important precondition for developing children who are good readers and who are interested in reading. It is one of the best things you can do to prevent later school failure and to help ensure academic success.

Noncompliance is one example of a maladaptive behavior that is too often inadvertently strengthened and maintained both at home and in school. Whether a child complies with an adult directive has as much to do with the way the command is framed and delivered as with the consequences, or lack thereof, that follow its delivery. The most commonly cited definition of noncompliance is by Schoen (1986): Noncompliance refers to a situation in which an adult makes a request or gives a command that directs another individual's behavior toward some end or goal, and (1) the individual refuses to comply with the request, (2) no response to the command occurs within a specified time (usually 5–10 seconds), or (3) some unrequested behavior occurs instead. If the command or request is given in response to an aversive behavior or act, it is usually in the form of a *terminating* directive designed to stop it. If the command or request is directed toward an appropriate task or goal, it is usually delivered in the form of an *initiating* directive designed to start or continue the behavior. Both parents and teachers frequently fall into the trap of issuing far more terminating than initiating commands. In the process, they focus too much on negative, inappropriate behavior and deliver too many critical statements. This is a cycle that is all too common in the interactions of parents and teachers with antisocial children and youths—one that ultimately reduces the social influence these agents can have in shaping their behavior toward positive ends.

It is also important to distinguish *alpha* from *beta* commands. Alpha commands involve a clear, direct, and specific statement with minimal verbalization and allow a reasonable time for compliance. Examples of alpha commands include

"Roberto, will you close the door, please?" and "Jenny, if you open your book to page 49, you'll find the answer to your question." In contrast, beta commands are vague, overly wordy directives that often contain multiple instructions to do something. Also, as a rule, they do not allow ample time or opportunity for compliance (see Forehand & McMahon, 1981; McMahon & Forehand, in press; Walker & Walker, 1991). Examples of beta commands include "Jamie, you are always talking when you're supposed to be working. How many times have I told you to do your work instead of talking all the time. I'm warning you; you'd better shape up!" and "Michiko, I don't care how many times you ask, I'm not going to let you go on the field trip until you change your ways. You're sassy and arrogant. When I see an attitude adjustment, we'll talk about it." Additionally, beta commands are usually accompanied by more anger and emotional venting than are alpha commands, which further reduces their effectiveness. As with the commonly observed ratio of terminating-to-initiating commands, adults often fall into a trap of giving far more beta than alpha commands. As a result, children may feel as if they are constantly being lectured to and reject the feedback as a matter of course.

Doing all they can to facilitate students' compliance with directives, and assisting parents to do the same, is one of the most important contributions teachers can make to students' social and academic development. Of course, children and youths should also be taught to discriminate the appropriateness of the commands they receive from their peers or strangers. Clearly, nonresponsiveness to inappropriate commands is an important skill to have and requires the exercise of good judgment.

Box 9.15 lists guidelines for giving commands that should be studied carefully and shared with parents as appropriate. Follow-up discussion of this material with parents is highly recommended. The teacher can request the parents' assistance in facilitating their child's compliance with teacher directives. The best way for parents to accomplish this is to implement these guidelines in their interactions with their children at home. This investment will be well worth the effort.

Preventing Abuse

Antisocial children and youths are masters at provoking parents and teachers into fits of anger and sometimes rage. They often find these outcomes rewarding and see adult anger as an indication of their social control over authority figures. Sometimes, the resulting escalated interactions between the adult and these children and youth can approach abusive levels and even become abusive. The information on child abuse prevention in Box 9.16 is designed to assist parents who may find themselves in this situation. Dissemination of such information to parents of antisocial children and youths is optional and depends on the teacher's judgment as to how it would be received.

Recommended Resources on Parenting Practices

Some excellent resources on effective parenting practices have been developed over the past two decades. Many of the best materials have been produced by Gerald Patterson and his associates at the Oregon Social Learning Center in Eugene. The reader can access information about these parenting materials through

---

Box 9.15   **Guidelines for Giving Commands**

1. Avoid beta commands at all costs—give clear, crisp alpha commands whenever possible.
2. Whenever possible, keep the ratio of initiating-to-terminating commands at 4:1 or 5:1.
3. Praise the child promptly following acceptable compliance with a command.
4. Give only one request or command at a time.
5. Be precise in your description and delivery of the command.
6. Use language the child can understand.
7. Ensure that the child understands exactly what is expected.
8. Ensure that the child is capable of doing what is being asked.
9. Do not reissue the command more than once.
10. Never allow yourself to be drawn into arguments or confrontations about the command.

Sources: Forehand and McMahon (1981); Morgan and Jenson (1988); Walker and Walker (1991).

---

the OSLC Web site: www.oslc.org. Sources for accessing additional parenting materials are listed following.

◆ *Blueprints for Violence Prevention.* The Center for the Study and Prevention of Violence at the University of Colorado at Boulder, under the direction of Del Elliott, Ph.D., has established rigorous scientific criteria for identifying violence prevention programs that have proved to work. So far, 11 programs have been identified and validated by the scientific panel that has been appointed to apply these rigorous standards. The most recent Blueprint Program is called *The Incredible Years,* which is a superb parenting program developed by Carolyn Webster-Stratton and her colleagues at the University of Washington. *The Incredible Years Parent, Teacher and Child Training Series* is a comprehensive set of curricula designed to promote social competence and to prevent, reduce, and treat conduct problems in young children (ages 2–8). In all three training programs, experts use videotape scenes to encourage group discussion, problem solving, and the sharing of ideas. There is a core parent training program called BASIC, which is the foundation for the series. The teacher and child components are also highly recommended. In addition, they afford the means to involve parents, teachers, and children in the interventions, which likely maximizes overall treatment outcomes. The teacher component strengthens classroom management skills, and the child component teaches specific violence prevention skills such as empathy, anger management, and conflict resolution. Information about The Incredible Years can be obtained by contacting Sharon Mihalic, Program Director, Center

PARENTS ON THE VERGE OF ABUSE

STOP and:

- ◆ Call a friend
- ◆ Go to your room and take ten deep breaths (and then ten more)
- ◆ Play some music
- ◆ Exercise
- ◆ Take a shower
- ◆ Sit down, close your eyes, and think of a pleasant place

NATIONAL CHILD ABUSE HOTLINE

(A FREE CALL)

1-800-422-4453

for the Study and Prevention of Violence, Institute of Behavioral Science, University of Colorado at Boulder, 910 28th Street, Boulder, CO 80303; phone 303-492-1266; fax 303-449-8479; email SharonMihalic@Colorado.edu; Web site www.colorado.edu/cspv/blueprints.

- ◆ *Northwest Media, Inc.* Northwest Media develops videotapes, manuals, and newsletters emphasizing practical skill-building tools for natural, foster, and adoptive parents and for children of all ages. They are also quite useful for related-services personnel and educators. Available materials address the following topics: creation of safe environments, study skills for success, young children in court, drug use during pregnancy, instruction in new behavior, parents and friends, confidence building, limit setting, problem solving, and preparation for school. Ordering information and a catalogue can be obtained by contacting Northwest Media, 326 West 12th Avenue, Eugene, OR 97401; phone 541-343-6636, toll-free 800-777-6636; fax 541-343-0177; email nwm@northwestmedia.com; Web site www.northwestmedia.com.

- ◆ *Castalia Publishing Company.* Castalia carries some of the best materials for teaching effective parenting skills. Available materials range from scientific research volumes to books, manuals, and videos designed specifically for parents. Castalia can be contacted at P.O. Box 1587, Eugene, OR 97440; phone 541-343-4433; fax 541-683-0871; Web site www.castpub.com.

- ◆ *Sopris West Publishing Company.* Sopris West is the leading publisher of high-quality programs and products for use with at-risk children and youths. The company's mission is to "positively impact the education of children and youth, particularly those at risk for school failure, by providing educators and parents with practical, affordable and theoretically sound products, programs and professional services." This company is somewhat unique among educational publishers in that it delivers high-quality training and technical assistance to parents and professionals regarding best practices associated with not only its own programs and products but also those of other publishers. Sopris has published an excellent resource guide for parents called *TIPS: Pamphlets for Parents*. This publication provides a series of one-pagers on over 99 target problems and skills distributed across the areas of home/family involvement, school performance, social skills/self-esteem, discipline/motivation, personal health/safety, independent living, and bilingualism/multiculturalism. It is a highly recommended parenting resource. The mailing address is Sopris West, 4093 Specialty Place, Longmont, CO 80504; phone 303-651-2829, toll-free 800-547-6747; fax 888-819-7767; email customerservice@sopriswest.com; Web site www.sopriswest.com.

♦ *Guilford Publications*. Guilford Publications produces a range of books and products that are marketed to professionals in psychology and education working with children and youths who have mental health problems and who are at risk for destructive psychological outcomes. They publish research-based books and materials ranging from ADHD and depression to school safety and ecological approaches to intervention. Guilford is the publisher of the second edition of a classic book on noncompliance for parents, *Helping the Noncompliant Child: Family-Based Treatment for Oppositional Behavior*. The first edition of this comprehensive book became a standard for family therapists and clinicians in the treatment of noncompliant, oppositional behavior in children and youths. This edition should be equally influential, covering such topics as child compliance and noncompliance, parent training methods, programs on reducing noncompliance, assessment procedures, adjunct interventions, adaptations for specific at-risk populations, and the treatment research and current directions in the area of noncompliant, oppositional behavior. This parent resource is highly recommended. Information about this book and other Guilford materials can be obtained from Guilford Publications, 72 Spring Street, New York, NY 10012; phone 212-431-9800, toll-free 800-365-7006; fax 212-966-6708; email info@guilford.com; Web site www.guilford.com.

♦ *Research Press Publishers*. Research Press has a long tradition of publishing excellent materials for clinicians, parents, and educators. They offer a broad array of materials for use in training parents in effective practices. Their address is Dept. 23W, P.O. Box 9177, Champaign, IL 61826; phone 217-352-3273, toll-free 800-519-2707; email rp@researchpress.com; Web site www.researchpress.com.

♦ *Channing Bete Company*. This company publishes an array of nationally acclaimed products and tested programs focusing on such areas as smoking prevention and cessation, prevention of child abuse, substance abuse and violence prevention, and school success. One of its showcase programs is *Families That Care—Guiding Good Choices,* which is a research-based drug prevention program that aims to reduce substance abuse among teens by teaching parents effective prevention skills before their children enter adolescence. The key element in the program's success is parent involvement. This program, developed by the highly respected research team of David Hawkins and Richard Catalano of the University of Washington School of Social Work, emphasizes bonding to family, school, and peers as protection against drug use, truancy, and other problem behaviors. The program's content and guidelines are delivered through a workshop training format conducted by an expert. By attending just a few workshop sessions, parents can significantly reduce the odds of drug use and lower its use if it is already a problem. This program is highly recommended. Information about *Families That Care—Guiding Good Choices* can be obtained from Channing Bete, One Community Place, South Deerfield, MA 01373-0200; phone 413-665-7611, toll-free 800-477-4776; email custsvcs@channing-bete.com; Web site www.channingbete.com.

Conclusion

This chapter focused on the importance of communicating effectively with parents regarding their children's school behavior and performance and utilizing parents as a resource for managing antisocial students in school. Though often a challenge, engaging such parents in school–home interventions designed to improve students' school achievement and behavioral adjustment can yield major dividends. Our experience indicates that the resulting outcomes are well worth the investment of time and energy.

Chapter 10 presents a number of case studies that highlight some of the best practices described in this book. Several of these cases illustrate the roles that parents can assume as effective partners with schools in responding to the behavioral challenges presented by antisocial students. The reader is urged to review these case studies carefully.

InfoTrac College Edition Research Terms

Blueprints for Violence Prevention

Child abuse prevention

Discipline techniques

Parent involvement

References

Eddy, J. M., Reid, J. B., & Curry, V. (2002). The etiology of youth antisocial behavior, delinquency and violence and a public health approach to prevention. In M. R. Shinn, H. M. Walker, & G. Stoner (Eds.), *Interventions for academic and behavior problems II: Preventive and remedial approaches* (pp. 27–51). Bethesda, MD: National Association of School Psychologists.

Epstein, M. H., & Sharma, J. M. (1998). *Behavioral and emotional rating scale: A strength-based approach to assessment—Examiner's manual.* Austin, TX: Pro-Ed.

Forehand, R., & McMahon, R. (1981). *Helping the noncompliant child.* New York: Guilford Press.

Katz, M. (1997). *On playing a poor hand well.* New York: Norton.

Kazdin, A. E. (Ed.). (1985). *Treatment of antisocial behavior in children and adolescents.* Homewood, IL: Dorsey Press.

Loeber, R., & Dishion, T. J. (1983). Early predictors of male delinquency: A review. *Psychological Bulletin, 94,* 68–99.

Loeber, R., & Farrington, D. P. (2001). *Serious and violent juvenile offenders: Risk factors and successful interventions.* Thousand Oaks, CA: Sage.

Lombardi, T. P., Odel, K. S., & Novotny, D. E. (1990). Special education and students at risk: Findings from a national study. *Remedial and Special Education, 12,* 56–62.

McMahon, R. J., & Forehand, R. (In press). *Helping the noncompliant child: A clinician's guide to parent training* (2nd ed.). New York: Guilford.

Patterson, G. R. (1982). *Coercive family process (Vol. 3): A social learning approach.* Eugene: Castalia.

Patterson, G. R. (1983). *Longitudinal investigation of antisocial boys and their families.* [Research grant from the National Institute of Mental Health]. Eugene: Oregon Social Learning Center.

Patterson, G. R. (2002). The early development of coercive family process. In J. Reid, G. R. Patterson, & J. Snyder (Eds.), *Antisocial behavior in children and adolescents: A developmental analysis and model for intervention* (pp. 25–44). Washington, DC: American Psychological Association.

Patterson, G. R., Reid, J. B., & Dishion, T. J. (1992). *Antisocial boys.* Eugene: Castalia.

Reid, J. B. (1993). Prevention of conduct disorder before and after school entry: Relating interventions to developmental findings. *Development & Psychopathology, 5,* 311–319.

Reid, J. B., Eddy, J. M., Fetrow, R. A., & Stoolmiller, M. (1999). Description and immediate impacts of a preventive intervention for conduct problems, *American Journal of Community Psychology, 27,* 483–517.

Reid, J. B., Patterson, G. R., & Snyder, J. J. (Eds.). (2002). *Antisocial behavior in children and adolescents: A developmental analysis and the Oregon model for intervention.* Washington, DC: American Psychological Association.

Schoen, S. (1986). Decreasing noncompliance in severely multihandicapped children. *Psychology in the Schools, 23,* 88–94.

Snyder, J., & Stoolmiller, M. (2002). Reinforcement and coercive mechanisms in the development of antisocial behavior: The family. In J. Reid, G. Patterson, & J. Snyder (Eds.), *Antisocial behavior in children and adolescents: A developmental analysis and model for intervention* (pp. 65–100). Washington, DC: American Psychological Association.

Strain, P. S., & Timm, M. A. (2001). Remediation and prevention of aggression: An evaluation of the Regional Intervention Program over a quarter century. *Behavioral Disorders, 26* (4), 297–313.

Wahler, R., & Dumas, J. E. (1986). "A chip off the old block": Some interpersonal characteristics of coercive children across generations. In P. Strain, M. Guralnick, & H. M. Walker (Eds.), *Children's social behavior: Development, assessment and modification* (pp. 49–91). Orlando, FL: Academic Press.

Walker, H. M., Nishioka, V. M., Zeller, R., Severson, H. H., & Feil, E. G. (2000). Causal factors and potential solutions for the persistent under-identification of students having emotional or behavioral disorders in the context of schooling. *Assessment for Effective Intervention, 26*(1), 29–40.

Walker, H., & Shinn, M. (2002). Structuring school-based interventions to achieve integrated primary, secondary, and tertiary prevention goals for safe and effective schools. In M. Shinn, H. Walker, & G. Stoner (Eds.), *Interventions for academic and behavior problems II: Preventive and remedial approaches* (pp. 1–26). Bethesda, MD: National Association of School Psychologists.

Walker, H. M., & Walker, J. E. (1991). *Coping with noncompliance in the classroom: A positive approach for teachers.* Austin, TX: Pro-Ed.

West, D. J., & Farrington, D. P. (1977). *The delinquent way of life.* London: Heinemann.

Case Study Applications of Best Practices with Antisocial Students

Introduction

This chapter presents case studies of effective practices with antisocial students in school. These case studies are based on real events that reflect the diverse experiences of the authors in designing and implementing school-based interventions. Those case studies that contain graphic presentations of data reflect direct observations of students' behavior recorded in classrooms and on playgrounds, analysis of existing school records, or informant ratings of the effects of interventions. Our intent is to illustrate a range of school interventions (both selected and universal) for addressing antisocial behavior patterns and to highlight the key features that account for their effectiveness.

Jamie: Reducing High-Risk Lifestyle Factors

Background

Jamie was a fifth-grade boy at Elmwood Elementary in Creswell, Oregon. Creswell is a small rural town of approximately 7,000 people. Three elementary schools serve the schooling needs of the Creswell population. The town economy is dominated by a lumber mill that has fallen on hard times as a result of the severe restrictions on timber cutting in the Northwest. Each year, the labor force in Creswell shrinks due to mill layoffs, and the unemployment rolls increase accordingly.

Jamie came from a difficult family situation. His father and mother were divorced when he was 3 years old, after years of abuse, conflict, intermittent poverty, and involvement with drugs and alcohol. Jamie's mother struggled to raise three children, Jamie and two younger sisters, on an income that was just above the poverty level. The family had been listed with the Oregon Children's Services Division because of the severe economic and social stresses and pressures the family had been suffering. Because of reports of severe parental neglect, Jamie's mother had had her parenting rights reviewed by the court on several occasions. Jamie had poor monitoring and supervision at home and in his neighborhood, and his behavior pattern reflected it. He was a troubled boy whose school history was a patchwork quilt of erratic attendance, high rates of discipline contacts with the principal, negative comments by his teachers in his cumulative folders, and frequent school suspensions; he had also repeated a grade. He had a negative reputation with most of his current and former teachers because of his sullen attitude, weak academic performance, tendency to engage in confrontations with adults that verged on being "out of control," and failure to respond to either teacher directives or teacher attempts to correct his academic mistakes. Things were not much better with his peers, who tended to avoid him whenever possible and to disengage rapidly when they got involved in social exchanges with him. Although Jamie pretended not to care about his negative reputation and social isolation, it was clear that he was extremely hurt by it. However, he had little idea about how to change the situation.

School officials at Elmwood reported that Jamie had had major behavior problems since the first grade, when he missed nearly a third of the school year because he disliked school so much. The slightest demands on Jamie would often result in defiance that, if responded to, would quickly escalate into violent tantrums. Through this process, Jamie learned that he could acquire a substantial degree of control over his school environment, and he engaged in the process at the slightest provocation. By the third grade, Jamie was largely alienated from his teachers, peers, and school. School officials indicated that, if an alternative school or day-treatment placement were available, Jamie would probably have been assigned to it several years earlier.

Jamie was even a major factor in the reassignment of the Elmwood vice principal, Mr. McDaniels. His behavioral episodes in his regular classroom, on the playground, in the hallways, and in the lunchroom resulted in so many visits to the vice principal's office that a computer program was developed to record his disciplinary infractions. The vice principal was frustrated with his inability to get Jamie to "listen to reason" and change his ways. At the beginning of the fifth grade, Jamie was testing his new teacher through subtle provocations and passive noncompliance. Mr. Rexius lost his patience and sent Jamie to the vice principal's office after a shouting episode that followed one of Jamie's more memorable tantrums. As Jamie walked into the office, Mr. McDaniels asked him, "Well, what've you done this time?" whereupon, Jamie replied with, "None of your business, you . . . !" Mr. McDaniels lost his temper and struck Jamie on the side of the face, breaking his jaw in two places. As a consequence, the vice principal was subjected to school board disciplinary actions and reassigned as a regular fourth grade teacher.

In the past year and a half, Jamie had been associating with several other boys who shared his background and many of his behavioral characteristics, though none approached his levels of defiance and alienation. On several occasions, they were suspected of being behind some incidents of vandalism at the high school, but sufficient evidence to corroborate their involvement was not available. A neighbor recently told Jamie's mother she had heard that Jamie and these boys are experimenting with alcohol and drugs.

Intervention

The principal and staff of Elmwood School were exasperated with Jamie. Everything they had tried seemed either to have no effect or to actually make Jamie's resistance to positive influence by adults greater. Home tutoring, suspensions, counseling, and values clarification had all been tried with Jamie to no avail.

Jamie was referred by his fifth-grade homeroom teacher, Mr. Rexius, for evaluation as emotionally disturbed according to the procedures and criteria of the Individuals with Disabilities Education Act (IDEA). The child study team reviewed the test results prepared by the school district psychologist, Ms. Moraga, and also examined Jamie's school history as part of the IDEA eligibility process. Although many of Jamie's behavioral characteristics suggested that he was socially maladjusted, and so ineligible for certification as emotionally or behaviorally disordered (EBD), there was sufficient evidence for a diagnosis of emotional disturbance because he (1) showed clear signs of depression, (2) was very

Antisocial behavior is often the result of a negative family history and poverty.

impulsive, and (3) had great difficulty controlling his anger and related emotions. Thus, Jamie was eventually certified under IDEA and declared eligible for its protections and services and the additional resources provided under this legal mandate.

It was decided that Jamie's counselor, in consultation with the school psychologist and child study team, should design an individually tailored program for Jamie that would attempt to reduce his risk of (1) school failure and dropout, (2) drug and alcohol involvement, and (3) delinquency. Jamie's counselor, Mr. West, spent the summer in a special institute learning how to work with high-risk youths such as Jamie. During his training, he discovered the following facts about risks faced by students like Jamie:

◆ Antisocial students tend to be at risk for multiple rather than single negative developmental outcomes. Thus, students who show signs of being at risk for conduct disorder are also very likely to be at approximately equal risk for drug, alcohol, and tobacco use; accidents; delinquency; and sexually transmitted diseases.

◆ Students who are antisocial or have deficits in their ability to regulate their own behavior have a greatly elevated risk for later involvement with drugs (Patterson, Reid, & Dishion, 1992; Patterson, Reid, & Snyder, 2002)

◆ Due to their alienation from adults and their ability to resist social influence attempts from adults, it is very difficult to change the behavior of these children.

Mr. West decided to make a long-term investment in Jamie by acting as a mentor, teacher, and resource to help Jamie learn the skills that would reduce his risk status. He made a commitment to work closely with Jamie for the five months remaining in the fifth-grade year and to follow up with the middle school counselor in the next academic year. Mr. West divided his approach into four phases: (1) relationship building and general counseling; (2) self-esteem building; (3) skill building in the areas of relating to others, achieving in academics, and refusing drugs, tobacco, and alcohol; and (4) development of self-control and self-regulation skills. The intervention program began with relationship building and followed in sequence through the remaining phases; however, elements of each previous phase were continued into the next so as to build on and maintain the gains realized in the earlier phases.

Mr. West was realistic enough to know that his efforts were unlikely to guarantee a reversal in Jamie's trajectory toward a life of trouble, failure, and frustration. However, he wanted to reduce Jamie's risk as much as possible in order to give him a chance to access a more positive life course.

Mr. West began by scheduling a regular meeting time each week with Jamie that lasted 60–90 minutes. Sometimes, they met in his office; other times, they performed a variety of activities (e.g., playing basketball or video games, taking walks, or simply talking). The counselor's goal was to establish a positive, trusting relationship with Jamie that would allow him to have some social influence with him. He counseled Jamie during these sessions in an indirect rather than direct way. Initially, he had been reluctant to attend the sessions with Mr. West, but he eventually began to look forward to them and to open up.

Jamie felt rejected, criticized, and devalued because of his negative family and school histories. Given the treatment he had received, his feelings in this regard were realistic. During the sessions in phase 1, it soon became clear that Jamie had an extremely low opinion of himself and had experienced little success in his young life. In self-report assessments administered by Mr. West, he showed clear signs of adolescent depression. Mr. West talked in general terms with Jamie regarding his strengths and his long-term potential. His most difficult task was to get Jamie to see that he had *any* value and that his problems stemmed from the behavioral choices he made. This was a difficult discrimination for Jamie to make, but he eventually seemed to realize and accept it, at least intellectually.

Mr. West had Jamie develop a list of his good points and strengths and then rank order them according to which he felt were his best and most valued attributes. Although this process took a great deal of time and effort and was difficult for Jamie, it proved to be a therapeutic exercise. Mr. West used Jamie's list as a means of pointing out examples of his competence and skills during some of their outings.

Skill building was the most difficult and time-consuming phase of Mr. West's intervention program. He believed that Jamie had to dramatically improve his competence in three crucial areas: (1) social relationships with peers and adults; (2) resistance to peer pressures to use drugs, alcohol, and tobacco and to engage in illegal activities; and (3) academic performance. Mr. West selected a well-known social skills curriculum to use in directly teaching Jamie social skills that would support his peer- and teacher-related social adjustments. He used a combination of role-plays, videotaped simulations, and homework assignments to teach Jamie social skills in the areas of solving problems, managing anger, resolving conflicts, making friends, coping with frustration, meeting teacher expectations, and maintaining a positive outlook.

To help him learn to deal with peer pressures, Mr. West decided to enroll Jamie in a schoolwide prevention program dealing with risk-taking behavior, developed by the Oregon Research Institute. This program teaches students (1) essential health facts associated with drug usage and high-risk behavior, (2) awareness of sources of influence that subtly push people to engage in these activities, and (3) knowledge and use of refusal skills for resisting social bids to become so engaged. As part of this program, students are taught a set of refusal skills that involve different ways to say no. Examples of these refusal skills include (1) refusing but giving a reason (e.g., "I'm on the track team, so I can't do it"), (2) changing the topic of the conversation, (3) thinking of another activity and suggesting it, and (4) saying you can't do it but giving the others permission to do so if they wish. In his counseling sessions with Jamie, Mr. West supplemented this instruction with material from Jamie's regular sex education classes.

In addition, Mr. West set up a monitoring and academic support system for Jamie with all his teachers. His daily academic performance was rated by each teacher, and the ratings were turned in to Mr. West. If Jamie achieved a certain average rating for the week, he earned a special reward. Mr. West also monitored Jamie's homework assignments and his completion of them.

Finally, Mr. West taught Jamie some strategies for monitoring his own behavior and making good decisions in difficult situations. A key strategy was called the triple-A routine. That is, whenever Jamie was confronted with a potentially difficult situation, he was taught to run through the following problem-solving procedure in his mind: (1) *Assess* the situation and collect information in order to make a sound behavioral choice; (2) consider alternatives, select one, and then *act* on it; and (3) evaluate how it worked and then *amend* his actions, if necessary, in order to better adapt to the situation. Assess, act, and amend became a reliable strategy that Jamie learned to apply to any situation that he perceived held potential problems for him.

Results

Jamie responded reasonably well to Mr. West's efforts. Most of all, he was flattered by the consistent, positive attention he received from Mr. West, who was the one individual Jamie felt had really tried to understand him. A genuine feeling of respect and affection developed between them.

Jamie lost his sense of helplessness and victimization through the efforts of his counselor. He learned skills that were functional and that he could apply in difficult situations. He even began to anticipate these difficult situations and to take preventive actions to deal proactively with them. In this sense, he felt empowered to cope with the daily challenges of living as never before.

Jamie still had occasional lapses with his temper and the surly attitude that resulted from his long-standing sense of alienation from and rejection by most of the people in his life. Though greatly improved in this respect, Jamie's lapses were just enough to provide justification for his teachers and peers to maintain their negative biases toward him. Jamie's most difficult problem seemed to be coping with the consistently negative expectations of him that his long pattern of aversive behavior had established. Mr. West spent a great deal of their counseling sessions on this issue and tried to get Jamie to see that eventually people would change their images of him if he continued along the positive, adaptive path he was following. Jamie wasn't so sure, but he did not argue the point.

Jamie had superior academic potential and responded well to the academic monitoring and support arranged by Mr. West. He began completing all his homework and generally received excellent marks on his schoolwork. His teachers were delighted with these signs but remained wary of his volatile behavioral repertoire. Jamie was pleased with their positive reactions to his academic success, but he tried hard not to show it.

Over the summer, Mr. West continued to call Jamie weekly unless he was out of town; they also got together occasionally. Jamie had some real worries about moving to middle school in the upcoming school year and encountering new teachers and new peers. However, Mr. West pointed out that this was a great opportunity to start fresh and to build a new, more positive reputation with peers and teachers. Jamie promised that he would try his hardest. He also wanted to stay in contact with Mr. West, who agreed to do so. And Mr. West promised that he would alert his new counselor to the arrangement they had had over the past year.

Discussion

Jamie fit the profile of the typical upper-elementary student on a path leading to antisocial behavior, conduct disorder, delinquency, and adult criminality. Mr. West made a good start at diverting Jamie from this path and invested an exceptional amount of effort in doing so; however, it is unlikely that Mr. West's efforts will be sufficient to turn Jamie around and to ensure his positive adjustment and school success. For this to occur, systematic efforts would have to be made to involve Jamie's mother and his peers directly in a comprehensive intervention program that spans multiple school years.

Jamie would have had a far greater chance of overcoming this unfortunate behavior pattern if Mr. West had implemented his program when Jamie was just beginning his school career (in kindergarten or grade 1). Jamie's unfortunate experiences with his teachers and peers actually strengthened the antisocial behavior pattern he brought to the school setting. Over the next five years, he learned that his coercive tactics and oppositional behavior allowed him to control, through aversive means, his social environment at school—and it became his primary means of coping. Jamie had little idea of the enormous social costs that this interactive style would hold for him in his future life.

Bobby and Greg: Increasing Positive Peer Interactions

Background

Bobby and Greg were referred to an ongoing project, directed by the senior author, on remediating aggressive behavior problems of students in grades K–3. These boys were enrolled in different second-grade classrooms at Twin Oaks Elementary School. This Eugene, Oregon, elementary school served a rural population. As a small school, it had a relatively low incidence of disciplinary problems, school safety was not an issue, and there were few recurring, serious behavior problems among its students.

Bobby and Greg stood out among their peers because of their tendency to bully and tease other children. Both boys were larger than most students of the same age. They were often abusive and negative in their interactions with classmates in the classroom, on the playground, in hallways, and in the lunchroom. Although they were enrolled in different classrooms with separate teachers and different peer groups, Bobby and Greg were best friends. They spent almost all their available time together at recess and tended to associate with a small number of at-risk children who seemed to share their aversive behavioral characteristics. Because of their negative and coercive behavioral tendencies, Bobby and Greg were often excluded from peer-controlled activities and rarely participated in structured games and activities at recess. Both boys were socially rejected by the vast majority of their peers, who tended to avoid them whenever possible.

Bobby's and Greg's teachers were thoroughly familiar with the behavior problems presented by these two boys and were distressed by their consistently aggressive behavior. Like most teachers, they were extremely intolerant of aggressive behavior, even when it was not directed at them. Teacher ratings of Bobby's and Greg's social behavior indicated a consistent pattern of engaging in provocative social behavior and using coercive tactics designed to force the submission of others. Their levels of aggressive, negative, and hostile behavior were rated by teachers as well above normal.

Because Bobby and Greg had spent all of their school careers at Twin Oaks, the entire school staff and most of the student body were well aware of their behavior patterns. Unfortunately, both boys had already developed well-established reputations as bullies and troublemakers by the second grade; they were well on their way toward school failure, even at this early point in their schooling experience.

The home backgrounds of Bobby and Greg showed some similarities. Bobby came from a chaotic family environment that placed him at serious risk. Greg's family situation was much less serious but still involved severe problems in supervision and monitoring. Bobby's parents were under tremendous stress from a host of problems including drug and alcohol abuse and long-term poverty, and Bobby's father had spent considerable time in jail. Bobby had two younger siblings who also showed the damaging effects of these family conditions. Bobby came to school with a strong pattern of oppositional and coercive behavior, but Greg's problems were of a more covert nature (e.g., taking things without permission while others weren't looking, lying, and escaping responsibilities for his actions through avoidance and denial).

A series of observations was recorded for Bobby and Greg in their homeroom and on the playground. These observations revealed that the two boys would qualify for and probably benefit from a systematic, structured program to teach them a prosocial, adaptive pattern of peer-related behavior. Preintervention observations conducted over a two- to three-week period indicated that, on average, 72% of Bobby's social interactions with peers were positive and 28% were negative; the comparable figures for Greg were 91% and 9%. As a rule, primary-grade students are approximately 95% positive in their interactions with peers across school settings (i.e., classroom and playground). Bobby had a more serious problem with negative-aggressive behavior than Greg; however, when he was having a bad day, Greg tended to engage in brief but violent episodes that seemed to come out of nowhere. Thus, both boys needed access to an effective intervention that would teach them a more adaptive approach to peer relations and also increase their overall rates of positive social interaction. A relatively intensive, selected intervention was designed and implemented to focus on their peer-related social behavior in the classroom; it could later be extended to other school settings.

Intervention

Although their patterns of negative-aggressive behavior were somewhat different, Bobby and Greg were exposed to the same intervention. This intervention appeared to be sufficiently versatile to accommodate the aggressive behavior problems of both boys. The intervention was implemented over four consecutive phases that ranged in length from 6 to 14 days and was individually tailored for each boy.

In the first phase, behavior-specific praise and accompanying points were awarded for positive social exchanges with peers; earned points were also simultaneously subtracted for each instance of negative-aggressive behavior directed toward peers. Earned points could be exchanged for individual rewards, delivered at home, and for a group activity reward shared equally with peers at school (e.g., a game of 7-up or Simon says). Thus, Bobby and Greg were earning points for positive social behavior and were also losing them for negative-aggressive behavior.

In phase 2, the intervention procedure was simplified in order to make it easier to manage. A total of 15 points was given noncontingently (i.e., awarded freely) at the beginning of the intervention period (1 point for each minute); the boys did not have to earn points as in the previous phase—they merely had to avoid losing them. Thus, the boys' task was to keep the points by not engaging in negative-aggressive behavior or playground rule infractions during the 15-minute intervention period.

In phase 3, only a praise and bonus-points procedure was in effect in which Bobby and Greg were awarded bonus points for outstanding examples of either positive social behavior or a refusal to respond to provocative situations that normally precipitated hostile or aggressive social behavior. Individual rewards were eliminated during this phase, and only an occasional group reward, shared equally with peers, was made available.

Finally, in phase 4, the point system was faded out, so that daily feedback from the teacher regarding peer-related social behavior was the only intervention in effect.

This intervention was coordinated and delivered by a behavioral consultant (the district behavioral specialist) who visited Twin Oaks on a daily basis. The intervention was in effect for only a brief 15- or 30-minute period daily and spanned approximately a two-month period. It was introduced for Bobby following the 14th day of baseline observations and for Greg following the 23rd day.

As a first step in implementing the intervention, the consultant carefully reviewed with Bobby and Greg the instances of negative-aggressive behavior that were of concern to their teachers and peers. These instances were role-played and debriefed, as were positive examples of social exchanges with peers. The intervention was explained in detail to Bobby and Greg and reviewed until they understood it. After all their questions had been answered, they helped the consultant and teacher present the plan to the entire class. Peers were encouraged to contribute ideas as to how they might help Bobby and Greg become more positive in their daily behavior. The intervention was then implemented in a daily activity period in the homeroom, where peer interactions were allowed to occur within the context of a variety of quasi-free-play activities involving low levels of classroom structure. Permission for Bobby's and Greg's participation in the intervention was obtained from their parents following a meeting in which the program was explained. As per the consultant's request, Greg's parents agreed to grant home rewards (e.g., extra TV time and special privileges) contingent upon his school performance. Bobby's parents were opposed to home rewards of any kind and refused to participate in this part of the program; however, they did not object to Bobby earning individual rewards at school (e.g., playing computer games).

Results

As Figure 10.1 shows, the intervention program had a powerful effect for both Bobby and Greg, dramatically increasing their rates of positive interactions with peers. It essentially eliminated negative-aggressive behavior for the two boys in the first three intervention phases. Bobby showed some slight decrease in his positive social interactions during the fading phase and during postintervention observations. Greg seemed to maintain a consistent pattern of positive social interactions with his peers throughout the study.

The daily observations shown in Figure 10.1 were recorded by professionally trained observers. These observers, who were not informed about any details of the study, achieved and consistently maintained an interobserver agreement standard of better than 80% across all phases of the study. Teacher ratings of Bobby's and Greg's behavior also showed improvements that were consistent with the observational results.

Following termination of the study, the teachers were coached in techniques for maintaining the behavioral gains over the long term. These techniques included (1) the consistent use of praise and approval for instances of positive social behavior involving peers, (2) covert monitoring of Bobby's and Greg's social behavior, (3) regular debriefing sessions on their peer relations, and (4) occasional, surprise group activity rewards for exceptional weeks of positive social interactions. Our experience indicates that the application of such techniques is necessary to maintain behavioral gains over the long term following even the most successful of interventions.

Discussion

The intervention in this case study proved to be highly effective for Bobby and Greg. But it was an expensive intervention and would require minor adaptations

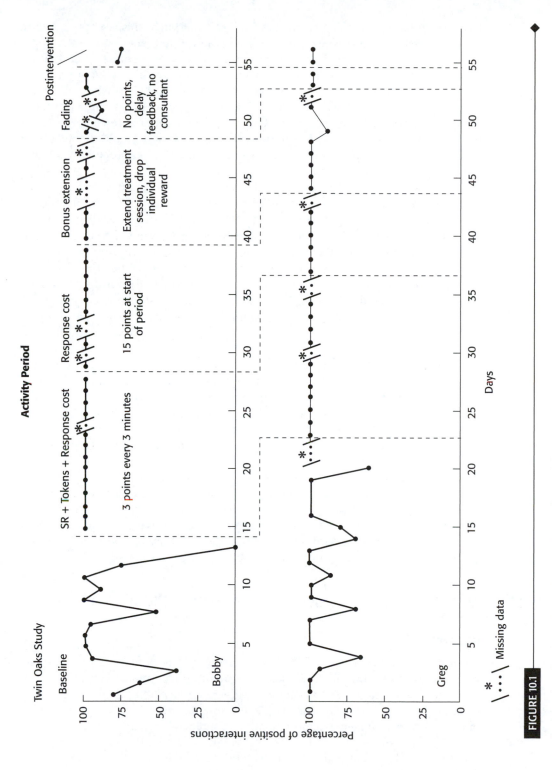

FIGURE 10.1 Increasing Positive Peer Interactions for Bobby and Greg.

to cover all settings throughout the school day. To address this issue, the authors have successfully used a procedure in which the full intervention is first applied in a homeroom period or in the first morning recess. It is then extended to other school settings and periods using a low-cost variation of the intervention procedure in which the teachers or supervisors in these settings simply rate the child's overall performance on a card as either $+$ or $-$ or, sometimes, on a 1–5 rating scale (1 = poor performance, 5 = excellent performance). The card is then returned to the homeroom teacher at the end of the school day, and the results are used to determine home and school rewards. This extension procedure is highly efficient and seems to work well.

According to a series of studies by this author on reducing negative-aggressive behavior among K–3 students, awarding points at the start of a period and then subtracting them as required for each rule infraction or for each instance of maladaptive behavior is as effective as simultaneously awarding and taking away points throughout the period. This is an important finding because the former procedure is far easier for teachers and other school personnel to manage. Chapter 2 contains a discussion of response cost (subtracting points), including recommended guidelines and issues to consider when using this highly effective technique. (See the online appendices that appear on your companion Web site for a series of studies on the application(s) and effectiveness of response cost.)

The key ingredient accounting for the power of this intervention was the combination of simultaneously applying praise and awarding points (exchangeable for home and school rewards) for positive social behavior and subtracting points (response cost) for instances of negative-aggressive behavior. Either one of these procedures, in isolation, would not have produced a treatment effect of this magnitude. However, it is a relatively complex and labor-intensive procedure, so it should be simplified, as in this example, as soon as possible. Reducing negative-aggressive social behavior initially requires an intensive intervention, but its intensity can be faded out relatively quickly if some variation of the procedures remain in effect over the long term (e.g., praise, careful monitoring, debriefing, and occasional school or home rewards). Positive-only procedures are highly effective for maintaining behavioral gains following the initial use of a combination of positive and mild punishment procedures.

Charlotte: Encouraging Positive Behavior at Home and School

Background

Charlotte was a third-grader at Mildred Elementary School who had experienced academic and social difficulties since kindergarten. Her attention span was limited, and, according to her first- and second-grade teachers, she often acted inappropriately during class and on the playground. Charlotte had a high frequency of classroom rule infractions and difficulties handling free play.

When working on an independent writing assignment, Charlotte could stay on-task for only 3–5 minutes. Then she would abruptly get out of her seat, walk to the back of the room, and start eating part of her lunch. When told to go back to her desk, Charlotte usually sneered and said something like, "I don't have to listen to you; I can do what I want." As a rule, further warnings were futile. Ms. Evans, Charlotte's teacher, typically handled the inevitable conflict by sending Charlotte to the principal's office, which only provoked Charlotte even more.

In the second grade, Charlotte had been evaluated for learning disabilities. However, the examining school psychologist decided that her difficulties were primarily social-behavioral in nature, which meant that she did not qualify under IDEA for any handicapping condition. The school psychologist recommended several small-scale, prereferral interventions, such as after-school friendship groups, so that Charlotte might learn to be more cooperative in the classroom and develop a better sense of self-esteem. Ms. Evans thought that she would do better in a resource or self-contained classroom and was disappointed when Charlotte was declared ineligible for special education. Although she stayed in her second-grade classroom for the remainder of that year, neither Charlotte's teacher nor the school psychologist noticed much improvement.

The teachers at Mildred and the school psychologist knew little about Charlotte's home life. Her mother did not attend the child study team meeting when the school psychologist presented his test results. Nonetheless, all of Charlotte's teachers had expressed concerns at one time or another about her home life. Her daily appearance indicated little in the way of consistent care or a daily routine. Her hair was usually uncombed, and most days she was tired when she arrived at school. She had great difficulty focusing and sustaining her attention, possibly because she suffered from poor nutrition. Her teachers believed that there was little discipline or effective supervision and monitoring in Charlotte's home. Ms. Evans did not try to call Charlotte's mother, mostly because past efforts by teachers and administrators had been unsuccessful. Ms. Evans did send home weekly schoolwide bulletins for parents and monthly classroom newsletters, but she doubted that Charlotte's mother reviewed the information.

Citing Charlotte's lack of progress and poor response to the classroom interventions proposed by the school psychologist, Ms. Evans expressed concern that Charlotte was falling so far behind academically that she was in danger of having to repeat third grade. Further, Charlotte's negative attitude and difficult behavior were taking up too much of Ms. Evans' time, hindering her ability to teach the other students in the class. And Charlotte had been sent to the principal's office at least once a week since October. Ms. Evans recommended to Mr. Otis, Mildred's new school counselor, either that Charlotte be assigned to a resource room or that arrangements be made to give her supplementary academic instruction.

Intervention

Although Mr. Otis could see that Charlotte was falling further and further behind, he thought they should try again to establish better home–school communication before referring Charlotte to the school psychologist. Mr. Otis offered to take charge of the communication process and development of subsequent intervention plans. He had some specific ideas in mind, and Ms. Evans was more than glad to have him take charge.

Meeting and interacting with a parent in the home environment is often the catalyst for improving home–school communication.

Mr. Otis' initial conversation with Charlotte's mother was tense but civil. The mother saw Charlotte's difficulties as a school problem and insisted that she had no behavior problems with Charlotte at home. Mr. Otis was genuinely interested in hearing more about how things worked in Charlotte's home and asked if he might visit with the mother in her home for about 30 minutes.

The home visit enabled Mr. Otis not only to see Charlotte's home environment firsthand but to be more persuasive as well. This face-to-face contact gave him a chance to talk with Charlotte's mother in her home, where she was more relaxed and comfortable. In this atmosphere, Mr. Otis had a chance to explain Charlotte's academic and behavior problems in greater detail. Charlotte's mother was more forthcoming, and he was finally able to persuade her to monitor Charlotte's daily school efforts through a weekly home–school report.

The plan was simple: The school would send home a weekly summary of Charlotte's school behavior that described how she performed across the following four areas for each of the five school days: (1) followed directions, (2) completed her homework, (3) kept her hands and feet to herself, and (4) raised her hand when there was a problem. Without using any incentives to encourage or increase her performance, Ms. Evans simply tracked Charlotte's behavior in each area and gave her a score of 1 (poor), 2 (fair), or 3 (excellent). Charlotte's mother had to sign the report and see that Charlotte returned it to school.

Results

The first week, Mr. Otis called to remind Charlotte's mother that the school behavior report was coming home. Two weeks later, Mr. Otis asked Ms. Evans to call Charlotte's mother and thank her for signing the school behavior notes. Mr. Otis was hoping to build up a more positive relationship between Ms. Evans and Charlotte's mother. Two weeks after that, Ms. Evans invited Charlotte's mother in for a meeting with her and Mr. Otis. The purpose of the meeting was to discuss the home–school behavior-note system and ways it might be improved.

Mr. Otis began the meeting by thanking Charlotte's mother for her participation and describing the purpose (or problem) of the discussion: "We greatly appreciate your support with Charlotte's school behavior notes. Charlotte is doing a fine job taking the notes between home and school. We wanted to meet today to talk about ways to improve the system." Fifteen minutes of brainstorming led to some creative solutions. Charlotte's mother, it turned out, wanted to see notes from school more often and wondered if she could provide a small reward if the notes were positive. Mr. Otis, Ms. Evans, and Charlotte's mother brainstormed some small home rewards that might be appropriate for good behavior. Ms. Evans agreed to send the notes home daily; she also asked if she could call home in about a week to see how the new system was working.

Another meeting was scheduled for the next month to follow up and make necessary changes in the home–school note system. Once Charlotte's mother was using the system consistently Mr. Otis planned to talk with her again about discipline issues and strategies at home. The goal was not to change her parenting style or her value system but to make essential information on parenting practices available to her.

Discussion

Charlotte's pattern of problem behavior could be classified as mildly antisocial at best; her problems were not severe enough to warrant a diagnosis of disordered or antisocial conduct. Her main problem seemed to be (1) noncompliant and occasionally oppositional behavior directed toward her teacher, (2) difficulty in focusing and sustaining her attention, (3) poor social skills, and (4) lack of motivation for academics and homework. Although not considered of an antisocial nature per se, these behaviors are problematic for teachers who must manage a class of 20 or 30 or even 40 youngsters.

The intervention proposed by Mr. Otis was on the lower end of the intensity scale and was only slightly intrusive in terms of classroom management. It was a largely private arrangement among Charlotte, her mother, her teacher, and Mr. Otis. As interventions go, it was not especially powerful; however, it was just the ticket in Charlotte's case, as she responded very favorably. The intervention involved all parties in a positive school–home monitoring procedure in which a great deal of positive attention was focused on Charlotte's school behavior and academic performance. It was also accomplished with only a minimal reliance on privileges and rewards; Charlotte responded well to adult praise, approval, and attention—which does not often occur with antisocial students. The cross-setting monitoring and accountability component of this intervention and the positive attention from adults were probably the factors that were most responsible for the positive outcomes. It is *extremely* important to continue this sort of monitoring and supervision, albeit at a reduced level, over the long term in order to solidify and preserve the gains.

Second Step: Implementing Classwide Social Skills

Background

Cliff Heights Elementary School is located in a working-class neighborhood in Chicago, Illinois, and serves approximately 800 students from low- and middle-income families. Violent behavior, including random acts of assault and vandalism and occasional drive-by shootings, characterized the daily life of this neighborhood. These volatile social conditions were spilling over into Cliff Heights and affecting what went on there.

Cliff Heights teachers and staff were frustrated with the number of students in their classrooms who had low academic skills and poor school adjustment records. The teachers also complained about having to spend most of their time dealing with behavioral issues. There were playground fights almost every day, despite the new requirement that two classroom teachers supervise recess, in addition to the three regular playground supervisors. There were also increasing concerns about children bringing weapons to school. The problem was so bad that children as young as 6 and 7 were being suspended for engaging in unacceptable playground behavior.

At the same time, a small, vocal group of parents was asking Cliff Heights to do something about the situation. They were very concerned about drugs, gangs, and the disrespectful behavior toward adults and property that they saw in the school. Cliff Heights was lucky to have Ms. Gilfrey, a full-time counselor, who ran anger management, social skills, and self-esteem student groups. They seemed to be effective and were popular with teachers, parents, and students; however, only a small number of students in the school were being reached by each group. Clearly, another strategy was needed if the problems at Cliff Heights were to be adequately addressed.

Intervention

Ms. Gilfrey, together with the principal, Ms. Abbott, decided to devote an entire staff meeting to a problem-solving session focused on what the school could do to decrease and prevent the high levels of negative, undesirable, and sometimes dangerous student behavior it was experiencing. Teachers expressed concern that the pattern of letting kids out of class to attend groups was becoming more and more difficult to accommodate. These were the very students who most needed academic instruction and support.

Ms. Gilfrey described a new violence prevention curriculum, called Second Step, designed for entire classes rather than for small groups of students. Second Step focuses on four core skill areas designed to prevent violent behavior: empathy, impulse control, conflict resolution, and anger management. The Cliff Heights teachers were interested in the program but were hesitant to take on anything more. They already felt extremely stressed by the demands and pressures of increasing class sizes, the complex needs of their students, reduced resources, and the diversity of backgrounds and behavioral characteristics of their students.

Ms. Gilfrey recommended that Second Step be used on a schoolwide basis and at every grade level. In this way, students would be more likely to learn the skills and concepts, and classroom expectations would carry over across grade levels.

Ms. Gilfrey was determined to make a violence prevention program work at Cliff Heights. She recognized how much more effective a classwide approach of this type could be as compared with the use of small pullout groups with five or six students each. Too often, she had helped at-risk students make positive behavioral changes, only to watch them confront negative peer group reactions and attitudes. Another recurring problem had been that, even when students were able to improve socially, the improvement tended to be restricted largely to her office (i.e., the training setting) and was reflected only in students' talk, and not in actual behavior. Further, generalization of these behavioral effects to other school settings tended to be difficult and ephemeral.

Following the staff meeting, however, Ms. Gilfrey decided that schoolwide implementation would have to be put on hold. Instead, after conferring with Ms. Abbott, she decided to approach only the third-grade teachers to conduct a trial test of the program.

Third grade marks a major change in how children are socialized. They depend much less on their parents for guidance and tend to look more to their peers for feedback and acceptance. As a corollary, they are increasingly influenced by what peers think, value, and do. Ms. Gilfrey believed, as did the developers of Second Step, that all children of this age could benefit from practice and training in mastering the Second Step core skills given the sometimes difficult changes and choices they face. Empathy, in particular, seems to be a skill or attribute in which many students are seriously lacking. Such skills can assist all children in building up their coping ability as they begin this new stage of socialization. Curricula like Second Step have the potential to help students feel better about themselves and get along with others, including their families.

Ms. Gilfrey met with the third-grade teachers and introduced Second Step. She agreed to take primary responsibility for preparing and teaching the lessons if the classroom teachers would make 30 minutes of class time available twice a week for a two-month period. The teachers were also asked to participate in all role-play activities included in the lessons. After two lessons, one third-grade teacher, Mr. Michaelson, decided that he would teach the curriculum himself. There were modifications he wanted to make, and he also wanted to teach the lessons at different times during the day. Ms. Gilfrey agreed and made herself available for support and assistance.

Results

After one month of leading students through the curriculum and demonstrating how to teach it, Ms. Gilfrey asked the other teachers to teach the lessons themselves. She offered to stay in the classroom and help when necessary as the teachers assumed teaching responsibility for Second Step. Apparently, the third-grade teachers had spoken with Mr. Michaelson, who was quite pleased with the program, and he had encouraged them to take charge of teaching it. It quickly became clear that Ms. Gilfrey's presence was not needed to teach and manage Second Step successfully. These teachers, all highly skilled, were able to integrate Second Step materials and instruction into their ongoing teaching activities. In addition, they were able to review, practice, and reinforce the skills taught as students displayed them throughout the school day.

During this time, Ms. Gilfrey provided a training session for all playground supervisors, as well as the school principal. Her goal was for everyone (herself included) to be in a position to help the third-grade students use and practice the key social skills they were learning—especially when conflict arose.

Mr. Michaelson, the three third-grade teachers, and the playground supervisors all reported that they saw some improvements in peer relations and the classroom adjustment of many of the students who were participating in Second Step. The fact that everyone got involved in Second Step (students, teachers, the principal, and Ms. Gilfrey) was a positive feature of the program. Within two months of Second Step's implementation, Ms. Abbott observed a substantial decline in office referrals and the number of playground incidents reported to the front office.

The plan was that, next year, the third-grade teachers would teach Second Step and even provide some guidance to teachers at two other grade levels. A new teacher assistance team was formed at Cliff Heights to support teachers' efforts to implement the curriculum. This committee is made up of a parent, two third-grade teachers, Ms. Gilfrey, Ms. Abbott, and one playground supervisor. The committee had the goal of effecting schoolwide implementation of Second Step, but for now they plan to take it one class at a time.

Discussion

Key features of the Second Step program include (1) the core skills areas it teaches, (2) the fact that it is a universal intervention to which all students are exposed in the same manner, and (3) its implementation at a schoolwide level. No skills are more important in the prevention of antisocial and violent, aggressive forms of behavior among children and youths than the ones in these domains. However, it is extremely important that each student be recognized and praised by teachers, counselors, playground supervisors, the principal, and school support staff for displaying these skills in natural school settings.

Second Step represents an important advance in the direct teaching of social skills that facilitate positive peer relations and that also contribute to meeting teacher expectations for classroom behavior and academic performance. It is designed for integration into the ongoing curricula of most elementary programs. Whenever possible, curricular content of this type should be taught to *all* students on a schoolwide basis. Universal interventions like Second Step are most important for those students who seem to be on the margins of school failure. That is, they show signs of adjustment problems and accompanying academic failure, but at a level that is still amenable to reversal and recovery. Those students with fully developed antisocial behavior patterns will usually require selected interventions that are more powerful and individualized in order to divert them from a path that too often leads to unfortunate long-term outcomes, including prison.

PeaceBuilders: Addressing the Root Causes of Violence Among Young Children

Background

For perhaps a majority of individuals who ultimately become violent, the path to this destructive behavior pattern begins early in their lives as a result of the attitudes, beliefs, actions, and toxic conditions they are exposed to. These include dysfunctional families; sexual, physical, and emotional abuse; deteriorating and crime-ridden neighborhoods; weak caregiving by parents; the modeling and demonstration of violent behavior in and outside the home; and drug and alcohol abuse by support group members. The root causes of youth violence often lie in the early-life experiences of at-risk individuals and their families. It is of the utmost importance to address these problems as soon as possible in their development so as to buffer, reduce, and eliminate their influence on the growing child.

The ideal solution to society's violence problem would be (1) to effect broad changes in our societal values and attitudes regarding the use of force, intimidation, and aggression for achieving social goals and (2) to motivate and empower families and caregivers to instill empathic attitudes and prosocial, responsible forms of behavior in their children. But we will never be able to realize these goals by focusing only on the family. A true collaborative effort involving parents, children and youths, their peers, schools and teachers, communities, social service agencies, and the larger society is, in our view, necessary to forge such a solution.

Schools are a key player in this mix, representing an ideal setting for creating a culture or climate that eschews violence and promotes caring, empathy, and prosocial behavior. Teaching alternatives to violence, both directly and by example, is one of the most important functions of schools. Schools and educators, however, have come to the table as partners in this effort only recently and, quite rightly, do not see themselves as primarily responsible for this massive social problem. However, they can have a remarkable impact by focusing on the precipitating factors and root causes of subsequent violent and aggressive behavior among young children in their care.

A highly recommended and carefully researched approach to this challenge is embodied in a universal intervention for use with K–5 students called Peace-Builders. PeaceBuilders was developed by the Heartsprings Institute of Tucson, Arizona, and is widely used to create positive school climates and to reduce conflict. This program seeks to create peaceful, caring school environments by teaching all students a common language, a set of positive values, and forms of behavior that move them in the direction of caring, altruism, self-regulation, and positive relations with key social agents in their lives (i.e., parents, teachers, and peers). All school staff and students participate in the program's implementation. The goal is to positively alter the climate and culture of the entire school by (1) changing characteristics of the school that can and do trigger aggressive, hostile behavior, (2) developing positive adult and child models of caring, positive behavior, (3) directly teaching nonviolent attitudes, values, and beliefs, and

(4) providing incentives for children to display these attitudinal and behavioral characteristics in their daily interactions in the school setting. All children and school staff learn five rules, as well as a common language for referring to them, which provides a clear focus for the intervention and its goals. They are as follows: (1) Praise others, (2) avoid putdowns, (3) seek wise people as advisors and friends, (4) notice and correct hurts that they cause, and (5) right wrongs (Flannery et al., 2003).

Teachers and other school staff are thoroughly trained in all phases and procedures of the PeaceBuilders program so that its principles and techniques permeate the school. When the program is fully installed, the school becomes a place in which positive rather than negative, destructive child behavior has a much greater likelihood of earning attention from adults and peers. PeaceBuilder rules and values are displayed throughout the school setting, and students are assisted in completing activities that teach key values, beliefs, and actions contributing to a positive school climate. School personnel constantly recognize, praise, and reward PeaceBuilder behaviors as they see them displayed by children in their daily interactions and activities. Children learn to write "praise notes" to each other as a way of expressing positive regard and friendship and, importantly, to reinforce peers for their positive, prosocial behavior. The impact of PeaceBuilders has been carefully researched and has been shown to increase positive behavioral rates and occurrences, to reduce aggression and negative behavior, and to substantially reduce the number of school nurse visits due to injuries from fighting (Embry & Flannery, 1999; Embry, Flannery, Vazsonyi, Powell, & Atha, 1996).

Intervention

Flannery and his colleagues (2003) have conducted a comprehensive intervention study of the PeaceBuilders program in eight matched schools involving approximately 4,000 students in grades K–5. These students were randomly assigned to either the PeaceBuilders program or to a wait-list control group, which received the intervention one year later. All students were followed up over multiple school years to assess both the short- and longer-term effects of the program. The sample of 4,000 participating students was highly diverse and included representation from Caucasian, African American, Hispanic-Latino/a, Native American, and Asian American subpopulations. Approximately 70% of the students in the study qualified for free or reduced-cost lunch.

The authors thoroughly assessed outcomes for the study. Their measures addressed social competence, aggressive-antisocial behavior, prosocial behavior, and PeaceBuilder behavior (target skills) using child self-reports in grades 3–5. The results of this study were quite powerful and very encouraging.

Results

Flannery et al. (2003) reported their results in the areas of social competence and aggression for the fall and spring of the 1994–95 school year to assess intervention effects as compared to nonintervention, wait-list controls and then, in the fall and spring of the following school year, to assess maintenance effects. Figures 10.2 and 10.3 show results for social competence and aggression

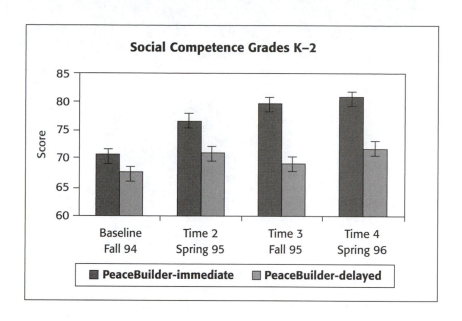

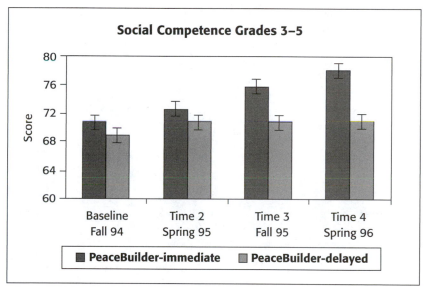

FIGURE 10.2

Results for Social Competence for Intervention (PeaceBuilder-Immediate) Participants and for Wait-List Control (PeaceBuilder-Delayed) Participants. *Source:* Flannery et al. (2003).

for intervention (PeaceBuilder-immediate) participants and for wait-list control (PeaceBuilder-delayed) participants, respectively. The data in these figures are based on teacher ratings of child behavior and reflect the teachers' appraisal of the students' behavioral characteristics and how they did and did not change

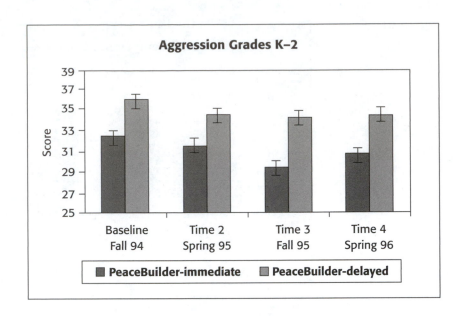

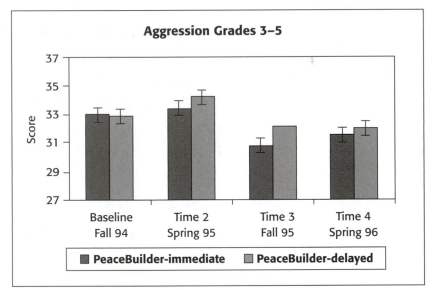

FIGURE 10.3

Results for Aggression for Intervention (PeaceBuilder-Immediate) Participants and for Wait-List Control (PeaceBuilder-Delayed) Participants.

Source: Flannery et al. (2003).

from fall to spring of each school year. They show highly significant results favoring the PeaceBuilder-immediate students over the PeaceBuilder-delayed students and are a tribute to the power and impact of this impressive universal intervention.

Discussion

PeaceBuilders is an exemplar of the kind of universal intervention that elementary schools should consider implementing to teach critical prosocial skills to all children. If programs such as PeaceBuilders were implemented in all feeder elementary schools, the social ecology of middle school settings would be qualitatively different in all the right ways. Young children love to participate in the program and view it as a fun experience. It gets everyone in the school to focus on positives, and it dramatically reduces office discipline referrals and the need for suspensions and expulsions. It is a highly recommended intervention that is easy to implement, takes very little teacher time, and costs less than $10 per student, per year to implement. PeaceBuilders is one of *the* most cost-effective investments that educators can make in the future of young children.

The First Step to Success Program: Early Intervention for the Prevention of Antisocial Behavior Among Kindergartners

Program Components

First Step to Success is a coordinated school and home intervention program designed to prevent the development of antisocial behavior patterns among at-risk children in the K–3 grade range who have an elevated risk for this disorder. First Steps was developed and tested over a four-year period, was supported by a federal grant to the senior author, and involved a collaborative partnership between the University of Oregon Institute on Violence and Destructive Behavior, the Eugene School District 4J, the Oregon Social Learning Center, and the Oregon Research Institute. First Steps addresses secondary prevention goals and outcomes in that it seeks to reduce and reverse the harm that has occurred as a result of the target child's exposure to multiple risk factors in the 0–5 age range and that is evident in his or her school performance and overall behavior.

First Steps consists of three interrelated modules that can be implemented separately or collectively. These modules were designed to be applied in concert with each other in order to provide a comprehensive screening and home–school intervention package coordinated within a single linked process. These modules focus respectively on (1) universal screening and early detection of behaviorally at-risk students in grades K–3, (2) implementation of a school intervention component that teaches an adaptive pattern of behavior for school success and the development of friendships, and (3) parent instruction in how to teach and reward school success skills at home. In combination, the First Steps program components provide a comprehensive and highly effective approach for the prevention of antisocial behavior patterns among young children. The program was designed to detect at-risk children when they begin their formal school careers and to work cooperatively with them and their parents, teachers, and peers intensively over a three-month period to ensure that they get off to the best start possible in their school careers. School success, in turn, serves as a protective factor against numerous destructive outcomes (e.g., teenage pregnancy, heavy drinking, delinquency) over the long term. Details of each of the First Steps components, which are set up and coordinated by a behavioral coach (i.e., an early interventionist, school counselor, psychologist, or behavioral specialist), are described next.

Universal Screening and Early Detection.   The screening component of First Steps is proactive in nature, involves multiple gates or screens, and is designed to give every child an equal chance to access the intervention based on their behavioral characteristics. Classrooms of students in kindergarten and the primary grades are systematically screened to detect behaviorally at-risk children who show signs of emerging antisocial behavior. Four screening options are provided ranging from inexpensive (teacher nominations) to more expensive (a three-stage, multiple-gating procedure involving teacher nomination and rank ordering, teacher ratings on measures of adaptive and maladaptive behavior and critical behavioral events, and direct observations recorded in classroom and playground settings). Information provided by the screening process is also used to determine whether behaviorally at-risk children, who emerge as potential candidates for the First Steps program, have problems that justify the expense and effort involved in the program's implementation.

The total cost of First Steps, including the coach's time and required materials, is approximately $400 per case. The coach invests approximately 40–50 hours of time over the three-month implementation period.

School Intervention.   The CLASS (Contingencies for Learning Academic and Social Skills) Program for Acting-Out Children comprises the school intervention component of First Steps (Hops & Walker, 1988). CLASS requires 30 school days for implementation. It is designed as a behavior-management template that overlays the curricula content and instructional routines of regular educational settings; however, it can be easily adapted to more restrictive placement settings (e.g., resource or self-contained settings, day-treatment centers, and residential programs).

CLASS is divided into two major phases: consultant and teacher. The consultant phase lasts five program days and is characterized by proximal and intense monitoring of the target student's classroom behavior. Red and green signaling cards are used for this purpose during two 20- to 30-minute periods daily; points and praise for following classroom rules and remaining academically engaged are awarded frequently during these periods (every 1–2 minutes). The red side of the card is used to signal inappropriate behavior or a lack of academic engagement. If the red side is showing when it is time to award a point, then the point goes on the red rather than green side and serves as a form of cost contingency (i.e., loss of points). Eighty percent of the available points have to be awarded on the green side of the card (i.e., for appropriate behavior) in order to earn a group activity reward, which immediately follows the period. If the target student meets the reward criterion for both daily sessions, then a special privilege or reward, prearranged with the parents, is delivered at home. The student takes the card home, signed by the teacher, as a record of the day's events and performance at school; the parents, in turn, review and sign the card. It is returned to school the next day.

The teacher phase of the CLASS program lasts from day 6 to day 30 and is divided into reward and maintenance conditions. The reward condition (program days 6–20) involves continued use of home and school rewards and the awarding of points. The maintenance phase (program days 21–30) relies only on teacher and parent praise to maintain the behavioral gains achieved in the previous phase. Brief time-out procedures (either in the classroom or in the school office) are implemented to deal with such things as teacher defiance, fighting, property destruction, and severe tantrums.

On program day 6, the regular teacher assumes primary control of the CLASS program's daily procedures, with the support and assistance of the teacher consultant (usually a school counselor, school psychologist, behavioral specialist, resource teacher, diagnostician, or other school professional). By this time, the monitoring, point awarding, and praising requirements of CLASS have been reduced to levels at which the teacher can manage the program as part of her or his regular teaching duties. The teacher phase begins with intermittent use of the red and green point card for monitoring and awarding points but this is completely faded out by day 15. The magnitude of available rewards at both home and school increases as the program progresses, as does the length of the intervals required to earn them. For example, during days 16–20, the student must work for five full school days in order to meet the reward criterion.

The CLASS program was developed and tested over a five-year period under the auspices of a large grant from the U.S. Office of Special Education Programs. It has been used extensively throughout the United States, Canada, and Australia; in addition, CLASS has been translated into Spanish and successfully replicated in Costa Rica. CLASS is a powerful intervention for changing the behavior of acting-out children in grades K–3 who are oppositional or defiant. It is geared primarily for those students who have problems with rule-governed behavioral demands imposed by teachers and other adults early in their school careers.

Family Support and Parent Training. The third component of First Steps is the parent-training module called Homebase. Homebase is a parent skill-building program based on over 30 years of research and clinical trials at the Oregon Social Learning Center, which conducts research on deviant families (i.e., those that produce antisocial, delinquent offspring). Homebase is a child-focused program for improving adjustment to kindergarten. The program includes six sessions in the home and a midweek call to discuss parent and child performance of the lesson content previously taught. Homebase is implemented over consecutive weeks to maximize parents' mastery of the material and corresponding parenting skills. The Homebase lessons, designed to complement the CLASS program, are organized around such key elements of good school adjustment as following rules, being ready for school, cooperating, accepting limits, and getting along with others.

Each in-home meeting follows a standard format. The skill is presented by the behavioral coach, and a rationale is provided for its importance. Then the parent and consultant complete a current skill-level assessment for the child. Some lessons are enhanced through videotape examples shown during the home visit. Activity cards and other instructional materials for the week's lesson are presented and reviewed with the parents. A daily time is chosen for practice of the skill. Barriers to practicing the exercises are then discussed, and strategies for implementation are developed that are fine-tuned to the parents' preferences and skill levels.

Following the six weeks of skill development, groups of parents may meet monthly to share their successes and discuss strategies for responding to difficulties they encounter during the daily practice sessions geared toward managing the child's behavior problems at home. Groups also discuss their successes and difficulties in collaborating with the school intervention component. This is an extremely important part of First Steps and is appreciated by the parents of kindergarten children in the program.

Box 10.1 contains a brief description of the content of each Homebase lesson, in the order in which the skills are taught.

Background

Jimmy was commonly referred to as a "terror" soon after entering kindergarten; it did not take him long to establish a reputation as one of the most difficult children in the school's morning and afternoon kindergarten classes. He entered school with a well-developed pattern of oppositional and extremely noncompliant behavior. Jimmy had a short attention span and was agitated much of the time—going off at the drop of a hat. Academic tasks and appropriate group behavior (e.g., participating in circle time and listening to the teacher in small groups) were extremely difficult for Jimmy. He could not seem to keep his hands off others and was constantly pestering his classmates.

Jimmy's peer relationships were a disaster. He was informally labeled as "undesirable" by peers because his highly aversive social behavior was so intolerable; they avoided him whenever possible, often going to extraordinary lengths to do so. Jimmy was aggressive, controlling, and bullying in his peer-related social behavior, and his peers responded in kind. Based on peer popularity ratings, he was the most disliked student in the class.

Ratings of Jimmy's aggressive behavior on the Achenbach Child Behavior Checklist showed that he scored in the 99th percentile for boys of his age on the aggression subscale. Observations of his playground and classroom behavior revealed a high rate of rule infractions and negative-aggressive social behavior and low levels of academic engagement. Jimmy easily qualified for the First Steps program, based on his screening–evaluation profile and the program's selection criteria.

Jimmy's parents had divorced when he was 2. They were both from Montana and came from ranching backgrounds. After the divorce, Jimmy's mother moved to Oregon with Jimmy and his older sister. They settled in a trailer home on the outskirts of Eugene, where Jimmy's mother raised wolves as a combined occupation and hobby. The family's income fluctuated between just above and just below the poverty level. Jimmy and his sister were left alone and unsupervised for long periods while their mother attempted to make ends meet.

When the First Steps coach conducted a home visit to explain the program and the parent's role in it, she was confronted by a pack of nine timber wolves who were wandering in and out of the house and yard. Jimmy's mother reassured her that they were harmless. She noted that Jimmy had difficulty under-

Box 10.1   Instructional Content of Homebase Lessons

Homebase is a brief program designed to serve as a bridge between home and school that helps parents guide children's behavior and support and supplement school programs and expectations. Homebase consists of a basic program for parents and a follow-up enhancement program. The basic program is delivered in the home over a six-week period.

The Six Skills Lessons

1. *Talking about school*—*"How's school?"* This involves gathering information, listening, and problem solving.

2. *Building self-confidence*—*"You're great and you can do it."* This reflects what parents can do each day to improve their child's self-confidence in school (encouraging school) by identifying and encouraging the child's strengths and helping him or her try out new activities and skills.

3. *Teaching cooperation*—*"I appreciate your cooperation."* This means teaching school-related skills of following directions, sequencing activities, and joining in activities.

4. *Teaching self-control*—*"Remember the rules."* In combination with cooperation, this involves instruction in being able to control and manage behavior and emotions in the classroom and on the playground according to the rules parents set up for good behavior.

5. *Problem solving*—*"Let's figure it out."* This simply means teaching the child to look at a problem as something to solve rather than as an obstacle. We provide some simple skills that parents can practice at home with their children. We also teach strategies to help children work out problems away from home.

6. *Playing well with other children*—*"If you're nice to them, they'll be nice to you."* This is always an important concern for parents, and one that they may not feel able to help with. We provide activities parents can do with their children to help in friendship initiation and maintenance.

standing why he could not take his favorite wolf, Tundra, to school for show-and-tell. From this point on, in staff meetings, the First Steps coach affectionately referred to Jimmy as the "wolf kid."

Jimmy's mother said that she did not care if he participated in the school intervention part of the program, but after hearing about the parent component of First Steps, she said she wanted no part of Homebase. She thought that her relationship with Jimmy was fine and that she did not need to develop her parenting skills further. The program coach agreed to implement the school intervention part of First Steps but asked Jimmy's mother to provide home privileges and rewards, as the CLASS program requires, and to monitor his school performance. She agreed to do so.

Intervention

The CLASS program was explained to Jimmy, his teacher, and his peers according to guidelines contained in the program. Jimmy's classmates were somewhat skeptical about the program's ability to improve his behavior—as was his kindergarten teacher, Mr. Spira. However, three months into the school year, he was willing to try almost anything to improve Jimmy's daily school behavior.

Jimmy made the reward criterion for the morning session of program day 1 but failed to make the second session's reward criterion. Thus, he earned an activity reward for himself and his classmates after the morning session but missed the afternoon reward opportunity and the home privilege for that day. He came to school in a sullen, agitated state on day 2 and failed to achieve the criterion for both sessions. At the beginning of day 3, the procedures for day 2 were repeated. Jimmy said that he did not think the program's available reward options were attractive enough and was not sure he wanted to continue.

The First Steps coach talked with him and pointed out that the available rewards in the CLASS program were the same for him as for other children who participate in the program. She agreed to review the list of school and home rewards and to add options that were of greater interest to Jimmy, but she refused to increase their magnitude, as Jimmy originally wanted. Jimmy seemed pleased with this proposal and agreed to continue the program. He made the daily reward criterion for all sessions for program days 3–5 after successfully completing day 2. On day 6, Mr. Spira assumed control of the program under the coach's supervision. Jimmy had some difficulty with this transition, failing to make the criterion for that day. However, he did well on days 7–10 when the program was extended to the playground, lunchroom, and gym.

On days 10–15, Jimmy had to repeat, several times, program blocks that are required in this part of the CLASS program in order to meet the reward criterion. However, he negotiated the more difficult, five-day program block (days 15–20) on the first try and did quite well in the process. He earned nearly all the available points for this five-day period and seemed to enjoy the recognition and praise he received from his peers and teachers and his mother. During the maintenance phase of the CLASS program (days 21–30), Jimmy was working for teacher and parent praise only. His performance was somewhat irregular over this 10-day period, but his overall behavioral level was still substantially above his preintervention level.

The CLASS program was terminated following this phase; however, the First Steps coach strongly encouraged Mr. Spira to continue praising Jimmy as much as possible for good academic work, appropriate classroom behavior, and positive social behavior toward peers. He agreed to provide a weekly review and debriefing for Jimmy regarding his social behavior and academic performance. The First Steps coach arranged with Jimmy's mother to make a surprise home privilege available from time to time when the reports of Jimmy's school performance were positive.

The program coach explained to Jimmy's mother that support from community agencies was available through the First Steps program. Jimmy's mother expressed considerable interest in this option and asked for further information on

TABLE 10.1 ◆

Profile of Jimmy's Classroom and Playground Behavior

Code Category	Preclass	During Class	Postclass
Academic engaged time	47%	82%	74%
Negative social behavior	17%	2%	7%
Playground rule infractions	0.27 per minute	0.06 per minute	0.09 per minute

available supports and services and ways to qualify for them. The coach promised to look into the matter and get back to her regarding specifics.

Results

Mr. Spira was asked to rate Jimmy's behavior on the Achenbach Aggression Subscale after the CLASS program had been concluded. His ratings indicated that Jimmy's overall level of aggression was reduced from the 99th to the 70th percentile. An analysis of archival school records for Jimmy showed that the number of discipline contacts with the principal's office averaged nearly 4.0 per week in the month immediately preceding the CLASS program; discipline contacts averaged 0.3 per week in the month following termination of the program. Table 10.1 provides a profile of Jimmy's classroom and playground behavior prior to, during, and following the CLASS program.

Jimmy's levels of maladaptive behavior showed substantial decreases across the various phases of the CLASS program; however, there was some recovery of preintervention baseline levels in the month following termination of CLASS. This is typical for antisocial children who are exposed to programs like CLASS. As a rule, there is substantial residual gain during follow-up if low-cost maintenance procedures are put into effect and remain in place over the long term.

Discussion

Although Jimmy had a reasonably positive response to the CLASS program, it was unlikely that the First Steps intervention alone, as implemented, would permanently turn him around. His risk of school failure and teacher and peer rejection was clearly reduced to some degree in kindergarten by exposure to this program. However, for him to be diverted from a path leading to negative school and nonschool outcomes, it is essential that an intensive coordinated home, school, and peer group intervention be implemented over the long term (i.e., across school years). It is rare for schools to make an investment of this magnitude in students such as Jimmy. However, results of our best efforts are increasingly leading us to the conclusion that such an early and comprehensive investment is necessary to divert children from a path leading to antisocial behavior, conduct disorder, delinquency, school dropout, adult criminality, and related problems.

Billy: Victim of Circumstances and Victimizer of Others

Background

Billy was born into a family that had lived on the margins of poverty for generations. Daily life in his family was chaotic, unpredictable, harsh, and often cruel; psychological and other forms of abuse (sexual and physical) were routine occurrences. Billy was severely beaten as a child for offenses that most children commit at one time or another (e.g., arguing, taking things without permission, refusing to comply promptly with requests, fighting with siblings and peers, and being late). He came to expect harsh punishments as a natural part of his life and developed a high tolerance for physical abuse and pain. His later responses to psychological therapy, however, would reveal that he did not tolerate well the severe psychological abuse that he experienced growing up.

Billy's parents, uncles, older siblings, and cousins had frequent contact with police due to a variety of offenses ranging from minor to extremely serious. Several of Billy's uncles were known drug dealers as well as users; they were frequently involved in disputes with their clients over drug money and the associated exchanges. Billy's family seemed to define itself in terms of criminal behavior and exhibited attitudes of alienation, hostility, exploitation, and manipulation for personal gain without regard for the consequences to others.

When Billy was 9 years old, one of his uncles shot and killed Billy's father in a dispute that escalated into a murderous rage. The uncle concealed the body and attempted to hide the crime from the attention of police. He managed to do so for approximately two weeks before word of the murder got out; he was arrested, charged, and eventually convicted and sent to prison. Billy was acutely aware of all these events as they unfolded; although their impact on him was severe, his overt behavior did not seem to change noticeably as a result of his exposure to them.

From about the age of 3, Billy was regarded by all who knew him outside the family as an extremely disturbed little boy. He exhibited the classic profile associated with the development of antisocial behavior patterns due to harsh punishments, infrequent monitoring and supervision, weak parent involvement, lack of positive parenting, and an inability to rely on family members for assistance in problem solving and crisis resolution. Billy had an aura of great sadness about him, but mixed in were anger and dangerous, passive-aggressive tendencies. In his interactions with strangers and acquaintances, he behaved much like an abused animal—wary, afraid, and equally ready to avoid contact or to strike first in anticipation of punishment from others. Billy suffered the classic symptoms of severe psychological distress, including bed-wetting, nightmares, delusional speech unconnected to actual events, arson, theft, and cruelty to animals.

Billy was referred for a psychological evaluation during the first month of kindergarten. Kindergarten was mandatory in the school district in which he lived, and this was his first experience with schooling. The school was shocked by much of Billy's characteristic behavior—his mix of bizarre, aggressive, and oppositional behavior was unacceptable to his teachers and peers. The school's attempts to further understand and work with Billy's mother regarding his school behavior were futile. Billy was quickly rejected by nearly everyone in his school;

he, in turn, viewed school as a hostile place in which people constantly picked on him for no good reason. He had mastered elaborate verbal schemes for justifying his own actions and blaming others for his problems.

Billy's school records file was nearly 3 inches thick by the time he was in middle school. It was filled with archival accounts and documentation of his unfortunate and destructive path through the school system. In the elementary school years, each teacher who was to receive Billy the following year dreaded having to deal with him. And they rarely underestimated the severity of the challenges that Billy presented. Although bright, Billy's performance always hovered around barely passing in his academic subjects; however, not a single teacher recommended that he repeat a grade.

Billy joined a gang in the fifth grade and had his first felony arrest within a year. He told his school counselor that he could have been arrested 15 times during this period but that he outsmarted the cops. Billy was exposed to virtually every available school-based service during his first five years in school—that is, counseling, values clarification, social skills training, resource room and self-contained placements, and referral to outside psychological and psychiatric services—all to no avail. In the sixth grade, he was the target of a court-ordered interagency hearing to determine the next step for him. A decision was made to send him, at public expense, to the secure-treatment unit of a residential facility for extremely disturbed and criminal children and youths. Assigned to this program for three and a half years, Billy was neither the worst nor the best student in the program.

Billy was considered a reasonable risk by the staff of the residential facility and was returned to his family and home district in his sophomore year. He seemed to adjust well for a while until he reconnected with his former peers—most of whom were now habitual, chronic juvenile offenders. During the summer between his sophomore and junior years, Billy was arrested for shooting at a local church with another student from his school. Eight shots from semiautomatic weapons were fired into the church. Fortunately, the shooting occurred during a week when the church was occupied only by staff, none of whom were injured. Billy and his accomplice were tried and sentenced to four years in prison.

Discussion

Billy was on a path to personal destruction and a chaotic, unfortunate life almost from birth. He had no chance for a normal upbringing, and he reacted to the conditions of his daily life as most children would—he adapted to them as best he could and learned from what he experienced. Unfortunately, the values he was taught and the survival skills he acquired are extremely dysfunctional in the normative mainstream of our culture.

An episode that occurred in one of his sessions with a psychologist illustrates the nature of the social ecology in which Billy was immersed. Billy and the psychologist were discussing his family, and Billy asked if the therapist would like to see a picture of his family. The picture, taken when Billy was about 8 years old, showed his father, older sister, and Billy with their arms around each other. Billy's 15-year-old sister was holding her year-old illegitimate daughter, and Billy and his father were each holding an Uzi.

Billy told the psychologist that he did know his sister, at least, loved him. The psychologist asked how he knew that, and he told the following true story: "One day, my sister and I were running from the cops after we robbed a store. As we came around this corner, the door on my side of the car flew open. She reached over, grabbed me, and kept me from falling out." Nothing about the situation appeared out of the ordinary for Billy.

It is unlikely that anything could have been done to save Billy from the path he followed and from the excruciating experiences of his life. The financial and social costs resulting from Billy's situation will be enormous and are, in many respects, essentially incalculable. Our society seems to be producing children and youths like Billy at a far higher rate than is generally known or believed. Each Billy we produce and fail to divert from the path to prison is a potential time bomb that will wreak enormous damage to our society and collective quality of life. Responding to the problems posed by the Billys of society involves far more than simply working with at-risk families; a coordinated federal, state, and local response is necessary to address the myriad stresses, dysfunctional attitudes, and unfortunate traditions of such child-rearing situations. Failure to do so puts our nation and our way of life at serious risk. Indeed, this is a national emergency that warrants development of a national plan to guide state and local efforts in addressing this critical problem.

Conclusion

With the exception of Billy, the preceding case studies are intended to provide helpful illustrations and details relating to the application of many of the principles described in this book. The procedures described represent best practices with antisocial students, as illustrated in the professional literature and as judged by the authors. As noted, the studies are based on real events and applications in which the authors have been involved. We hope that they are of value to the reader in bridging the often difficult gap between knowledge and effective practice.

Chapter 11 addresses an issue that is assuming paramount importance in our schools and the larger society—that is, school violence and school safety. We are experiencing an epidemic of violence among school-age children and youths, and societal concern about its potential impact is at an all-time high. The seeds that spawn this violence are sown at national, state, and local levels, and each level of government must play a role in its reduction. Until a coordinated national plan is developed to systematically address this problem, schools must take the necessary steps to protect themselves and to work collaboratively with parents and community agencies in realizing this goal and preventing future school violence.

 ## InfoTrac College Edition Research Terms

Achenbach Child Behavior Checklist

PeaceBuilders

Positive peer interactions

References

Embry, D. D., Flannery, D., Vazsonyi, A., Powell, K., & Atha, H. (1996). Peace-Builders: A theoretically driven, school-based model for early violence prevention. *American Journal of Preventive Medicine, 12,* 91–100.

Embry, D., & Flannery, D. (1999). Two sides of the coin: Multilevel prevention and intervention to reduce youth violent behavior. In D. Flannery & C. R. Huff (Eds.), *Youth violence: Prevention, intervention and social policy* (pp. 47–72). Washington, DC: American Psychiatric Press.

Flannery, D., Vazsonyi, A., Liau, A., Guo, S., Powell, K., Atha, H., Vesterdal, W., & Embry D. (2003). Initial behavior outcomes for the PeaceBuilders universal school-based violence prevention program. *Developmental Psychology, 39*(2), 292–308.

Hops, H., & Walker, H. M. (1988). *CLASS: Contingencies for Learning Academic and Social Skills.* Seattle: Educational Achievement Systems.

Patterson, G. R., Reid, J. B., & Dishion, T. J. (1992). *Antisocial boys.* Eugene: Castalia.

Patterson, G., Reid, J., & Snyder, J. (2002). *Antisocial behavior in children and adolescents: A developmental analysis and model for intervention.* Washington, DC: American Psychological Association.

CHAPTER 11

Youth Violence, Gangs, and School Safety: Reducing Risks and Enhancing Protections

Introduction

Violence is a public health and safety issue that has infused all levels of our society. Youth violence, in particular, has been and continues to be the focus of concern from parents, school leaders, legislators, professionals, and policymakers. Violence includes physical and nonphysical harm that causes damage, pain, injury, and fear. The FBI classifies four types of criminal acts as violent: murder, aggravated assault, rape, and robbery. Many sectors of our society define violent acts as involving *both* physical and nonphysical harm that results in damage, pain, injury, and fear (e.g., child abuse, severe bullying, threats, and intimidation). Violence, and the threat of it, is also highly disruptive to the school environment and interferes significantly with the teaching–learning process.

Although there have been numerous attempts to identify genetic and biological markers for violence, the scientific consensus is that violence is best thought of as a condition that is responsive to environmental intervention. Current public policy overwhelmingly emphasizes social rather than biological factors in accounting for violent behavior (see Stone & Kelner, 2000). The National Institute of Mental Health promotes and advocates the search for effective therapies and empirically based prevention initiatives to address this problem, as opposed to behavioral profiling techniques and personality checklists to identify potential violent offenders. The downside of such an approach is huge, and it has no proven efficacy. However, it remains a tempting and popular option for school administrators who are concerned about protecting and securing the school setting.

This chapter addresses the volatile issue of violence, particularly as it affects our school systems and the quality of life of students and school staff. School violence, gangs, and personal safety are strongly linked dimensions of a larger societal problem for which we seem to have no solutions. Schools are no longer the safe havens they once were. In many urban and suburban centers, they are primary sites for the exchange of weapons and drugs, as well as centers of gang activity and recruitment. A number of observers have noted that violence seems endemic to our society and is increasingly a normative form of behavior for many.

As we have noted on several occasions in this book, violent, aggressive, and antisocial forms of behavior represent a national emergency, and we need a national plan of action to address it. The National Centers for Disease Control have concluded that violence is one of our society's chief public health concerns. Billions of dollars are spent annually to pay for the medical and health-related costs of interpersonal violence.

This chapter characterizes violence, profiles its recent trends, describes the conditions that seem to be associated with its occurrence, and presents recommended approaches and strategies for coping with violence both in and outside of schools. The chapter also examines gangs and gang activity—characteristics, types, and activities, as well as recommended strategies for dealing with them. Finally, the chapter describes school safety issues, risk and protective factors, and practices designed to ensure that school safety risks to students and school staff are minimized.

Violence in U.S. Society

Violence is usually thought of as an extreme form of physical aggression, sometimes involving weapons, that is directed toward others. Vandalism is also considered a form of violent behavior, but against property as opposed to people. Increasingly, verbal harassment and intimidation are also defined as violent. Physical and psychological violence is destructive both to individuals' self-esteem and to their emotional well-being; it places severe constraints upon normal, day-to-day activities. This is particularly true of intimidation and harassment directed toward females. Box 11.1 presents some useful assumptions and facts regarding violence, as developed by the School Violence Advisory Panel of the California Commission on Teacher Credentialing (Dear, Scott, & Marshall, 1994).

As we have noted elsewhere, violent acts are much like earthquakes or tornadoes in that they are difficult to predict, seem to come out of nowhere, do incredible damage, and require long periods for recovery. If there were such a thing as a "behavioral Richter scale," these events would likely register at very high levels in terms of their impact and potential for damage. Youth violence, in particular, has been of great concern in our society because it has a different trajectory from adult violence since the mid-1970s. Figure 11.1 shows the number of violent offenders per 100,000 of population for individuals age 14–17, age 18–24, and age 25–34 for the period 1976–96. Youth violence surged at the beginning of the 1990s, reached its peak in 1993, and has been in a slow decline since then.

This increase in violence was largely driven by the crack cocaine epidemic and by a dramatic surge in the number of youths carrying weapons, particularly handguns (Helmuth, 2000). Although these risk conditions have abated somewhat and are correlated with a decline in youth violence since 1993, experts are concerned about the possibility of a resurgence of youth violence due to (1) the number of youths who confidentially report directing severe acts of physical aggression toward others, as well as the number who report being victimized by such acts, and (2) their belief in the utility of violent acts in achieving social goals, redressing grievances, and coping with frustration. Should youths resume carrying weapons on a broad scale, as in the 1980s and early 1990s, experts believe that these practices and beliefs could provide fuel for another surge in youth violence. This may be a public health problem just waiting to happen. It is important to note the findings of epidemiologists in this context, who report that violence in U.S. society has peaked at regular intervals in the past (i.e., in the early 1960s, 1970s, 1980s, and 1990s) (see Helmuth, 2000).

Handguns and easy access to alcohol and drugs provide an explosive and often lethal mixture that accounts for a large proportion of the violent acts that occur between people. Farrar (1994) notes that approximately a thousand guns are purchased daily in California. And it is estimated that there are more firearm dealers in California than teachers.

U.S. Violence Rates Versus Those of Other Developed Countries

The rate of youth homicide in this country is far beyond anything observed in other developed societies. Figure 11.2 profiles the homicide rates of males, age 15–24 per 100,000 population for the United States compared to 22 other developed countries. These results are consistent with many other comparisons of interpersonal violence in showing that U.S. society is extremely violent by international standards. These tragic outcomes are no doubt attributable to the toxic social conditions of our society, but they are also likely a function, in part, of U.S. youths' involvement with alcohol and drugs.

Approximately 14% of incarcerated U.S. juveniles are considered to be violent offenders (DeComo, 1994). Of these violent offenders, 50% report that they were under the influence of alcohol when they committed violent acts. A Los Angeles study of homicides showed that 79% of violent offenders had drugs or alcohol in their systems at the time of arrest. There is a tendency for alcohol to be associated with violent crimes, and illegal drugs with property crimes.

Truancy is also a factor that indirectly exacerbates the occurrence of both violent and nonviolent acts. Over 90% of daytime burglaries are committed by truant youths. If these individuals are also using drugs and alcohol and are carrying weapons, the possibilities for the commission of violent crimes are substantially increased.

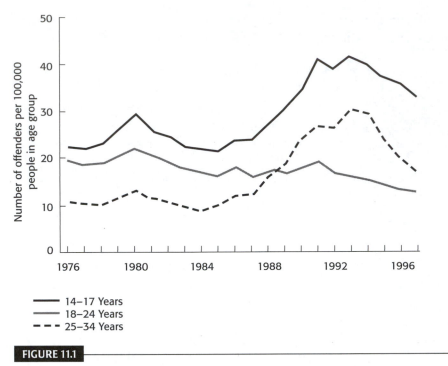

FIGURE 11.1

Trends in Youth Versus Adult Violence.

Source: Science, vol. 289, p. 582 (7/28/2000). ©2000 The American Association for the Advancement of Science. Reprinted with permission.

Increases in Aggravated Assault and Incarceration Rates

Beginning in the mid-1960s, the aggravated assault rate in U.S. society began to increase. This was followed about a decade later by a similar increase in the rate of imprisonment. Figure 11.3 illustrates these trends for the period from 1957 to 1992. The question can be posed as to why this substantial increase in the aggravated assault rate was not reflected more strongly in the homicide rate during this period. Grossman (1995) argues that it is due, in large part, to advances in medical technologies that can keep severely wounded individuals alive when they might previously have died from their wounds. The disrupted lifestyles, social costs, and long-term medical and rehabilitative care that these individuals require is a major ongoing tragedy in our society.

Characteristics, Causal Influences, and Trends

The conditions and outcomes just described provide an overview of the dimensions of violence in our society, particularly as they relate to violent juvenile crime. Violence is an unfortunate behavioral response that some individuals acquire as an option for dealing with certain highly charged interpersonal situations. It is not an inevitable feature of our society that we are unable to address and are obligated to accept as the status quo. But the presence of drugs, alco-

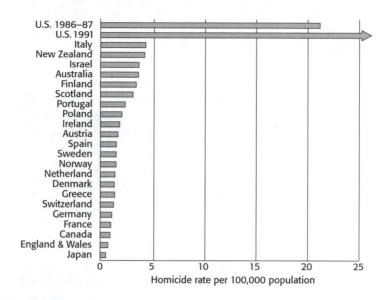

FIGURE 11.2 ◆

International Comparisons of Homicide Rates,
Males 15–24 Years of Age, 1988–91.

Source: National Center for Injury Prevention and Control (1994).

hol, weapons, and triggering events greatly increases the chances that violent acts will be committed by volatile, at-risk youths. Family situations and environmental toxins also play key roles in the development of violence on a case-by-case, individual level. Box 11.2 details the tragic case, reported in the *New York Times*, of a 10-year-old boy who murdered a 3-year-old after kidnapping him from a public library. The roots of this tragedy can be traced to the 10-year-old's unfortunate family situation.

As many experts have noted, we must teach our children and youths to eschew violence in all its forms and to develop alternative strategies for solving problems and resolving disputes and conflicts with others. This instruction needs to occur in all settings and at all ages, but it is especially important that we begin to build it into our core curricula in school and to encourage parents to teach it as part of socializing their children to the norms and values of our society. Excellent tools are now available for accomplishing this goal in family, school, and mental health settings (Committee for Children, 1993; Flannery et al., 2003; Thornton, Craft, Dahlberg, Lynch, & Baer, 2000). These tools need to be made widely available and made a normative part of the values, principles, and skills that we teach to all our children and youths.

Complex causes associated with violence involve social, environmental, and individual conditions and factors. Specific causal influences can include: (1) poverty, (2) prejudice and discrimination, (3) unemployment, (4) despair and hopelessness, (5) access to drugs, alcohol, and weapons, (6) gang membership and

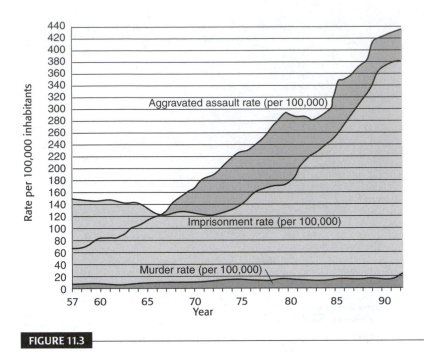

FIGURE 11.3 ◆

The Relationship Between Aggravated Assault, Murder, and Imprisonment Rates in America Since 1957.

activities, (7) association with antisocial peers, (8) modeling of interpersonal violence in the family, (9) the presence of mob violence, (10) cultural values, and (11) media violence (i.e., exposure to repeated violent episodes and images depicted in the mass media) (see American Psychological Association, 1993; Huesman, Moise-Titus, Podolski, & Eron, 2003; Petitt & Dodge, 2003). Satcher (2001) provides an excellent compilation and analysis of the risk factors associated with youth violence at different points in the developmental age span.

Violent acts can also be precipitated by three events or factors: (1) temporal proximity, (2) situational risk factors, and/or (3) activating events. Temporal proximity refers to predisposing factors that precede the violent event. Situational risk factors are circumstances that inform an encounter between persons and that increase the chances that violence will occur. Finally, activating events are those that immediately precede the violent act and trigger its actual occurrence (see Roth, 1994). For example, suppose Jamie is a fifth-grade boy who has a history of severe antisocial behavior problems in school and who has suffered teacher and peer rejection (temporal event). Of late, Jamie has been teased by some of his classmates about his appearance, especially his style of dress (situational risk factor). At recess, several boys are looking at him, pointing, and laughing (activating event). Jamie walks over in a rage and attacks one of the boys.

High levels of agitation and feelings of alienation are strong precursors of violent behavior, particularly among youths. If these factors lead to membership in a deviant peer group or a gang, there is a dramatic escalation of criminal

Box 11.2   The Tragic Story of 3-Year-Old Amir Beeks

The story of Amir appeared in a Sunday edition of the *New York Times* in 2003. He was an innocent 3-year-old boy who lived with his family in Woodbridge Township, New Jersey. Only days before moving to Georgia with his family, Amir was kidnapped from the local library and murdered by a 10-year-old boy. He was clubbed to death with a baseball bat and left in a storm drain at the edge of the older boy's yard. His alleged murderer did not know Amir. He simply happened to bump into him, and the tragic event ensued for no apparent reason. Investigators could not identify a motive for Amir's murder.

The older boy lived alone with his father, who was blind. His mother had succumbed to breast cancer when he was 5 years old, and he was apparently distraught by her death. The boy's father had a difficult time providing monitoring and supervision of his activities and behavior. Neighbors reported that he caused trouble frequently. He would pelt dogs with rocks, tear out shrubs and pound them with his baseball bat, and pull siding off homes, and he bullied and verbally abused his classmates. He was rude to adults and would break things intentionally in the homes of his playmates. Some parents were so concerned about this behavior that they refused to allow their children to play with him.

Due to his incessant misbehavior, several neighbors reported him to the state's Division of Youth and Family Services and to the police. An investigation found no evidence of neglect or abuse, so no action was taken. A series of boarders stayed at the family home who, neighbors said, made frequent visits to the nearby liquor store.

The 10-year-old became increasingly isolated, appeared sad and depressed, and could be seen crying while keeping to himself at school. He carried a great deal of anger and agitation and was a serious disciplinary problem. After hitting another student with his baseball bat and throwing a small desk at his teacher, he was expelled from school. His father confided that he was having problems with him and was considering a military school placement just before the incident with Amir happened.

This story that ended so tragically for Amir and his family appears to be a pattern that is seen increasingly within chaotic family and neighborhood environments in which young children are exposed to crime, victimization, cruelty, injury, and sometimes death. The lack of parental supervision and monitoring in this case, mixed with the loss of a parent and the presence of strong agitation, appear to have been triggering events for this terrible tragedy. In retrospect, it appears that the state Division of Youth and Family Services should have looked beyond the absence of evidence for abuse and neglect and taken the neighbors' concerns and complaints more seriously. This boy needed to be in a different environment with more structure that could have provided adequate monitoring and supervision. The termination of parental rights and supervision along with placement in a foster home may have been indicated had such an investigation been conducted. A thorough investigation with a hearing before a family court judge would have been necessary to produce this change. With 20/20 hindsight, it seems that it may have been the only way to prevent the loss of one young life and the destruction of another.

Suppression strategies, like incarceration, are relied upon heavily to manage youth violence. Prevention and intervention strategies at the community and school levels, however, may be more effective for addressing violent acts committed by antisocial and delinquent youth.

behavior—much of it violent in nature (Jensen & Yerington, 1997; Klein, 1994; Patterson, Reid, & Dishion, 1992; Reid, Patterson, & Snyder, 2002). As noted previously, drug and alcohol use, especially when combined with limited skills for resolving disputes and conflicts, provides a potent mixture that can easily trigger violence.

Violence, particularly youth violence, remains an extremely serious social problem in this country. In 1990, 23,438 Americans were murdered—a rate of 9.4 per 100,000 population. An estimated 2.9 million nonfatal violent acts (rape, robbery, aggravated assault) also occurred in 1990. In 1997, 3,700 individuals age 19 and younger died from violence—an average of 10 per day. Each year, approximately 5,000 children and youths die from wounds caused by guns—many of which are accidental in nature (see Osofsky, 1997).

Nearly all studies of violent criminal behavior show that it has remained fairly stable or actually increased over the past two decades or so (see Figure 11.1), in spite of harsher sanctions meted out during this same period. However, evidence also shows that rates of violent juvenile crime (e.g., aggravated assault and robbery), unlike adult violence, have increased substantially over the past several decades (Satcher, 2001). For example, juvenile arrests for violent crimes increased 41% from 1982 to 1991; during this same period, the number of arrests for murder and aggravated assault increased by 93% and 72%, respectively (Wilson & Howell, 1993).

Societal Changes Associated with Increases in Violent Behavior

Antisocial behavior and the conditions associated with it (e.g., stressed families, weak parenting practices, poverty, social fragmentation, and dysfunctional families) provide a fertile breeding ground for juvenile crime and violence, gang membership, and drug and alcohol use (Loeber & Farrington, 2001). The huge increase in the juvenile crime rate in the past 50 years is primarily the result of the deteriorating social and economic conditions of our society. Since 1987, the crime rate for 14- to 17-year-olds has doubled even as their percentage of the population has declined. By 2005, however, the cohort of 14- to 17-year-olds will increase by approximately 23% (Coie, 1994), a demographic trend that has ominous social consequences.

John Coie, a noted researcher on antisocial behavior and violence, delivered a seminal address on the prevention of violence at a national conference (Coie, 1994). He described some key facts and societal changes, which hold true today, that partially account for the sharp increases we have witnessed in juvenile crime and violence; they are summarized in Box 11.3.

Approaches for Addressing Youth Violence

As a society, we have become heavily invested in the use of suppression strategies (e.g., incarceration) to cope with the increasing tide of violence, especially juvenile violence. Many experts now argue that we need a science of prevention for addressing violent behavior and its many ramifications. The U.S. Society for Prevention Research comprises a broadly accomplished group of social scientists who are experts in the prevention of youth violence and who have made important contributions to solving this problem in recent decades. Coie (1994), an exemplar of these professionals, makes a persuasive case that the complex problem of juvenile violence will not yield to either simple or unidimensional solutions. Most experts in the areas of law enforcement, corrections, juvenile justice, criminology, and psychology agree on the following points:

◆ Incarceration alone does not work, and we cannot build a sufficient number of incarceration facilities to solve the problem.

◆ By the time the legal system actually punishes juvenile offenders, they have too extensive a criminal history to be turned around.

◆ Most of our suppression programs are punitive in nature and often turn out to be training grounds for later offending due to the aggregation of deviant individuals, who socialize with each other to new forms of deviance.

◆ Boot camps do not affect recidivism rates more favorably than other programs for antisocial and delinquent youths.

◆ Day-treatment programs, with educational and rehabilitative components, appear to be far more effective than incarceration but are only rarely available for juvenile offenders.

◆ The best time to intervene with this population is as early as possible in their lives; preschool and kindergarten are especially effective contexts for mounting coordinated home–school intervention programs.

Box 11.3 Key Facts and Changes Associated with Increases in Juvenile Violence

◆ Adolescents are killing their friends. Of juvenile homicides, 55% involve friends and acquaintances; only 30% involve assaults on strangers.

◆ There has been a surge in reactive aggression among children and youths that is qualitatively different from anything we have seen before. This surge is associated with the following developments: (1) Youths today are much more likely to respond with a rage reaction to situations in which they feel violated or victimized; (2) the anger flashpoint has lowered dramatically—youths today take offense much earlier and to things that were previously ignored; and (3) youths feel an obligation to retaliate when they perceive provocations from others.

◆ In recent decades, youths have moved from fists, to knives, to handguns, to automatic weapons in settling their conflicts.

◆ There are two pathways to the development of a violent behavior pattern among children and youths. Both pathways show a rise in violence with a subsequent drop-off after age 17. The more serious path involves the early-starter group (age 6–8), who are more violent and are likely to continue their violent behavior into young adulthood. The other path involves later starters (early adolescence), who are less violent and whose violence does not persist.

◆ Two key risk factors associated with the development of violent behavior are (1) children with high irritability and temperament problems and (2) stressed families with primary caregivers who feel pressured and overwhelmed. This mix often leads to a highly negative and coercive pattern of family interaction resulting in violent episodes.

◆ Parents of such children have a firm belief that, the harsher the punishment they mete out, the more likely the child is to remember it, and the more effective it will be. Such parents were often exposed to harsh punishment themselves and tend to replicate it with their own children.

◆ Antisocial, violent children and youths often go to overcrowded schools where there is a high density of students like themselves. They tend to use aggression to solve problems with their peers and to suffer rejection by peers as a result. These students then bond with others like themselves—a bonding that provides the foundation for deviant peer group affiliation, with associated violence and gang activity.

Box 11.3   *(Continued)*

◆ Schools with high concentrations of antisocial, violent students tend to have poor resources and to employ teachers who are inexperienced and who become overly stressed and burned out. These teachers' frustrations in dealing with such students parallels the students' home experiences involving child irritability and overly stressed parents with weak child management skills. Such teachers become highly frustrated, are often unsuccessful, and react angrily to these difficult students.

◆ These students view teacher and peer rejection as unfair and undeserved, and they react accordingly. If they perceive bad things happening to them, they (1) get angry, (2) think the other person meant it, and (3) retaliate, often with violent behavior. This behavior, in turn, confirms teacher and peer expectations of them.

◆ Children who are antisocial at home and at school are 50% more likely to become violent by age 6 or 7. Parent–teacher conferences to resolve these emerging problems often escalate, degenerate into blame fixing, and further polarize the school–family relationship.

◆ During the elementary school years, parents gradually lose the ability to influence and control such children effectively. Parents start giving up hope by early adolescence and begin to reduce their involvement with the child. This translates into reduced monitoring and supervision of the child's activities, whereabouts, and affiliations. Consequently, the risks for juvenile violence, involvement with drugs and alcohol, criminal behavior, gang membership, and use of weapons can escalate dramatically.

Source: Adapted from Coie (1994).

An effective, overall strategy for coping with the complex problem of juvenile crime and violence will require some changes in the way many of our key agencies and institutions respond. For example, the juvenile justice system has a characteristic practice of warning rather than sanctioning first-time juvenile offenders—especially if they are young. This practice is based on the quite reasonable assumptions that (1) first-time offenders should be given second chances and (2) admonishments from a judge and parents may be effective in this regard. However, this approach may be the exact opposite of what is needed in many cases (Patterson et al., 1992; Reid et al., 2002).

In an ongoing longitudinal study of 80 boys who were at elevated risk for antisocial behavior, Walker and his colleagues found that the two best predictors of these boys' arrest patterns in grades 6–12 were (1) the severity of the first arrest and (2) the boy's age at the time of the first arrest. The more severe the first offense and the younger the boy when it occurred, the greater the number of arrests in grades 6–12. Using first-arrest severity (among other factors) and age of onset as predictors, we obtained a better-than-chance prediction of their subsequent arrest frequency.

This result suggests that the first arrest should be taken very seriously by prosecutors and the juvenile court system—particularly if it is for a severe offense and occurs early. It is likely that such children and youths will require direct attention to their emerging criminality, which could involve appropriate sanctions, parent obligations, careful monitoring and supervision, and probation. Assignment to day-treatment or other rehabilitative programs may be indicated as well. Such a reversal of traditional practices has significant implications for resource allocation decisions, juvenile accommodations, and many current professional practices with this population.

School practices will also have to change as part of any overall effective strategy for addressing this problem. Traditionally, (1) schools have tended to resist assuming ownership of this problem (i.e., responsibility for solving it); (2) students showing such signs are typically exposed to control, containment, punishment, and push-out strategies; and (3) in many cases, they are denied access to therapeutic support services during their school careers, which puts them even further at risk.

With 4 to 6 million of these students currently populating our schools, we can no longer afford the luxury of such problem avoidance and neglect. Specifically, schools should (1) be the focal point of coordinated, comprehensive interventions involving families and other agencies; (2) begin identifying, monitoring, and intervening with at-risk students early in their school careers; (3) assume a proactive, supportive posture with these students and their families rather than a rejecting, punishing one; and (4) stop assuming that such students can solve their problems without assistance from school professionals. Changes along these lines will go a long way toward giving at-risk children and youths a reasonable chance of achieving school success—a critical ingredient in realizing a productive life in today's world.

Two recommended strategies for prevention–intervention efforts operate at the societal-community and the individual-school levels.

The Societal-Community Level.   In a thoughtful discussion of the problem of violence in our society, Kauffman (1994) argues, like other experts, that violence and aggression have no single cause or single solution. He notes further that as a society we must make a commitment to become less violent and to implement, on a broad scale, the actions that we know will achieve this goal. Box 11.4 lists the seven steps Kauffman suggests be taken in this regard; his suggestions make a great deal of sense.

These recommendations have broad policy implications and, if adopted, could have a substantial impact on this societal problem. Their adoption will require both development of a national consensus and a broad-based commitment and overall strategy to ensure they have an impact. Our educational system and media resources will be key instruments in any effort to realize this goal through the process of social marketing. The success of media and educational campaigns to reduce tobacco, alcohol, and drug use are good examples of what can be accomplished.

Steinhart (1994) suggests four basic elements that must be included in a comprehensive strategy to prevent violence: (1) a recognition that violence

Box 11.4   Steps for Reducing Violence in Our Society

1. Provide effective consequences of aggression.
2. Teach nonaggressive responses to problems.
3. Stop aggression early, before it takes root.
4. Restrict access to the instruments of aggression.
5. Restrain and reform public displays of aggression.
6. Correct the conditions of everyday life that foster aggression.
7. Offer more effective instruction and more attractive educational options in public schools.

Source: Kauffman (1994).

---

arises from multiple risk factors, including child abuse, school failure, family criminality, media violence, and drug abuse and its ramifications; (2) the application of different strategies to address multiple risk factors; (3) an early start to intersect the trajectory of children and youths headed toward a violent lifestyle; and (4) the involvement of whole communities. The American Psychological Association's Commission on Violence and Youth offers a number of universal recommendations, summarized in Box 11.5, that are invaluable and should be considered in addressing the individual and social factors that contribute to youth violence (American Psychological Association, 1993).

School systems are having to invest in extremely restrictive educational programs to accommodate at-risk children and youths who are potentially dangerous. The growth in alternative school settings and placements for this population has been substantial in recent years and continues to accelerate. And increasingly, these placement programs are having to be established at the elementary school level as more and more children manifest comparatively mature forms of violent and deviant behavior.

The macrolevel strategies described thus far are essential for addressing violence and its prevention at the societal level. At best, schools are collaborative partners with a host of other agencies in implementing such complex strategies. Obviously, they cannot do it by themselves. However, there are things that schools can do on an individual basis to address their share of the problem and to make themselves safer and more productive environments for academic achievement and social-emotional development.

The Individual-School Level.   Proactive, school-based strategies for preventing violence generally focus on curricula, staff development, and administrative procedures. It is essential that units on violence prevention be incorporated into curricula that address (1) peer mediation, (2) conflict resolution, and (3) the social and emotional skills for managing anger, negotiating with others, adopting another child's perspective, and developing alternative solutions to disagreements

Box 11.5   American Psychological Association's Recommendations for Reducing Violence

1. Teach all families and child-care and health-care providers how to deal with early childhood aggression via early childhood interventions in the form of extensive support services and training.

2. Provide developmentally appropriate school-based interventions in classroom management, problem solving, and violence prevention.

3. Promote sensitivity to cultural diversity through community involvement in the development of violence prevention efforts.

4. Solicit media cooperation to both limit the depiction of violence during child viewing hours and educate children about violence prevention efforts.

5. Limit accessibility to firearms for youths, and teach firearm violence prevention.

6. Reduce alcohol and other drug use among youths.

7. Provide mental health services for perpetrators and victims of and witnesses to violence.

8. Fund prejudice reduction programs that defuse hate crimes.

9. Mount cooperative mob violence prevention efforts through police and community leaders.

10. Obtain individual and professional commitment from the psychological community to reduce youth violence.

Source: American Psychological Association (1993).

(Van Steenbergen, 1994). The National Association for Mediation (NAME), an advocacy organization for mediation approaches, indicates that many schools have set up conflict resolution programs over the past decade. The state of Oregon has an Office of Conflict-Dispute Resolution that provides services across a range of state agencies including public schools. The advantages of mediation approaches are listed in Box 11.6.

Increasingly, curricula are available that include units specifically geared toward violence prevention and that provide direct instruction to students in how to cope with violence. The Second Step and PeaceBuilders universal interventions, described in Chapter 10, are examples of such curricular-based programs. Ways need to be found to incorporate this instruction into academic curricula so that all students are exposed to it at each grade level.

Staff development training is essential to instruct teachers in how to prevent and cope with violence at an individual, teacher–student level. It is important that they know how to recognize when students are becoming agitated, when they are likely to escalate, when not to press them on an issue, and how to develop and maintain positive interactions with all students. Teachers are also key participants in the development of a positive school climate such that all stu-

Box 11.6   Advantages of Peer Mediation

- ◆ Mediation is more effective than suspension or detention in promoting responsible behavior.
- ◆ Mediation reduces violence, vandalism, and absenteeism.
- ◆ Mediation reduces the time teachers and administrators must spend dealing with discipline problems.
- ◆ Mediation promotes peace and justice in our multicultural world through mutual understanding of individual differences.

Source: Van Steenbergen (1994).

dents, and their families, are made to feel welcome and valued. Development of a schoolwide discipline plan and, where necessary, a violence prevention plan is essential in creating and maintaining such a school climate.

It is essential that a responsive and prompt crime-reporting system be developed by each school. Schools have been criticized for underreporting crimes occurring on their campuses but also for failing to distinguish between school misconduct and criminal behavior (Fein et al., 2002; Maddox, 1994). Recent task force reports on school safety and violence have provided guidelines and criteria for use by educators in distinguishing between a school-based, disciplinary issue and an illegal incident that requires a referral to law enforcement (see Fein et al., 2002; O'Toole, 2000).

Violence and Crime in U.S. Schools and Responses to the Problem

Gottfredson and Gottfredson, and their colleagues (2000) have conducted the most extensive study to date describing school crime and conduct problems and the approaches that schools typically use to cope with them. A national sample of 1,279 schools was gathered by these researchers to investigate critical dimensions relating to each of these problem areas during the 1997–98 school year. School-based crime and victimization, as well their frequencies of occurrence in the school setting, were reported for both teachers and students. Results indicated a relatively high level of school crime. For example, 42% of teachers reported having obscene gestures and remarks directed toward them by a student; 28% experienced damage to personal property worth less than $10; 24% had property worth less than $10 stolen from them; 21% were threatened by a student; 14% experienced damage to personal property worth more than $10; 13% had property worth more than $10 stolen; and 3% were physically attacked. To put these data in perspective, the authors noted that 7.9 teachers per 1,000 were attacked and had to visit a doctor, which translates into an estimated 12,100 teachers nationally who were so victimized in that school year.

Students participating in this study were asked to confidentially self-report on their problem behavior, delinquency, and drug use. Based on their results, Gottfredson et al. (2000) concluded that interpersonal violence is an especially common occurrence in middle schools. They found that 32% of high schoolers and 41% of middle schoolers reported having hit or threatened to hit another student in the past year; 16% of all students reported damaging or destroying school property; 9% of middle schoolers and 17% of high schoolers reported having come to school intoxicated one or more times; 9% of all students reported having stolen something; and 5% reported having hit or threatened a teacher. Finally, nearly one in five students reported being threatened with a beating (22% for middle schoolers, 16% for high schoolers); 19% of middle schoolers and 10% of high schoolers were physically attacked; and 5% of high schoolers reported being threatened with a knife or gun.

Gottfredson et al. (2000) found that schools typically implement a broad array of prevention activities and approaches simultaneously. However, the effectiveness of a majority of these activities and programs has not been established through empirical research, and their value or impact in reducing school problem behavior is not clear. These authors identified 23 prevention practices that were commonly used in the schools sampled; 17 were "environmental" practices, and six were "individual" practices addressing skill deficits and/or behavioral excesses. Environmental practices focus on changing the structure or administrative management of the school (e.g., communicating expectations, enforcing rules, and recognizing certain forms of conduct); individual practices, in contrast, focus on teaching individual skills (e.g., teaching social skills and self-regulation and providing counseling services). Box 11.7 contains a classification of the types of prevention activities identified and the percentage of schools in the Gottfredson et al. sample using each type of activity to reduce problem behavior or promote school safety.

The research of Gottfredson et al. (2000) shows that a relatively large amount of criminal and problem behavior takes place in today's school settings. They urge school leaders to focus much more strongly on careful implementation of effective intervention approaches and to consider using a combination of environmental and individual practices in order to produce maximal effects. Greenberg, Domitrovich, and Bumbarger (2001) have catalogued a range of universal and selected intervention approaches, either proven or promising, for accomplishing this goal. In addition, the U.S. Centers for Disease Control have developed a sourcebook for youth violence prevention that provides a framework for selecting and implementing best practices (see Thornton et al., 2000). *Best Practices of Youth Violence Prevention* is a detailed compendium of research-based principles and procedures in four areas: (1) parent and family-based strategy, (2) home-visiting strategy, (3) social-cognitive strategy, and (4) mentoring strategy. Implementation guidelines in the sourcebook are well developed, and proven model programs are identified and illustrated. Access information is given for each of the model programs cited within the four strategy areas.

The Fast Track program, designed to prevent antisocial behavior and violence within the context of families and schools, involves family members, teachers, and professionals in a coordinated intervention to accomplish this goal. This

Box 11.7   School-Based Prevention Activities Used to Reduce Problem Behavior and to Promote School Safety

Category

Direct Services to Students, Families, or Staff

Provision of isolated information	90
Prevention curriculum, instruction, or training	76
Counseling/social work/psychological/therapeutic interventions	75
Behavioral or behavior modification interventions	64
Recreational, enrichment, and leisure activities	64
Individual attention/mentoring/tutoring/coaching	58
Services to families	55
Treatment or prevention interventions for administration, faculty, or staff	49

Organizational or Environmental Arrangements

Reorganization of grades, classes, or school schedules	81
Architectural features of the school	76
Use of external personnel resources in classroom	72
Distinctive culture or climate for interpersonal exchanges	66
Improved instructional methods or practices	62
Improved classroom organization and management methods or practices	57
School planning structure or process—or management of change	57
Improvements to intergroup relations or interaction between school and community	57
Alter school composition	32

Discipline or Safety Management Activities

Rules, policies, regulations, laws, or enforcement	100
Security and surveillance	55
Youth roles in regulating and responding to student conduct	400

model program represents one of the most comprehensive efforts ever initiated to prevent these unfortunate outcomes. Fast Track is a multisite, collaborative program funded by the National Institute of Mental Health to prevent antisocial behavior patterns, violence, and juvenile crime by (1) identifying at-risk children and families as early as possible and (2) intervening intensively with parents and schools at the point of school entry.

Neighborhoods with high crime rates are selected initially, and students who are enrolled in the schools serving them are then screened and identified at the end of the kindergarten school year. Children identified as antisocial both at home and in school are selected for Fast Track participation.

Both universal and selected target interventions are used in this prevention effort. Schoolwide interventions are implemented in target schools designed to make the classroom and school environment more accepting, more instructionally effective, more disciplined, and more socially responsive to the needs of children. Selected target interventions for the at-risk children include academic tutoring, social skills training, and problem-solving sessions. Parent groups are held regularly; in these groups, parents are assisted in helping their children make a good transition from kindergarten to first grade. The focus is on what parents can do. Teachers also participate in these parent focus groups to foster the development of effective partnerships in a noncrisis atmosphere. Teachers are given training, support, and technical assistance from Fast Track staff to assist them in more effectively teaching and managing the participating at-risk students. Finally, the target children are followed up intensively and given support at key transition points (e.g., at entry into middle school).

The authors of Fast Track expect to follow up on these students through 2005. This study is a well-designed prevention effort and should greatly enhance our knowledge about whether and how we can achieve cost-effective prevention outcomes in this area. If the program succeeds, ways will have to be found to adapt it and bring it to scale so its key features can be adopted by professionals in family, school, and community contexts.

Our current knowledge base concerning the reduction and prevention of school crime and violence far exceeds our level of adopting that which has proved to work. It is essential that we continue to promote effective, evidence-based interventions and provide professional consumers with the means to access and implement them.

A Case Study of a School Shooter

In May 1998, Kip Kinkel, a Thurston High School student in Springfield, Oregon, shot his father in the back of the head while he was reading and waited quietly for several hours for his mother to come home from work. When she did, he greeted her by saying, "I love you, Mom," and then fatally shot her as well. The next morning, he drove to school armed with multiple weapons, killed two of his classmates, and wounded over two dozen others before being disarmed by several students. As he was being subdued, he yelled out to his classmates to kill him.

Kinkel was a textbook case of the difficult child from the first day of his life. He had severe anger control problems from early on in his development, and he was a challenge for his parents to manage. His parents, who were both teachers, were alarmed by some of his actions and sought help from a variety of agencies. His teachers reported that he often complained of hearing voices and that some of his essays contained disturbing imagery. Following the shootings, he was diagnosed by several mental health professionals in Oregon as paranoid schizophrenic. He was sentenced to over 99 years in prison for his crime.

Things had come to a head when Kinkel brought a gun to school that was discovered by school officials. After he was suspended from school, his father decided to enroll him in a military-type boot camp program in Bend, Oregon, that emphasized strict discipline. This may have been the final triggering event that caused him to embark on his rampage.

Kinkel had pressured his parents relentlessly to purchase guns for him. Finally, his father relented and purchased him a gun on the condition that he enroll in a gun safety class. At the time of the shooting, Kip possessed a number of weapons.

Kinkel and his friends displayed remarkable cruelty toward animals. Reportedly, they would mix up pool chemicals and dip house cats head first into them. He also spent hours on the Internet exploring its darker side. One of the skills he acquired in this process was bomb building. Upon searching the Kinkel home following the tragedy, investigators found 18 bombs or bomblike devices in various stages of assembly.

It was apparent that Kinkel's parents felt helpless to deal with him. They became detached in their supervision of his activities and increasingly desperate in their search to find professional help for his problems. Their lax supervision and monitoring doubtless gave him the space he needed to build bombs, collect weapons, and plan his assault.

So far, experts have been unable to identify *any* behavioral profile of attributes that will predict, beyond chance levels, whether an individual will commit a violent act. However, the FBI and the U.S. Secret Service have extensively studied the shooters who were involved in the school shooting tragedies of the 1990s, and a solid knowledge base has emerged from retrospective analyses of these incidents. For example, (1) such incidents of targeted school violence are rarely sudden, impulsive acts but are carefully planned over time; (2) prior to most incidents, others know about the attacker's intentions and/or specific plans; (3) most attackers do not threaten their targets directly prior to the attack; (4) most attackers engage in some form of behavior, prior to the incident, that causes concern or indicates a need for help; and (5) most attackers have access to weapons before the attack (see Fein et al., 2002; O'Toole, 2000).

The tragedy of Kip Kinkel is that he ruined so many lives through the expression of his own rage and anger. It is not clear in retrospect whether his actions could have been prevented. His parents' attempts to secure help for him were frustrated at every turn by society's response—that little could be done in the absence of his committing a violent or illegal act. His story is a wake-up call that we must do better in assisting those youths whose actions indicate that they may be on a path to violent or destructive behavior.

Reactive Responses of U.S. Schools to the School Shooting Tragedies of the 1990s

The public's shock, outrage, and concern reached a crescendo with the Columbine High School shooting tragedy in Littleton, Colorado in April 1999, in which one teacher and 12 students were killed by students Eric Harris and Dylan Klebold. At the end of their rampage, the attackers killed themselves.

The director of the U.S. National Institute of Mental Health, Steve Hyman, M.D., suggests that Columbine was the turning point that led to a substantial expansion of the federal government's investment in research on youth violence prevention (*Science Magazine*, July 2000). This program of research is ongoing and is contributing to a greater science-based understanding of the forces that propel at-risk youths toward violence. The public demand for answers in this area has been intense and has prompted three key responses from school, mental health, and law enforcement personnel: (1) increasing school security, (2) profiling the potential school shooter, and (3) analyzing and attempting to predict violent episodes through the development of threat assessment approaches.

Increasing School Security

Perhaps the most common reaction of school leaders to the threat of continuing school shootings and a perceived lack of school safety was to invest in mechanical forms of school security and in school resource officers. Metal detectors, video surveillance cameras, locker searches, and public safety personnel thus have become standard fare in many suburban and rural schools. These forms of security have long been in evidence in many urban schools, which, unfortunately, have had to turn themselves into fortresslike structures in an attempt to provide adequate levels of school safety.

This development has been controversial in that some critics and experts argue that such measures cannot prevent a school shooting tragedy if a dedicated attacker wishes to penetrate a campus. Indeed, we do not have the means at present to absolutely certify a school's safety from all potential threats. The argument goes that, because preventing a school shooting tragedy is impossible, the use of this approach to improve school security is not worth the associated negatives of intrusiveness and cost. However, we would argue that, if a school has an inadequate level of school safety and exists within a dangerous, high-crime neighborhood, the investment in such security measures is well worth the effort and *can* improve the school building's overall safety. There has been a substantial drop in the number of school shooting incidents in recent years, and many point to schools' investments in school security measures as a major reason for this outcome. Although it is impossible to verify this claim, neither can it be ruled out as a partial explanation for improved school safety.

In many cases, school security technology is in place but not properly operated in today's schools. It was widely reported, for instance, that Columbine High School, a relatively new structure, had a state-of-the-art video surveillance system. However, the system was not being used at the time of the attack because no school personnel were assigned to monitor the cameras. It is not clear, however, whether such monitoring would have prevented the Columbine attack, although it likely would have detected the attackers bringing homemade bombs into the school.

The National Institute of Justice (NIJ) and the Office of Safe and Drug-Free Schools of the U.S. Department of Education have jointly commissioned the development of a resource document for school administrators for addressing physical security problems. This resource guide focuses on the *appropriate* and *effective*

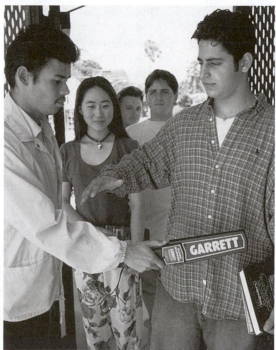

Effective and appropriate use of surveillance systems, metal detectors, and security personnel is expensive and intrusive, but may improve overall school safety.

use of school security technology (Green, 1999). The guide was prepared by Sandia National Laboratories of Albuquerque, New Mexico, the principal provider of research, design, development, and testing of leading-edge technologies to solve physical security problems at high-risk U.S. facilities. Information about the availability of this guide can be obtained by calling 800-851-3420 or visiting the NIJ Web site at www.ojp.usdoj.gov/nij.

The guide is extremely thorough and addresses the following school security dimensions: (1) the nature and use of video surveillance systems; (2) metal detection involving walk-through systems, hand-held scanners, and X-ray baggage scanners; (3) school entry control technologies including limiting entry/exit points and setting up entry control approaches; and (4) duress alarm devices and their role in crisis management. The guide also lists additional resources on school security technology.

The decision to invest in physical school security is a difficult one; the systems can be expensive and certainly are intrusive. However, if the decision *is* made to go this route, it should incorporate the best knowledge available on how to do it effectively.

Profiling the Potential School Shooter

During and following the school shooting tragedies of the 1990s, school leaders came under enormous pressure to profile and identify potential school shooters.

This approach assumes that some stable set of behavioral attributes (e.g., cruelty to animals, anger control problems, substance use, lack of empathy, dehumanization of others) can be used to predict future violent acts. This is simply *not* the case! The FBI and the U.S. Secret Service have been adamant that picking out an individual from a larger group who is likely subsequently to commit a violent act simply is not possible. No agreed-upon set of attributes can be used to predict individual violent acts beyond chance levels. Further, school shooters share a large number of behavioral attributes with the vast majority of students who have not and will not commit a violent act. These facts, however, have not deterred many school administrators from being receptive to behavioral profiling techniques and checklists of attributes that purport to identify potential school shooters.

Experts have commented extensively about the potential downsides of the behavioral profiling trend. Students can have their reputations damaged beyond repair through the profiling process. Being labeled as a potentially violent youth or a possible school shooter is clearly a violation of one's basic civil and human rights. It can also lead to a student being barred from schooling.

It is important to distinguish between behavioral profiling and threat assessment, which is discussed in the next section.

Implementing Threat Assessment Approaches

Threat assessment refers to an investigative and analysis protocol that comes into play when a student actually threatens to commit a violent act. The FBI and the Secret Service have both developed procedures for conducting these assessments *after* a threat has been made. These comprehensive documents detail threat assessment approaches and procedures based upon extensive study and analysis of school shooting incidents. The FBI analyzed 18 school shooting incidents, and the Secret Service included 37 shootings that occurred between 1974 and 2000 in its analysis. These agencies used their extensive experience in dealing with threats to public figures as a foundation for developing their task force reports and protocols. The FBI report is titled *The School Shooter: A Threat Assessment Perspective* (see O'Toole, 2000); the Secret Service report is titled *Threat Assessment in Schools: A Guide to Managing Threatening Situations and to Creating Safe School Climates* (see Fein et al., 2002). These are highly recommended resource documents for use by school administrators and law enforcement personnel.

The FBI report identified four categories of threat: direct, indirect, veiled, and conditional. Critical factors in threat assessment include (1) the existence of specific, plausible details relating to the threat; (2) the emotional content of the threat; and (3) precipitating stressors (circumstances, reactions, or situations) that can trigger a threat. Threats are coded by the FBI as low, medium, or high. Threats that are direct, detailed, highly specific, and plausible pose the highest level of danger and have the highest likelihood of occurrence. Once a plausible threat has been validated, the FBI threat assessment process involves four prongs: (1) the personality of the student, (2) family dynamics, (3) school dynamics and the student's role in these dynamics, and (4) social dynamics. Investigations are initiated in each of these four areas to collect information that may be critical in evaluating, managing, and preventing a threatened violent act.

The Secret Service task force report on threat assessment presents a series of key findings from the agency's analysis suggesting that some school attacks may be

◆ Principle 1: Targeted violence is the end result of an understandable, and often discernible, process of thinking and acting.

◆ Principle 2: Targeted violence stems from an interaction among the person, the situation, the setting, and the target.

◆ Principle 3: An investigative, skeptical, inquisitive mind-set is critical to successful threat assessment.

◆ Principle 4: Effective threat assessment is based on facts rather than characteristics or "traits."

◆ Principle 5: An integrated systems approach should guide threat assessment investigations.

preventable based on the fact that most attackers engage in preincident planning behavior and share their intentions with others. Key findings include the following:

◆ Incidents of targeted violence at school rarely are sudden, impulsive acts.

◆ Prior to most incidents, other people know about the attacker's idea and/or plan to attack.

◆ Most attackers do not threaten their targets directly prior to launching the attack.

◆ There is no accurate or useful "profile" of students who engage in targeted school violence.

◆ Most attackers engage in some behavior, prior to the incident, that causes others concern or indicates a need for help.

◆ Most attackers have difficulty coping with significant losses or personal failures, and many have considered or attempted suicide.

◆ Many attackers felt bullied, persecuted, or injured by others prior to the attack.

◆ Most attackers had access to and had used weapons prior to the attack.

◆ In many cases, other students are involved in the attack in some capacity.

◆ Despite prompt law enforcement responses, most attacks are stopped by means other than law enforcement intervention, and most are brief in duration.

The report notes that the central question in threat assessment is not whether a student *makes* a threat but whether the student actually *poses* a threat. It is of critical importance to make this distinction accurately. The Secret Service threat assessment protocol is geared toward implementing investigative procedures to achieve this goal. Box 11.8 contains a list of underlying principles that guide the threat assessment process.

Threat assessment inquiries are the responsibility of the school's threat assessment team. If the results of this inquiry indicate that the threat is credible, involves an illegal act, and is potentially dangerous, law enforcement is brought in to conduct a thorough threat assessment investigation.

Box 11.9 **Components of a Safe/Connected School Climate**

1. Assess the school's emotional climate.
2. Emphasize the importance of listening in schools.
3. Take a strong but caring stance against the code of silence.
4. Work actively to change the perception that talking to an adult about a student contemplating violence is considered "snitching."
5. Find ways to stop bullying.
6. Empower students by involving them in planning, creating, and sustaining a school culture of safety and respect.
7. Ensure that every student feels that he or she has a trusting relationship with at least one adult at school.
8. Create mechanisms for developing and sustaining safe school climates.
9. Be aware of physical environments and their effects on creating comfort zones.
10. Emphasize an integrated systems model.
11. Recognize that all climates of safety ultimately are "local."

In terms of preventing school violence, the report notes that creating cultures and climates of safety is essential, as is providing a solid foundation for the threat assessment management process. The Effective Behavioral Support program, the Second Step Violence Prevention Program, and PeaceBuilders (reviewed earlier in this volume) are all universal interventions that can be used to achieve this outcome. Each has a strong evidence base and is recommended for this purpose.

The report also identifies the major components involved in creating a safe/connected school climate. They are listed in Box 11.9.

Gangs and Gang Activity

The control of gang activity on school campuses, as well as the symbols of such activity, is critical. Often, gangs are infused into the social structure of a school before staff are fully aware of the problem. The National School Safety Center has developed the Gang Assessment Tool to assist communities in determining the extent of gang activity in the vicinity of a school. For more information, contact the National School Safety Center, Pepperdine University, 4165 Thousand Oaks Boulevard, Suite 290, Westlake Village, CA 91362. This assessment tool, presented in Box 11.10, is highly recommended.

Each "yes" response on this tool earns the indicated number of points. The total score is an overall assessment of the severity of the problem and can suggest the possible need for school security measures: 0–15 points indicate no significant gang problem; 20–40 points indicate an emerging gang problem; 45–60 points indicate a significant gang problem for which an intervention–prevention strategy

Box 11.10   Gang Assessment Tool

1. Do you have graffiti on or near your campus? (5)

2. Do you have crossed-out graffiti on or near your campus? (10)

3. Do your students wear colors, jewelry, [or] clothing, flash hand signals, or display other behavior that may be gang-related? (10)

4. Are drugs available near your school? (5)

5. Has there been a significant increase in the number of physical confrontations or stare downs within the past twelve months in or around your school? (5)

6. Is there an increasing presence of weapons in your community? (10)

7. Are beepers, pagers, or cellular phones used by your students? (10)

8. Have you had a drive-by shooting at or around your school? (15)

9. Have you had a "show-by" display of weapons at or around your school? (10)

10. Is the truancy rate of your school increasing? (5)

11. Are there increasing numbers of racial incidents occurring in your community or school? (5)

12. Is there a history of gangs in your community? (10)

13. Is there an increasing presence of "informal social groups" with unusual names—for example, "Woodland Heights Posse," "Rip Off and Rule," "Females Simply Chillin'," or "Kappa Phi Nasty"? (15)

Source: National School Safety Center (1992).

should be developed; and 65 points or higher indicate an acute gang problem that requires urgent attention and intervention.

In recent decades, U.S. society has become increasingly socially fragmented and divided into factions. This process has been referred to as "the Balkanization" of our culture—we divide ourselves by ethnicity, religion, gender, sexual orientation, class, politics, and so on. As a result, our society has experienced unprecedented social conflict. These developments have provided a fertile breeding ground for gang affiliations wherein youths seek social support, shared values, and a sense of family and acceptance provided by the gang structure.

In many ways, gangs are an expression of modern tribalism. Anthropology has much to offer us in understanding the tribal structure and dynamics of modern gangs. Some shared features between ancient tribes and organized street gangs include (1) dialects, (2) visual signs, (3) dress, (4) territory marking, (5) codes of behavior, (6) intertribal conflict, (7) peace treaties, and (8) tribal cohesion and loyalty of tribal members. Developing attractive alternatives to such powerful affiliations is a daunting challenge. Box 11.11 lists gang characteristics, types, and activities. This list represents a synthesis of some of the core knowledge regarding gangs and their activities and so has

Box 11.11   Fact Sheet on Gang Characteristics, Types, and Activities

- Gangs have been with us since the beginning of organized society. The Book of Proverbs contains descriptions of elders being victimized by youth groups.

- Gang proliferation and growth are associated with a breakdown of the family, increased urbanization, the advent of crack cocaine, budget measures that eliminate youth programs, the loss of meaningful jobs for youths and young adults, and racial discrimination, alienation, and conflict.

- Gang members are three times more likely to be violent than nongang members.

- Gang violence is a community problem that requires a multi-agency, community-based solution. It is not exclusively a police or school problem.

- Incarceration and suppression strategies alone will never solve the U.S. gang problem; community organization, outreach programs, and vocational training programs are also required to effectively treat and prevent gang problems.

- Much of gang activity is driven by control issues (of members, neighborhoods, and turf) and by manipulation of others' fear. Gangs capitalize on the natural fears community members have of them.

- In the past decade, 11,000 individuals have been murdered by gang members and 15,000 have been seriously injured.

- Gangs are highly cohesive and communicate through marking, graffiti, dress, language (verbal and nonverbal), tattoos, hand signals, and behavioral codes or rules.

- Over four-fifths of the largest U.S. cities ($N = 79$) report having a gang crisis.

- Male gang members outnumber female gang members by 20 to 1; however, female gangs are a fast-growing problem.

- There are two major types of gangs: (1) traditional (neighborhood based) and (2) nontraditional (profit oriented and organized around drug dealing, car theft, and burglary).

- Ethnic orientation, among other factors, can be an organizer for gang development and identification and often leads to gang-related, racial violence.

- Schools are heavy recruiting sites for new gang members. Gangs are often the leading competitors with communities for the hearts and minds of young people. Peer pressures to join gangs can be extremely powerful and difficult to resist.

Box 11.11   *(Continued)*

◆ Incentives for gang membership include recognition, peer status, social support, shared values, family tradition or history, protection, and perceived opportunity.

◆ In recent decades, the U.S. gang problem has worsened significantly in several dimensions: (1) Instruments of war (Uzis, AK-47s) are now being used by gangs; (2) victims are often shot multiple times with these weapons; and (3) many gang members are totally desensitized to violence and care nothing for their victims.

◆ Gang members generally range in age from 12 to 40. The average age of gang members is increasing, with many maintaining their gang membership well into their 30s.

◆ Hate crimes committed by loosely affiliated youth groups and gangs are increasing rapidly in our society.

◆ Gang members have a low rate of participation in school activities. Rarely do gang members bond or identify with a significant adult at school.

◆ Neither programs nor people change gang membership. Individual gang members must see a window of opportunity to change and be supported in that decision. Youths need alternatives to gang membership that are attractive and accessible.

◆ Currently, Latino/a gangs are the most populous in the United States.

considerable relevance for educators in understanding and coping with the challenges of gang activity.

A prevention–intervention strategy for gangs should be developed in close collaboration with parents, law enforcement authorities, and other agencies as appropriate. Gang insignias, clothing, graffiti of any kind, jewelry, or other gang symbols should not be allowed on campus. In addition, formal programs should be in place to divert students from gang membership.

Box 11.12 contains guidelines and recommended strategies for preventing and intervening with gang activity on school campuses. Both universal (e.g., gang prevention curricula) and selected (e.g., graffiti removal) strategies should be incorporated into a comprehensive gang strategy. In addition, a strategy needs to be in place for responding immediately to gang incidents at school that involve violence or drugs. Law enforcement must be a key player in this strategy.

The reader is referred to two superb sources on strategies for coping and intervening with gangs on school campuses. Natalie Salazar, coordinator of community partnership programs for the Los Angeles County Sheriff's Office, is a nationally recognized expert on gang prevention–intervention. She has developed a model program, Rising Above Gangs and Drugs, through a grant from the U.S.

Box 11.12 Recommendations for Schools in Preventing and Intervening in Gang Problems

1. Begin gang prevention efforts as early as possible in a child's school career—some kindergartners and first-graders show clear signs of emerging gang involvement. Early intervention is more likely to divert children from later gang involvement.

2. Improve the social cohesion of neighborhoods and communities. Schools are important partners with families, police, churches, courts, corrections, and social service agencies in working toward this goal.

3. Develop a comprehensive interagency system for sharing records and information to effectively address gang problems that will allow early intervention and guide prevention efforts.

4. Build three components into the gang prevention–intervention strategy: (a) a strong law enforcement component that allows detection and detention of chronic gang members, (b) an intervention component that controls gang activity on school campuses and allows gang members to escape gang involvement, and (c) a prevention component to positively influence vulnerable children and youths who are on the cusp of gang activity.

5. Expose students vulnerable to recruitment by and involvement in gangs to (a) adult and peer mentoring, (b) academic tutoring and added support as needed, (c) strategies for fully engaging them in the schooling process including participation in school activities, (d) social skills training geared toward building and maintaining friendships, and (e) effective home–school communication and collaboration.

6. Teach multicultural sensitivity, awareness, tolerance, acceptance, and respect. Ensure that the behavior of school staff and students reflect these values on a daily basis.

7. Reinstitute the teaching of morals, values, and socially responsible decision making in the school curriculum.

8. Provide after-school recreation and leisure programs to students and their families.

9. Maintain sports programs whenever possible.

10. Provide at-risk students with access to computers, labs, and instructors.

11. Strengthen school service clubs and make them broadly accessible.

12. Develop a reasonable and enforceable dress code.

13. Avoid a false sense of security that leads to denial of the subtle signs of emerging gang activity.

14. Make strong, positive role models available at school.

15. Be cautious about transferring gang members between schools, as such transfers may help spread gang activity.

Box 11.12   *(Continued)*

16. Consider developing a gang prevention policy on campus in collaboration with law enforcement officials and other agencies as appropriate. Implement a gang prevention curriculum as part of this effort.

17. Confront and immediately remove *all* graffiti on school buildings. Gang-related graffiti found on students' persons should be confiscated. Building graffiti should be removed within 12 hours.

18. Be sure a comprehensive set of gang prevention–intervention school strategies includes (a) clear behavioral expectations, (b) visible staff, (c) parent involvement, (d) in-service training, (e) graffiti removal, (f) cooperation with law enforcement, (g) existence of a gang prevention plan, and (h) community involvement and coordination.

◆

Department of Justice. This model program is packaged in a highly readable, user-friendly operational manual. Information about this program can be obtained by writing to Natalie Salazar, Community/Law Enforcement Partnership Programs, 4700 Ramona Boulevard, Monterey Park, CA 91754-2169. The National School Safety Center's *Gangs in Schools* publication is another excellent resource for schools in developing gang prevention–intervention strategies. It is available from the NSSC, 4165 Thousand Oaks Boulevard, Suite 290, Westlake Village, CA 91362.

Assessing School Safety

School safety should be assessed, whenever possible, using multiple indicators. Dimensions that should be considered in this regard include the number and type of disciplinary referrals that occur within the school, the rate of suspensions and expulsions for challenging student behavior, and the perceptions of the school's safety by staff members. In addition, specific features of the physical setting should be inspected according to whether they deter or allow criminal or dangerous forms of behavior. A large number of entrances to and exits from a school building is a major weakness in terms of school safety, as is a lack of easy and natural visual surveillance of the school grounds. The senior author and his colleagues have developed a resource guide for conducting these assessments that also provides guidelines for correcting problem areas and situations revealed through the assessment process (Schneider, Walker, & Sprague, 2000). The role of architectural design features in school safety is a major focus of this resource guide; this topic is briefly discussed in a later section of this chapter.

Box 11.13 contains a crime assessment tool that can be used to assist schools in measuring their crime vulnerability status through the self-reports of school staff. This instrument was developed by the National School Safety Center. Ideally,

Box 11.13   School Crime Assessment Tool

The National School Safety Center has developed the following school crime assessment tool to assist school administrators in evaluating their vulnerability to school crime issues and potential school climate problems.

1. Has your community crime rate increased over the past 12 months?
2. Are more than 15% of your work-order repairs vandalism-related?
3. Do you have an open campus?
4. Has there been an emergence of an underground student newspaper?
5. Is your community transiency rate increasing?
6. Do you have an increasing presence of graffiti in your community?
7. Do you have an increased presence of gangs in your community?
8. Is your truancy rate increasing?
9. Are your suspension and expulsion rates increasing?
10. Have you had increased conflicts relative to dress styles, food services, and types of music played at special events?
11. Do you have an increasing number of students on probation in your school?
12. Have you had isolated racial fights?
13. Have you reduced the number of extracurricular programs and sports at your school?
14. Has there been an increasing incidence of parents withdrawing students from your school because of fear?
15. Has your budget for professional development opportunities and in-service training for your staff been reduced or eliminated?
16. Are you discovering more weapons on your campus?
17. Do you have written screening and selection guidelines for new teachers and other youth-serving professionals who work in your school?
18. Are drugs easily available in or around your school?
19. Are more than 40% of your students bused to school?
20. Have you had a student demonstration or other signs of unrest within the past 12 months?

Scoring and Interpretation

Multiply each affirmative answer by 5 and add the total.

0–20	Indicates no significant school safety problems
25–45	An emerging school safety problem (safe school plan should be developed)
50–70	Significant potential for school safety problem (safe school plan should be developed)
Over 70	School is a sitting time bomb (safe school plan should be developed immediately)

it should be administered twice annually (e.g., October–November and March–April). An elevated score indicates the need to develop a comprehensive school safety plan, perhaps in cooperation with law enforcement personnel, as the situation warrants.

Sprague and his colleagues have developed a more comprehensive instrument, The School Safety Survey, for assessing school safety that examines risk and protective factors in this context (see Sprague, Walker, Nishioka, & Smith, in press). A series of risks that lower school safety and a series of protective factors that enhance it are rated by key school staff in terms of their presence or absence within the school. This instrument should be used as a follow-up assessment to the School Crime Assessment Tool when a moderate-to-high score is obtained on that scale. The School Safety Survey can be quite useful in pinpointing where to invest effort and resources in making the school safer. A copy of this instrument can be obtained by contacting the Institute on Violence and Destructive Behavior (IVDB), 1265 University of Oregon, College of Education, Eugene, OR, 97403-1265. It is also available on the IVDB Web site: http://darkwing.uoregon.edu/~ivdb.

Figure 11.4 illustrates the risk and protective factors that can move a school in the direction of either greater safety or reduced safety. This figure also profiles the characteristics of safe versus unsafe schools that have emerged from the professional literature. It is important to note that schools can move from safe to unsafe depending upon the extent to which the ratio of risks to protective influences changes over time.

Sources of Vulnerability in Terms of School Safety

Typically, at-risk students are regarded as posing the primary threat to a school's safety. It is certainly true that the attitudes, values, beliefs, and behavioral characteristics that students bring to school have a major influence (negative or positive) on their performance in this setting. The at-risk conditions of our society are reflected in the ecology of schools through the exposure that vulnerable students have to these conditions. Long-term exposure to these risks leads to negative effects that are behaviorally manifested by these students as they begin their school careers.

However, other risks also impact the vulnerability of schools in terms of their safety and security. These are (1) the design, use, and supervision of school space, (2) the administrative and management practices of the school, (3) the nature of the neighborhood(s) served by the school, and (4) the behavioral characteristics of students served by the school. Figure 11.5 profiles these sources of vulnerability and lists key indicators for each area.

It is beyond the ability of schools and educators to influence some of these societal risk conditions (e.g., poverty, abuse, neighborhood crime levels, domestic violence). However, in many cases, schools can play an important role in buffering or offsetting the impact of risk exposure through the development of social resilience and essential skills and through the provision of emotional support. With regard to the first area in Figure 11.5, schools can do a great deal by applying the knowledge base that currently exists in Crime Prevention Through

Unsafe Schools
(Lack of cohesion, chaotic, stressful, disorganized, poorly structured, ineffective, high risk, gang activity, violent incidents, unclear behavioral and academic expectations)

Safe Schools
(Effective, accepting, freedom from potential physical and psychological harm, absence of violence, nurturing, caring, protective)

School-Based Risk Factors

- Poor design and use of school space

- Overcrowding

- Lack of caring but firm disciplinary procedures

- Insensitivity and poor accommodation to multicultural factors

- Student alienation

- Rejection of at-risk students by teachers and peers

- Anger and resentment at school routines and demands for conformity

- Poor supervision

School-Based Protective Factors

- Positive school climate and atmosphere

- Clear and high performance expectations for all students

- Inclusionary values and practices throughout the school

- Strong student bonding to the school environment and the schooling process

- High levels of student participation and parent involvement in schooling

- Provision of opportunities for skill acquisition and social development

- Schoolwide conflict resolution strategies

FIGURE 11.4 ◆

Bipolar Dimensions and Attributes of Unsafe and Safe Schools with Associated Risk and Protective Factors.

Environmental Design (see Crowe, 1994; Schneider, Walker, & Sprague, 2001). This information makes it possible to retrofit and design the physical structure of schools so as to minimize problematic and/or criminal forms of behavior. Further, through careful examination of school schedules and patterns of supervision, especially in low-traffic areas of the school, it is possible to substantially reduce the amount of conflict among students and the frequency of problem behavior. With respect to how the school is managed and administered, there is a cohesive knowledge base from the "effective schools" literature on ways to create positive, inclusive, and well-led schools. The work of Gottfredson et al. (2000) has great relevance in this regard. Forging partnerships with public safety

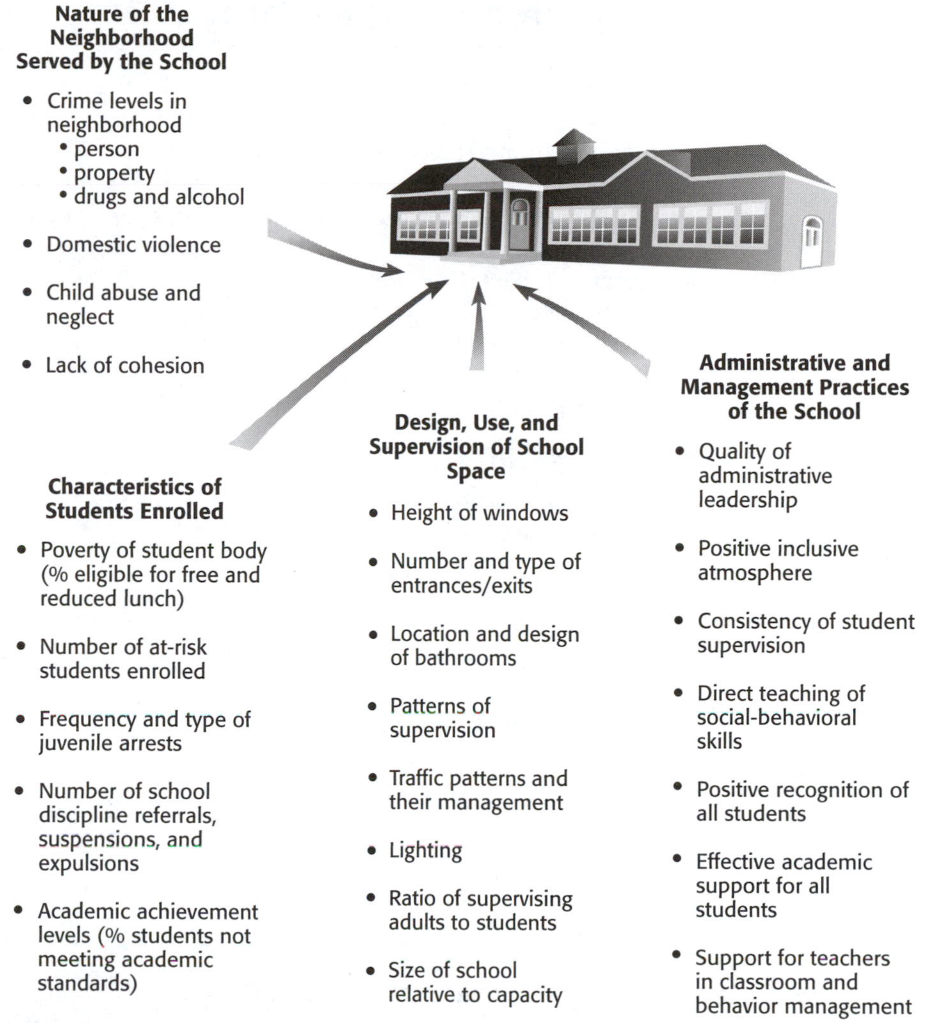

Nature of the Neighborhood Served by the School

- Crime levels in neighborhood
  - person
  - property
  - drugs and alcohol

- Domestic violence

- Child abuse and neglect

- Lack of cohesion

Characteristics of Students Enrolled

- Poverty of student body (% eligible for free and reduced lunch)

- Number of at-risk students enrolled

- Frequency and type of juvenile arrests

- Number of school discipline referrals, suspensions, and expulsions

- Academic achievement levels (% students not meeting academic standards)

Design, Use, and Supervision of School Space

- Height of windows

- Number and type of entrances/exits

- Location and design of bathrooms

- Patterns of supervision

- Traffic patterns and their management

- Lighting

- Ratio of supervising adults to students

- Size of school relative to capacity

Administrative and Management Practices of the School

- Quality of administrative leadership

- Positive inclusive atmosphere

- Consistency of student supervision

- Direct teaching of social-behavioral skills

- Positive recognition of all students

- Effective academic support for all students

- Support for teachers in classroom and behavior management

FIGURE 11.5

Sources of School Vulnerability.

and social service agencies is also important in addressing some of the problems listed in the third area of Figure 11.5. However, realistically, schools can be only minor players in this effort.

Our schools continue to invest in numerous interventions and practices to improve the behavioral and academic performance of students, with varying degrees of success. As we have noted several times herein, we need to implement proven and promising practices that have been validated through research much more extensively than is currently the case.

Generic Strategies for Enhancing School Safety

Walker, Sprague, and Severson (in press) described a set of strategies that should be considered in moving schools in the direction of greater safety. The following strategic approaches can reduce the likelihood over time of a school tragedy occurring: (1) secure the school, (2) address the peer culture and its problems, (3) involve parents in making the school safer, (4) create a positive, inclusive school climate and culture, and (5) develop a school safety and crisis prevention–response plan. The more at risk a school is perceived to be, the more important these topical areas become, and the greater the investment that should potentially be made in them. Their importance and relevance increases as students move from elementary to middle to high school.

Securing the School

The most immediate and direct method of addressing school safety issues is to physically secure the school. The three primary approaches to consider in this regard are (1) the appropriate use of school security technology, (2) employment of school resource officers, and (3) the applicatoin of Crime Prevention Through Environmental Design principles and techniques. Used in combination, these three approaches can be effective in reducing the likelihood or probability of a school shooting tragedy. Considerable progress has been made in the development and appropriate use of security technology to make schools safer without turning them into fortresslike structures—technology that is increasingly being used in schools across the country. As noted earlier, an excellent resource on this topic has been developed and published (see Green, 1999). School administrators should be aware of the status, advantages, and limitations of this technology when considering implementation of school safety strategies.

Addressing the Peer Culture and Its Problems

A primary target for violence prevention and safer-school efforts should always be the peer culture. Unfortunately, the norms, actions, beliefs, and values within broad sectors of today's youth culture are socially destructive and demeaning. Many young people experience a trial by fire in negotiating the complex and difficult social tasks involved in finding their place in this peer culture. And far too many fail this critical test, become lost within it, and wander aimlessly while seeking acceptance that generally is not forthcoming. They become "homeless persons" within the larger peer group; and their lack of fit is generally well known among peers. This process forces many marginalized youths to affiliate with atypical or deviant peer groups, which can prove destructive to themselves and to the school.

Transforming this destructive peer culture is perhaps our most formidable task in the area of school safety. This culture is not of the schools' making, but schools are perhaps the only social institution, excluding the family, capable of addressing it effectively. Five ongoing strategies are recommended in this regard.

1. *Adopt and implement the Students Against Violence Everywhere (SAVE) and the Ribbon of Promise school violence prevention programs By Kids, For Kids (BK4K) and Not My Friends, Not My School.* These programs are designed to transform students' attitudes and beliefs about violence, to make them aware of the risks to school safety resulting from the "code of silence" ethic among peers that prevents them from reporting their school safety concerns to an adult, and the importance of taking ownership, with school leaders, in making the school safe. These programs promote ownership by peers of the tasks involved in preventing school tragedies and are highly recommended as a first strategy for enlisting a school's peer culture in this effort. The U.S. Secret Service task force report on threat assessment strongly recommends involving peers in this manner and creating a school environment in which there is two-way communication between adults and students, and students feel that adults are listening to them. Information on accessing the SAVE and Ribbon of Promise programs is given later in the chapter.

2. *Bully-proof the school setting by adopting effective antibullying/harassment programs such as Bully-Proofing Your School and Steps to Respect.* The best antidote for bullying, mean-spirited teasing, and harassment is sunlight. That is, these events need to be defined as clearly unacceptable in the school by everyone (administrators, teachers, other school staff, students, and parents) and made public when they occur. Students should be given strategies for reporting and resisting them in an adaptive fashion, and the reporting of those who commit these acts should be made acceptable. The previously cited programs incorporate these principles and strategies.

3. *Teach anger management and conflict resolution techniques as part of regular curricular content.* The Second Step Violence Prevention Program, developed by the Committee for Children in Seattle, is one of the best means available for creating a positive peer culture of caring and civility. It is also useful for teaching specific strategies that work in controlling and managing anger and resolving conflicts without resorting to coercion or violence. This program was recently rated as *the* most effective of all those currently available for creating safe and positive schools by an expert panel of the Office of Safe and Drug-Free Schools of the U.S. Department of Education.

4. *Refer troubled, agitated, and depressed youths to mental health services, and ensure that they receive the professional attention they need.* Youths with serious mental health problems and disorders, who are alienated, socially rejected, and taunted by peers, can be dangerous to themselves and others. These students, who are often known to peers and staff, should be given the appropriate professional and parental attention, access to services, and social supports. Having mental health problems, combined with being the target of severe bullying and taunting by peers, has proved to be a dangerous combination in the context of some school shootings.

5. *Ask students to sign a pledge not to tease, bully, or put down others.* Reports from schools that have tried this tactic indicate that it makes a difference in the number of incidents that occur and in the overall school climate.

Involving Parents in Making the School Safer

With each new school shooting tragedy, parents of school-age children and youths seek greater assurances that their child's school is safe and, increasingly, are seeking a voice and role in helping the school attain this goal. Recently, a prosecuting attorney, the mother of four children, described a plan for creating a parent-based advocacy group on school safety that would rate the safety of schools and make this information broadly available to all parents. Under the federal No Child Left Behind legislation of 2001, parents have the option of transferring their child to a new school if the old school is deemed persistently dangerous. Parents have much to offer and can be an effective force in bringing greater safety and security to the school setting.

Four strategies are recommended for facilitating parent involvement:

1. *Create a parent advisory–planning group at each school devoted to school safety issues for that school.* Such an advisory group can bring valuable knowledge, experience, and advocacy to the process of dealing with local school safety challenges. It can also serve as a forum for reacting to district- and state-level policy directives in this area.

2. *Advocate for parents to teach their children adaptive, nonviolent methods of responding to bullying, teasing, and harassment at school and to avoid encouraging them to fight back.* In the vast majority of cases, fighting back is not effective and may, in fact, escalate the situation to dangerous levels. It is certainly more likely to increase the probability of the offensive behavior occurring again rather than reducing it. An antibullying program at school that has parental support and involvement will be much more effective.

3. *Advocate for the securing of weapons at home and for gun safety instruction for all family members.* Given the society we live in and the number of guns in U.S. homes, it is imperative that everyone have some understanding of the dangers involved in handling guns and in being in proximity to those who are doing so. Trigger locks and secured gun cases are essential elements for securing weapons in the home, with the keys to same also secured. The National Rifle Association offers some excellent information on gun safety that can be accessed by anyone. In connection with these efforts, young children need to be taught about the sanctity of life and the hard fact that guns are deadly, life-ending instruments.

4. *Make available to parents the best information on effective parenting practices, and provide access to those parents who seek training and support in more effective parenting.* Generic parenting practices that are instrumental in determining how children develop include discipline, monitoring and supervision, involvement in children's lives, positive family management techniques, and crisis intervention and problem solving. (Box 9.14 explains these techniques in some detail; see also Figure 11.6. A number of parent-training programs address these parenting practices.)

Creating a Positive, Inclusive School Climate and Culture

There is solid evidence that effective schools are safer schools, and vice versa. The research of Gottfredson et al. (2000) has shown that a school climate that is

Effective Family Management Techniques

The following rules are offered for your consideration in parenting your children. They can be helpful in the prevention of adjustment problems later.

1. Set up a daily debriefing time in which you review your children's day. Questions like: "Tell me what you did today" "What did you do that was fun or interesting?" "Who did you play or talk with?" and "Did anything happen that was a problem or that you didn't like?" are excellent ways to conduct such a debriefing. Why should you debrief? First, it tells your children that you care for them and are concerned about what happens in their lives. It is also an excellent method for screening to detect problems that you might not discover otherwise. Once children start school, it is extremely important to conduct a daily debriefing of this type.

2. Monitor your children's activities, behavior, schedules, whereabouts, friendships, and associations very carefully. It is important to provide such monitoring in a positive, caring manner, but to do so in a way that is neither smothering nor unpleasant. Careful monitoring of this type can be a very powerful protective factor in the child's life. As children grow and mature, such monitoring may have to change form and become more subtle and less direct. However, it is extremely important that it occur, especially as they enter adolescence, when risks of problems are so much greater.

3. Teach your children positive attitudes toward school. School should be perceived as a highly valued activity. A pattern of cooperative, prosocial behavior will do a great deal to foster a good start and ensure both academic achievement and social development over the long term.

4. Teach your children prior to entering school, to listen as you read to them. Your children should see the material you are reading and associate the sound of the words with their symbols on the page. This activity is an important precondition for developing children who are good readers and who are interested in reading. It is one of the best things you can do to prevent later school failure and to help ensure academic success.

FIGURE 11.6 ────────────────────────────────◆

Effective Family Management Techniques.

positive, inclusive, and accepting is a key component of an effective and safer school. Recommended strategies for addressing this component of school safety include the following:

1. *Create and promote a set of school-based positive values that include civility, caring, and respect for the rights of others.* It is unfortunate that schools have to teach civility in addition to everything else they do, but such is now the case. Children and youths are daily exposed to models of incivil behavior in adult society. Making civility a core value of the school's culture

may help reduce some of the coarseness of the peer culture that has become such a problem in our schools—and our society.

2. *Teach all students how to separate from their own lives the exaggerated media images of interpersonal violence, disrespect, and incivility to which they are exposed daily.* School curricula exist that teach media literacy relative to interpersonal violence. It is especially important that young children learn how to make the disconnect between media displays of violence and their own behavior and actions.

3. *Establish schoolwide rules and behavioral expectations.* The Effective Behavioral Support (EBS) program is an excellent and proven vehicle for accomplishing this goal. EBS is being broadly implemented in school districts across the country. It is a highly recommended approach for schools to use in creating orderly, positive, well-managed school environments.

Developing a School Safety and Crisis Prevention–Response Plan

In today's environment, it is essential that every school go through a planning process designed to reduce the likelihood of a school tragedy and to manage a crisis when it occurs. Dwyer (2002) and Paine (2002) have contributed excellent resources and guidelines in these two areas, respectively.

Recommended Resources on Youth Violence and School Safety

The following selected resources can be of value to professionals in coping with youth violence, gangs, and school safety problems. Publication or access information is provided below for each listed resource.

BOOKS

Osher, D., Dwyer, K., & Jackson, S. (2004). *Safe, supportive and successful schools: Step by step.* Longmont: Sopris West Educational Services, Inc., 4093 Specialty Place, Longmont, CO, 80504.

Reid, J. Patterson, G., & Snyder, J. (2002). *Antisocial behavior in children and adolescents.* Washington, DC, American Psychological Association.

Loeber, R., & Farrington, D. (2001). *Child delinquents.* Thousand Oaks, CA: Sage.

Shinn, M., Walker, H., & Stoner, G. (2002). *Interventions for academic and behavior problems II: Preventive and remedial approaches.* Bethesda, MD: National Association of School Psychologists.

Walker, H., & M. Epstein, M. (2001). *Making schools safer and violence free: Critical issues, solutions, and recommended practices.* Austin, TX: Pro-Ed.

Jensen, M., & Yerington, P. (2000). *Gangs—Straight talk, straight up: A practical guide for teachers, parents, and the community.* Longmont, CO: Sopris West.

PUBLIC AGENCY REPORTS AND SYNTHESES OF CURRENT KNOWLEDGE

Satcher, D. (2001). *Youth violence: A report of the Surgeon General.* Washington, DC: U.S. Public Health Service, U.S. Department of Health and Human Services.

Thornton, T., Craft, C., Dahlberg, L., Lynch, B., & Baer, K. (2002). *Best practices of youth violence prevention: A sourcebook for community action.* Atlanta: U.S. Centers for Disease Control.

WEB SITES AND RESOURCES

U.S. Office of Juvenile Justice and Delinquency Prevention: www.ncjrs.org/pdffiles/fs9878.pdf.

U.S. Office of Safe and Drug-Free Schools: www.ed.gov/offices/OSDFS/index.html.

Early Warning/Timely Response: A Guide to Safe Schools: available from www.ed.gov/offices/OSERS/OSEP/Products/earlywrn.html.

Safeguarding Our Children: An Action Guide: available from www.ed.gov/offices/OSERS/OSEP/Products/ActionGuide/.

Ribbon of Promise programs: Contact Cindy Brown at 541-726-0512 or www.ribbonofpromise.org.

By Kids, for Kids, Not My Friends, Not My School, and Students Against Violence Everywhere (SAVE), available at www.nationalsave.org.

JOURNALS

Gerler, E. (Ed.). *The Journal of School Violence.* Haworth Press.

ORGANIZATIONS

The National School Safety Center. Ron Stephens, Director: 141 Duesenberg Drive, Suite 11, Westlake Village, CA 91362; phone 805-373-9977; fax 805-373-9277; Web site www.nssc1.org/.

COMPACT DISKS

Safe and Secure: Guidelines to Creating Safer Schools. Available from the Northwest Regional Educational Laboratory, 101 SW Main Street, Suite 500, Portland, OR 97204; toll-free 800-268-2275; Web site www.safetyzone.org.

Conclusion

Policy generally lags well behind the research that validates evidence-based approaches that can inform and guide policy decisions and practices based upon them. This is especially true in the area of school safety and violence prevention—the focus of this chapter. The pressures and demands of the moment force many school administrators into making decisions about school safety strategies and tactics that may appear promising but are not, as yet, proved through the research process. Gottfredson et al. (2000), in their national survey of school practices in dealing with school problem behavior and crime, found that a majority of practices being used by educators have not been empirically validated through rigorous research. The knowledge base on effective environmental and individual intervention practices, however, has expanded substantially in the past decade. It is incumbent upon school leaders to access and implement these methods effectively in order to create and sustain effective, safe schools.

InfoTrac College Edition Research Terms

School safety

School violence

School violence prevention

Students Against Violence Everywhere

References

American Psychological Association. (1993). *Violence and youth: Psychology's response. Volume I: Summary report of the American Psychological Association Commission on Violence and Youth.* Washington, DC: American Psychological Association.

Coie, J. (1994, July 21). *Antisocial behavior among children and youth.* Keynote address presented at the OSEP National Research Director's Conference. Washington, DC: U.S. Office of Special Education Programs.

Committee for Children. (1993). *Second Step: A violence prevention curriculum.* Seattle: Author.

Crowe, T. (1994, July). *A statistical profile of juvenile crime.* Paper presented at the Institute on Gang and Drug Policy, Office of Juvenile Justice and Delinquency Prevention. San Jose, CA.

Dear, J., Scott, K., & Marshall, D. (1994). An attack on school violence. *National School Safety Center News Journal, 3,* 4–8.

DeComo, R. (1994, May). *Reinventing juvenile corrections.* Paper presented at the Council of State Governments Conference on School Violence. Westlake Village, CA.

Dwyer, K. P. (2002). Tools for building safe, effective schools. In M. R. Shinn, H. M. Walker, & G. Stoner (Eds.), *Interventions for academic and behavior problems II: Preventive and remedial approaches* (pp. 167–211). Bethesda, MD: National Association of School Psychologists.

Farrar, D. (1994, May). *Violence, guns and alcohol: Tailoring the solutions to fit the problems.* Paper presented at the Council of State Governments Conference on School Violence. Westlake Village, CA.

Fein, R. A., Vossekuil, B., Pollack, W. S., Borum, R., Modzeleski, W., & Reddy, M. (2002). *Threat assessment in schools: A guide to managing threatening situations and to creating safe school climates.* Washington, DC: U.S. Department of Education, U.S. Secret Service.

Flannery, D., Vazsonyi, A., Liau, A., Guo, S., Powell, K., Atha, H., Vesterdal, W., & Embry, D. (2003). Initial behavior outcomes for the PeaceBuilders universal school-based violence prevention program. *Developmental Psychology, 39*(2), 292–308.

Gottfredson, G. D., Gottfredson, D. C., Czeh, E. R., Cantor, D., Crosse, S. B., & Hantman, I. (2000). *Summary: National study of delinquency prevention in schools.* Ellicott City, MD: Gottfredson Associates.

Green, M. (1999). *The appropriate and effective use of security technology in U.S. schools.* Washington, DC: U.S. Department of Justice, Office of Juvenile Justice Programs.

Greenberg, M. T., Domitrovich, C., & Bumbarger, B. (2001). *Preventing mental disorders in school-age children: A review of the effectiveness of prevention programs.* Available from the Prevention Research Center for the Promotion of Human Development, College of Health and Human Development, Pennsylvania State University, State College, PA.

Grossman, D. (1995). *On killing.* Boston: Little Brown.

Helmuth, L. (2000). Has America's tide of violence receded for good? *Science, 289*, 582–585.

Huesman, L., Moise-Titus, J., Podolski, C., & Eron, L. (2003). Longitudinal relations between children's exposure to TV violence and their aggressive and violent behavior in young adulthood: 1977–1992. *Developmental Psychology, 39*(2), 201–221.

Jensen, M. M., & Yerington, P. C. (1997). *Gangs: Straight talk, straight up. A practical guide for teachers, parents, and the community.* Longmont, CO: Sopris West.

Kauffman, J. (1994). Violent children and youth: A call for action. *Journal of Emotional and Behavioral Problems, 3*(1), 25–26.

Klein, M. (1994, May). *Gangs and gang violence.* Paper presented at the Council of State Governments Conference on School Violence. Westlake Village, CA.

Loeber, R., & Farrington, D. P. (2001). *Serious and violent juvenile offenders: Risk factors and successful interventions.* Thousand Oaks, CA: Sage.

Maddox, J. (1994). Bringing down the information wall. *National School Safety Center News Journal, 3*, 28–30.

Osofsky, J. D. (Ed.). (1997). *Children in a violent society.* New York: Guilford.

O'Toole, M. E. (2000). *The school shooter: A threat assessment perspective.* Quantico, VA: Critical Incident Response Group (CIRG), National Center for the Analysis of Violent Crime (NCAVC), FBI Academy, Federal Bureau of Investigation.

Paine, C. K. (2002). Preparing for and managing school crises. In M. R. Shinn, H. M. Walker, & G. Stoner (Eds.), *Interventions for academic and behavior problems II: Preventive and remedial approaches* (pp. 993–1019). Bethesda, MD: National Association of School Psychologists.

Patterson, G. R., Reid, J. B., & Dishion, T. J. (1992). *Antisocial boys.* Eugene: Castalia.

Petitt, G., & Dodge, K. (Eds.). (2003). Violent children [Special issue]. *Developmental Psychology, 39*(2).

Reid, J. B., Patterson, G. R., & Snyder, J. J. (Eds.). (2002). *Antisocial behavior in children and adolescents: A developmental analysis and the Oregon*

Model for Intervention. Washington, DC: American Psychological Association.

Roth, J. A. (1994, February). Understanding and preventing violence. *National Institute of Justice Research in Brief.* Washington, DC: U.S. Department of Justice, Office of Justice Programs, National Institute of Justice.

Satcher, D. (2001). *Youth violence: A report of the Surgeon General.* Washington, DC: U.S. Public Health Service, U.S. Department of Health and Human Services.

Schneider, T., Walker, H. M., & Sprague, J. R. (2000). *Safe school design: A handbook for educational leaders.* Eugene: ERIC Clearinghouse on Educational Management, College of Education, University of Oregon.

Science. (2000, July 28), p. 582.

Sprague, J. R., Walker, H. M., Nishioka, V., & Smith, S. G. (in press). *School safety and prevention strategies: Proven and practical solutions for educators.* New York: Guilford.

Sprague, J. R., Walker, H. M., Sowards, S., Van Bloem, C., & Eberhardt, P. (2002). Sources of vulnerability to school violence: Systems-level assessment and strategies to improve safety and climate. In M. R. Shinn, H. M. Walker, & G. Stoner (Eds.), *Interventions for academic and behavior problems II: Preventive and remedial approaches* (pp. 295–314). Bethesda, MD: National Association of School Psychologists.

Steinhart, D. (1994, May). *What can state legislators do to curb youth violence?* Paper presented at the Council of State Governments Conference on School Violence. Westlake Village, CA.

Stone, R., & Kelner, K. (Eds.). (2000). Violence: No silver bullet [Special section]. *Science, 289,* 545, 569–594.

Thornton, T. N., Craft, C. A., Dahlberg, L. L., Lynch, B. S., & Baer, K. (2000). *Best practices of youth violence prevention: A sourcebook for community action.* Atlanta: Centers for Disease Control and Prevention.

Van Steenbergen, N. (1994). "If only we could . . ." *National School Safety Center News Journal, 3,* 20–22.

Walker, H. M., Sprague, J. R., & Severson, H. H. (in press). Schools and youth violence: What educators need to know about developing healthy students and safe schools. In R. H. A. Haslam & P. J. Valletutti (Eds.), *Medical problems in the classroom: The teacher's role in diagnosis and management* (4th ed.). Austin, TX: Pro-Ed.

Wilson, J., & Howell, J. (1993). *A comprehensive strategy for serious, violent, and chronic juvenile offenders.* Washington, DC: Office of Juvenile Justice and Delinquency Prevention, U.S. Department of Justice.

Text Credits

Page 9, Table 1.1: Lindberg, Boggess, and Williams (1999).

Page 13, Figure 1.1: From "A Construct Score Approach to the Assessment of Social Competence: Rationale, Technological Considerations, and Anticipated Outcomes," by H. M. Walker, L. K. Irvin, J. Noell, and G. H. S. Singer, in *Behavior Modifications, 16*(1992), 448–474. Reprinted with permission.

Page 14, Figure 1.2: Patterson et al. (1992).

Page 19, Table 1.2: Walker et al. (1987).

Page 20, Table 1.3: Walker et al. (1987).

Page 21, Table 1.4: Walker et al. (1993).

Page 24, Figure 1.3: From G. Patterson, J. Reid, & T. Dishion, *Antisocial Boys,* © 1992 Castalia Publishing Company. Reprinted with permission.

Page 26, Figure 1.4: From H. M. Walker & J. R. Sprague, "The Path to School Failure, Delinquency, and Violence: Causal Factors and Some Potential Solutions." *Intervention in School and Clinic, 35*(2), 67–73. Reprinted with permission of PRO-ED, © 1999.

Page 27, Table 1.5: Leober et al. (1993).

Page 30, Figure 1.5: Satcher (2001).

Page 46, Box 2.1: Lieberman (1994).

Page 55, Figure 2.3: Bullis and Walker (1994).

Page 56, Figure 2.4: H. M. Walker, V. M. Nishioka, R. Zeller, H. H. Severson, & E. G. Feil, "Causal Factors and Potential Solutions for the Persistent Underidentification of Students Having Emotional or Behavioral Disorders in the Context of Schooling," *Assessment for Effective Intervention, 26*(1), 29–39. Reprinted with permission.

Page 63, Figure 2.5: Adapted with permission from Walker et al. in *Journal of Emotional and Behavioral Disorders, 4*(4), 194–209. © 1996 PRO-ED.

Page 92, Table 3.3: Office of Juvenile Justice and Delinquency Prevention (1995). *Guide for Implementing a Comprehensive Strategy for Serious Violent and Chronic Juvenile Offenders.* Washington, D.C.

Page 94, Table 3.4: K. Bennett, E. Lipman, S. Brown, Y. Racine, M. Boyle, & D. Offord, "Predicting Conduct Problems: Can High-Risk Children Be Identified in Kindergarten and Grade 1?" *Journal of Clinical and Consulting Psychology, 67*, 470–480. © 1999 The American Psychological Association. Reprinted with permission.

Page 96, Figure 3.1: Figure 1 from E. G. Feil, H. M. Walker, & H. H. Severson, "The Early Screening Project for Young Children with Behavior Problems,"

Journal of Emotional and Behavioral Disorders, 3, 194–202, 213. © 1995 PRO-ED. Reprinted with permission.

Page 104, Box 3.1: F. M. Gresham, K. Lane, & K. Lambros, "Comorbidity of Conduct Problems and ADHD: Identification of 'Fledging Psychopaths,'" *Journal of Emotional and Behavioral Disorders, 8,* 83–93. © 2000 PRO-ED. Reprinted with permission.

Page 107, Form 3.1: J. C. Witt, E. Daly, & G. H. Noell, *Functional Assessments: A Step-by-Step Guide to Solving Academic and Behavior Problems.* © 2000 Sopris West. Reprinted with permission.

Page 128, Figure 4.1: Olds et al. (1999).

Page 131, Table 4.1: W. Bennett, *The Perry Preschool Program and Its Long Term Effects: A Benefit-Cost Analysis.* © 1985 High/Scope Press. Reprinted with permission.

Page 132, Table 4.2: W. Bennett, *The Perry Preschool Program and Its Long Term Effects: A Benefit-Cost Analysis.* © 1985 High/Scope Press. Reprinted with permission.

Page 138, Figure 4.2: Horner et al. (2001).

Page 140, Figure 4.3: R. H. Horner, G. Sugai, A. W. Todd, & T. Lewis-Palmer, "School-Wide Positive Behavior Support: An Alternative Approach to Discipline in Schools," in L. Bambara & L. Kern (Eds.), *Positive Behavior Support.* © 2004 Guilford. Reprinted with permission.

Page 142, Box 4.4: S. Schoenwald & M. Rowland, "Multisystematic Therapy," in B. Burns & K. Hoagwood (Eds.), *Community Treatment for Youth: Evidence-Based Interventions for Severe Emotional and Behavioral Disorders.* © 2002 Oxford University Press. Reprinted with permission.

Page 150, Figure 5.1: E. T. Gershoff, "Corporal Punishment by Parent and Associated Child Behaviors and Experiences: A Meta-Analytic and Theoretical Review," *Psychological Bulletin, 128,* 538–579. © 2002 The American Psychological Association. Reprinted with permission.

Page 155, Box 5.1: A. M. Golly's unpublished Doctoral Dissertation, University of Oregon.

Page 165, Figure 5.2: U.S. Office of Juvenile Justice and Delinquency Prevention (OJJDP) (1999).

Page 183, Table 6.1: Adapted with permission from P. Caldarella & K. Merrill, "Common Dimensions of Social Skills of Children and Adolescents: A Taxonomy of Positive Social Behaviors," *School Psychology Review, 26*(2), 264–278. © 1997 NASP.

Page 184, Figure 6.1: F. M. Gresham, "Best Practices in Social Skills Training," in A. Thomas & J. Grimes (Eds.), © 2002 NASP; and F. M. Gresham, "Teaching Social Skills to High-Risk Children and Youth: Preventive and Remedial Strategies," in M. Shinn, H. Walker, & G. Stoner (Eds.), *Interventions for Academic and Behavior Problems II: Preventive and Remedial Approaches* (pp. 403–432), © 2002 NASP. Reprinted with permission.

Page 189, Box 6.1: Adapted with permission from F. M. Gresham, "Teaching Social Skills to High-Risk Children and Youth: Preventive and Remedial Strategies," in M. Shinn, H. Walker, & G. Stoner (Eds.), *Interventions for Academic and Behavior Problems II: Preventive and Remedial Approaches* (pp. 403–432), © 2002 NASP.

Page 190, Box 6.2: F. M. Gresham & S. N. Elliott, *Social Skills Rating System.* © 1990 American Guidance Service. Reprinted with permission.

Page 191, Table 6.2: F. M. Gresham & S. N. Elliott, *Social Skills Rating System.* © 1990 American Guidance Service. Reprinted with permission.

Page 192, Box 6.3: Walker and McConnell (1995).

Page 193, Box 6.4: K. W. Merrell, *School Social Behavior Scales (SSBS-2),* 2nd Edition. Reprinted with permission.

Page 197, Box 6.5: Adapted with permission from F. M. Gresham, "Social Skills Training with Children: Social Learning and Applied Behavioral Analytic Approaches," in T. S. Watson & F. M. Gresham (Eds.), *Handbook of Child Behavior Therapy.* © 1998 Kluwer Academics/Plenum Publishers.

Page 208, Box 7.1: Adapted with permission from F. M. Gresham, "Social Skills Training with Children: Social Learning and Applied Behavioral Analytic Approaches," in T. S. Watson & F. M. Gresham (Eds.), *Handbook of Child Behavior Therapy.* © 1998 Kluwer Academics/Plenum Publishers.

Page 218, Box 7.2: Reid and Eddy (2002).

Page 220, Box 7.3: Adapted with permission from F. M. Gresham, "Teaching Social Skills to High-Risk Children and Youth: Preventive and Remedial Strategies," in M. Shinn, H. Walker, & G. Stoner (Eds.), *Interventions for Academic and Behavior Problems II: Preventive and Remedial Approaches* (pp. 403–432), © 2002 NASP.

Page 223, Box 7.4: Adapted with permission from F. M. Gresham, "Social Skills Training with Children: Social Learning and Applied Behavioral Analytic Approaches," in T. S. Watson & F. M. Gresham (Eds.), *Handbook of Child Behavior Therapy.* © 1998 Kluwer Academics/Plenum Publishers.

Page 230, Box 7.7: Adapted with permission from S.N. Elliott & F.M. Gresham, *Social Skills Intervention Guide: Practical Strategies for Social Training.* © 1991 American Guidance Service.

Page 239, Box 8.1: School Safety News Service (2001); U.S. Department of Education (1998).

Page 246, Table 8.2: Sjomm et al. (1987).

Page 249, Table 8.3: From "Bully/Victim Problems Among School Children: Basic Facts and Effects of a School-Based Intervention Program," by D. Olweus. In D. J. Pepler & K. H. Rubin (Eds.), *The Development of Childhood Aggression* (pp. 411–446). Copyright © 1991 Lawrence Erlbaum. Reprinted with permission.

Page 250, Box 8.2: U.S. Department of Education (1998).

Page 261, Figure 8.2: Walker et al. (1987).

Page 270, Table 8.7: From *RECESS: A program for Reducing Negative-Aggressive Behavior,* by H. Walker, H. Hops, and C. Greenwood. Copyright © 1993 by Educational Achievement Systems, Seattle, WA. Reprinted with permission.

Page 271, Table 8.8: From *RECESS: A program for Reducing Negative-Aggressive Behavior,* by H. Walker, H. Hops, and C. Greenwood. Copyright © 1993 by Educational Achievement Systems, Seattle, WA. Reprinted with permission.

Page 272, Table 8.9: From *RECESS: A program for Reducing Negative-Aggressive Behavior,* by H. Walker, H. Hops, and C. Greenwood. Copyright © 1993 by Educational Achievement Systems, Seattle, WA. Reprinted with permission.

Page 311, Box 9.15: Forehand and McMahon (1981); Morgan and Jenson (198); Walker and Walker (1991).

Page 337, Figure 10.2: Flannery et al. (2003).

Page 338, Figure 10.3: Flannery et al. (2003).

Page 353, Box 11.1: Dear, Scott, and Marshall (1994).

Page 354, Figure 11.1: *Science,* vol. 289, p. 582 (712812000). © 2000 The American Association for the Advancement of Science. Reprinted with permission.

Page 355, Figure 11.2: National Center for Injury Prevention and Control (1994).

Page 356, Figure 11.3: D. Grossman, *On Killing: The Psychological Cost of Learning to Kill in War and Society,* p. 300. © 1996 Little, Brown, & Co. Reprinted with permission.

Page 361, Box 11.3: Adapted from Cole (1994).

Page 363, Box 11.4: Kauffman (1994).

Page 364, Box 11.5: American Psychological Association (1993).

Page 365, Box 11.6: Van Steenbergen (1994).

Page 367, Box 11.7: G. D. Gottfredson, D. C. Gottfredson, E. R.Czeh, D. Cantor, S. B. Crosse, & I. Hantman, *Summary: National Study of Delinquency Prevention in Schools.* © 2000 Gottfredson Associates. Reprinted with permission.

Page 373, Box 11.8: R. A. Fein, B. Vossekuil, W. S. Pollack, R. Borum, W. Modzeleski, & M. Reddy, *Threat Assessment in Schools: A Guide to Managing Threatening Situations and to Creating Safe School Climates, 2002.* Washington, D.C.: Department of Education, U.S. Secret Service.

Page 374, Box 11.9: R. A. Fein, B. Vossekuil, W. S. Pollack, R. Borum, W. Modzeleski, & M. Reddy, *Threat Assessment in Schools: A Guide to Managing Threatening Situations and to Creating Safe School Climates, 2002.* Washington, D.C.: Department of Education, U.S. Secret Service.

Page 375, Box 11.10: National School Safety Center (1992).

Page 382, Figure 11.4: H. Walker & J. Sprague, *Oregon School Study Council Bulletin,* 1998.

Page 383, Figure 11.5: J. R. Sprague, H. M. Walker, S. Sowards, C. Van Bloem, & P. Eberhardt, "Sources of Vulnerability to School Violence: Systems-Level Assessment and Strategies to Improve Safety and Climate," in M. R. Shinn, H. M. Walker, & G. Stoner (Eds.), *Interventions for Academic and Behavior Problems II: Preventive and Remedial Approaches* (pp. 295–314). © 2002 National Association of School Psychologists. Reprinted with permission.

Photo Credits

This page constitutes an extension of the copyright page. We have made every effort to trace the ownership of all copyrighted material and to secure permission from copyright holders. In the event of any question arising as to the use of any material, we will be pleased to make the necessary corrections in future printings. Thanks are due to the following authors, publishers, and agents for permission to use the material indicated.

Page 3: © Bonnie Kamin/PhotoEdit; page 6: © Dennis MacDonald/PhotoEdit; page 58: © Richard Hutchings/PhotoEdit/PictureQuest; page 67: © Jeff Greenberg/PhotoEdit; page 86: © Michael Newman/PhotoEdit; page 100: © Terri Wright; page 127: © Rob Crandall/Stock Connection/PictureQuest; page 151: © Robert Brenner/PhotoEdit; page 154: © Mary Kate Denny/PhotoEdit; page 180: © Rudi Von Briel/PhotoEdit; page 186: © Dennis MacDonald/PhotoEdit; page 210: © Cleve Bryant/PhotoEdit; page 224: © David Young-Wolff/PhotoEdit; page 245 (left): © Michael Newman/PhotoEdit; page 245 (right): © David Young-Wolff/PhotoEdit; page 263: © Bob Daemmrich/Stock, Boston Inc./PictureQuest; page 281: © Amy Etra/PhotoEdit; page 286: © David Young-Wolff/PhotoEdit; page 320: © Michael Newman/PhotoEdit; page 330: © Michael Newman/PhotoEdit; page 358: AP/Wide World Photos; page 371 (left): AP/Wide World Photos; and page 371 (right): © Michael Newman/PhotoEdit

Name Index

Subject Index

youth violence and, 28–31
See also Behavior problems; Conduct disorder
Antisocial personality disorder, 10
Antisocial risk index, 12
Arrests, juvenile, 29, 30, 358, 361–362
Assault rates, 354, 356
Assertive behavior, 163, 183, 219
Assessment
 assumptions in, 84–87
 classification and, 99–105
 decision making in, 82–84
 early identification/screening and, 93–108
 functional behavioral methods of, 105–108
 identifying risk and protective factors in, 89–92
 indirect vs. direct methods of, 186, 187–188
 measurement errors in, 86–87, 93–94
 multiple gating procedures in, 94–99
 office disciple referrals and, 109–111
 problem-solving model of, 87–89
 purposes of, 83
 school safety, 379–381
 social skills, 187–199
 strengths-based, 61
 technical considerations in, 93–94
 threat, 372–374
At-risk students
 academic skills of, 18, 19
 aggression and, 15
 classroom behavior of, 20
 comorbidity and, 9
 early identification of, 18, 340
 interventions for, 9–10, 206–207
 long-term outcomes for, 12, 14
 playground behavior of, 21–22
 school-based support for, 32–33
 social resilience and, 61
 violent behavior and, 29
Attention deficit/hyperactivity disorder (ADHD)
 antisocial behavior and, 50–51, 71
 media violence and, 45
 medications used for, 50, 158, 159
Autistic children, 128–129
Aversive behaviors, 151
Avoidance strategy, 167–168

BASIC training program, 311
Behavioral contracts, 227, 228
Behavioral definition of social skills, 180–181
Behavioral Disorders journal, 105
Behavioral hypotheses, 108
Behavioral profiling, 371–372
Behavioral rehearsal, 222–223, 224, 226
Behavioral standards, 258–259

Behavior chains, 156
Behavior Education Program (BEP), 135
Behavior management
 blaming and, 157–158
 counseling/psychotherapy and, 159–160
 ineffective techniques of, 160–162
 medications used for, 158–159
 proven strategies for, 162–172
 See also Classroom management
Behavior modification, 159
Behavior problems
 case study on, 328–331
 externalizing vs. internalizing, 4, 95
 ineffective management of, 160–162
 intervention strategies for, 162–172, 329–330
 procedures for reducing/removing, 227–228, 230–231
 results of interventions for, 330–331
 social skills deficits and, 184
 typical approaches to managing, 157–160
 See also Antisocial behavior
Behavior rating scales, 188
Best practices
 for changing maladaptive behaviors, 105
 for giving teacher commands, 172
 for school-based interventions, 69–74
 for youth violence prevention, 366
Best Practices of Youth Violence Prevention (Thornton et. al), 366
Beta commands, 155, 170–172, 310
Blaming others, 157–158
Blueprints for Violence Prevention, 311–312
 Bullying Prevention Program, 248, 272
 Incredible Years Program, 311
 Multisystemic Therapy, 139, 141
Boys
 antisocial behavior of, 12, 14, 22–23
 bullying by, 239, 240, 244, 245
 See also Gender differences
Bullies and Victims in Schools: A Guide to Understanding and Management (Besay), 274
Bullying, 237–249
 definitions of, 238–239
 developmental pathway of, 245
 gender differences and, 239, 240, 244
 harassment distinguished from, 239–240
 peer reactions to, 245–247
 policies, statutes, and laws on, 240, 241–243
 prevention programs for, 272–274, 385
 RECESS program and, 265–272
 resources for addressing, 274–275
 role dynamics of, 240, 244
 statistics and facts about, 239